How to Make Whips

Silas Hobson
with the whip he made
Lockhart River Nov 1995

Other books by Ron Edwards:

BUSHCRAFT 1 *Australian Traditional Bush Crafts*
BUSHCRAFT 2 *Skills of the Australian Bushman*
BUSHCRAFT 3 *Making Do in the Bush*
BUSHCRAFT 4 *Using What Is Available*
BUSHCRAFT 5 *Developing Your Skills*
BUSHCRAFT 6 *Old Ideas for Use Today*
BUSHCRAFT 7 *Preserving Old Secrets*
BUSHCRAFT 8 *Bush Leatherwork*

These titles are available from

Ron Edwards
Rams Skull Press
12 Fairyland Road
Kuranda, Queensland 4872
Australia

How to Make Whips

written and illustrated by

Ron Edwards

CORNELL MARITIME PRESS
A Division of Schiffer Publishing, Ltd.
Atglen, Pennsylvania

Copyright © 1997 by Ron Edwards
Reprinted by arrangement with
The Rams Skull Press

Library of Congress Control Number: 2010920964

All rights reserved. No part of this work may be reproduced or used in any form or by any means—graphic, electronic, or mechanical, including photocopying or information storage and retrieval systems—without written permission from the publisher.
The scanning, uploading and distribution of this book or any part thereof via the Internet or via any other means without the permission of the publisher is illegal and punishable by law. Please purchase only authorized editions and do not participate in or encourage the electronic piracy of copyrighted materials.
"Schiffer," "Schiffer Publishing Ltd. & Design," and the "Design of pen and inkwell" are registered trademarks of Schiffer Publishing Ltd.

First Cornell Maritime Press edition, 1998; third printing, 2010

ISBN: 978-0-87033-513-6
Printed in China

Schiffer Books are available at special discounts for bulk purchases for sales promotions or premiums. Special editions, including personalized covers, corporate imprints, and excerpts can be created in large quantities for special needs. For more information contact the publisher:

Published by Schiffer Publishing Ltd.
4880 Lower Valley Road
Atglen, PA 19310
Phone: (610) 593-1777; Fax: (610) 593-2002
E-mail: Info@schifferbooks.com

For the largest selection of fine reference books on this and related subjects, please visit our web site at
www.schifferbooks.com

We are always looking for people to write books on new and related subjects. If you have an idea for a book please contact us at the above address.

This book may be purchased from the publisher.
Include $5.00 for shipping.
Please try your bookstore first.
You may write for a free catalog.

In Europe, Schiffer books are distributed by
Bushwood Books
6 Marksbury Ave.
Kew Gardens
Surrey TW9 4JF England
Phone: 44 (0) 20 8392 8585; Fax: 44 (0) 20 8392 9876
E-mail: info@bushwoodbooks.co.uk
Website: www.bushwoodbooks.co.uk

Contents

Foreword.................................... 8

Introduction................................ 9

**Chapter 1: *Whipmaking Book 1*—How to
Make a Basic 4-Plait Stockwhip**........ 11
A Good Basic Whip........................... 12
    Whip Names............................. 12
    Styles of Whip......................... 12
    Types of Leather....................... 12
    Choosing the Leather................... 13
    Points to Watch........................ 13
    Buying a Strip of Leather.............. 14
4-Plait Basic Whip.......................... 14
Step 1: Making the Belly.................... 14
Step 2: Cutting Out the Whip................ 15
    Using a Pair of Dividers............... 15
    Using a Template....................... 16
    Using Fingers as Guides................ 16
    Cutting Methods........................ 16
    Cutting and Skiving.................... 16
    Splitting the Strands.................. 16
    Skiving................................ 16
    Angled Cut............................. 17
    Cutting on the Beam.................... 18
Step 3: Plaiting the 4-Plait Whip........... 19
    Working in a Confined Space............ 19
    Plaiting Soap.......................... 20
    Leather Dressing....................... 20
    Cleaning Tallow........................ 20
    Use of Acid in Cleaning Fat............ 20
    Plaiting the Whip...................... 21
Step 4: The Fall............................ 21
    Cutting the Slit in a Whip Fall........ 21
    Common Fall Hitch...................... 23
    Rolling the Whip....................... 23
    Resin Board for Whip Rolling........... 23
Step 5: The Cracker......................... 23
    Speeding Up the Job.................... 24
    Finishing Off the Cracker.............. 24
    Fastening the Cracker to the Fall...... 24
    Attaching the Cracker—Another Method... 25
    Cracking the Whip...................... 25
Step 6: Making the Handle,.................. 25
    Half-Plaited Handle.................... 25
    Straightening a Whip Handle............ 26
Step 7: Covering the Handle................. 26
Handle with Dog's Knot...................... 26
Forming the Knob............................ 27
Crown Knot.................................. 27
Wall Knot................................... 28
Final Crown Knot............................ 28
Handle with an 8-Plait and Turk's Head...... 29
12-Plait Handle............................. 29

8-Plait for Half-Plaited Whip Handle........ 30
Square Start for Half-Plaited Handle,
    12-Plait............................... 31
Wraparound Handle........................... 32
Secret Plait Worked into a Whip Handle...... 32
Binding on the Keeper....................... 33
Rib Rattling................................ 34
French Grapevine............................ 35
3-Part, 4-Bight Turk's Head................. 36
Attaching Whip and Handle................... 37
6-Plait Basic Whip.......................... 38
Beginning a Round 6-Plait................... 39
Round 6-Plait............................... 40
Reducing from 6-Plait to 4-Plait............ 40
The Built-in Belly.......................... 41
Kangaroo-Hide Whips......................... 41
Kid's Whip.................................. 41
Slit Braid.................................. 42

**Chapter 2: *Whipmaking Book 2*—How to Make an
8-Plait Kangaroo Stockwhip**............ 43
Two Main Groups of Whips.................... 44
Some Styles of Whips........................ 44
    Stockwhip of Kangaroo Leather.......... 44
    Redhide Whip........................... 45
    Bullwhip............................... 45
    Snake Whip............................. 45
    Bullockie's Whip....................... 45
First Rule about Whipmakers................. 45
Whipmaking Terms............................ 46
Plaiting or Braiding?....................... 46
    Plait.................................. 47
    Braid.................................. 47
12-Foot Shot-Loaded Stockwhip............... 47
How to Make a 2.3-Meter 8-Strand Kangaroo
    Stockwhip with a Full-Plaited Handle... 47
    Materials Needed....................... 48
    Selecting the Kangaroo Skin............ 48
    Using Precut Lace...................... 48
    Testing for Stretch.................... 48
Step 1: The Core or Filler.................. 49
    Redhide Core........................... 49
    Kangaroo Core.......................... 49
    Lead Loading........................... 51
Step 2: The Belly........................... 51
    The Filler and Belly Plait............. 51
    Belly from Redhide..................... 53
Step 3: The Bolster......................... 54
Step 4: Cutting Out the Top Plait or Overlay.. 55
    Number of Strands to Cut............... 55
    Cutting Out Strands.................... 55
    Stretch in the Leather................. 56
    Length of Strands in Overlay........... 56
    Knife Sharpness........................ 56

Cutting with the Thumbnail	56
Type of Roo	58
Cutting with the Side of the Thumb	58
Cutting to a Marked Line	59
Cutting with a Strand Cutter	59
Homemade Strand Cutter	59
Cutting Out Tight Corners	59
Splitting the Strands	60
Skiving	60
Leather Chattering While Skiving	60
Holes in Leather	61
Leather Dressing and Greasing the Strands	61
Pull Tight, Plait Loose	61
Step 5: Plaiting the Overlay	62
Round 8-Plait, Whipmaker's Method	62
Round 8-Plait	63
Bundles	63
Self-Greasing Lace Holder	64
Looseness in Plaiting the Overlay	64
Gaps in the Plaiting	65
Plaiter's Knot	65
Broken Strands	66
Dropping Strands	66
Changing from 8-Plait to 7-Plait	66
Changing from 7-Plait to 6-Plait	67
Uneven Taper	68
Lumps	68
Narrow Sections	68
Round 6-Plait	68
Finishing Off the Thong	68
Step 6: The Fall	69
Attaching the Fall	69
Replacing the Fall	69
Step 7: Making the Cracker	71
Finishing the Cracker	72
5-Part, 4-Bight Turk's Head on the Thong	74
Step 8: The Handle (or Stock) Foundation	75
Using Bush Timber	75
Step 9: The Overlay for the Handle	76
Tying the Set to the Stock	76
Long Whipping	77
Step 10: The Knob on the Handle	79
Shaping the Knob	80
The Shape of the Knob	80
5-Part, 4-Bight Turk's Head	80
Gaps in the Turk's Head	82
Finishing the Knob	82
Turk's Head on Keeper End	82
Spanish Ring Knot	83
A More Elaborate Handle	84
Two-Tone Work	84
Fitting the Handle and Thong Together	84
Care of the Whip	84
A Few Tips	86
Broken Strands	86
Joining without Glue	86
Another Method	86

Adding in a Strand	87
Adding in Two Strands	88
Portable Plaiting Rack	88
Chapter 3: How to Make a Bullwhip	89
Making a Bullwhip	90
The Handle	90
The Belly	90
Round 4-Plait	90
Handle Loop	92
Plaiting the Overlay	92
Precut Lace	92
12-Plait, Under 2 Sequence	93
12-Plait, Under 3 Sequence	94
Changing from 12-Plait to 10-Plait	94
Round 10-Plait	94
Changing from 10-Plait to 8-Plait	95
Changing from 8-Plait to 6-Plait	95
Attaching the Fall	95
Making and Attaching the Cracker	95
Rolling the Whip	95
The Knob	95
Turk's Head on the Handle	96
5-Part, 4-Bight Turk's Head	96
Pineapple Knot	96
Chapter 4: How to Make a Snake Whip	97
Method 1: Lead-Loaded	98
Handle Loop	99
Method 2	101
Whip as a Weapon	101
Handle	101
A Quick Snake Whip	103
The Belly	103
Building Up the Knob	103
Turk's Head	103
Miniature Whip Hatband	104
Riding Crop	104
Chapter 5: Whip Handle Designs	105
Twisted Handles	108
Carved Timber Handles	109
Cowtail Handle	110
Lunging Whip	110
Designs for Whip Handles	111
Plaiting Soap	111
Cowtail or Whipmaker's Plait	112
Doubled Herringbone	113
Short Herringbone	113
Chessboard Plait	114
Double Diamond	115
Irregular Herringbone, 12-Plait, Round	115
Triple Diamond	116
4-Strand Diamond, Coachwhipping	116
Bracelet	117
Double Bracelet	118
Stairstep	119

Double Stairstep. 120
Two Methods for Complex Plaiting. 120
    Alternate Strand Method. 120
    Spiral Method. 120
Solid Band. 121
Bird's Eye, 12-Plait, Round 122
Egyptian Eyes 123
The Sun 124
Flowers and Zigzag 125
Double Zigzag. 126
Flowers 126
Interlocking Diamonds, 16-Plait, Round 127
The Ship of the Dead 128
Two-Seam Plait 129
Vee Pattern, Whipmaker's Plait 129
Barber's Pole Plait 130

Chapter 6: Plaiting Names in Whips 131
Name Plaiting 132
    Joining One Pattern to the Next 132
    Plaiting Names with Short Pieces. 132
    Working the Letters into the Weave. . . . 132
    Colors to Use 132
    Never Believe What You Are Told. 133
    Using Precut Lace 134
    Chessboard Start: Calculating the Length
      of the Lace 134
    Locking the Back 135
    Working in the Letters 135
    White-on-Black Letters. 137
    Vertical and Horizontal Letters 137

Plaiting Long Words 138
    Setting Out 138
    Amount Needed. 139
Whip Handle Clamp. 140
Stitching Stool. 141

Chapter 7: Some Useful Tips. 142
Making a Whip with Bought Lace 143
    The Belly 143
    Covering the Core 143
    The Overlay, Quantity Needed. 144
    Plaiting the Keeper 144
    Round 12-Plait 144
Whip Cracker Knots. 146
    Overhand Knot 146
    Small Cracker Knot. 146
    Blood Knot Variation. 147
    Napranum Hitch 147
    Attaching the Cracker 148
Fall Hitches 149
    Morris Doohan's Hitch 149
    Snake's Head Hitch 150
    Nymboida Hitch. 152
    George's Hitch 153
3-Part, 4-Bight Turk's Head. 154

Appendix. 155

Index 161

People Named in This Book 166

Foreword

It is a pleasure to write a foreword to this book. Ron Edwards is a folklorist, and his Bushcraft series of books have the place in Australia that the Foxfire books have in the United States. Coming from a family in the saddlery trade, he has a particular insight into leatherwork and has collected much on whips and plaiting, as well as general leatherwork.

The Australian whipmaking industry developed in the latter half of the nineteenth century, as the cattle industry expanded. The majority of the early craftsmen were English thong makers who had learned their craft as apprentices. In England they had worked principally with cowhide or foalskin, and were familiar with both the coarse work of heavy hunt and cattle thongs, and the fine work of light coach thongs. In Australia they found kangaroo hide (an outstanding leather for whips) and a large and expanding market for cattle whips. The English-style whip, with a stock of 18 to 20 inches, soon developed into the Australian stockwhip. Conditions in Australia were harsh, the apprenticeship system still widespread, and the trade highly competitive. With a large and discerning market, conditions were right to encourage the steady development of the stockwhip, leading to superb cattle whips unequaled elsewhere in the world.

The trade flourished up to the onset of World War II, but has declined since then. There are now very few fully trained whipmakers, and none being trained, but there remain numbers of part-time or off-season country plaiters and amateurs who carry on the tradition. Many have benefited a great deal from the professional craftsmen of past times. Ron Edwards has collected from these remaining plaiters methods and patterns in a wide variety of styles and qualities as an illuminating record of whipmaking in Australia.

Americans reading this book should bear in mind that the Australian whip is the stockwhip. Much can be learned from the discussions of stockwhips. Bullwhips and snake (shot) whips, on the other hand, are seldom used in Australia and are made largely for Americans. Less is to be learned from the discussions of these whips.

Ring work and plaiting names in whip handles is a specialty of the Australian whipmakers. This subject has not been well covered in the American literature, and the presentation here will be welcomed by a wide range of braiders.

—David Morgan
Author of *Whips and Whipmaking*

Les Turner.
Dec 1994

Introduction

The Australian stockwhip is the best in the world; not because we as a race are smarter than other nations, but because we have been blessed with abundant quantities of excellent whipmaking materials, and we have a very long tradition of whipmaking that has never been allowed to die out, as has happened in many other places.

I have been president of the Australian Whipmakers and Plaiters Association from its founding in 1985 until the present day (1997), and in that time I have seen membership grow from a handful of enthusiasts to well over two hundred, including quite a number of professional whipmakers.

In recent years we have had regular get-togethers of members, where beginners could gather round to watch and learn from the experts and in turn share their own knowledge. Even before our association had been formed, I had written a couple of small books on whipmaking. However, after watching our top whipmakers in action, I felt it necessary to fully revise and enlarge these books (both of which are still in print and have also been incorporated into this book).

As a result of the activities of our members, and perhaps also as a result of the association's interesting and informative quarterly journal, interest in the subject of whips and whipmaking seems to have grown a lot in the past years—so much so that I thought it was about time that I gathered together a lot of the material that I have prepared on the subject and brought it all out as one book.

Even a beginner should be able to make a good working whip by following the instructions in this book, but I would advise mastering the first section before attempting anything more elaborate. As for cracking the whip, there is nothing on that subject to be found in these pages, for while the making of a whip can be taught from a book, the cracking can only be learned by practice.

—Ron Edwards
Kuranda
January 2, 1997

A Long Drink

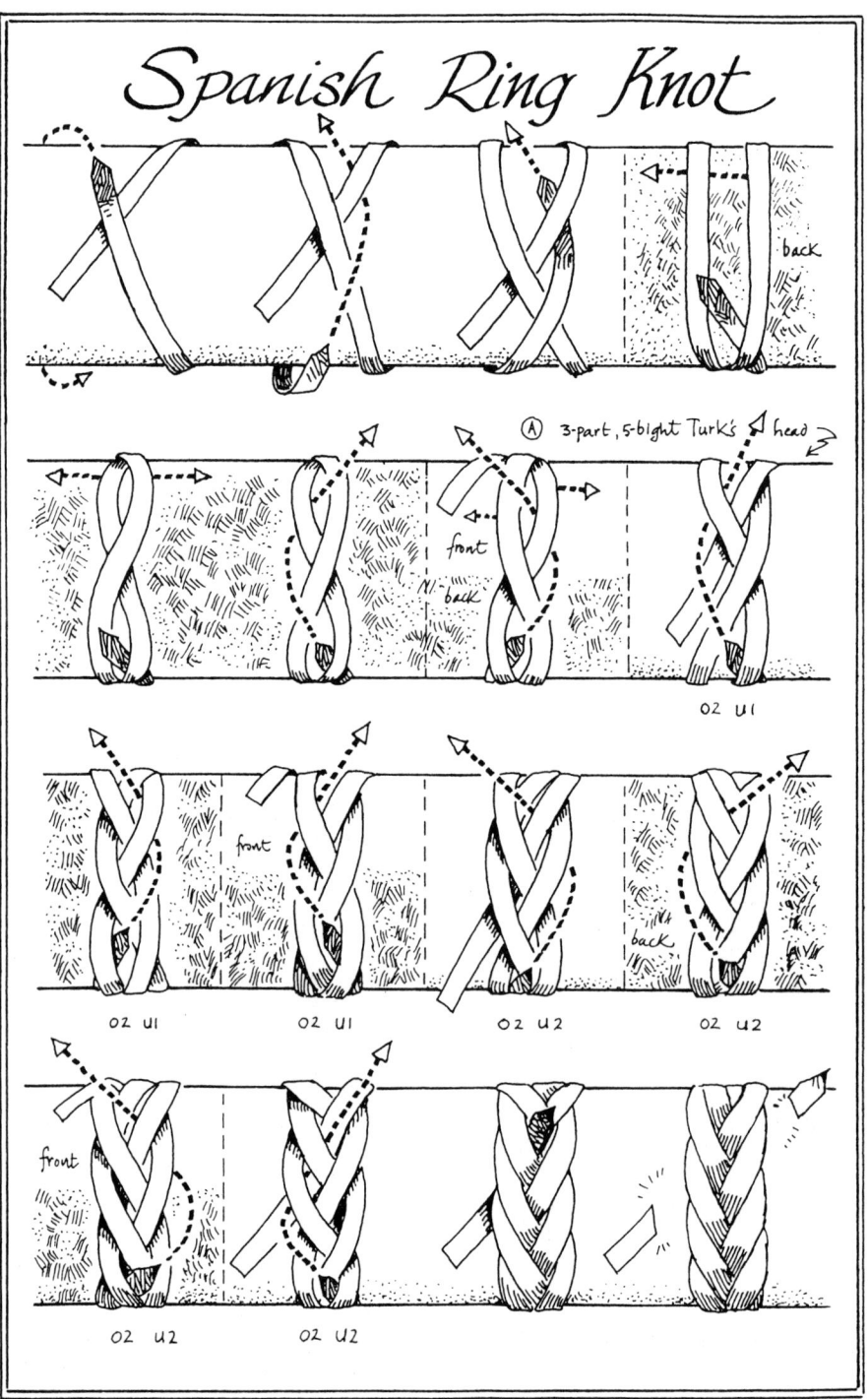

Chapter 1

Whipmaking Book 1
How to Make a Basic 4-Plait Whip

A GOOD BASIC WHIP

This is not only an instruction book on how to make stockwhips but is also the result of research into a traditional Australian craft. Unlike many other traditional bush crafts, the art of whipmaking is far from dead, and there are still many whipmakers working in different parts of the country. I have had the honor to be the President of the Australian Plaiters and Whipmakers Association from 1985 up to the present (1997), and the membership in 1996 was over two hundred and still growing.

In *Bushcraft 1* I gave some simple instructions for a whip, but that was over twenty years ago and a lot of water has flowed under the bridge since then. Over the years the Australian Plaiters and Whipmakers Association has published a quarterly journal and members haven't stopped arguing about what makes a good, standard whip. In *Bushcraft 1* and in the early editions of *Whipmaking Book 1* (now chapter 1 of this book), I wrote about the 6-strand whip, but today the 4-strand is the most common for a yard whip.

My original book has been revised here in order to simplify the system for the beginner. This has been achieved by adding extra drawings to more fully explain some of the basic steps. For the beginner I would suggest starting with a 4-plait whip. I would also suggest that for a first whip you make the strands just the length of the side of leather rather than curving it around in order to gain more length.

All you need for a start is a piece of leather, a sharp knife, a steady hand, and some patience. If you can spare the time, it is a good idea to think of your first couple of whips as presents for other people, and by the time you get to your third one you will probably have improved to the stage of wanting to keep it for yourself.

Whip Names

Considering what an apparently simple thing a basic 4-strand whip is, there is an immense amount of difference between one maker and another. Even the name of such a whip is open to controversy.

Whipmaker Glen Denholm calls such a 4-strand a team whip, because in the days of horse teams this was the common term for them. In many parts of inland Queensland they are known as yard whips, because they are mainly used as the basic knockabout whip in the cattle yards, while many other people refer to them as stockwhips. Still others insist that a stockwhip can only be of kangaroo lace (this last argument is wrong, as early saddler's catalogs list all whips with a stock, that is to say a handle, as stockwhips, even down to 4-plait whips of cowhide).

Some wholesalers call them redhide whips, but this only refers to the material that they are made from, and the same whip may be made of redhide, whitehide, greenhide, or rawhide. My advice is to go along with whatever name is common in your area, but be prepared to allow others the right to use whatever term is the common one for them.

Styles of Whip

There is no such thing as one correct length, width, or shape for a 4-strand whip. Some people want long thick whips, others want shorter, lighter whips. Both styles are equally correct and neither is better than the other; it is just a question of the intended use for the whip.

A few years ago our saddlery made ordinary long whips for our shop and very short thick whips for a group of graziers in western New South Wales. They wanted something short enough to be just thrown across the pommel of a saddle rather than being carried on the shoulder, and this was the style of whip that suited them but which they could not buy readily.

People who want a whip for cracking will require a different style from those who want one for working stock, and people who work stock in the yard will want a different style of whip from those who work from horses in the bush.

Types of Leather

If you do not have a full side of leather to work with, then you should go to a saddler and buy a wide strap the full length of the hide. A strap 50 mm wide should give you enough for a whip, the fall, and still leave enough left over to do a half-plaited handle.

Redhide is the usual leather for the basic whip, but you can also use greenhide, or any other strong leather. Redhide is properly tanned greasy leather that has been heavily oiled during the tanning process. It is red in color.

Greenhide is simply made by pegging out a fresh hide, covering it with a layer of salt, and leaving it to dry for a few days. This is greenhide, as it is known in my part of the world.

Rawhide is the skin as it comes off the beast, dried without salting. Both greenhide and rawhide become hard when dry and have to be oiled and worked a lot to keep them flexible. Because these hides are basically raw meat, they can also provide food for dogs and mice. Early polar explorers used rawhide for dog harnesses, one reason being that when things got tough the explorers could chew the harness for some nourishment. (There is some disagreement about the terms rawhide and greenhide. I won't go into the various arguments except to note that whipmakers all have their own terms for their work as well as their own methods and all, without exception, insist that they are the only one who is right.)

Whitehide can make good whips, and home-cure methods can be found in *The Australian Whipmaker,* vol. 1, p. 19, and vol. 4, p. 921 (inquiries may be addressed to the Editor, 12 Fairyland Road, Kuranda, Australia 4872). The great disadvantage of home-cured whitehide is that in humid conditions it will weep salty liquid.

Chrome-tanned leather. Some people (including a few writers) confuse greenhide with chrome-tanned leather. Chrome leather is light gray in color but when cut the inside is blue-green, hence the confusion. This leather can be used for whips, but is not highly regarded.

Bark-tanned leather (also called vegetable tanned). Bark-tanned leather can be used for whips as long as it is well oiled, strong, and flexible. Old saddler's catalogs list whips made from kip and similar bark-tanned leather.

Stockwhips are also made from kangaroo hide, and the making of these whips is described in chapter 2.

Choosing the Leather

When choosing a side, it is best to avoid thick leather—try and get it around 2.5 to 3 mm thick, and also make sure that it is not soft and spongy. Leather that is cut from the belly part of the hide is often very weak and will break easily when cut into thin strands.

On the other hand, thick leather is hard to plait well, and needs to be skived down. So, the aim is to go for leather that can be plaited nicely and that remains strong even in the thinnest sections.

Cut a narrow strip from the leather you are thinking about using, taper it down to a thin point, and then see how easily it breaks. If the break has a loose, hairy look about it, then the leather at that part of the hide is not good enough for whipmaking.

The sections that have been under the animal's armpits are often weak, but the leather 100 mm above this may be quite strong. Leather that can be stretched is usually not suitable. If you pull a strap of redhide and one section of it changes color to a pale shade of pink and then goes back to red when you let go, that means the strap has a weak section of leather at that point. This can sometimes still be used, but not if it occurs where the fine strands are to be cut.

These soft sections of leather need not be wasted; after all, you probably paid good money for them. They can be used for the belly of a whip, and can often be used for the plaiting on the handle, as this does not need the strength that the thong will need.

Points to Watch

The drawing is meant to show the parts of a side that you should look at when choosing one.

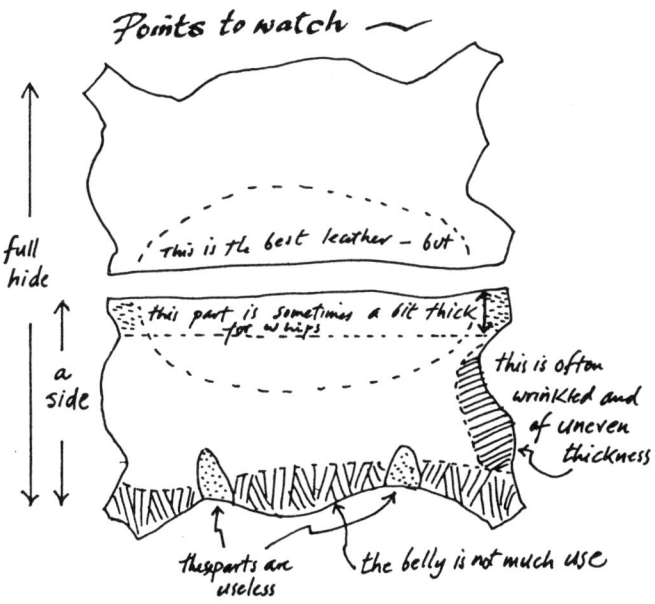

The section nearest the backbone is the best part of the hide, but sometimes this is a bit thick and may be better used for reins and similar jobs. The tanner divides the hide along the backbone before tanning, and the result is called a side. Leather is bought by the side.

On one end you will sometimes find a wrinkled section, and this may be of uneven thickness. This may be no problem at all if used for the start of the whip, but can cause problems if you try to cut thin strands out of it.

The belly can sometimes be used for whips as long as the leather is sound, but just watch out for that section that was under the armpits.

13

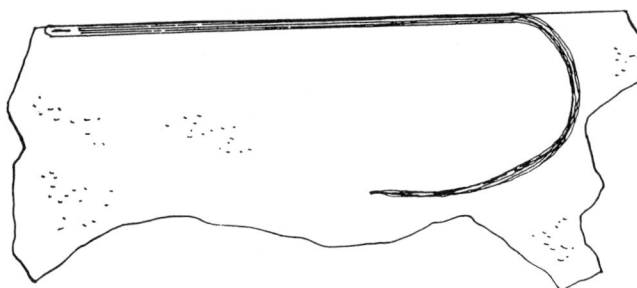

Fig. 2. There are two ways of cutting out the leather for a whip. For a long whip the cut will run along the straight side and then curve down. However, professional whipmakers only cut like this when they have an order for a long whip, because each whip cut out shortens the length of the side and so makes the cutting out of the next one that much more difficult.

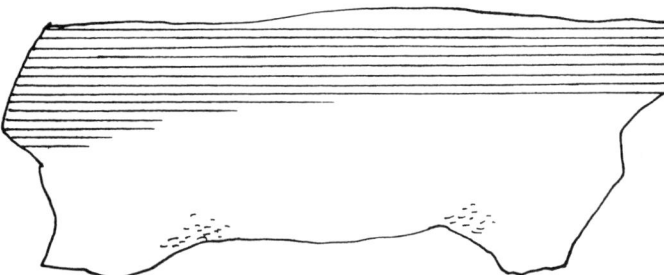

Fig. 3. Professional whipmakers, with few exceptions, cut straight across the length of the side as shown. In this way they can get the maximum number of whips from the side with the minimum amount of waste. Because of the irregular shape of the side, each whip will be a different length.

All the thin, weak parts of the belly are discarded before marking out begins. Some whipmakers then use a straight edge to get a line before marking out the first whip.

Others simply follow the general shape of the leather. Many years ago when I first saw this done by a local saddler I was very surprised, but the old fellow said that it saved a lot of leather and made no difference to the final job.

Buying a Strip of Leather

This is a useful method for the beginner who does not have the money or need to purchase a full side of leather. Leather shops will not usually cut out fancy shapes except for fancy prices, but they will sell a 50-mm strip cut the full length of the side, and this is what the beginner should start with.

Such a strip will provide the leather for the whole whip, including the thong, the fall, and enough to do a bit of a plait on the handle.

Ask for redhide and try and make sure that it comes from the upper part of the side and not from the weak belly section. The stretch test is the easiest way to check on a strip of leather. Give it a pull and if sections change from red to pink and get narrow, then the leather has too much stretch.

4-PLAIT BASIC WHIP

The most common whip for everyday use is the 4-plait. This can be made with the keeper and belly in one piece, or with the belly added as a separate piece. For your first whip I would suggest one with the belly added, as this is the type made today by professional whipmakers, and this is what I will describe here.

STEP 1: MAKING THE BELLY

The belly is needed to give weight and density to the whip. Round plaits are, by the nature of their construction, hollow, even when the strands are pulled very tight; so a whip made without a belly will be light and will not crack well.

Whips made of kangaroo leather usually have a plaited belly, but redhide whips do not, because of the thickness of the leather that is used for the outer covering of the whip. If you were to make a plaited belly for a redhide whip, the finished product could very well look like a pregnant sausage.

Unless you want a very heavy whip the belly need not be very thick, 4 mm at the widest is common, and that is thinner than a pencil. There are three ways to prepare the belly, according to the thickness of the leather that is available.

Whichever method is used you will find that the job will be easier if you soak the leather in water for five minutes or so before you roll it smooth. Remember to give it a good coating of leather dressing once it has dried out, in order to replace any oil that was lost during the soaking.

Method 1. If the leather is very thick, a strip may be cut and tapered each end as shown. A sharp knife is then used to round off the corners and it is then rolled firmly under a board until it is round all the way down its length.

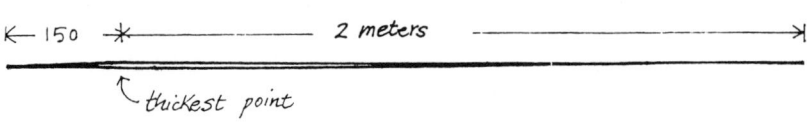

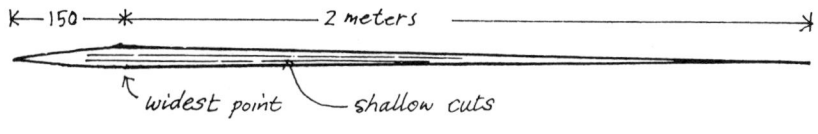

Method 2. Fig. 5. The second method is for leather that is not thick enough for the first method, perhaps 2-3 mm thick. Cut out a teardrop shape as shown and score it down its length to help make it roll up easier. Soak it in water and then roll it firmly under a board until it is as tight as it can possibly be.

Let it at least partly dry and give it a heavy coating of fat or leather dressing. Put it to one side while you go to the next step.

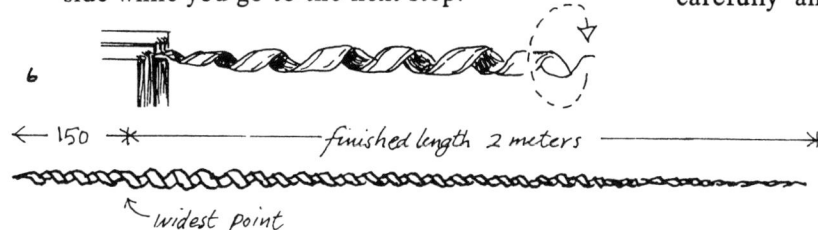

Method 3. Fig. 6. This method is not so common because it takes a little longer, but it is handy if you only have thin leather to use for the belly. The strand can be 4-5 mm wide, the same shape as the previous method, and should be given a good soaking in water.

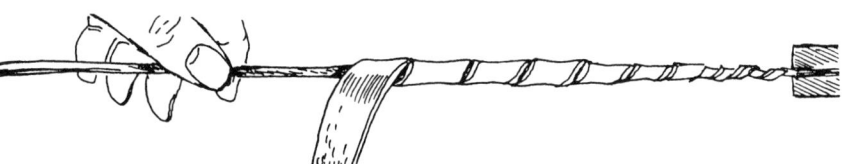

Fig. 7. Twist the strand into a spiral. It should not be hollow, so if it seems to be developing a hole down the center, the strand should be wrapped around a thin rounded strand of leather.

When fully wound up it is pulled out tight and tied or tacked down at each end. When dry it should be given a good rolling and well covered in leather dressing or fat.

Fig. 8. A long fine tapered belly can be made in this way.

STEP 2: CUTTING OUT THE WHIP

Fig. 9. Some professionals cut out whips by eye without needing to make any measurements at all, but the beginner should not attempt this because it is a skill developed from years of practice. Mark carefully and cut equally as carefully and you will have fewer problems. Maurice Doohan, a professional who makes beautifully tapered whips, always marks the leather and then cuts.

There are a few ways to mark and cut out leather, and I will describe some of them here and you can make your own decision about which you would like to use.

Using a Pair of Dividers

This is a common method and will suit most people. The dividers are set to the desired width and will make a clear groove in the leather.

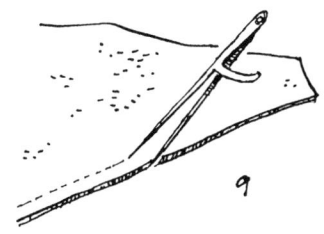

15

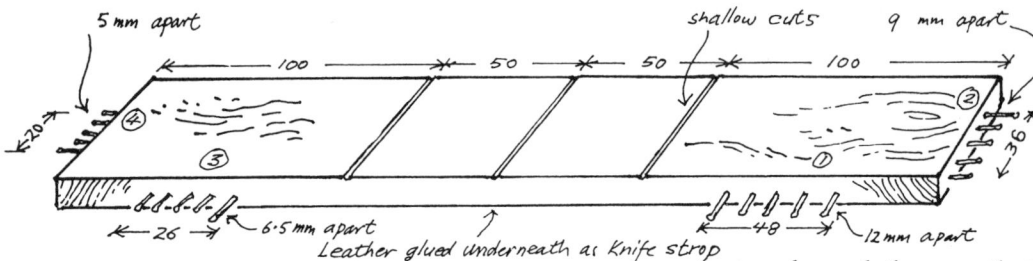

Using a Template

Fig. 11. If you are going to make a number of whips it might be worthwhile to make up a simple template. This is nothing more than four groups of five small tacks hammered into a scrap of timber. One of the outer tacks is left higher than the others to act as a guide.

Fig. 12. A template is simple to use: first divide the leather into four sections and use the tacks to press a series of grooves into the leather. The change from one width to the next will not be seen when the strands are cut out.

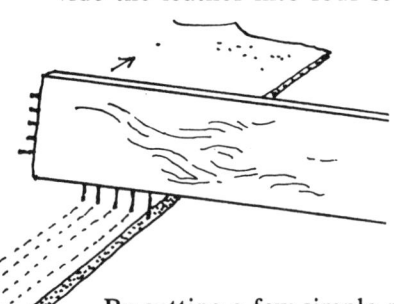

By cutting a few simple marks into the timber it can also be used to measure the leather. I also have a piece of leather stuck on the underside to use as a knife strop.

Using Fingers as Guides

Fig. 13. Marking out can be done using only your fingers as guides, and this is a skill that does not take very long to learn. First mark out the measurements at the points that are shown on the plan of the whip.

Now with a pencil, pen, or even a nail or piece of wire begin to mark starting from these measured points. Three fingers hold the pencil, and two run along the edge of the leather to act as a guide. You will find that you can soon learn to widen or narrow the line as you go along so that it will taper the whip strands correctly.

When you have marked out the whip, check it to make sure that the tapers look even and all strands are the same width. It is easy to correct your lines now—not so easy after you have cut them out.

Cutting Methods

There are two ways to cut out the strands, and the one that you choose will depend upon your skill with a knife.

Straight cut. This is the most obvious way to cut, with the knife blade cutting straight down through the leather. After cutting, the strand will require skiving.

Angled cut. This is harder to do, but it uses less leather, and after you have done it the strands will not need skiving. It is described later.

Cutting and Skiving

Having been marked, the four strands are now cut out, and here we are describing the straight cut.

Splitting the Strands

Once the strands have been cut, some professionals run them through the leather splitter to get them all to a uniform thickness. For a beginner this can be a traumatic job, as the slightest change of pressure or a blade that is not razor-sharp can result in slit strands. In any case, the average beginner will not have a splitter, and I know of a few professional whipmakers who do not use them, so this is really a matter of choice.

Skiving

Having cut out the strands, whipmakers take pride in carefully skiving the edges. (Skiving rhymes with diving, and means to take off the sharp corners). This makes for a much smoother finish when the plaiting is done. However, skiving calls for a steady hand and an amazingly sharp knife.

In the bush rough greenhide whips are sometimes left unskived, and even plaited with the hair still intact, or only roughly scraped off, the theory being that it will wear off with use.

Fig. 14. In our saddlery we have a stropping board about 500 mm long on which a piece of leather has been glued rough side up (some prefer it smooth side up). Jeweler's rouge is rubbed into this to provide a strop to keep the knives sharp. The rouge comes in stick form and some leather shops keep it in stock. Valve grinding paste can also be used.

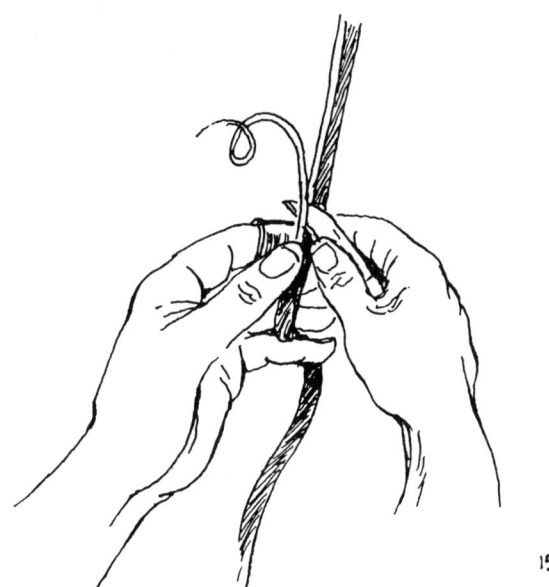

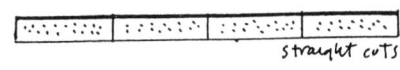

For the home workshop the rouge can be rubbed on the rough side of any small scrap of leather and this is then used as a strop. Only when the knife is sharp enough to shave the hairs on an arm can skiving begin.

Fig. 15. Everyone develops his or her own method of holding the leather and knife when skiving, and the sketch shows a typical style.

As you skive you walk backwards, so make sure the area behind you is clear and that the whip is firmly tied to something. Warn people not to walk behind you—if you bump into something you can cut yourself badly. Also wrap something around your forefinger or make a small fingerstall so that the knife will not cut you if it slips.

If the knife is really sharp, then skiving is easy; if not, then continue sharpening the knife. I have seen an Aboriginal stockman friend spend a full hour patiently sharpening a knife before starting work.

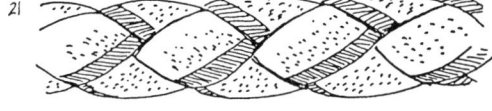

Fig. 16. There are three popular ways to skive the strands, and they are shown in the sketch. The first is convenient but rarely used by professionals: the leather is skived on either side of the face side.

Most professional whipmakers like to skive the underside of the leather as shown in the second drawing, but this can often be a problem if the leather has a furry back.

The third method is seldom used.

Angled Cut

In this method the strands are skived and cut at the same time. You might think this would be faster than the cut first and skive second method, and in the hands of an expert it can be, but a beginner will find it both slow and difficult, with a greater chance of cutting through a strand or getting uneven ones.

Fig. 17. The angled cut also saves leather. The top drawing shows a cross-section of leather with vertical cuts made in it so as to form four strands. If each strand was going to be 15 mm wide the full width would be 60 mm.

The second drawing shows the strands cut out with angle cuts.

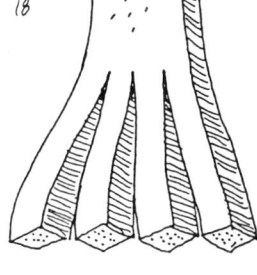

Fig. 18. When spread out, each strand will still cover 15 mm, and the four together will cover 60 mm, even though they have been cut out of a piece of leather only 40 mm wide.

Fig. 19. A whip cut in this way from redhide can be easily recognized because it shows two colors. In the sketch, the shaded part is the red surface of the hide and the dotted part the inner pink color of the hide.

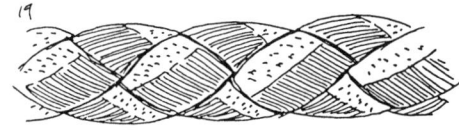

Fig. 20. Some professionals develop this skill to a fine art. They cut from thicker than normal hides and use extreme angle cuts. In this way they can cut four 15-mm strands from only 30 mm of leather!

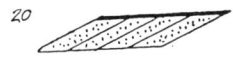

Fig. 21. When you look at a whip made in this way there is only a very narrow strip of the red surface of the hide showing, and the rest is the inner part. This is not as strong as the method shown in figure 19.

If you wish to use angled cuts, remember that the widths given in the drawing earlier will need to be modified according to the angles that you are cutting. In other words, measure and cut out the strands one at a time to the correct widths for each strand rather than drawing out the complete plan on the leather.

at an angle to the leather so that the greater the angle, the more tapered the skive. For the first whip from a side, a skive must be first put on the leading edge, but after that the final cut of each whip set will automatically produce a skived edge for the next set.

The cutting is done a section at a time, the section being as long as the whipmaker finds convenient to cut in one action (usually about 500 mm). Cutting the four strands out in this way makes it easier to get them evenly matched, and is also faster than cutting one complete strand out at a time.

The drawing shows James Hill (Jimmy the Whip) of the well-known whipmaking family, using this technique at Jondaryan in 1994. He was cutting extra-long whips and so his side of leather had become oval.

He used both redhide and chrome-tanned leather, and his knife had to be extremely sharp in order to cut the long bevel that is needed for this technique.

This is a difficult skill to master, and I would advise beginners not to bother with it until they have made a number of whips using the first method.

Cutting on the Beam

Professionals who use the technique of cutting out strands at an angle usually "cut on the beam," as the saying goes. That is to say, the side is thrown over some sort of rail—it might be over the top rail of a fence or over a special length of timber fitted into the workshop.

The leather is held in place with the side of the body—one hand holds out the strand being cut and the other hand holds the knife. Cutting commences from the narrow end of the whip. The knife is held

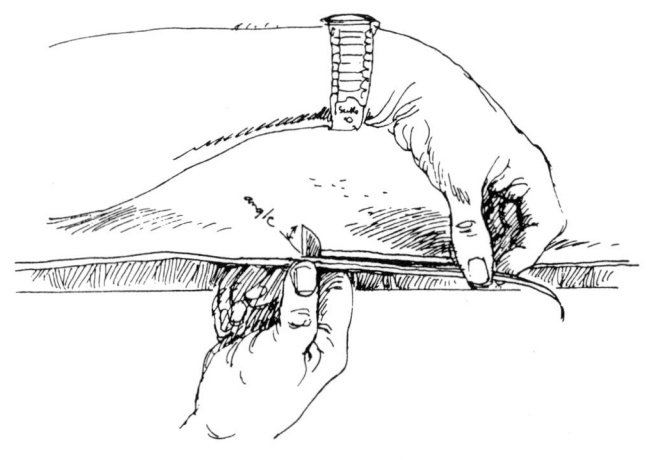

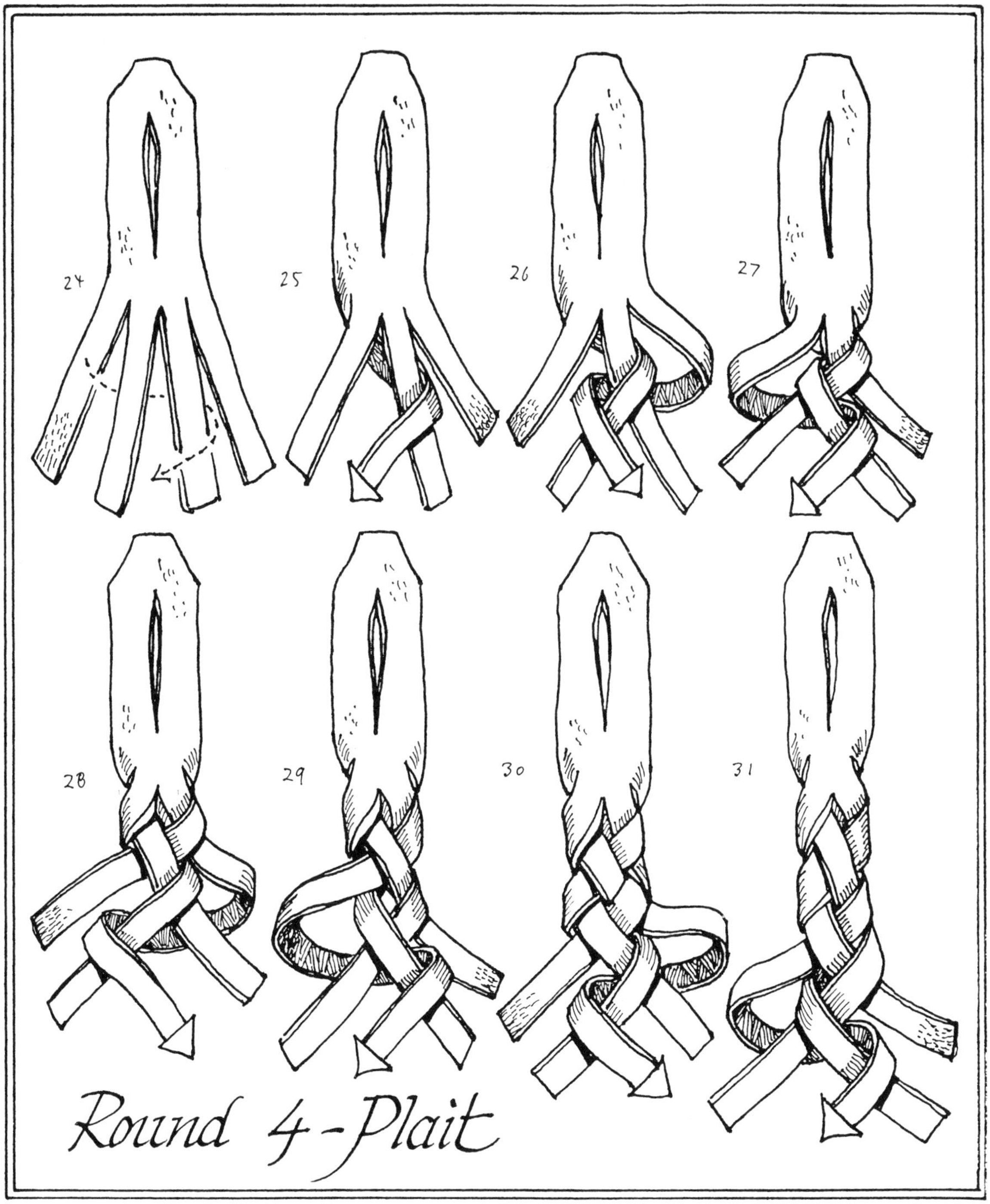

Round 4-Plait

STEP 3: PLAITING THE 4-PLAIT WHIP

Figs. 24–31. The 4-plait is an easy one to remember and use. Find a firm hook or a nail on which to hang the whip while you are plaiting it, or use a piece of cord tied to something firm. You will need to pull the plait tight, and so it will have to be fixed to something that will not move. It should also be at a convenient height for you to work from.

Fig. 32. Put the belly in the center and work around it. When a little more plaiting has been done the belly can be pulled down inside the whip so the upper end is not showing.

Working in a Confined Space

When working in a confined space, you should plait as much as you can and then tie a cord around the plaited section and loop this over your nail or hook. In this way you do not need to have the full whip stretched out.

Plaiting Soap

When you begin a whip you will usually find it difficult to pull the plaiting tightly together and make a neat job, and in that case the use of plaiting soap or leather dressing is necessary. After applying dressing you may find your hands

slipping when you try to tighten the strands, but you will soon develop a good grip to solve this problem.

Ordinary plain soap makes a satisfactory plaiting soap and also acts as a type of leather dressing, but the most common substance used in the bush is ordinary fat, because it does the job and is easy to obtain. Mutton fat is traditionally considered to be better than other fats, but in cattle country beef fat is used. Mix a little kero (kerosene) with it to prevent rats and insects chewing on the finished whip.

There are a number of sorts of leather dressings which can be bought and which do the job well, but professionals usually make up their own mixtures in order to save money.

Leather Dressing

Dressing 1
Clean fat
Neatsfoot oil

Add just enough oil to the fat to make a good working mixture. Temperature plays a part in this, and in cold weather more neatsfoot will be needed to get the right consistency. A small amount of kero, teatree oil, or eucalyptus oil will help prevent vermin from chewing the leather.

Dressing 2
4 parts clean fat
1 part beeswax
2 parts glycerin

Melt together and then set aside to cool. Stir a couple of times while the mixture cools to prevent the ingredients from separating.

Plaiting Soap
4 parts clean fat
1 part soap
3 parts water
(all by volume)

Plaiting experts often make up their own plaiting soaps, which they consider better than plain fat, and this is a common recipe:

Slice the soap up as finely as possible so that it will dissolve faster or, if you have the time, let the soap sit in the water overnight until it has dissolved.

Heat the water and soap and stir until the soap has all dissolved. Add the fat and let the mixture boil, stirring it well all the while. After a few minutes it can be set aside to cool.

When cool it should be firm but light to the touch and may be full of tiny bubbles. If it is watery, put it back on the heat and continue stirring until the water has reduced a little more. Do not overfill the pan or leave it unattended on the stove.

I sometimes add one part beeswax to this mixture, as this gives the leather a dressing at the same time.

Plaiting soap is also a great help when plaiting belts, and its use will result in a much tighter job.

Cleaning Tallow

You need good clean fat or tallow for making both leather dressing and soap, including plaiting soap and saddle soap. Tallow is made by rendering down fat and the fat must be clean and free from impurities if it is to be of any use.

It can be made by rendering down the trimmings obtained when cleaning up a hide before tanning, or from a beast that is being butchered—but most people get it from the family roast. However it is obtained, it usually has some impurities in it.

The normal way to render the fat is to add water to it and then boil it. The amount of water needed will depend on the amount of fat, but for ordinary home use about double the quantity of fat to water is a good rule of thumb. You can use less water, but then you need to make sure that it does not boil away.

Scoop off all the scum as it is boiling and then let it cool. The rubbish that has not been scooped off should then settle down into the water and when it has cooled the fat can be skimmed off.

Fat can also be easily bought clean and ready to use.

Use of Acid in Cleaning Fat

Joe Baxter, late of Packer's Tannery, Narangba, Queensland, passed on an additional hint some years ago which helps produce good quality tallow: When the mixture is boiling and the rubbish has been scooped off, sprinkle a little sulfuric acid (battery acid) onto the mixture. This will cause all the other impurities to settle so that clean tallow will result.

Caution. Care should be taken when doing this; otherwise the mixture may foam up. Noxious fumes can also be released if too much acid is used or it is thrown in carelessly.

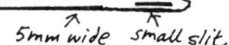
600mm long   5mm wide small slit

Plaiting the Whip

The 4-plait is very easy once you have learned it. Whipmakers have a saying: "Pull tight and plait loose." This means that when you pick up the next strand to be worked in, you first pull it tight before working it into the next position. This is the secret to plaiting a good tight whip.

The other secret is to have a good firm belly around which to plait.

Study your work as you go if you want to end up with a good-looking whip. There are a couple of things to watch out for.

Strands bunching up. If the strands start to get too crowded together and bunch up it may mean that you are pulling at too acute an angle, but it is more likely that the strands are too wide for the size of the belly. At this stage it will be too late to narrow the strands, and so a thicker belly should be used. Some flat strands of thin leather can be used to build up its thickness.

When making kangaroo whips, a strip of thin kangaroo leather, called a bolster, is wrapped around the belly to build up its diameter if this is needed.

Gaps forming. If there are gaps in the plaiting it may be that your strands are all of different widths, and there is little that can be done about this. Or it might be that you are pulling the strands down at too long an angle. If it is neither of these then it probably means that your belly is too fat for the size strands that you are using, and you should trim it down or replace it.

Although the plaiting of the whip may take the longest time, it is the shortest step to write about, since the same plaiting sequence continues for the whole length of the whip. Every now and then you will need to untangle the strands, but that is about all. For very long whips you may want to make the strands up into bundles to stop some of the tangles. This is discussed in chapter 2. However, this is hardly necessary for the average redhide whip.

Keep plaiting until only about 100 mm of the strands are left. If you are a beginner, it is a good idea to use some thread to put a temporary tie around the end of the plaiting at this stage. This will leave your hands free to put on the fall. With a little more experience you will be able to do away with this tie, but it will help with your first whip.

STEP 4: THE FALL

The fall is a strip of leather attached to the end of the whip. The end of the whip gets a lot of knocking around, so it is better to have a fall that can be replaced rather than let the plaited section take the damage.

The fall is usually made from redhide because it does not dry out and crack as readily as greenhide (but greenhide falls are all right as long as they are well greased).

The exact dimensions are according to taste, but 600 mm long is average. The width is decided by the thickness of the leather—it should be both thin and strong.

Cut the fall from the best and thickest part of the side, along the backbone, and it can then be made almost square in section for most of its length.

For the sake of appearance the edges should be skived and then a scrap of leather wrapped around the fall (which has been well greased with whatever dressing you are using) and pulled vigorously up and down to round off the edges. The fall is made a little wider at the top and a slit is put in it just large enough to take the end of the whip.

Cutting the Slit in a Whip Fall

Cutting the slit in a whip fall is simple—all you need is a sharp knife and a single cut. However, in our saddlery business we sometimes make up a lot of falls at one time, and then I look around for some way to speed up the work. This simple tool is a great help because it gives a cut of exactly the right length.

I often make whip falls when I have to straighten the long edge of a new side of redhide. This is the best part of the leather and so ideal for the job, and these trimmings would otherwise be wasted.

This simple tool can be made from any piece of scrap steel. The size of the slit will depend on what your customers want; I usually cut it about 13 mm long to suit the sort of whips that are most common here.

It is possible to quickly and easily shape the cutting edge on a grindstone, but for a properly tempered one you will need some heat.

I heat up the scrap in the forge and then hammer it to a taper and at the same time hammer it out to the desired width. Nearly all the shaping can be done with the hammer rather than the grindstone. Once it has been shaped it should then be hardened and tempered.

A rough and ready way to do this is to heat up the tool to red-hot. Now dip just the cutting edge in water and move it around quickly for a few seconds. When it is lifted from the water there should still be a lot of heat in the main part of the handle. If the cutting part of the tool is not bright and shiny, then use a file to clean a section with a couple of quick strokes. Do this in the shade, as you now need to study the colors moving in the steel.

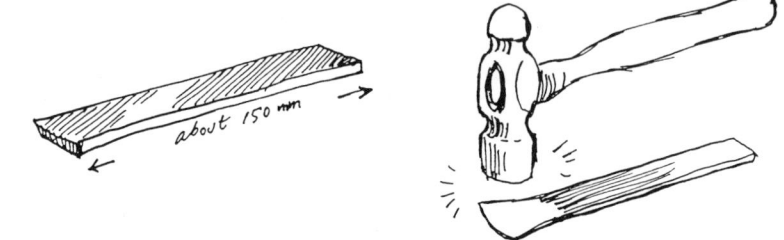

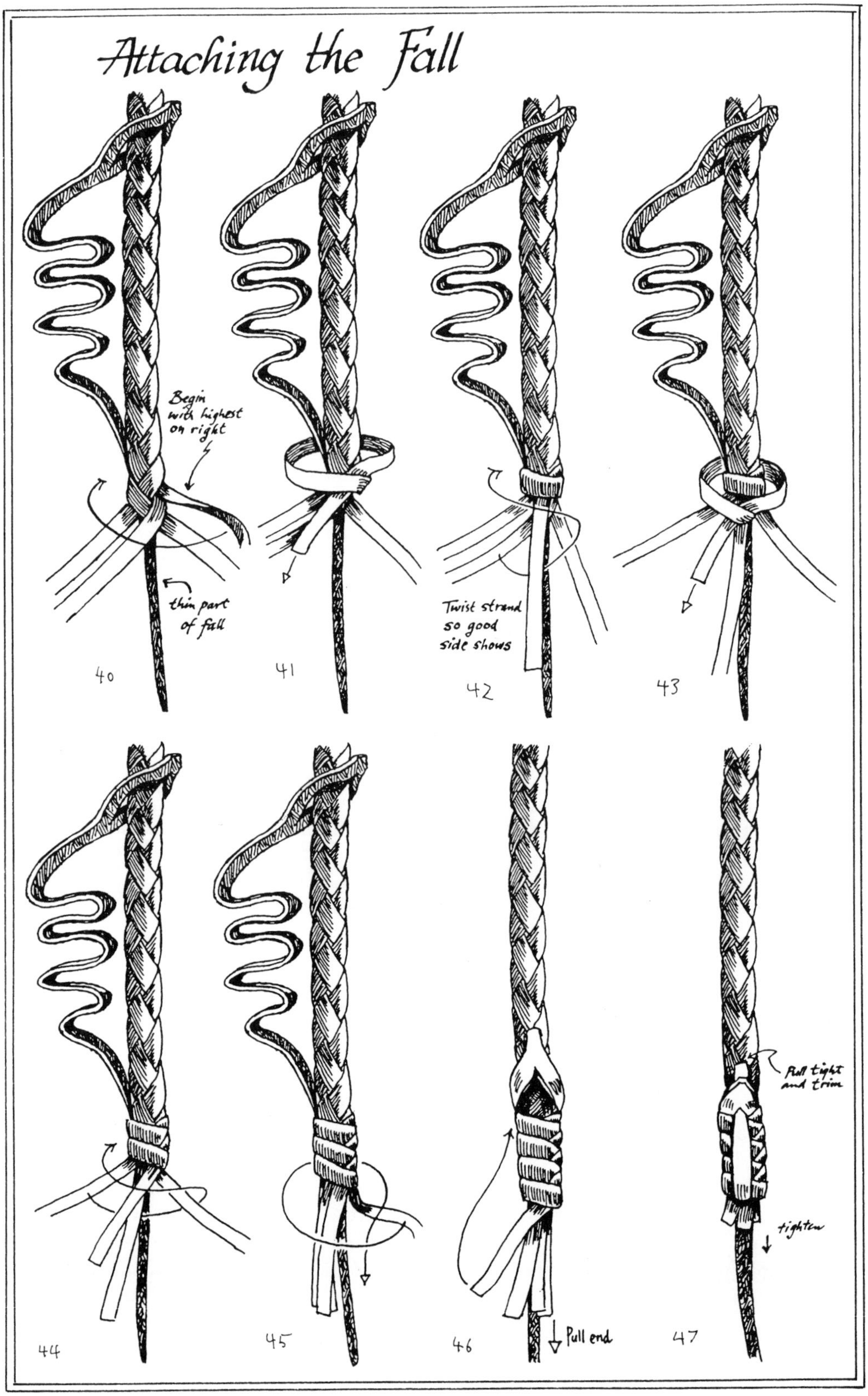

Attaching the Fall

40 — Begin with highest on right / thin part of fall
41
42 — Twist strand so good side shows
43
44
45
46 — Pull end
47 — Pull tight and trim / tighten

The heat from the middle part of the tool will now start to spread towards the cutting edge. First you will see what blacksmiths call yellow, but what is really just a dull yellowish tint that can hardly be seen. This will spread towards the cutting edge and be followed by a blue band of color that is a bit easier to see. When the yellow band has reached the cutting edge and the blue

48

band is just about to get there, plunge the tool back into the water and move it around until it is cool.

A grindstone can be used to get an edge on the tool. When cutting the slits in the fall, using a wood or leather hammer will avoid burring the end of the tool. Hammer into a block of wood.

Common Fall Hitch

Figs. 40-47. The fall is tied on as shown on the previous page. When the last hitch has been made, the end of the hitch is put through the slit as shown in the second to last drawing and then the fall is pulled down hard. This prevents it from coming loose.

49

Rolling the Whip

Fig. 49. When the fall has been attached, the whip should be rolled. This should be done as firmly as possible, using a board on the bench or between two boards and putting all your weight behind it. The effect will be to produce a good smooth finish on the whip.

Resin Board for Whip Rolling

Newly made whips are usually greasy from leather dressing—redhide whips particularly so—and after a few whips the board on which the rolling is done becomes slippery and it is difficult to roll a new whip. For a once-a-year whipmaker this is no problem, but for the professional it is a real nuisance.

Maurice Doohan has an old sock filled with powdered resin (bought from a sports store). By shaking this over the whip a light dusting of resin is deposited and this allows the board to get a good grip on the whip.

STEP 5: THE CRACKER

When a whip is cracked, a sharp noise is caused when the speed of the cracker at the end of the whip breaks the sound barrier.

Traditionally the cracker is made from horsehair, which the stockman pulls directly from the horse's mane or tail.

Nylon twine also makes excellent crackers and we use spools classed as 210/18 ply in our saddlery. Other materials can also be used, including most synthetic twines. In the old days silk thread was popular, but today many professionals use baling twine.

The traditional way of making a cracker is to take a few lengths of horsehair or twine around 700 mm long and grip one end firmly in the teeth while twisting the other. The sketch shows a couple of friends doing this at Lockhart River, November 1995.

The direction of the twist does not matter with horsehair, but with twine it is thought best to twist it in the opposite direction to which it has been made. However, for all practical purposes, this does not matter.

50

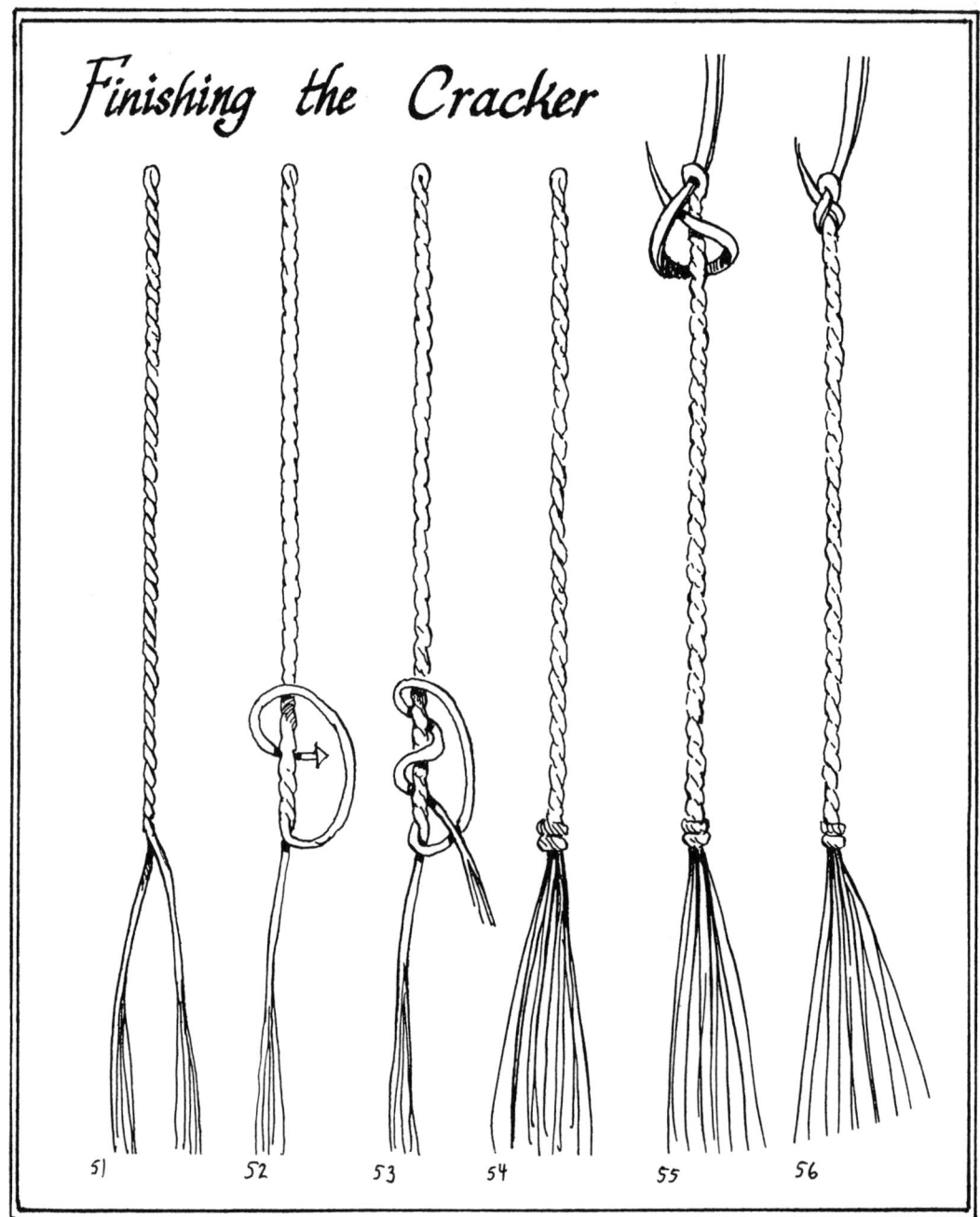

After a certain amount of twisting has been done the cord thus formed will be seen to begin to kink. At this stage it is grasped in the middle as shown on the left of the sketch of crackers being made, and the two ends will be seen to spiral around each other as if by magic.

Speeding Up the Job

If a number of crackers are to be made, the job can be speeded up by bending a small crank from a scrap of fencing wire with a small hook bent into the end of it. This takes only a few seconds, and all that is then needed is a nail or hook to take the other end of the twine (this cannot be done with horsehair, as the twine has to be in a loop to go around the hooks). This is illustrated on page 71.

Finishing Off the Cracker

Figs. 51–56. When the cracker has been twisted, it looks like the left-hand sketch. Many people then simply tie an overhand knot to stop it from unraveling. A neater way to tie it is shown in the second and third sketches. This is a variation of the blood knot (see next page), and allows the loose strands to point downwards instead of to one side.

Fastening the Cracker to the Fall

The cracker is fastened to the fall with a simple bend, as shown in the last two sketches.

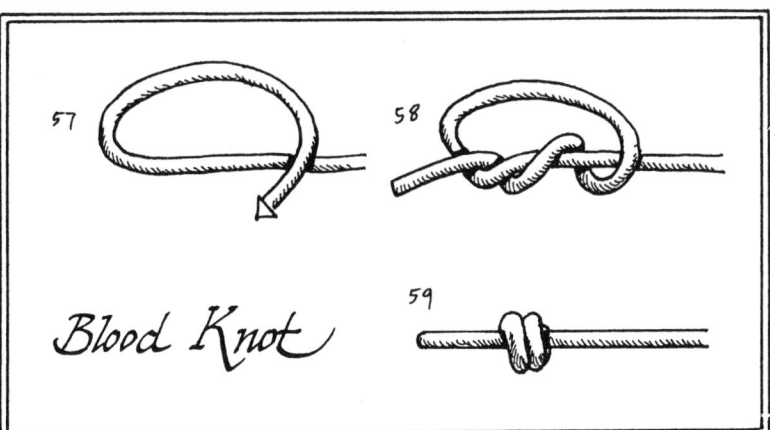

It is a good idea if making a whip for sale or for someone else to give it a few cracks before you get rid of it, as sometimes the cracker will fly off at the first couple of cracks unless you have this bend nice and firm.

Attaching the Cracker—Another Method

Figs. 60–63. Here is another method of attaching the cracker that is used by some whipmakers. They argue that if the cracker is to be replaced you lose less of the tip, but in practice they all seem to cut off the whole knot whichever method was used to attach it. Like many things, I think that it is just tradition, and this is the way they have been taught.

Cracking the Whip

Having just mentioned cracking the whip reminds me that I sometimes get phone calls from people asking where they can get a book that gives instructions for cracking a whip. Unfortunately, this is a skill that cannot be explained in words or pictures and can only be gained by practice.

STEP 6: MAKING THE HANDLE

Any strong timber can be used for a whip handle, but old stockmen warn against using any wood that splits into long, sharp slivers, as this could cause injuries in a fall from a horse.

A wide variety of timbers are suitable for whip handles, and certain woods are considered the best in different areas. You should be able to find a suitable timber without too much trouble if you first inquire. The best idea is to ask old bushmen in your district. An unusual handle of bush timber is illustrated here, made by Ross Grierson of Mount Pleasant station, Queensland.

Half-Plaited Handle

Cane is popular for whip handles. In north Queensland this can be obtained from the lawyer vine that grows in the jungle. Offcuts can also be obtained from the makers of cane furniture.

Length is to taste, but is usually around 500 mm. Diameter is around 20 mm.

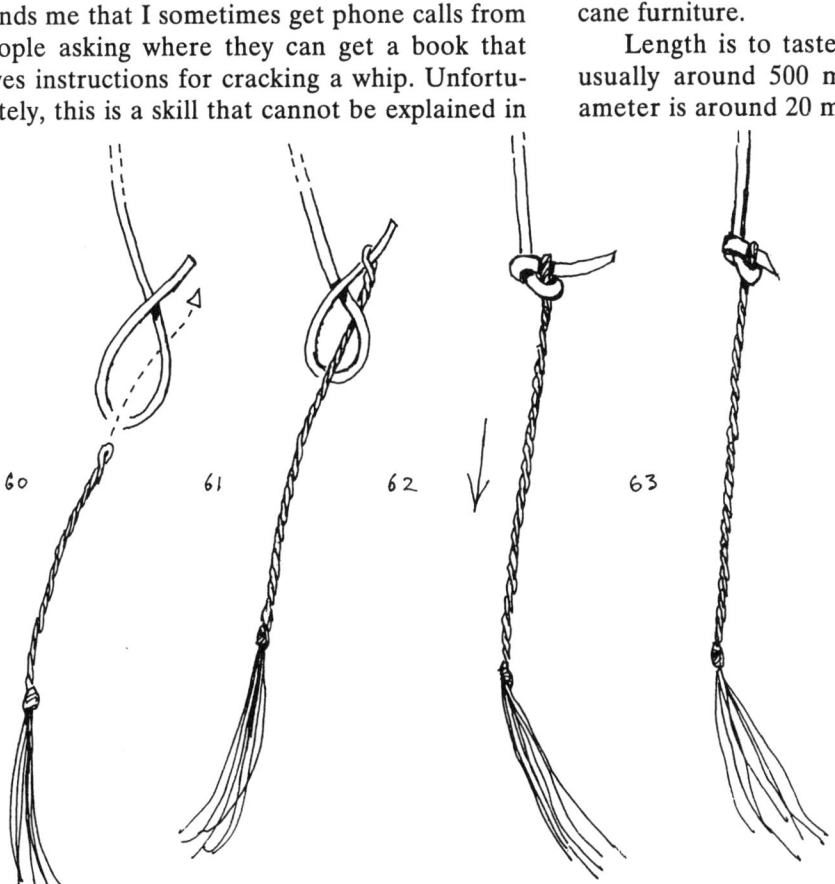

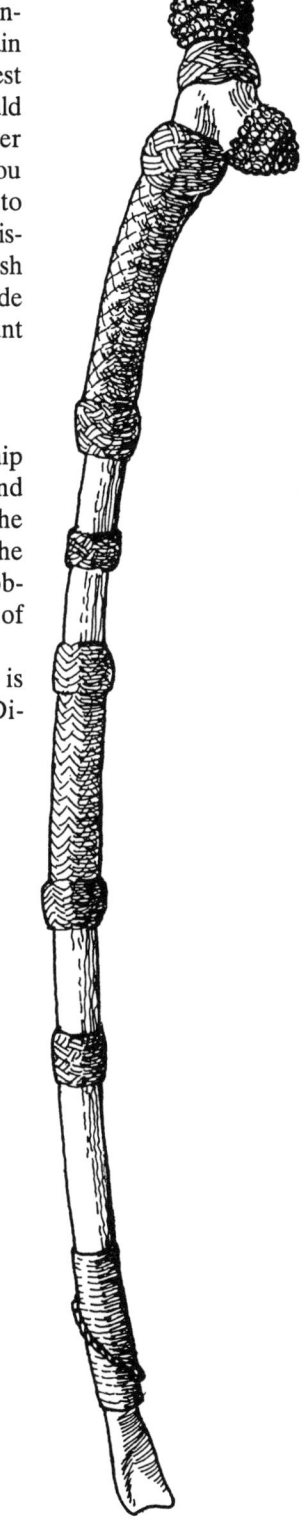

Straightening a Whip Handle

Straightening a cane whip handle is a job that the whipmaker should not have to do, because it should have already been done by the cane supplier. However, what few whipmakers ever consider is the fact that the cane is the product of a jungle vine, and in its natural state it curves and winds its way around tall jungle trees.

When harvested, it is cut into lengths and roughly straightened for convenience of transport. When it has been dried and seasoned, any remaining curves are removed (or should be removed) before it is sold.

The cane that whipmakers use is the same cane that is used to make cane furniture, and the makers of this material use simple tools to remove any curves. One of these is a tool made of iron rather like a wrench, but with the jaws fixed. If you were going to do a lot of this work it would be worthwhile to make one up, but the average whipmaker only has to deal with bent cane from time to time.

Cane can be straightened in a vice, or with an ordinary wrench, but if you try it you will soon see that the corners of the tool will mark the cane. For that reason any tool that you use must have rounded corners.

The simple wooden tool illustrated here was based on the one used by the professionals. Don't pay any attention to the fancy shape of the handle, or the swelling at the top—that just happened to be the shape of the scrap of timber that I picked up.

All that is needed is enough length for leverage and a hole with rounded edges large enough to take the cane. A bending action is used to straighten the cane.

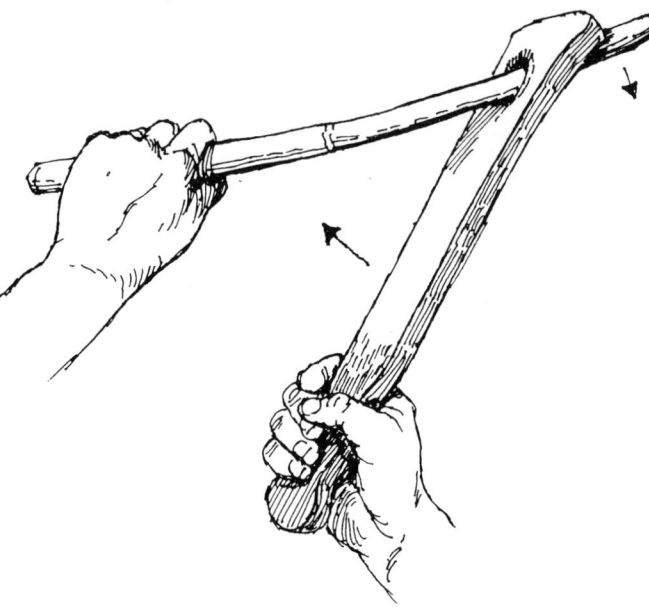

Sometimes the cane starts to resume its natural curve in humid weather. Recently in our saddlery a bunch of whip handles bent quite a bit during one wet month. A lot of problems can be avoided in the first place by binding the handles together into a firm bunch when you buy them rather than leaving them around loose.

Heat. Some whipmakers use heat to speed up the straightening of cane. The bent part is held over a flame or heat of some sort and it can then be straightened easier than doing it cold.

STEP 7: COVERING THE HANDLE

The half-plait handle is much easier and quicker to make than the full-plait handle described in *Whipmaking Book 2* (see chapter 2). When properly done it can look very attractive.

Two methods of covering the handle are given here. The first is the simpler method and is suitable for a rough old whip to use in the yards. The second method gives a much better looking product but takes a lot longer.

HANDLE WITH DOG'S KNOT

The leather for covering the handle can be taken from the thinnest part of the hide. Cut two strips of redhide, each one meter long, or longer if the handle is extra thick.

Fig. 67. Trim them down to half width in the middle, as shown.

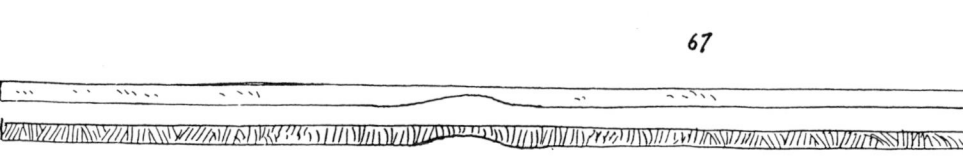

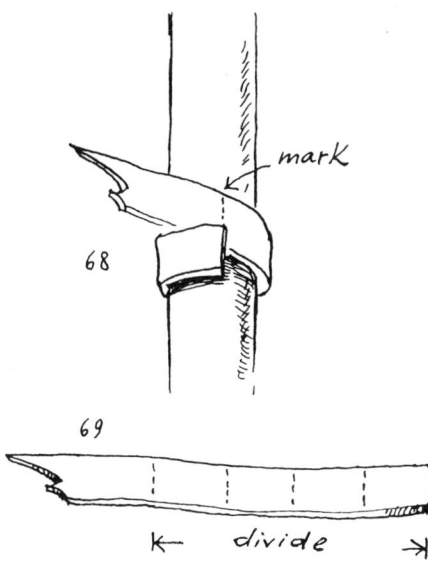

Fig. 68. The width of the strands is calculated by wrapping a scrap of the same leather around the handle and making a mark. Now add about 25 percent (one quarter) to this.

Fig. 69. Divide this measure into four parts to calculate the width of the strands. They will be around 15 mm. It looks better if the edges are skived before the plaiting is done.

Fig. 70–73. Wrap the strands around the handle 200 mm from the end and begin plaiting as shown. This is the same 4-plait as was used to make the whip.

Fig. 74. When the end is reached, put a tack in either side to hold the strands firmly in place. If you are working in the bush with no tacks handy, then cut a groove in the handle and tie twine tightly around the strands, making sure that the twine sits flush in the groove.

Fig. 75. Now give the handle a good roll with a scrap of timber to flatten and smooth the plaiting.

FORMING THE KNOB

The knobs formed on fancy whips are quite complicated, but this is a simple one. It is an elaboration of the crown knot, but is usually known in the bush as a dog's knot (in bush slang dog's testicles are called dog's knots).

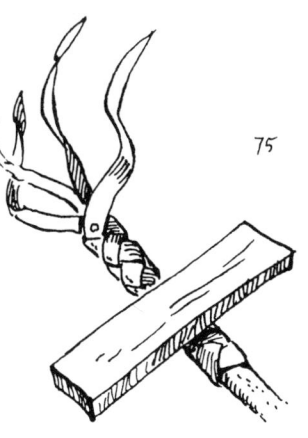

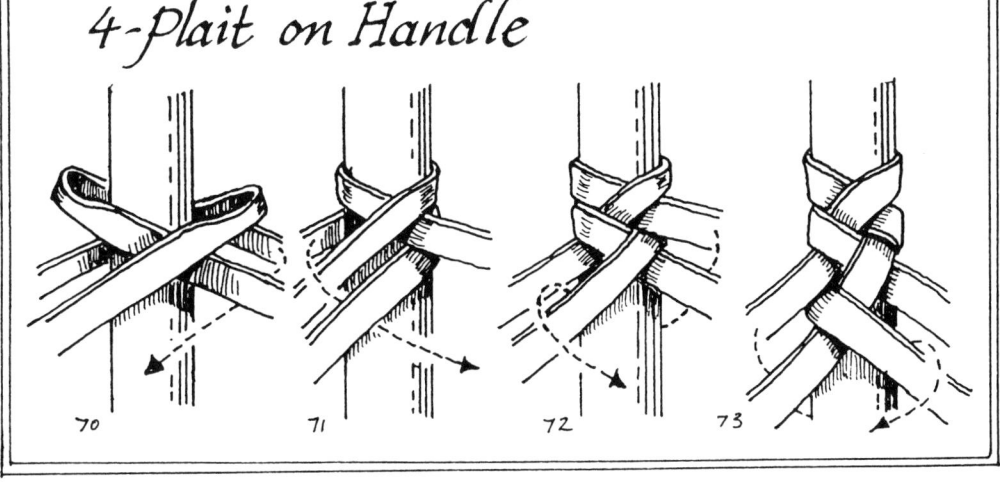

Fig. 76. If you tack a scrap of leather around the top of the handle this will help bulk out the handle, but if the leather is thick this may make the knot too large.

CROWN KNOT

Figs. 77–80. The knob is formed in three moves. First tuck each strand under the one next to it as shown below. This is a crown knot.

27

Due to the angles at which the strands come out from the handle plait, this knot may begin by looking a bit uneven and one-sided.

Figs. 81–82. The small sketch shows how the knot should look when seen from above, and to encourage it in this direction it should be given a few good thumps on a firm surface.

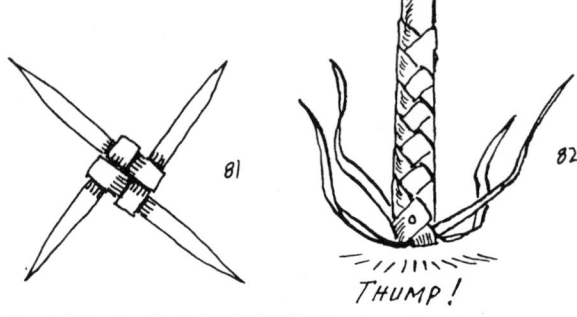

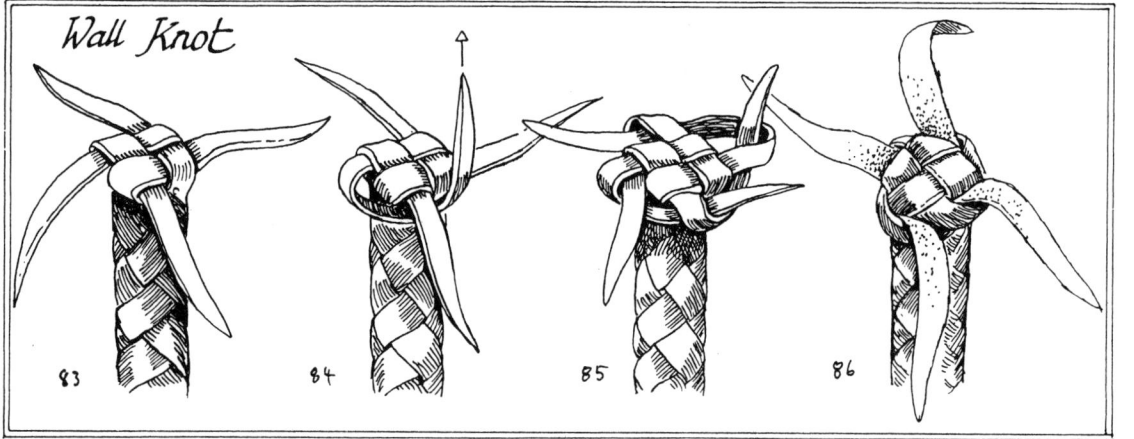

WALL KNOT

Figs. 83–86. The second move consists of passing each strand under the one next to it. This is known as a wall knot.

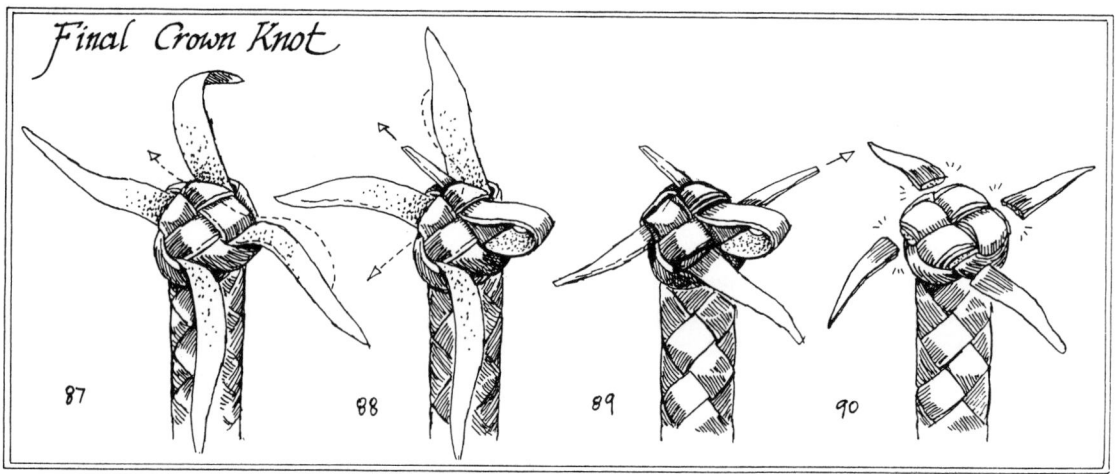

FINAL CROWN KNOT

Figs. 87–90. The third move follows the first move as shown and is another crown knot. In this way, each strand is locked under the strands that were put down first.

A fid or a screwdriver will be needed to open up the plaiting to make this move.

Fig. 91. When all four ends have been tucked through they can be trimmed flush and should look like the handle in the sketch.

Roll the knob firmly beneath your hand on a flat surface to get it smooth. This knob must be formed as tightly as possible.

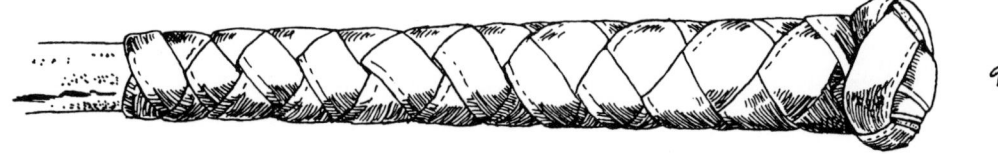

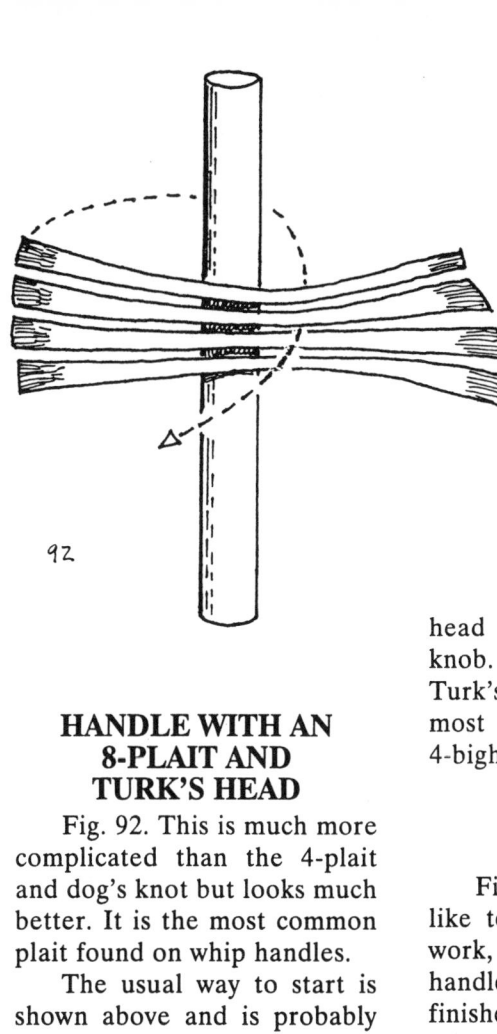

92

HANDLE WITH AN 8-PLAIT AND TURK'S HEAD

Fig. 92. This is much more complicated than the 4-plait and dog's knot but looks much better. It is the most common plait found on whip handles.

The usual way to start is shown above and is probably so common because it is easy to remember. Four strands are taken and laid one on top of the other as shown. A normal whipmaker's plait is then started, beginning as shown by the dotted line.

Figs. 93–104. This method, however, is not as neat as it could be, and the full page that follows shows a better method of beginning this plait.

A half plait can be as long or short as you like. Some commercial whips have them so short that they are little more than a hand grip, but most whipmakers like to cover about half the handle, and so the work is started about 250 mm from the knob end of the handle.

Amount needed. If you start 250 mm up the handle and the handle is of average thickness, you will need four strands each a meter long and 8–10mm wide, depending on the diameter of the handle. Narrow the width down in the center for a neater beginning, as shown in the first drawing on the next page.

Fig. 105. By the sixth step you will be making a normal whipmaker's plait, and continue in this way until the end of the handle is reached. Then tie or tack the strands to keep them in place. This is hidden by the Turk's head that goes over the knob. A 3-part, 4-bight Turk's head is one of the most common, or a 5-part, 4-bight, for a deeper knot.

12-PLAIT HANDLE

Fig. 106. If you would like to try some even finer work, you could cover the handle with a 12-plait. When finished, it should look like this.

I call this Doug's start because it was suggested to me by Doug Tarrant and Doug Kite. The idea proposed by the "Dougs" was to use a square start to go around a cylinder. This is much stronger and faster than tying a heap of strands onto the handle.

The method is shown in figures 107–116, and the rest of the explanation follows that.

Amount needed. To plait half the length of the handle, cut six strands, each double the full length of the handle (1 meter long), and 6 mm wide. This will make a 12-plait handle. (If you wish to use more strands than this, it is better to add 2 more rather than 1, so as to go up to a 16-plait.)

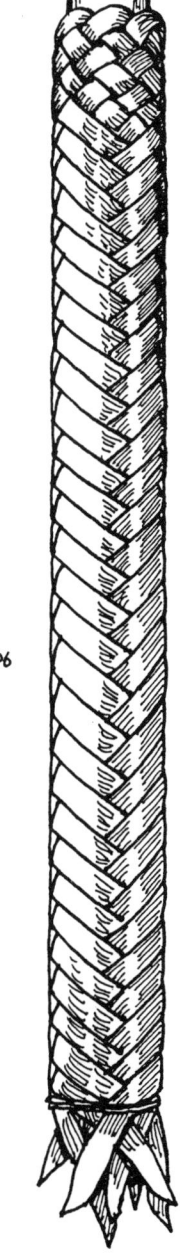

106

29

8-Plait for Half-Plaited Whip Handle

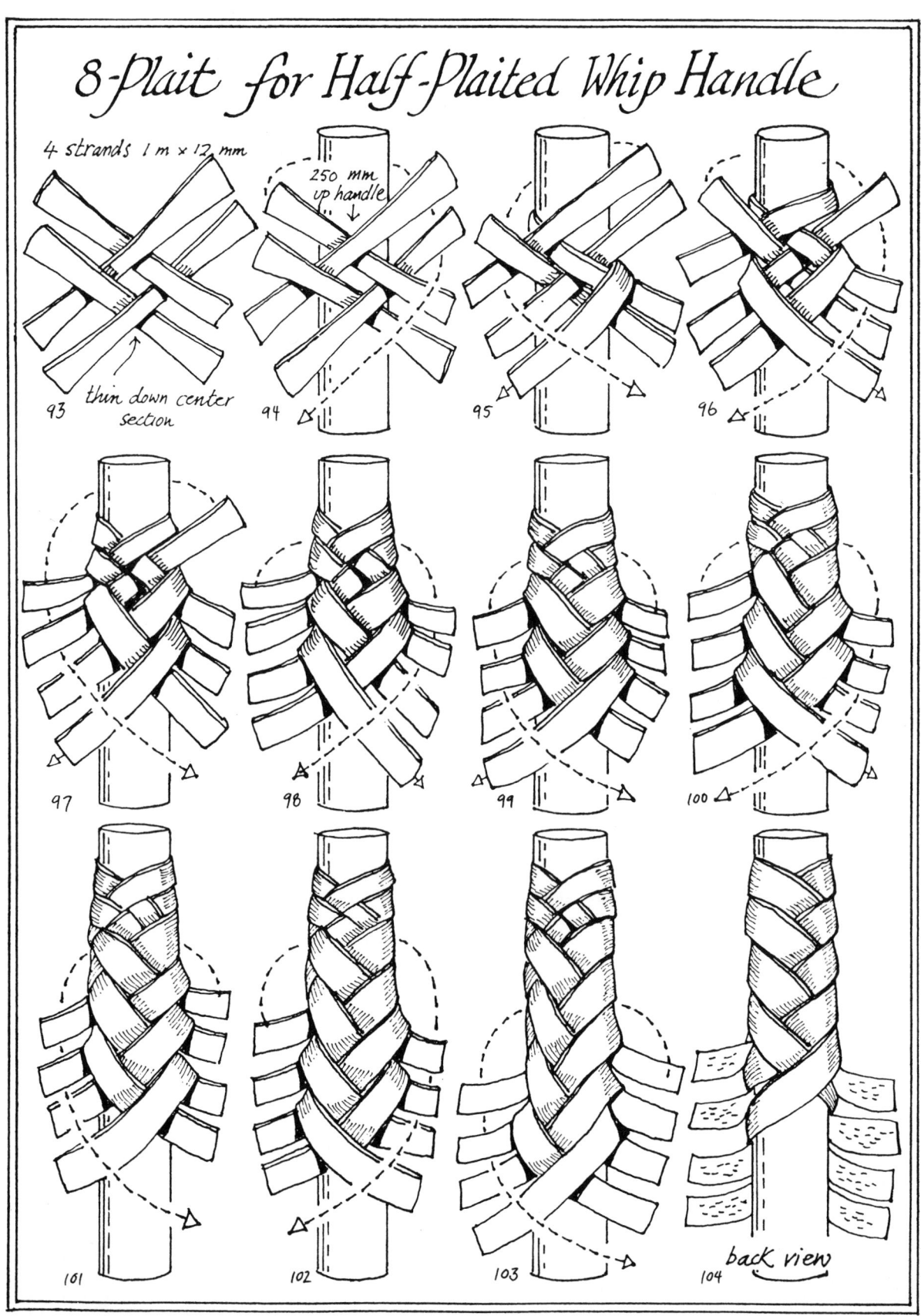

Square Start for Half-Plaited Handle   12-PLAIT

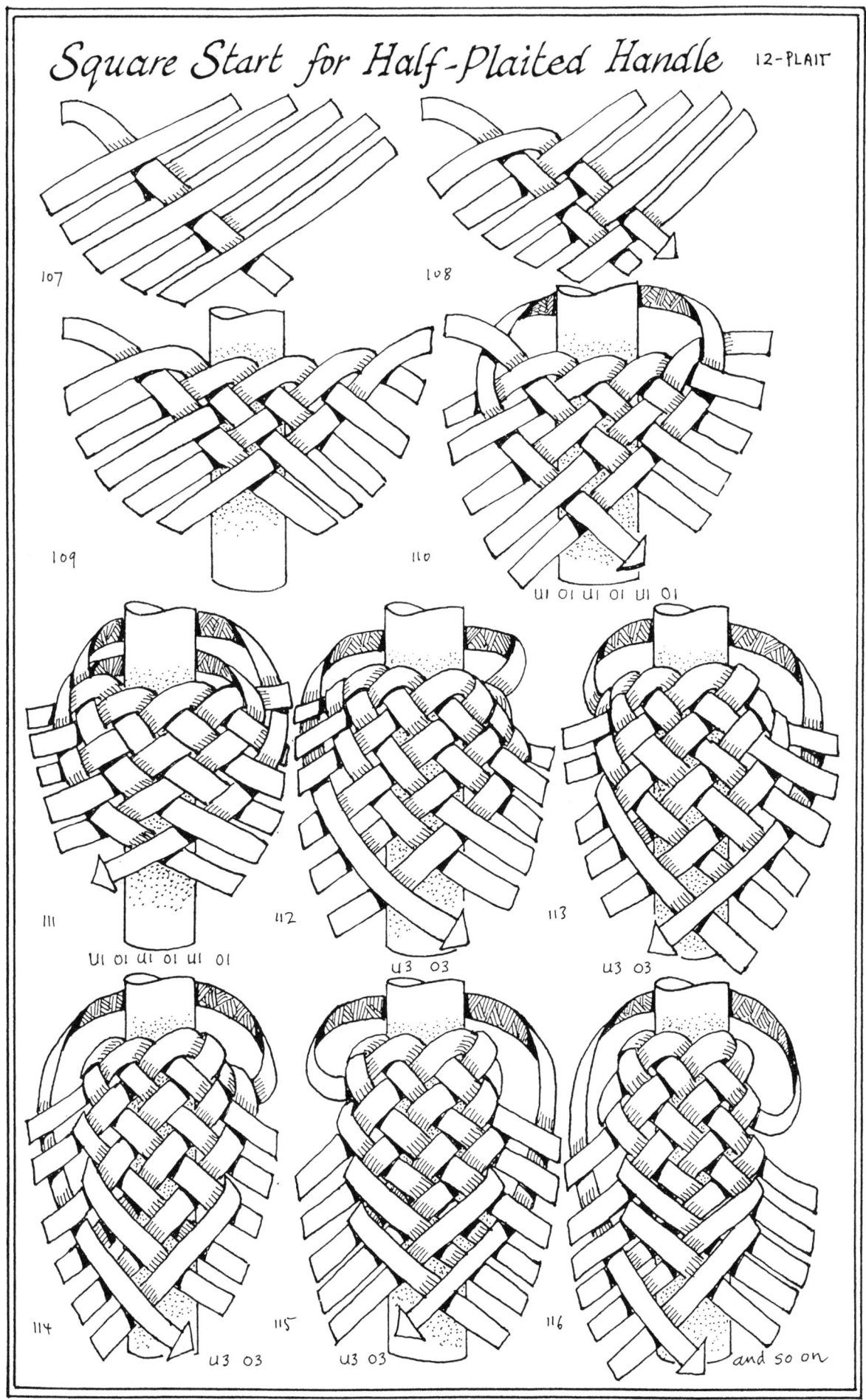

107 108 109 110 U1 O1 U1 O1 U1 O1
111 U1 O1 U1 O1 U1 O1 112 U3 O3 113 U3 O3
114 U3 O3 115 U3 O3 116 and so on

31

Figs. 107–116. The first step is to form the square end, and this can be done in the hand. Next lay this on the whip handle at the halfway mark, take one end around the back, and continue as shown in the drawings.

When you have brought all the strands around and got them in place, carefully tighten up the whole job and make it nice and even before continuing.

The ordinary whipmaker's 12-plait consists only of the two actions shown in the last two drawings. Continue this to the end of the handle and then firmly tie it before cutting off the ends.

This will be covered later with a Turk's head, and a 5-part, 4-bight will look good on this handle. This may be found on page 81 or you can use the 3-part, 4-bight on page 36 or page 154 (another method).

WRAPAROUND HANDLE

Fig. 117. I feel a bit ashamed about even mentioning this form of whip handle covering, as it is only seen on very cheap whips. However, as it is also commonly found on drafting canes, it should be given some space.

The method could not be simpler: a length of leather is taken and the ends trimmed to a point as shown. It is tightly wrapped around the handle and tacked at each end. To make it look a bit more acceptable, a small Turk's head or Spanish Ring knot (page 83) should be put on the bottom to cover the tacks and a proper knob should be put on the end.

SECRET PLAIT WORKED INTO A WHIP HANDLE

Simply wrapping a length of leather around a cane will give a whip handle a grip, but it looks rather plain. An interesting texture can be worked into the handle by using the secret plait in one section of the leather as illustrated.

(The method of forming the secret plait is explained in a booklet of that name that I have written and in the appendix starting on page 155.

Figs. 118–19. The leather is slit and the plait worked into it and then the whole strap is wrapped around the handle and tacked at each end. Additional prominence can be given to this plaited section by wrapping a scrap of leather around the handle just at the point where the secret plait is wrapped—this will make it bulge out a little.

Fig. 120. A normal knob and Turk's head is then put on the end and a small Turk's head or a Spanish ring knot is put at the spot where the wrapping is finished on the handle. In this case I used a headhunter's knot, but anything will do.

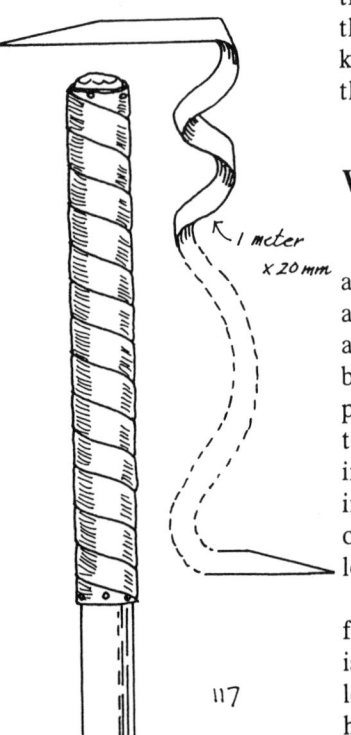

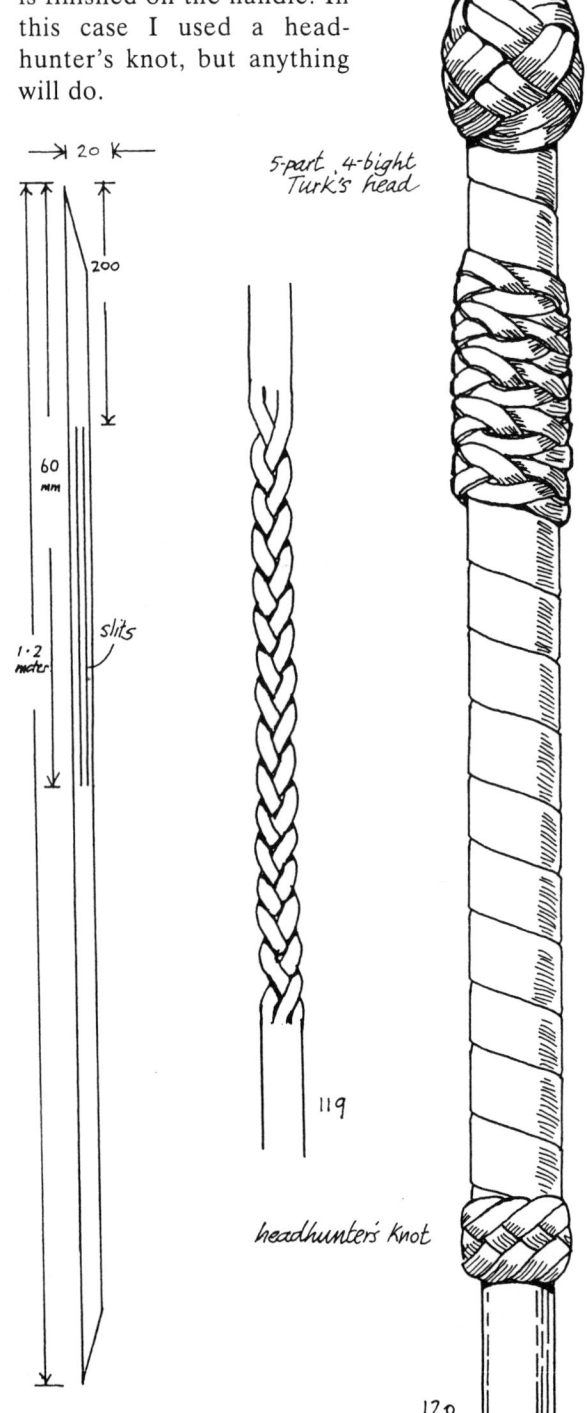

BINDING ON THE KEEPER

Fig. 121. The end of the handle should have a groove cut or filed into it so that the twine that holds the keeper will not come loose.

Fig. 122. A strip of heavy kangaroo hide 180 mm long by 30–40mm wide is used for the keeper, or a strip of redhide 180 × 20 mm. The edges are trimmed down so that they do not overlap each other when placed on the handle. The ends are also skived thin so that they will not make a bulge in the finished job.

Fig. 123. The keeper is tied on with strong thread. Today strong synthetic twine is used, but if you do wish to use natural twine it should be waxed to help preserve it. In order to get a tight job, one end of the thread is made firm to something and the whipmaker winds the thread on as shown, moving forward as he or she winds.

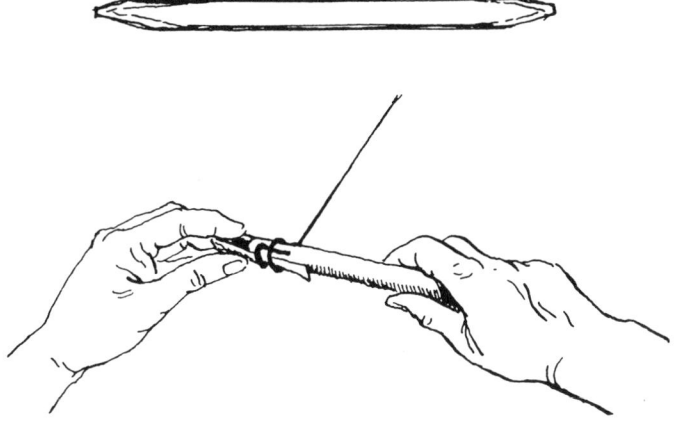

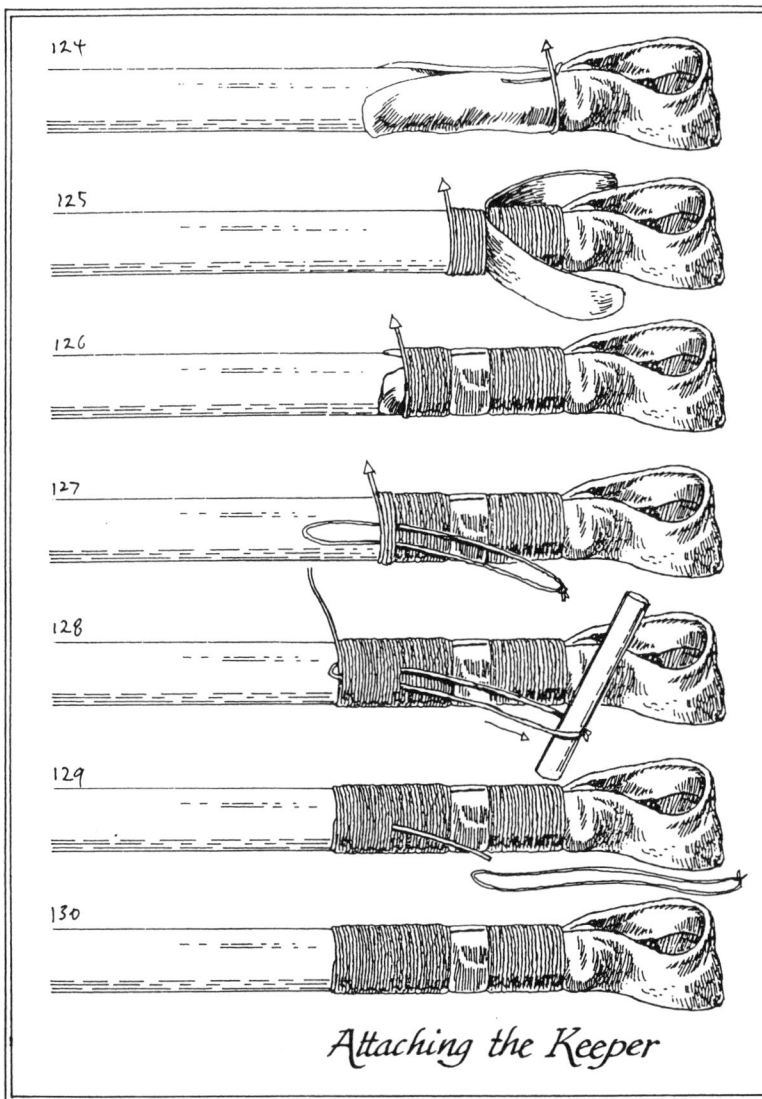

Attaching the Keeper

You get a stronger job if you wind the handle around the twine instead of winding the twine around the handle.

Here are three ways to tie on the keeper. The first is probably the most common one used today.

Method 1. Figs. 124–130. Begin as shown, and when there is only about 15 mm to go, drop a loop of strong twine onto the job and wrap the twine around this, leaving either end of the loop sticking out.

When enough has been wound on, the end of the twine is pushed through one end of this loop. Grasp the other end with the pliers and pull until the loop has been removed and the end of the thread will be ready to trim off.

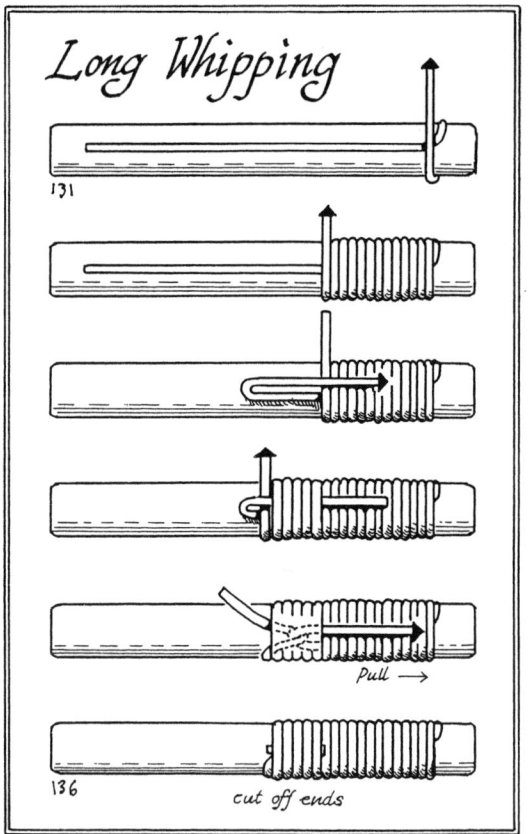

Long Whipping

Method 2. Figs. 131–36. This method is probably a little faster than the previous method because there is no need to make or find a loop.

If the end is pulled too hard when finishing up, both ends will come out together. Though this will not weaken the knot, it does tend to make a gap on the job.

Method 3. Figs. 137–41. The last method is an old one dating from the days of natural thread, when care had to be taken not to put too much pressure on it. It is slower than the previous methods but some people still use it.

If there are no pliers handy, a loop is put into the end of the twine and a piece of stick is pushed through this to provide a handle that can be pulled.

Begin by tucking one end of the thread under and begin winding. When most of the winding has been done, undo the thread from whatever it is tied to and cut it off with about 500 mm left hanging.

Form a bridge, as shown by the arrow, and wind the thread back towards the keeper. Grasp the bridge at the point shown by the arrow and tightly wind it around the handle. When all the thread has been wound on, pull the end tight and cut it off flush.

RIB RATTLING

The sketch shows Jimmy the Whip "rib rattling," as he called this old-fashioned

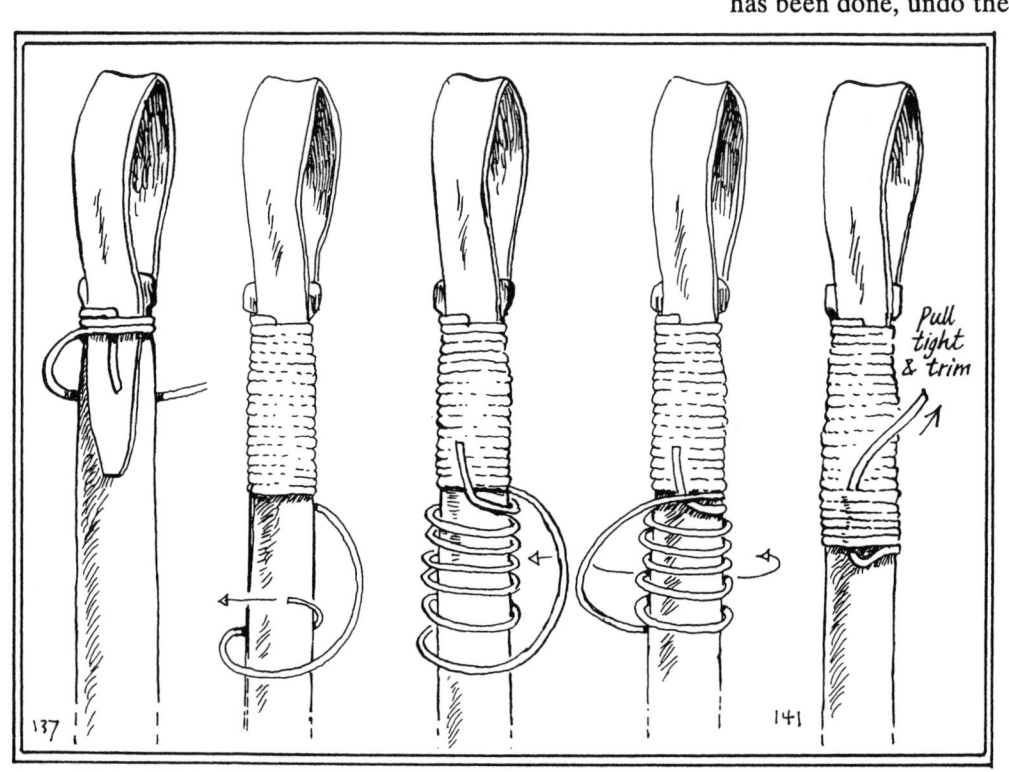

method of tying on the keeper. This was the method used in the old days before very strong synthetic twine came on the market. If natural twine was put in the vice as shown earlier and a little too much pull put on it, it would break.

To overcome this problem the pressure was only put on a short section of the natural twine. The whipmaker held the handle under his arm with one hand. In the other hand he had some cloth to prevent the twine cutting into his skin, and with this he kept the pressure on the twine. The handle was turned with the left hand to wind the twine onto the handle.

Jimmy said that when he was younger he had to make dozens of these every day and his ribs would become very sore. Even when I did the sketch in 1994 he was still using the same method.

FRENCH GRAPEVINE

This next step is just for decoration and would not normally be put on a whip for everyday use. It is also known as French whipping or grapevine service. It also looks good when tied in cord and has long been a favorite among sailors for covering railings.

If put on a whip handle very tightly it would hold the keeper by itself, but I think it is a safer idea to first bind on the keeper with twine and only use this for a decorative touch.

Figs. 143–47. Take a length of kangaroo lace and work it as shown. It should cover all the thread below.

Figs. 148–49. The lace is finished off in the same way as the twine in method 3, previous page.

Fig. 150. The spiral pattern is lost in these few last turns and there is no sign of the thread in the finished job.

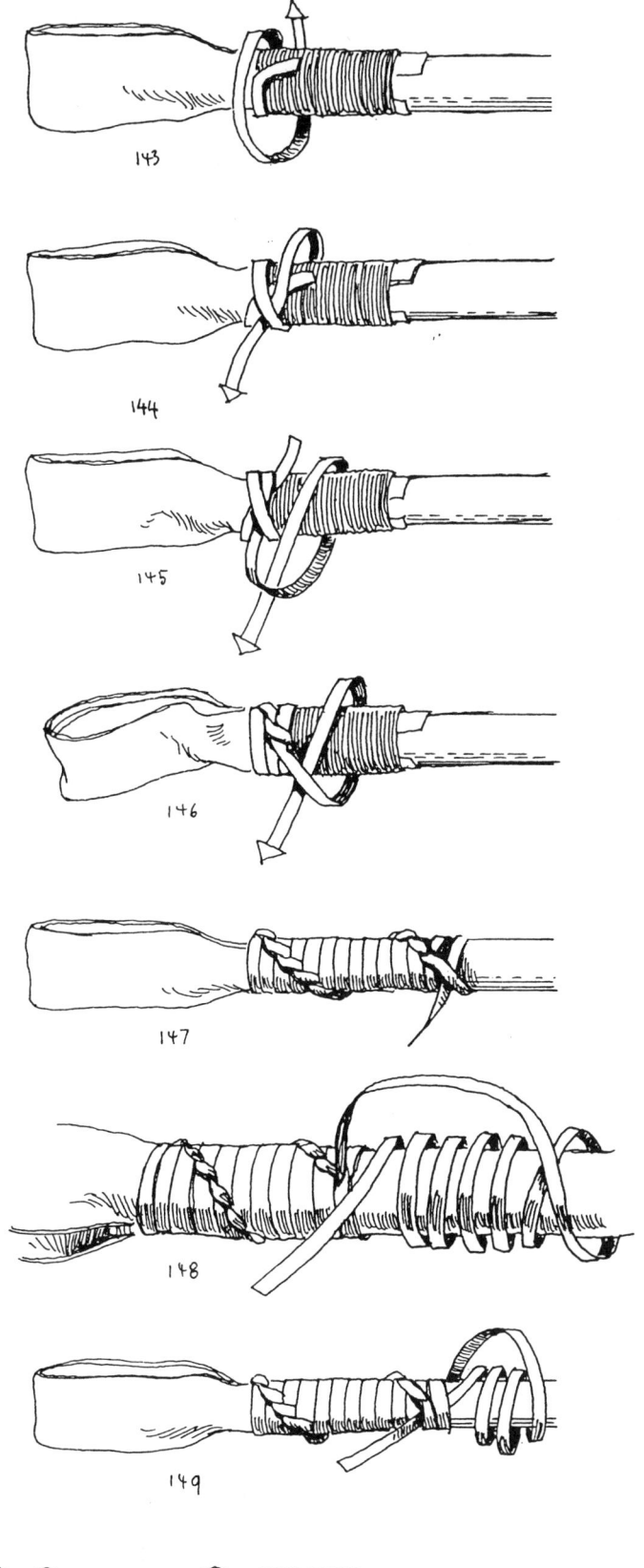

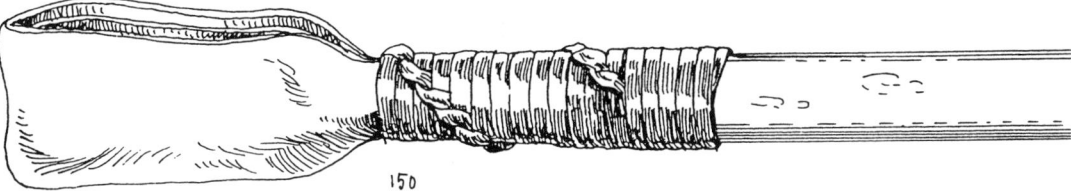

3-Part, 4-Bight Turk's Head

152

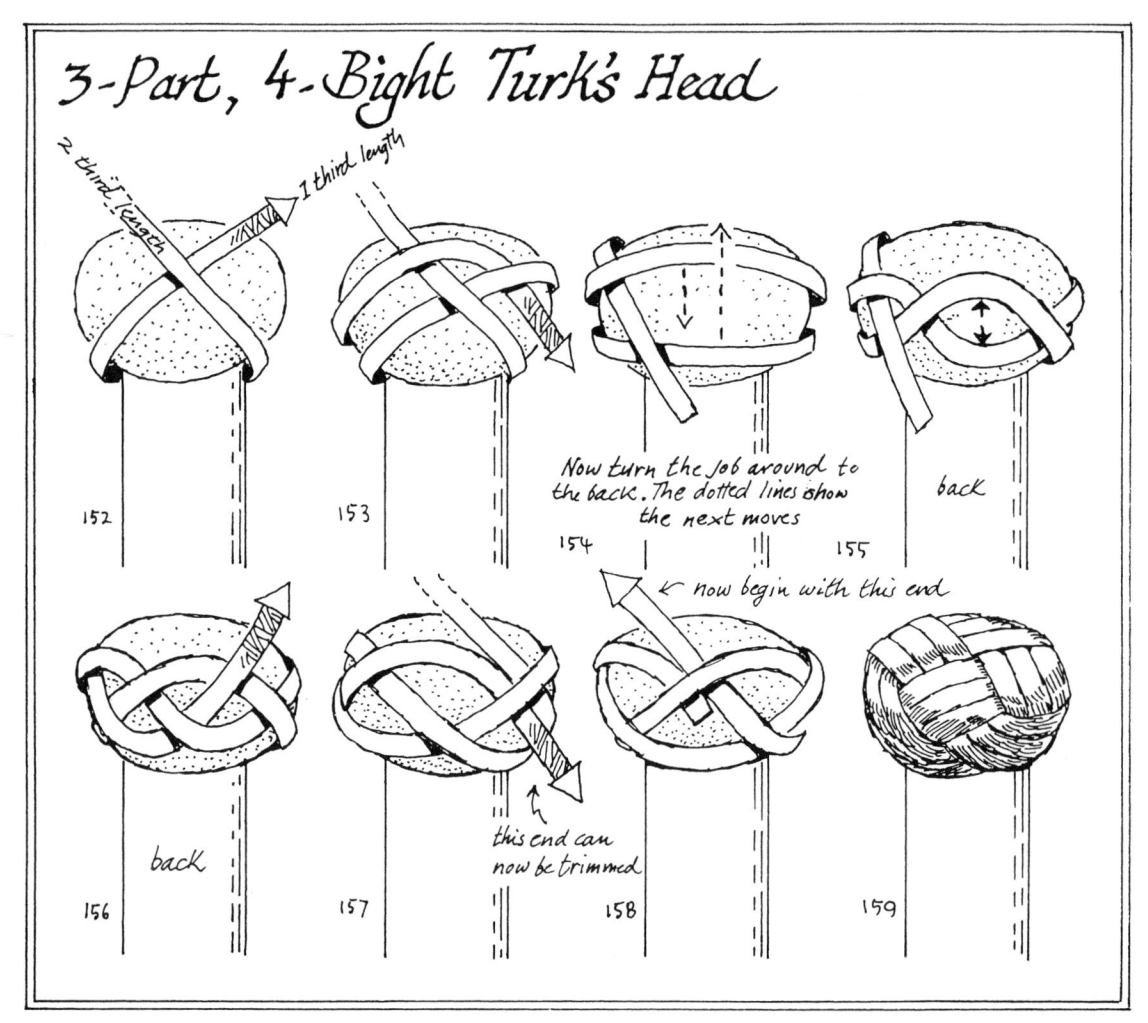

153

Now turn the job around to the back. The dotted lines show the next moves

154

155 back

156 back

157 this end can now be trimmed

158 now begin with this end

159

Form the shape of the knob as shown on page 80; then cover it with a Turk's head.

3-PART, 4-BIGHT TURK'S HEAD

(Another method is shown on page 154.)

Normally a Turk's head is tied by beginning at one end of the lace and continuing on in one direction until the knot is completed. This means that when you begin the knot you have to handle a long length of lace and this slows the job down. Whipmaker Maurice Doohan got around this problem by beginning one third of the way along the lace and working back towards the short end. When the knot has been fully formed, the longer end is used up for the second and third passes.

The advantage of this method is that the second and third layers (as shown in figure 159) go above rather than below the start (as shown in figure 158). This is the most common knot found on whip-handle knobs, not because it is the best Turk's head for the job, but because it is the fastest to tie.

Amount needed. The amount needed is impossible to say, since it all depends on the size of the knob that you are covering. A knob 25 mm in diameter might take just under 1 meter of 5-mm lace, while a knob 30 mm in diameter would take just over a meter. A knob 35 mm in diameter will take about 1.1 meters if using 6-mm lace.

The beauty of this method is that you can leave the long end of your lace still attached to the hank and need not cut it off until you have gone around the knob once, and can then judge what length has been used up.

Start with a bit over a meter of 5-mm lace or 6-mm if the knob is a large one of 35-mm diameter or more. Divide this into thirds, and begin with one-third, leaving the long end hanging. If you have trouble at the start, you can put a tack into the lace to hold the end firm, but once you learn the knot you will be able to do it without this.

Fig. 152. Go around once.

Fig. 153. Go around again and tuck the end in.

Fig. 154. Turn the job around.

Fig. 155. Cross the strands over each other.

Fig. 156. Put the end through the hole.

Fig. 157. Bring it home against the other end and the Turk's head is complete.

Fig. 158. Now to the long strand: this was two-thirds of the length, so you will now know whether you are going to have more than enough by the amount of the shorter end left over. Take the long end and work back following alongside the first strand.

Fig. 159. When you have made three passes in all, the knob should be fully covered. If there is still a gap, you can go around one more time. I have seen some whipmakers cover a narrow gap by going around with a thinner strand of lace, and one of a different color. This looks very good and makes an error of calculation look like a well-designed display of style and skill.

ATTACHING WHIP AND HANDLE

Figs. 160–61. The handle and whip are looped together as shown.

Your finished whip should now look something like this if you made the handle with a dog's knot. If it was made with a Turk's head on the handle, it should look like the drawing on the next page.

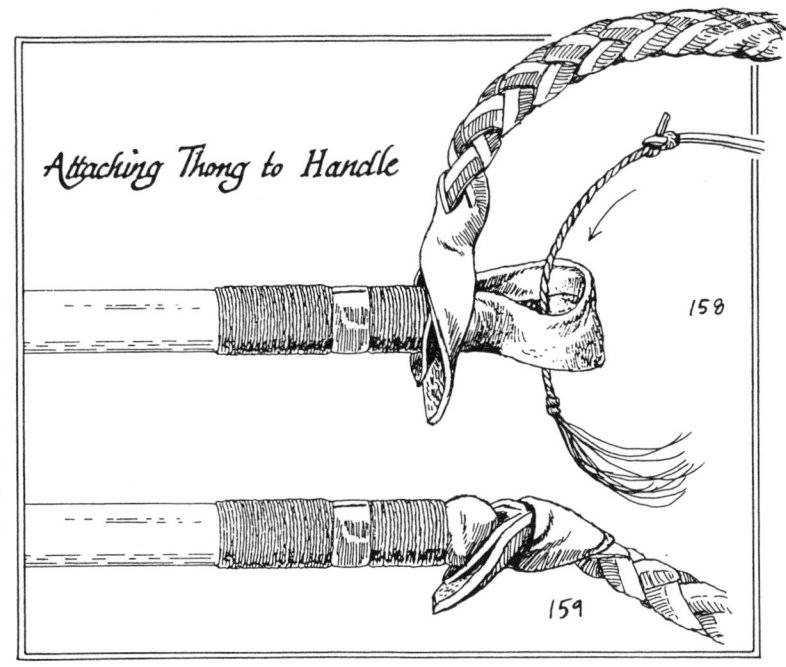

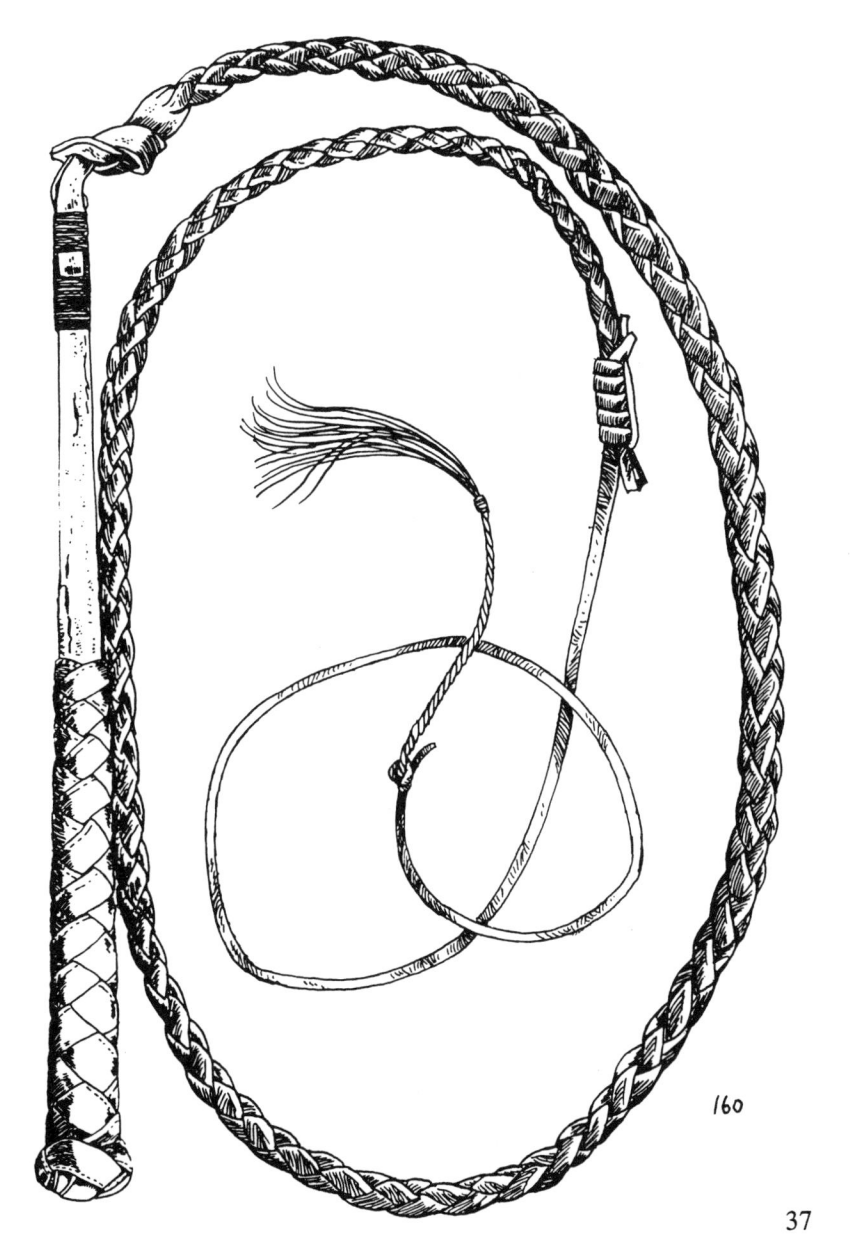

37

6-PLAIT BASIC WHIP

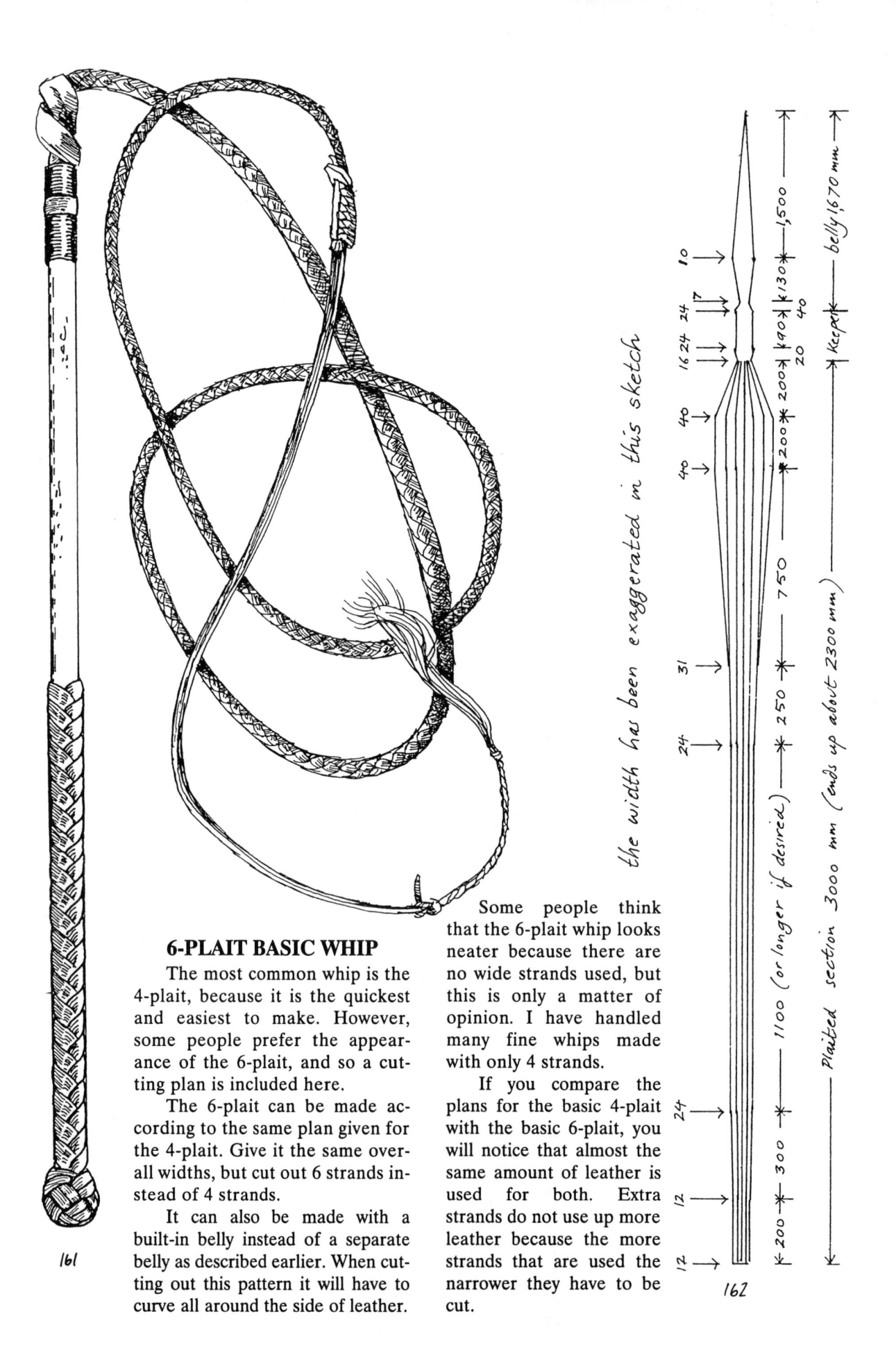

The most common whip is the 4-plait, because it is the quickest and easiest to make. However, some people prefer the appearance of the 6-plait, and so a cutting plan is included here.

The 6-plait can be made according to the same plan given for the 4-plait. Give it the same overall widths, but cut out 6 strands instead of 4 strands.

It can also be made with a built-in belly instead of a separate belly as described earlier. When cutting out this pattern it will have to curve all around the side of leather.

Some people think that the 6-plait whip looks neater because there are no wide strands used, but this is only a matter of opinion. I have handled many fine whips made with only 4 strands.

If you compare the plans for the basic 4-plait with the basic 6-plait, you will notice that almost the same amount of leather is used for both. Extra strands do not use up more leather because the more strands that are used the narrower they have to be cut.

161

162

Round 6-plait

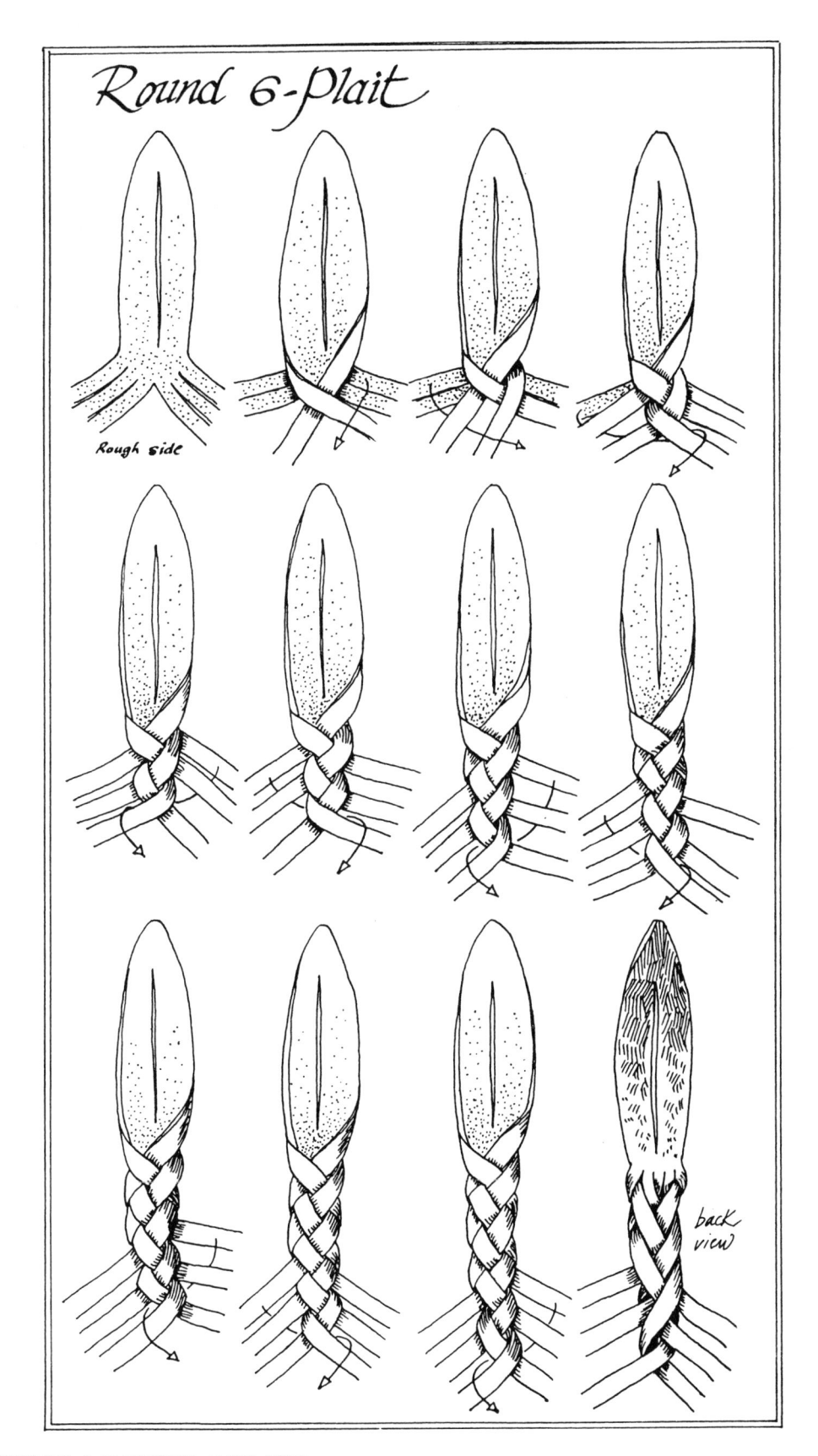

BEGINNING A ROUND 6-PLAIT

There are several ways to begin a 6-plait, and it is not hard to work out other methods, but this will do for a beginner.

Two other methods of working the 6-plait can be found on the next page. The chessboard pattern is the neatest, but it is also the slowest to do.

Two 6-Plait Methods (Round)

177 178   *Irregular Herringbone*

179 180   *Chessboard pattern*

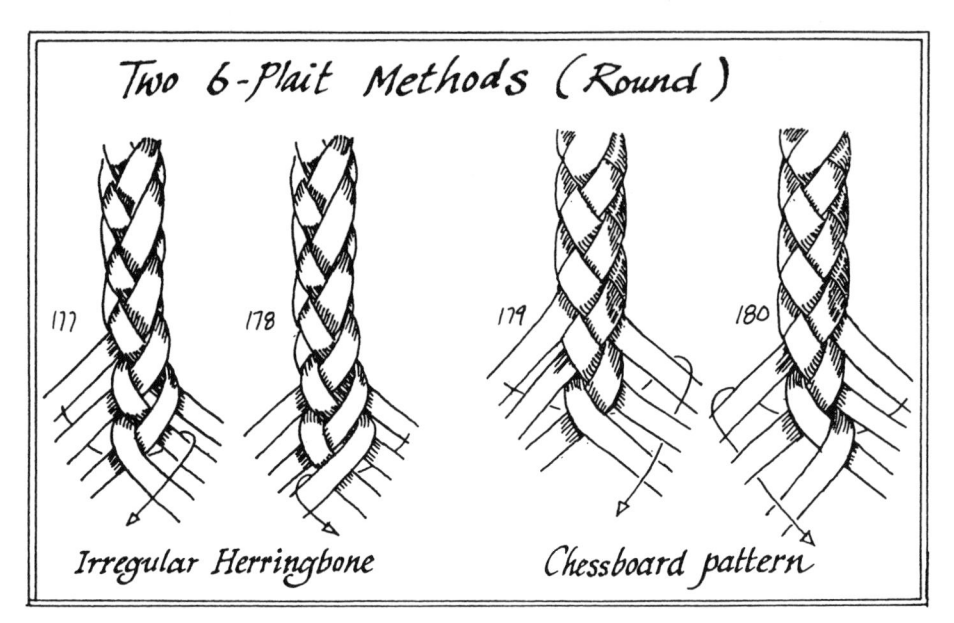

ROUND 6-PLAIT

Figs. 177–80. Above are two other methods of working a 6-plait.

REDUCING FROM 6-PLAIT TO 4-PLAIT

Figs. 181–88. When you are partway down the whip you will find that you are getting towards the end of the two shorter strands, and so it is time to reduce from 6-plait to 4-plait.

The short strands are dropped as shown, and the plaiting goes around them so that the ends are hidden from sight. Now a 4-plait continues for the rest of the whip.

This method suits a beginner, but people who have had some practice at plaiting whips will usually cut the 6 strands to run the full length of the whip, tapering the strands quite fine towards the end.

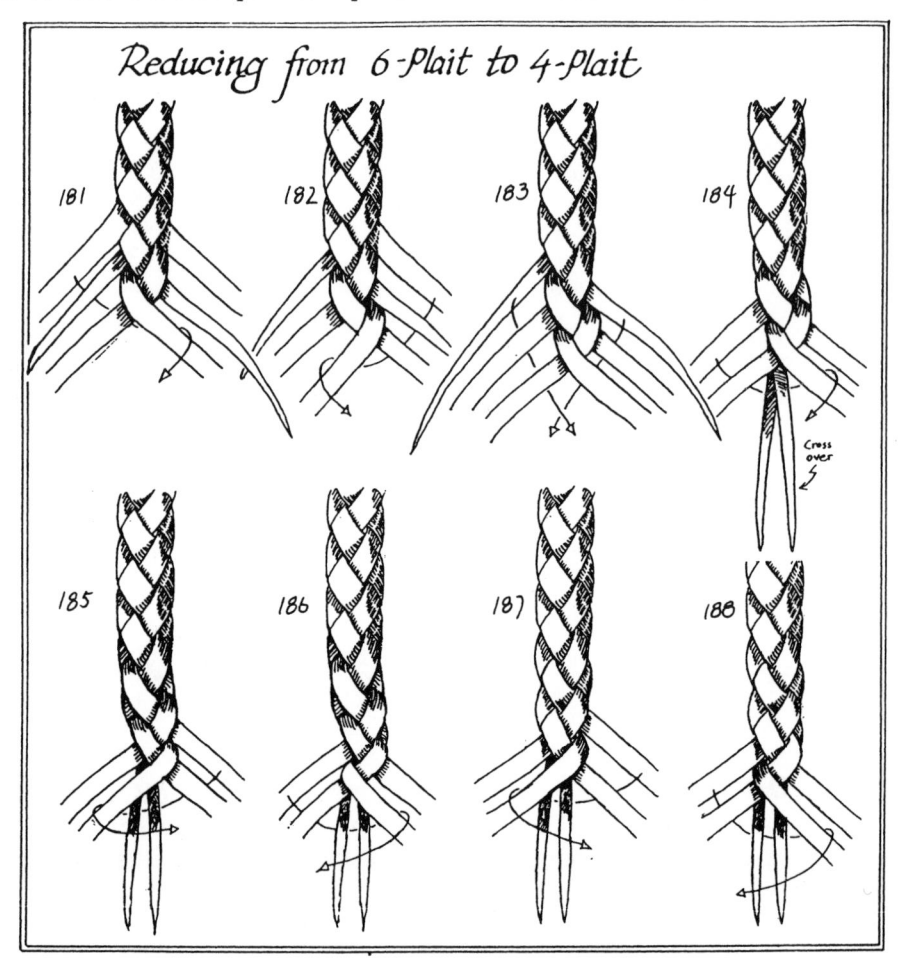

Reducing from 6-Plait to 4-Plait

181 182 183 184

185 186 187 188

THE BUILT-IN BELLY

When making a whip with a built-in belly to the plan shown on page 38, the belly section is bent over and the strands plaited over it, leaving a loop of leather which forms the keeper.

KANGAROO-HIDE WHIPS

Anyone can make a reasonable 4-plait whip if they take the time, but the kangaroo-hide whip is another matter. For the beginner I would suggest that you spend time making basic whips and not even consider beginning a kangaroo-hide whip until you can make a really smooth and even 4- or 6-plait whip.

Many beginners think that when they have made one basic whip they are ready to move to advanced work, but it does not work that way—skills must be developed first.

When you have made a number of good basic whips of the type described in this section, you may feel that you want to move to the next stage and work in kangaroo leather. Instructions for the making of kangaroo whips will be found in chapter 2.

For even more information on the making of good quality whips I suggest that you join the Australian Plaiters and Whipmakers Association and read their journal. Write to me at the address on page 2 for more details.

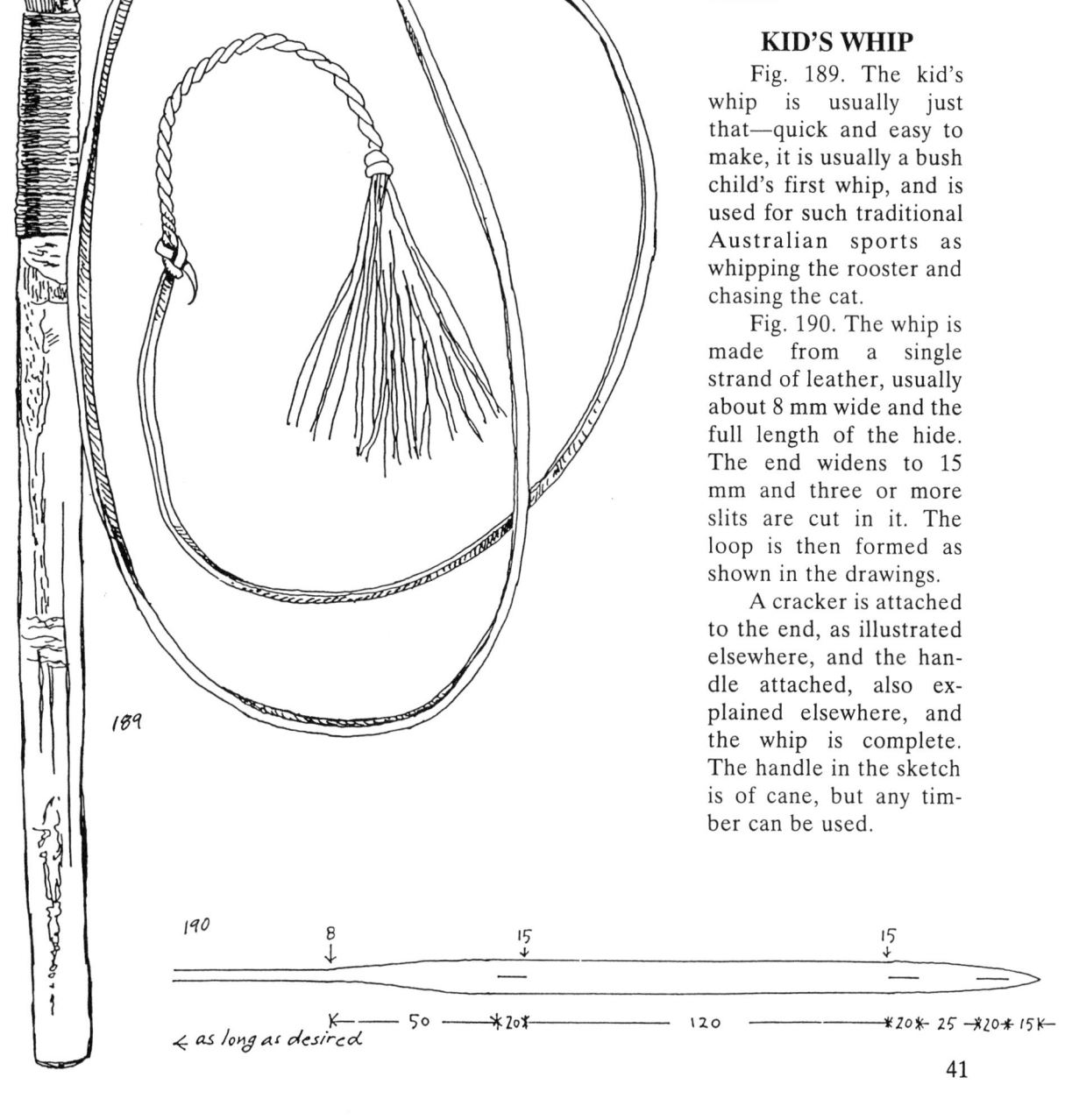

KID'S WHIP

Fig. 189. The kid's whip is usually just that—quick and easy to make, it is usually a bush child's first whip, and is used for such traditional Australian sports as whipping the rooster and chasing the cat.

Fig. 190. The whip is made from a single strand of leather, usually about 8 mm wide and the full length of the hide. The end widens to 15 mm and three or more slits are cut in it. The loop is then formed as shown in the drawings.

A cracker is attached to the end, as illustrated elsewhere, and the handle attached, also explained elsewhere, and the whip is complete. The handle in the sketch is of cane, but any timber can be used.

Slit Braid

191   192   193   194

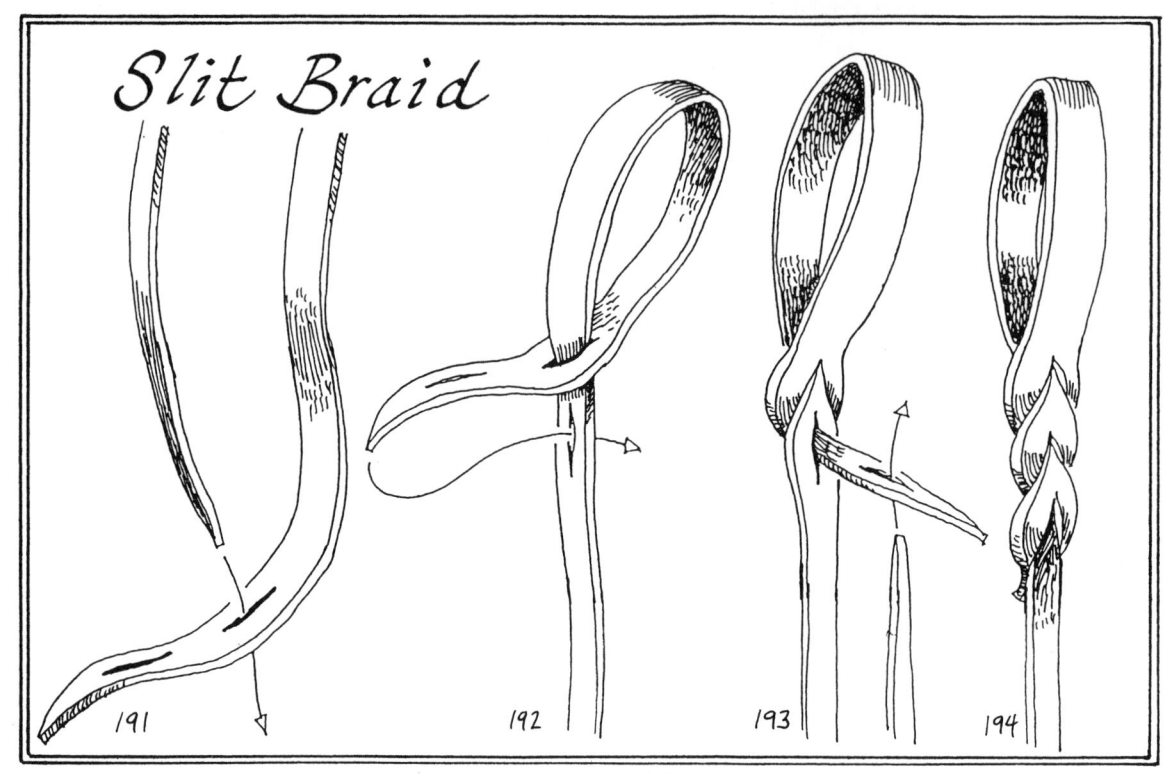

SLIT BRAID

Figs. 191–94. The loop is formed with a simple form of slit braid. Longer slit braids can easily be made by making more holes in the leather, and South American quirts are sometimes made with the slit braid going almost the full length of the lash.

Although shown here as a child's whip, this type of whip can also have practical uses. The driver of the horse coach that used to drive tourists around the streets of our village of Kuranda always had one of them.

Fig. 195. He used a handle made from a length of fiberglass fishing rod and it was much cheapter, and just as efficient, as a proper coach whip. The sketch shows him in the main street with the traces slack as the vehicle was coming down a slight slope.

Chapter 2

Whipmaking Book 2
How to Make an 8-Plait Kangaroo Stockwhip

TWO MAIN GROUPS OF WHIPS

Although primarily intended as an instruction manual, this book is also a serious study of one of Australia's important bush crafts, the making of whips. The traditional Australian stockwhip differs from whips made in other parts of the world, especially in the finely plaited examples. In great measure this has been due to the abundance of kangaroo hide, said to be the world's strongest leather for its thickness. This leather has allowed finer whip-plaiting techniques to evolve, as well as unique construction techniques, methods that would not be possible with weaker types of leather.

One of the Australian stockman's most prized possessions is his stockwhip. A top-quality whip takes a long time to make, and because of this it can be very expensive. With this book you should be able to make your own whip for a fraction of the cost.

Stockwhips can be classed into two main groups. The first is the basic whip, which may be called a yard whip, or team thong, or given a name according to the material from which it is made, such as a greenhide whip, a whitehide whip, or a redhide whip. In old saddlers' catalogs these whips were also referred to as stockwhips, a point to remember if anyone ever tries to tell you differently. Basic whips are both strong and simple to plait, and the making of them is explained in chapter 1.

The second group represents the most highly prized (and priced) stockwhips and consists of those made from kangaroo hide. These whips are so much more expensive because they are much more complicated to make and take considerably longer than the whip made of greenhide or redhide.

If you have never ever made a whip before, you would be better off to begin with chapter 1. Life will become a lot easier. The kangaroo-hide whip is complicated for two reasons: it uses much finer strands than is the case with cowhide whips; and it could be described as two whips in one, for in a good whip the belly of the whip is a 4-plait whip over which another whip with more strands is plaited.

Fig. 1. As a comparison between the simple redhide whip and the kangaroo whip, this first drawing shows the way a plain stockwhip is often made—nothing but a 4-plait of redhide over a belly of either rolled or solid leather.

Fig. 2. Just look at how much is involved in a good kangaroo whip. The sketch shows a kangaroo-hide whip, which can consist of more than nine layers in a thick whip. A whip of this type will probably take five times as long to make as a plain stockwhip, but the final result should almost be a work of art as well as a very practical whip.

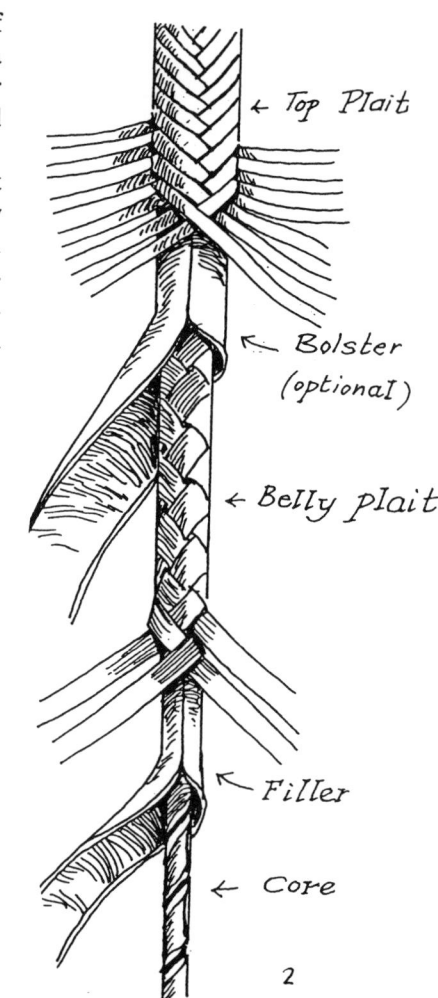

SOME STYLES OF WHIPS

Stockwhip of Kangaroo Leather

This is the prince of whips and this section deals with the making of them.

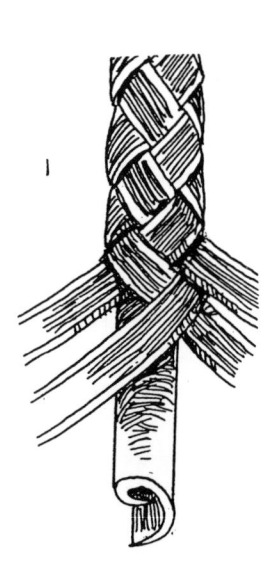

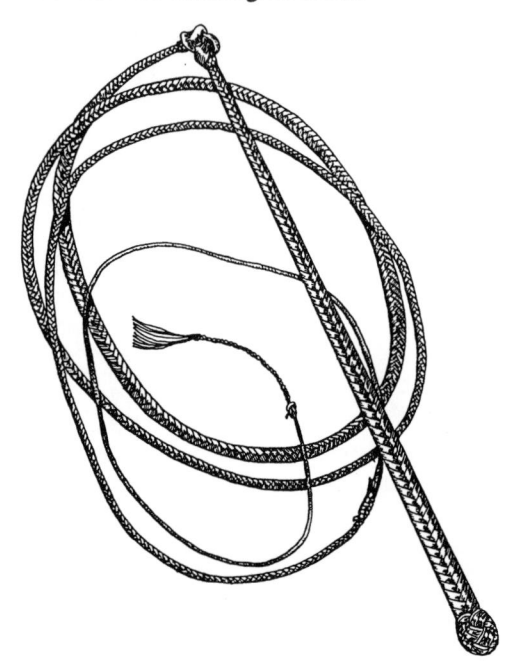

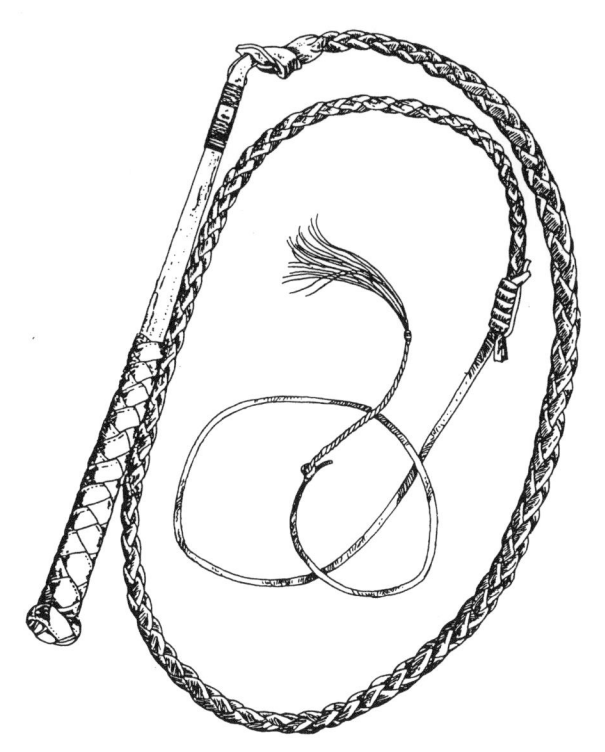

Redhide Whip

Here is a typical 4-plait redhide whip. Instructions for the making of this kind of whip may be found in chapter 1.

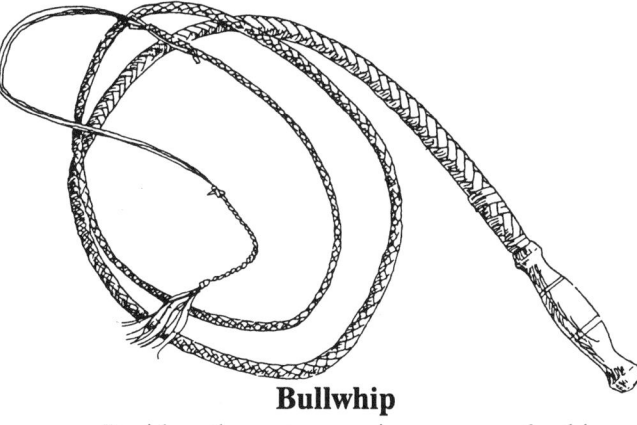

Bullwhip

Besides these two main groups of whips there are others such as the bullwhip, popular with Americans. In this type of whip the handle and thong are all part of a single unit, the solid part of the handle being very short (see p. 89).

Snake Whip

There is also the snake whip, which is like a short flexible bullwhip that can fit into the pocket (see p. 97).

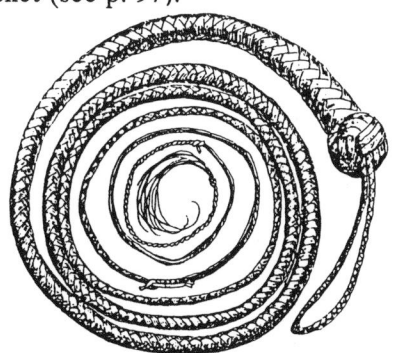

Bullockie's Whip

At the other extreme is the bullockie's whip, which often had a handle taller than the bullock driver himself, and a thong twice as long as that found on a stockwhip. The making of these whips is described in *Bushcraft 3,* page 95 and in the appendix starting on page 155.

FIRST RULE ABOUT WHIPMAKERS

In the eleven years that passed between the first and this present edition of *Whipmaking Book 2*, I met quite a few whipmakers through the Australian Plaiters and Whipmakers Association. Their ideas have brought about a major revision of this material in a way that should make it much easier for the beginner to make a good whip at first attempt.

Every whipmaker has his own special way of doing things, and insists that this is the only true and correct way of doing it. *This is the first rule*, and as a beginner you have to remember it. Talk to ten old whipmakers and you will get ten different sets of rules. This is why old whipmakers always look down on other whipmakers, for they know that they are the only ones who are doing it properly.

When I first wrote *Whipmaking Book 2* in 1984, getting information from these old possums was like pulling teeth. Fortunately, in 1985, the Australian Plaiters and Whipmakers Association was formed and this brought about a great sharing of knowledge among the whipmakers and a grudging admission by many of the old-timers that some of the other whipmakers were not all that bad.

I, too, have changed my ideas during the twelve years between writing the first edition and preparing this one, due to a lot of good advice from professional whipmakers. As a result there is considerable difference between the 1984 edition and this one. I am sure that this edition is better and will, I hope, produce a better whip for the beginner.

WHIPMAKING TERMS

Not all whipmakers use the same terms for the parts of the whip, and this can be confusing for the beginner. Out of interest I consulted some old saddlers' catalogs (mostly from the 1920s and 1930s) in order to find out the traditional terms used in Australia in the old days and came up with this list.

Stock crop or stock. This was the name given to the whip handle, and a stocker was the man who made the stock. However, the term handle was also used in some catalogs.

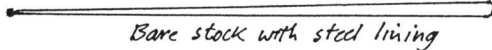

Steel-lined handle or stock. This refers to the length of spring steel found in the center of many handles.

Grip or plaited grip or hand part. Today often called a half-plaited handle, grip referred to handles which were only plaited far enough down to give a grip to the hands, the rest of the stock being left bare. The term "hand part" was used in one catalog for the same thing.

Thong or stock thong. The term thong is still used to refer to the main part of the whip, and the length of the thong is used to describe the whip as in an old advertisement: "thong 8 ft × 12 plait." The length of the handle and fall are not included when referring to the length of a whip.

Belly. The same term is used today. Good whips had a plaited belly but not all stockwhips had a plaited belly. One catalog of 1933 notes:

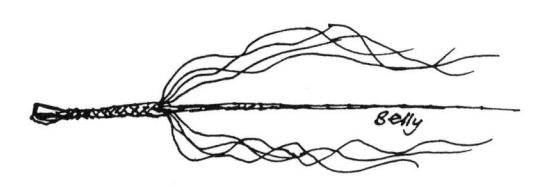

"These thongs are made with plain inside belly not plaited and are quite suitable for dairy or farm work where a high grade cattle drafting whip is not necessary."

Fall. This has the same meaning today and refers to the strip of leather attached to the end of the thong. A 1935 catalog mentions only "white or yellow hide whip falls," which supports Maurice Doohan's suggestion that redhide is a more recent product in the making of whips.

Cracker. The short, detachable end of the whip. Traditionally made from silk or horsehair, it is today more often made from synthetic twine of various types.

Stock whip or stockwhip. There is some argument today about this term, and some people insist that it only refers to the whip made from kangaroo leather. However, the old catalogs make it quite clear that this was not the case. One refers to "Stock Thongs—Kangaroo" as well as "Stock Thongs—Whitehide or Greenhide." There was also an ad for a "Stock Whip 6 ft × 6 plait, yellow kip hide."

While many people think that the term stockwhip comes from its use in working stock, it is more likely that it refers to the stock or handle, which makes the difference between the American bullwhip, which has no separate handle or stock, and the Australian stockwhip.

Team thongs. In the old catalogs this term seems to be used for basic whips, but they could still be of good quality materials, for a 1935 catalog lists team thongs in 4- and 6-plait kangaroo as well as 4- and 6-plait greenhide and whitehide. The term is still in use today by whipmakers such as Glen Denholm.

PLAITING OR BRAIDING?

The traditional Australian term is plait (because it is pronounced plat, some early writers used that spelling, and I have noticed it as plaitt in one old catalog, but plait was and is the common spelling). I have not seen the word braid used in any old Australian saddler's catalog.

However, in recent years the popularity of Bruce Grant's *Encyclopedia of Rawhide and Leather Braiding* has introduced the American custom of calling what is traditionally a plait in Australia a braid.

It could be argued that for the sake of uniformity we should drop our own traditional term of plait and adopt the American one of braid, but I would prefer to stick to our own usage.

Plait

Out of interest I looked up both words in the *Shorter Oxford Dictionary*. It notes that Shakespeare used the word plat: "Her haire nor loose nor ti'd in formall plat," and also notes platted as late Middle English spelling. It gives plait as the common spelling today.

Braid

Braid is given as being derived from the Old Teutonic *bregdan* "to pull quickly hither and thither," and part of the definition is given as "to make by plaiting." This would suggest that plaiting is the senior term.

In my experience braiding was only used in Australia to refer to very fine work, such as horsehair braiding, or to applying patterns in lace onto solid leather belts. Belts made entirely of kangaroo lace were always referred to as being plaited and, as noted earlier, all whips were referred to in old catalogs as being plaited.

12-FOOT SHOT-LOADED STOCKWHIP

We still get orders for these in our saddlery, and I had a couple of urgent phone calls from an aggressive New Yorker in the Bronx who insisted that this was the normal stockwhip and wanted me to send him one.

But times change and so do fashions, and I had to tell him that such a whip is today classed as a special order (he didn't believe me and got even more annoyed). Shorter and lighter whips are now the most popular, and, according to contributors to *The Australian Whipmaker's Journal,* our association journal, this is because the shorter and lighter whip moves faster and produces a louder crack. I would not like to get into an argument about that, but it is a fact that few professionals make the longer and heavier whips except as special orders. (See page 98 for more on loading whips.)

HOW TO MAKE A 2.3-METER, 8-STRAND KANGAROO STOCKWHIP WITH A FULL-PLAITED HANDLE

The beginner is advised to start with 8 strands, as this will make a handsome whip without the problems of dealing with a large number of very fine strands. Once the 8-plait has been mastered you can later make whips with as many strands as you wish.

Whipmaker Bruce Cull made a good point in one of his articles in *The Australian Whipmaker's Journal* when he said that the best way to learn was to make a whip, then see where it could be improved and make another. I don't think that anyone could make a good whip the first time from any book—in the end you must learn from your own experience.

This is why so many of the old whipmakers were so mean about passing on information, because they had learned the hard way themselves and did not see why they should pass anything on.

These whipmakers were forgotten when they died, but the whipmakers who have been free with their help will be remembered with affection for years to come.

Materials Needed

A full kangaroo hide.

A very sharp knife and the means to keep it sharp.

(Optional: A strand-cutter for those who are unable to learn to cut by eye.)

Plaiting soap or fat with a few drops of kero (kerosene) in it or leather dressing.

A 1.6 meter × 10 mm strip of 3 or 4 mm thick redhide for the core and the fall. If you wish to make the core out of kangaroo, then you will need only a 600 × 6-mm length of redhide for the fall.

Poly binder twine or nylon cord or horsehair to make the cracker.

Fine strong black waxed thread to tie the keeper on.

500 mm of cane or timber for the handle.

Whips can be made to any desired length. In this case the instructions are for a whip of 2,300 mm with a 600-mm fall, an average sort of whip. Whipmakers develop different techniques, and each man thinks that his method is the best. The methods described here are probably the most popular.

Selecting the Kangaroo Skin

Ask for one that is drum-stuffed and explain that you are going to use it for whipmaking. Most kangaroo is sold with a glazed surface that is not the best for a whip, while the drum-stuffed hide has a dull finish and a slightly oily feel.

Don't worry too much about bullet holes and cuts as these can be worked around, but look out for large areas of scars and scratches and also try to avoid skins that have too many tick scars on them. These are little hard patches about the size of a match head.

If you don't have a leather splitter (and you can make a good whip without one) make sure that the skin is of even thickness throughout and reasonably smooth on the back.

Using Precut Lace

No professional whipmaker would ever use precut lace for two good reasons, the first being the difficulty of getting a taper on it and the second the expense. However, I know from experience that some people who buy this book only want to make one whip for themselves and have access only to precut lace.

It is possible but difficult. Begin with 6 strands, start in the middle, and with flat plaiting form the keeper. Fold this and join the laces together and do a 12-plait round. Work down and drop strands (as explained on page 94) to get the right taper—and good luck.

Details on making a whip with precut lace may be found on pages 143–45.

Testing for Stretch

Fig. 7. Even the best kangaroo skin will have parts where there is a lot of stretch, and the sketch gives an idea of where they may be found. The sketch shows the neck at the top and the base of the tail at the bottom. The area around the armpits has the most stretch.

Pull the leather; if it changes color and becomes lighter between your hands as you pull, then there is a lot of stretch in that part, and you might have to cut strands up to twice as wide as they are to finish up. If there is some stretch but no change of color, then the strands may have to be cut perhaps a third wider. The best way to find out is to trim a little of the outer edge and test it yourself.

Before beginning a whip, all the strands should be given a good stretch in the hands to get them as dense as possible, for unstretched leather will make a loose-plaited job.

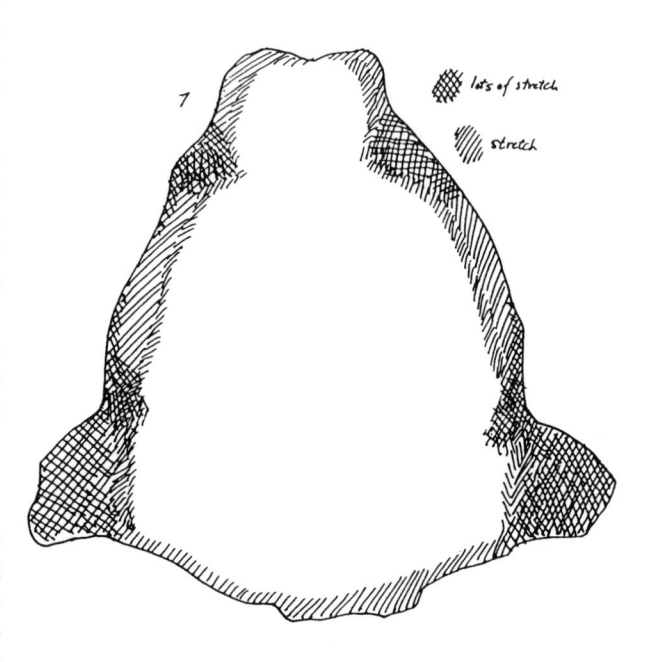

STEP 1: THE CORE OR FILLER

The core can be made either from cowhide or kangaroo; in the hands of a good whipmaker both will do a good job. In *The Australian Whipmaker's Journal,* page 354, Bruce Cull says that "redhide is ideal for cores as you can select natural thickness and taper," while on page 375 Maurice Doohan explains how he made cores from three pieces of kangaroo, his feeling being that "a roo hide whip should contain all roo hide." As both are expert whipmakers you can take your pick.

Redhide Core

Fig. 8. This is simple to make. As the core has to be round, the strip that is cut should be not much wider than the thickness of the leather, only 3–4 mm. It is tapered at either end with a short taper at the top and then a long taper at the bottom, the same shape as the finished whip.

Some whipmakers make this core the full length of the finished whip, while I have measured others under a meter. Ours will measure somewhere between 900 mm and 1.5 m.

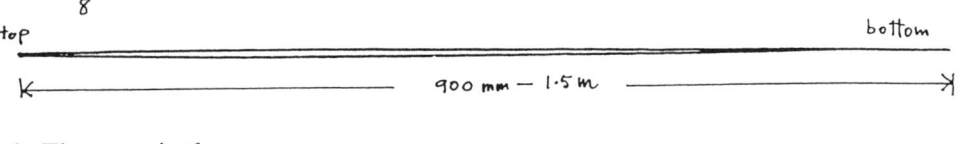

Fig. 9. The core is then skived on all edges until it is round. (Skive rhymes with dive, and means to take a shaving off the edge with a very sharp knife.)

Fig. 10. While redhide is the best, the core can also be cut from an ordinary hide of any strong leather 3–4 mm thick. No attempt is made to cut it from a straight strip of leather; the strip is simply cut by running around the outer edge of the leather, whatever shape it is. It will pull out straight quite all right later. Soak it in water for ten minutes and then give it a good rolling under a board and this will help in getting it round. A good rubbing with leather dressing will be needed after the rolling; otherwise, the wet leather will tend to dry a little hard. If you don't have leather dressing, use fat with a little kero in it.

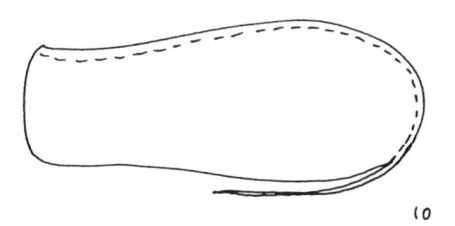

If your core or belly has any lumps, bumps, or hollows, these will show up on the finished whip. So make sure that you trim and roll it as evenly as you can.

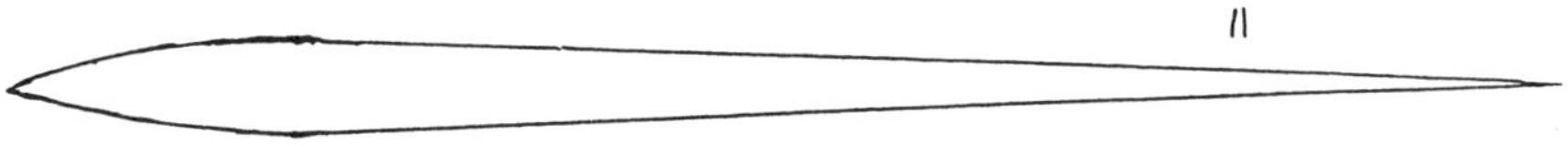

Kangaroo Core

There are at least three ways of doing this, and as the whole aim is to get a dense and solid core you should pick the one that works best for you. All of them use the most flexible leather that you can find, so this is a good chance to use up the outer edge of the kangaroo skin.

Fig. 11. The first method is to cut a long teardrop-shaped piece of kangaroo—the length can be 900 mm. The width will depend on the thickness of the leather, but 20 mm at the thickest part will probably be enough.

Rub it well with the fat mixture and then roll it into a hard core. If it will not roll easily then use a sharp knife to cut a few shallow scores in the leather and this will make it easier to roll. The finished job should be quite dense.

Use scraps of thread or lace to make a few ties around it to stop it unrolling as you work with it; they can be discarded as the plaiting takes place.

Fig. 12. The second method is to cut out three small pieces of flexible leather. Give them a heavy coating of fat or leather dressing.

Roll up the smallest one, and then roll the other two around it. Roll the whole thing as tightly as possible and leave it to dry before using it. Use some scraps of lace or thread to tie it tightly together if it looks like it might come unrolled. These can be removed later as you are plaiting around it. (If you have any problems with getting the pieces rolled tightly, soak them in water first and then a heavy layer of fat).

Fig. 13. The third method is really the same as the previous one, and this is the one that I saw Maurice Doohan using in 1995. Instead of using three small pieces of leather, he left them all connected at the top. This meant that he could put the end into the vice and then roll them by putting a scrap of leather around them and rubbing up and down briskly, using plenty of leather dressing.

Fig. 14. Another method of making a core is to take a strip of leather about 5 mm wide, soak it in water for ten minutes, and then twist it. This can be done by hand or with an old-fashioned drill.

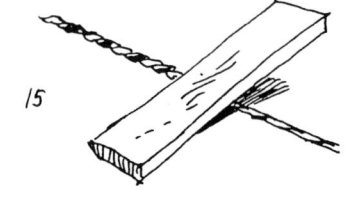

Fig. 15. When all the pieces are twisted up, they can be pulled tight and left to dry for a short time, and then given a good hard rolling.

Fig. 16. This should result in a tight dense string like this.

Fig. 17. **Thick core for a heavy whip**.

For your first whip, make a core using one of the previous methods—not this one, which is only for later reference should you ever need to make a very heavy whip.

Round a strip of redhide about 300 mm long. Soak a long strip of leather about 5 mm wide and wrap this around the redhide. When the redhide is all covered, keep twisting the rest of the strip as described above.

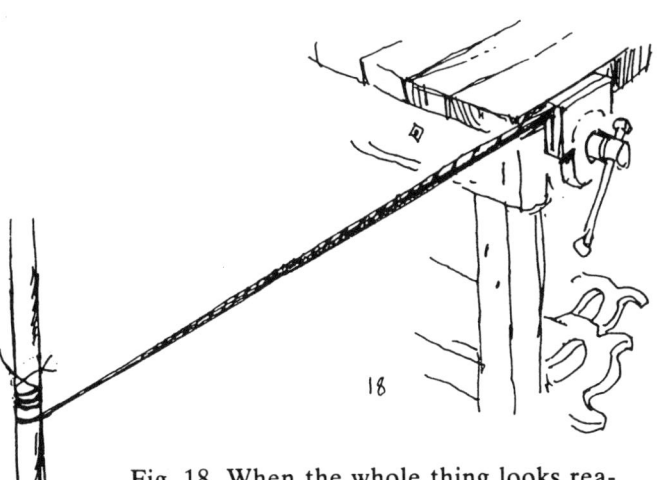

Fig. 18. When the whole thing looks reasonably smooth and even, pull it tight and tack it down at each end or leave it in the vice as shown until it is all but dry. Then put it on the bench and give it a good hard rolling until it is smooth and even.

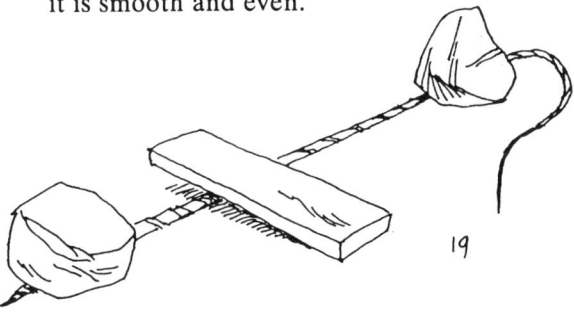

Fig. 19. It may be necessary to slightly dampen the leather again if it will not roll properly. After rolling the core put some sort of weights on it so that it will not unwind. Once properly rolled it will remain in this form permanently.

The life of a whip will depend upon regular oiling, and this should start right from the beginning. Use leather dressing of any type, or even fat (with a little kero in it to stop cockroaches and rats eating it), and thoroughly oil the core and then roll it again before plaiting over it.

Lead Loading

In the old days lead loading was all the rage, but many whipmakers today think that it slows down the whip and that a loaded whip will not crack as well as an unloaded one. To load a whip a small cotton or fine leather tube filled with lead shot would be built into the end of the whip instead of the core.

Once this was done it was also then necessary to pour some lead (about 50 grams) into the handle at the knob end in order to balance the whole thing.

STEP 2: THE BELLY

The Filler and Belly Plait

Planning ahead is important if you are to get the best use out of your kangaroo hide. As mentioned earlier, you will probably find it best to cut the strands for the handle from the tail section, across the bottom part of the roughly triangular shape of the skin. Pieces such as cores and bolsters can be cut from the soft and stretchy section around the edge of the skin where the armpits were, and then the strands for the belly can be cut. This should trim the skin down to the good leather that will be needed for the outer layer of the whip.

Fig. 20. The filler and belly plait are cut from one single strip of kangaroo. The method of cutting out the kangaroo hide is illustrated further on.

The plan given here has been exaggerated in order to make it easier to understand, and so the taper of the strands is not as severe as it looks—they taper from 10 mm wide at the thickest down to a point.

The filler should be the length of the finished whip—in this case, make it 2.5 meters, and the width should be just enough to wrap around the core, tapering down to only about 4 mm at the end.

You don't want it to overlap around the core, for that will cause a lump; nor do you want it to only go part of the way around the core, for that will spoil the roundness of the job.

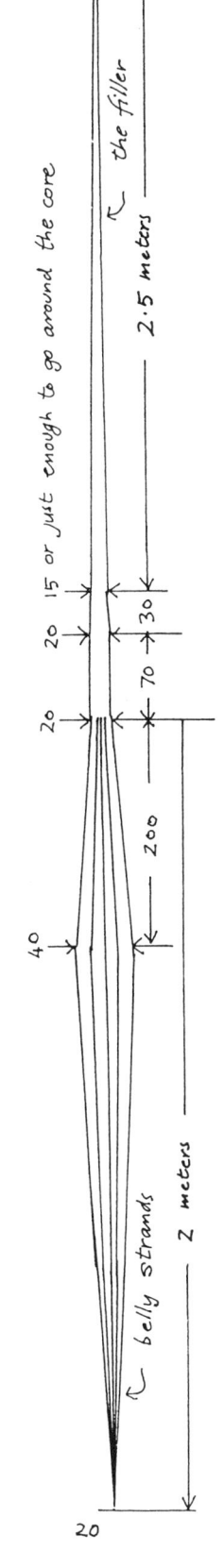

51

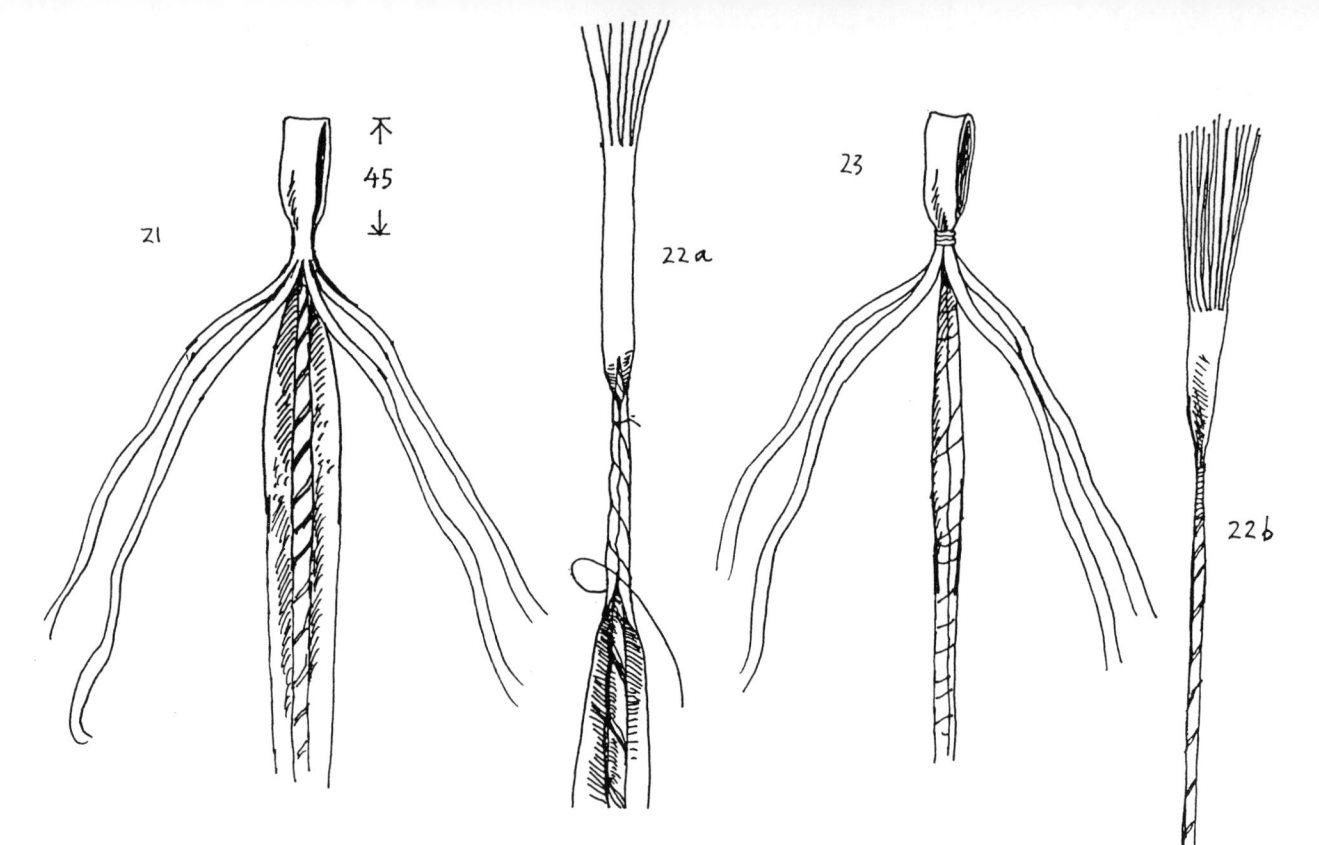

Fig. 21. Place the core on the filler so that the end of the core is in this position.

Fig. 22a. Beginners will find it convenient to use fine cotton thread to tie the filler up before beginning to plait. Professional whipmakers omit this step and simply fold the filler around the core as they are doing the plaiting, but this takes practice and we want to make the first whip as easy as possible.

Fig. 22b. The fully wrapped core.

Fig. 23. Fold over the leather to form a loop and tie it in place. This loop will be part of the keeper of the whip. (As you get more proficient you will not have to bother about tying this but will just begin plaiting).

The loop that is formed should be big enough to put a couple of fingers through. With the filler tied up and in place around the core plaiting can now begin.

Figs. 24–27. A 4-plait is now worked over the filler. When you get to figure 27 just keep repeating steps 26 and 27 to continue plaiting. The sequence is to take the top strand around the back and between the two strands on the other side and back to the original side.

Use plaiting soap, leather dressing, or some fat with a little kero in it in order to get the strands well greased. This will allow you to plait much tighter than with dry strands.

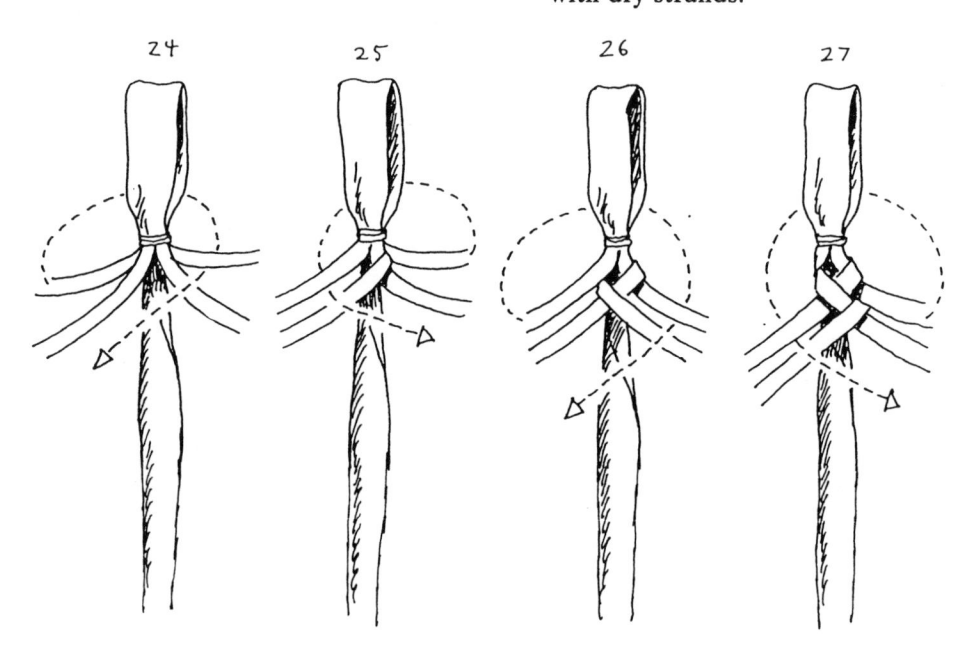

Fig. 28. When all the strands have been used up, the ends are tapered and thinned down if necessary, and then tied down with fine thread. Make sure to get a smooth line when doing this—abrupt changes in outline will show up on the finished whip.

There will still be the one long strand from the filler hanging down. Grease this well and then wrap a scrap of leather around it tightly and rub it up and down until the strand is well rounded. Look at the finished job and make sure that you have a good taper all the way. It may be that you will have to undo the end again and trim and taper the strands a little more to get a good-looking job, but don't let this worry you; a little extra work to get the belly looking good will be well worthwhile later.

Fig. 29. The completed belly is rolled to make it smooth and even. At every stage in making a whip there is some rolling to do. If at any point you find a bad lump or a thin part, it must be remedied before going on to the next stage.

The whip will thrash about when being rolled and knock almost everything off the bench. One way to stop this is to hang down a couple of lengths of cord. The whip can easily slip through the loops in the cord, and they will help restrain it.

Fig. 30. Another way to restrain the whip is to stretch it out and tie the ends, or get a couple of friends to hold the ends.

Belly from Redhide

In a good whip the belly is plaited from kangaroo leather over a core as described earlier. However, if you look at early saddlers' catalogs you will find that not all kangaroo whips had a plaited belly. For instance, in Uhl's catalog of 1935 the advertisement for a Henderson whip notes that it is "made with a plaited belly that is a double whip, there is no fear of the belly breaking. It costs a little more but the whip lasts twice as long."

Some of the cheaper whips did not have a plaited belly and most likely used a solid strip of tanned cowhide that could dry out in time and crack. People who do whip repairs have reported all sorts of rubbish being used as a belly, including things such as strips of cloth or rope, or even old singlets.

Bruce Cull tells the story of a Gulf Country ringer who had a whip with a rope belly and, after some time, the rope's fibers began to poke up through the plaited outer layer. The ringer said that he never knew which to shave first in the morning, himself or his whip!

Today there are some whipmakers who make the belly from redhide. A tapered strip is cut from the thickest available hide, as long as the finished whip is going to be. It is often soaked in water for ten minutes or so and rolled until it is quite round. It is then heavily treated with leather dressing or fat. As this will not provide a very thick belly it is sometimes covered with a bolster of kangaroo leather. This bolster is wrapped around it until it is built up to the desired thickness.

When I asked Maurice Doohan why the whipmakers in the old days did not use redhide for the belly he said that it was not available in the old days. He thought that redhide only came into general use halfway through the twentieth century. He also pointed out that if you wish to make a good whip, it should have a plaited belly. Bruce Cull confirmed this, stating that "a 4-strand plaited belly is not only the best belly but is easier and quicker to make than many of the other forms" (*Australian Whipmaker's Journal* p. 354).

STEP 3: THE BOLSTER

The purpose of the bolster is to build up the exact shape that you are looking for in the whip. According to the size of the belly, it might be that you will not need a bolster, for quite often the beginner will already have made a thick belly, and in that case there is no point in making it even thicker.

Some whipmakers cut the bolster out of one piece of leather, others use two, but all insist that they are correct. Whichever is done, great care is always taken to taper down the edges so that there is no ridge on the finished job. The bolster is of thin kangaroo, and this is often the way that the outer stretchy pieces of the skin are used up.

Fig. 31. The method that we are going to use is to cut a bolster that will not go right around the belly but will leave a gap about 4 mm wide. This space will later be filled by the second part of the bolster, which is the end part of the top plait.

The bolster is roughly teardrop-shaped and about a meter long, as shown in the upper sketch.

Fig. 32. While a professional whipmaker might simply lay the bolster onto the job and plait around it, the beginner is advised to use some fine thread to bind it into place. Use dark thread and dark leather, as light colors will be very obvious if there are any small gaps in your final plaiting.

Fig. 33. Once this is done the whole thing should be rolled again. In this way you can see at a glance if the shape is smooth and the taper is even. If there are any uneven patches, now is the time to fix them before going ahead with the final covering.

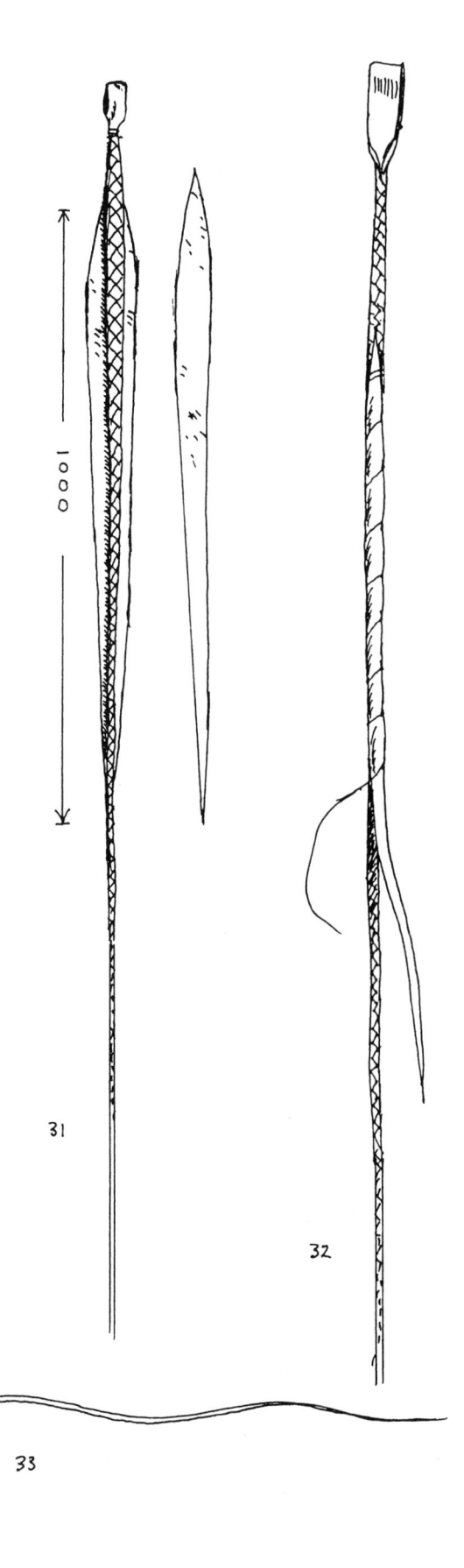

31

32

33

STEP 4: CUTTING OUT THE TOP PLAIT OR OVERLAY

Number of Strands to Cut

A kangaroo stockwhip can be made of any number of strands; 8 and 12 strands are common, but some of the old experts used to take great pride in using as many as possible and would work with up to 24 strands, each as narrow as 2 mm.

As this is a book for beginners I am going to describe the making of an 8-strand whip, and this will produce a strong and handsome whip. When you have fully mastered the 8-strand whip, you will have no problems in splitting each of these strands down the middle in order to make a 16-strand whip if you wish to.

But there is nothing wrong with an 8-strand whip, and one of my favorite whips is an 8-strand two-tone whip made by Maurice Doohan.

Cutting Out Strands

Fig. 34. As any person who runs around a sports ground will tell you, the inside of the track is a shorter distance than the outside, and it is the same thing when cutting out strands—the inside strand will be shorter than the outside one, unless you allow for it. If you are cutting out from a new, large skin this will not be a big problem, but as you get to the center of the skin the difference increases.

To prove this I cut an 8-strand whip set out from a small circle of kangaroo skin, ending up with nothing except a circle about the size of a fifty-cent piece. The outer strand was 3 meters long but the inner one was 700 mm shorter and ended up only 2.3 meters long! As an experiment this did not matter, but with a real whip it would have been a problem.

The small sketch shows how the strands were cut, beginning them all together. The sketch next to it shows what the result was with the strands short on one side and long on the other.

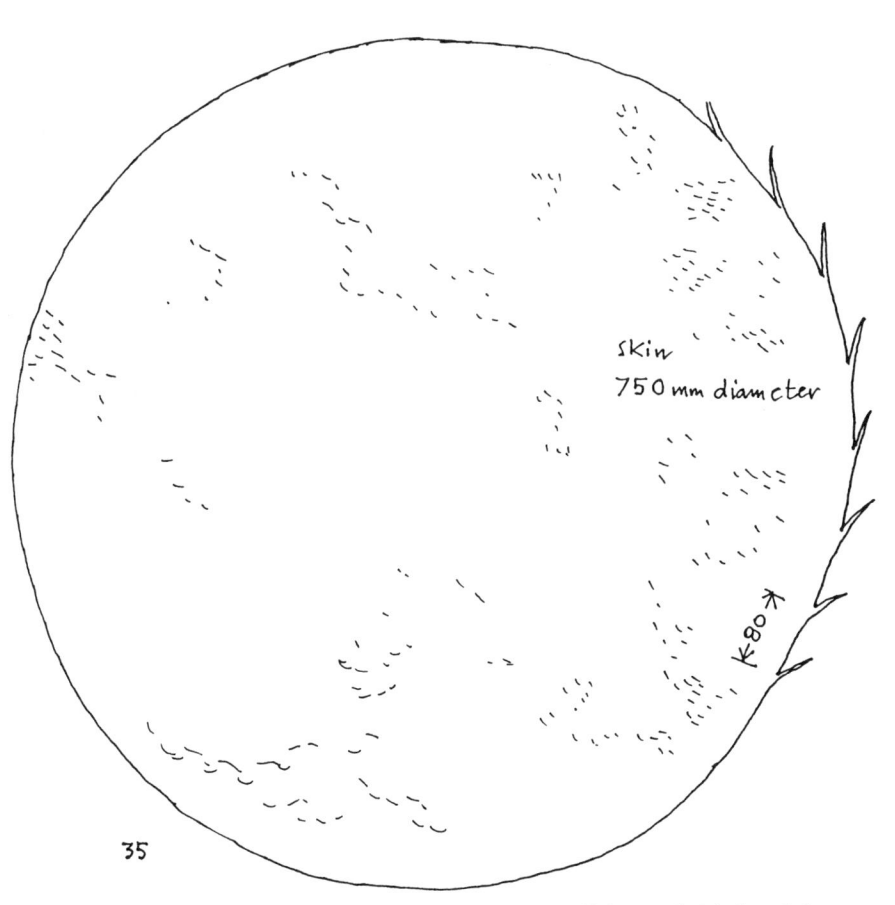

Fig. 35. In the earlier editions of this book I illustrated a cutting-out system that I had been taught and which worked well enough but was rather complicated to understand. This present method is much easier to remember and works just as well.

If the skin is roughly 750 mm in diameter, start cutting each strand 80 mm apart. For a skin of larger diameter the strands could start a little closer together, and for a smaller circle they could be a little farther apart, but this is a good general guide.

You should measure both the inner and outer strands as you cut them out to check that they are all the same widths at the same lengths.

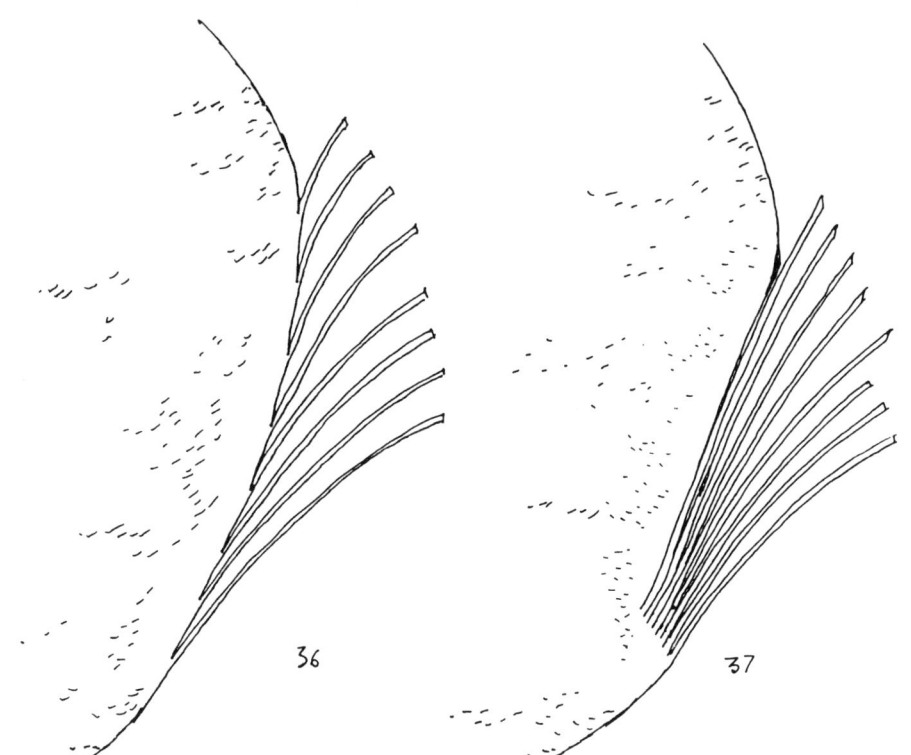

Figs. 36. As you start cutting out the strands, they will gradually widen as cutting continues.

Fig. 37. Continue the inner cuts to bring the whole lot together, then go to the outer strand and cut this for another short distance, whatever is convenient, and do the same to the rest of the strands. Continue cutting around the skin until all the strands are three meters long.

Stretch in the Leather

As explained earlier, when cutting out strands the whipmaker takes into account any stretch in the leather (see figure 7). For instance, a 4-mm strand cut from the best part of the skin will end up as 4 mm wide. However, a 4-mm strand cut from the softest part of the skin can stretch so much as to end up as only 2 mm wide after being plaited into the job.

Your overlay should use the best part of the leather, but even so you may have to use a skin with some stretch in it. Try to work out where the skin has stretch in it and allow for this. In these areas the strands are cut wider than needed and are then stretched by pulling them. This will bring them down to the proper width without loss of strength.

Length of Strands in Overlay

For the sake of this example we are cutting the 8 strands at 3 meters long each. The size of the belly, the degree of pull you use to plait, and the amount of stretch in the leather will all alter the finished length of the thong, but it should end up about 2.2 meters, or roughly 7 feet.

Fig. 38. This is the plan of the top plait for the whip. Of course, you can make it longer and the strands wider if you wish; this is only intended as a guide. I think it is a better plan than that given in earlier editions of this book, and is certainly much easier to cut out and plait.

The professional whipmaker might cut only 6 of the strands to 3 meters and leave two of them shorter, because the whip is going to begin as an 8-strand plait and finish as a 6-strand plait. However, the beginner is advised to cut all strands to the same length, as this means that you can later choose which strands to drop, or you might even just drop them and let them become part of the belly.

Knife Sharpness

When cutting out kangaroo leather the knife must be sharp enough to shave with (see page 16).

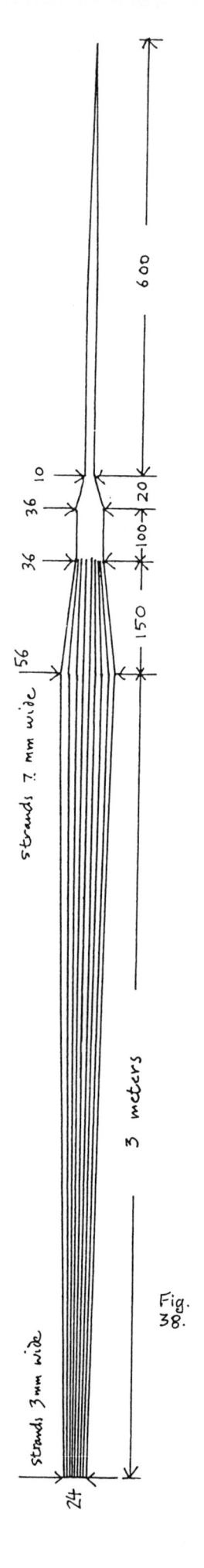

39

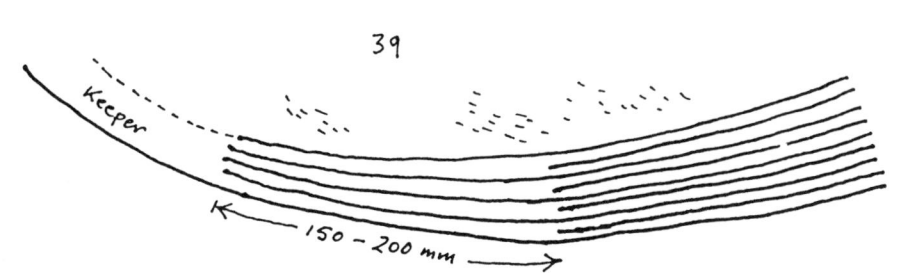

keeper

150 - 200 mm

There are a number of ways to cut out the set (the group of strands that make up the outer covering is known as the *set*). The great advantage of this method, which includes a 600-mm strip at the top that will form part of the bolster, is that the keeper can never be pulled loose, as it is permanently locked into place. The keeper is the 100-mm section shown in the upper half of figure 38.

Fig. 39. Some beginners who have not had much experience in cutting out thin strands run into problems when it comes to narrowing the strands down towards the keeper. One way to get around this is to cut 8 strands up to the widest part of the job, and then continue with only 4 strands for the last 150 or 200 mm.

If you do this, begin plaiting a 4-plait (the same as for the start of the belly), and then switch to 8-plait when you come to the 8 strands. It is quite simple to make the change from 4-plait to 8-plait.

The cutting out of the strands would be much easier if kangaroo skins were five meters long and straight along one side, but they are not, so the cutting has to work around whatever shape the skin happens to be.

Fig. 40. When you buy a skin it will have a rough edge and so the first thing to do is to trim off the sides so that they are a series of smooth curves.

Fig. 41. There are two quite different approaches to cutting a set. The first method is to taper the strands along their entire length as shown in figure 38. This calls for great skill, and though it is not recommended for the beginner it is the method that you will eventually learn to use.

The second method is to use a pair of dividers to mark out an even width, then cut strands of uniform length for 750 mm. The dividers are then widened a fraction and the next 750 mm marked and cut out, and so on until the whole strand has been cut up to the widest section.

In the sketch I have exaggerated the width of the strand so that there is a visible jump from one size to the next, but in practice this will not be seen, as the difference in each section is only just over a millimeter.

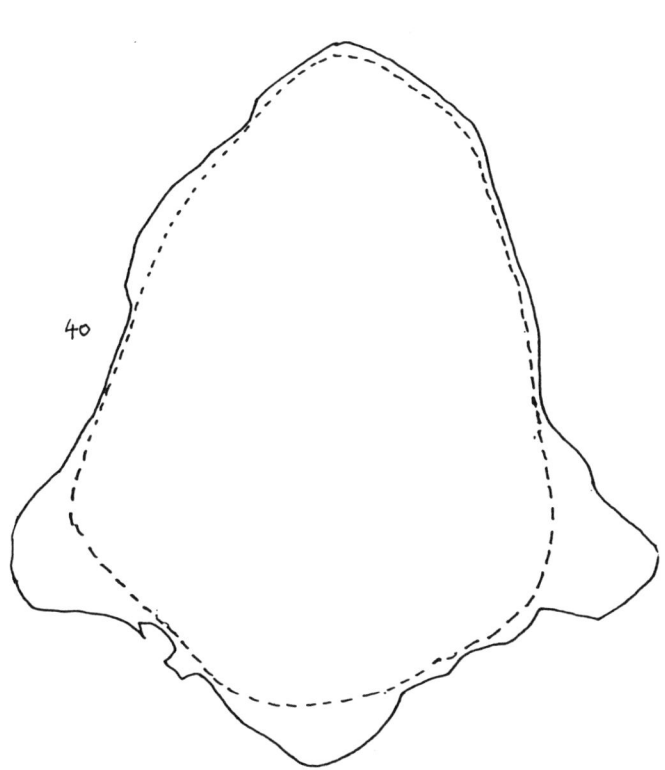

40

taper down to keeper
750 — 7 mm wide
750 — 5.5 mm wide
750 — 4.25 mm wide
750 — 3 mm wide

Fig. 41

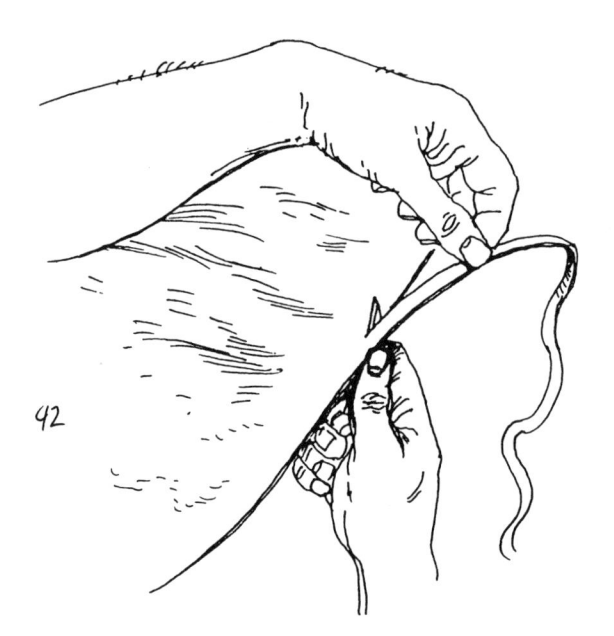

Cutting with the Thumbnail

Fig. 42. This is the technique used by most professionals, but it is difficult for the beginner as it takes a lot of skill and practice. The skin is placed on the bench or on the lap, and the thumbnail, which is grown long for the job, runs along the edge of the leather and acts as a guide allowing the whipmaker to cut very accurate strands.

It requires skill, steady hands, and a very sharp knife to cut strands in this way.

Maurice Doohan (*The Australian Whipmaker's Journal*, p. 165) points out that the nail does not have to be very long—just long enough to hold down the edge of the leather.

Type of Roo

Maurice goes on to add, "there are two main species of roo, the reds (and the female blue) and the greys." He has used the grays for whips up to 12-plait and the reds for finer whips.

Cutting with the Side of the Thumb

This may suit the beginner better. The method is the same as the above, but instead of the thumbnail, the edge of thumb is used as the guide. It is not as accurate as using the nail, but it may be the only way that the beginner can do it.

Cutting to a Marked Line

Professionals do not mark the skin; they all seem to cut by eye. As mentioned above, the beginner may find it better to use a pair of dividers and put a mark on the skin before starting to cut.

If cutting with the thumb is difficult, mark a line with dividers and cut it out on a cutting board.

Cutting with a Strand Cutter

Although most professionals cut with the thumbnail, I have heard of one who makes a large number of whips a year and cuts them all out with a strand cutter. I have not seen him in action, but presume that his cutter does not have a top guide or roller, so that he can quickly change from one strand to the next. I was told that the cutter could be easily adjusted so that the taper could be made in the strands as the cutting took place.

Fig. 43. This is the best type of strand cutter. It is a small metal tool fitted with a blade, and it fits over the thumb. R.M. Williams (the stockman's outfitter) distributes these cutters, and any leather shop should be able to order one. They come with their own blades, but as these become blunt, ordinary razor blades can be used.

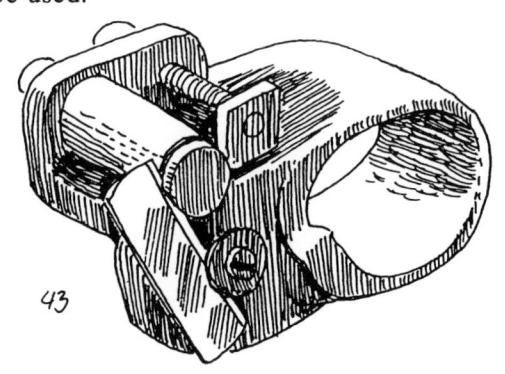

Fig. 44. The cutter is held like this. Some people use it on one of their fingers if their thumb is too large to fit in the loop.

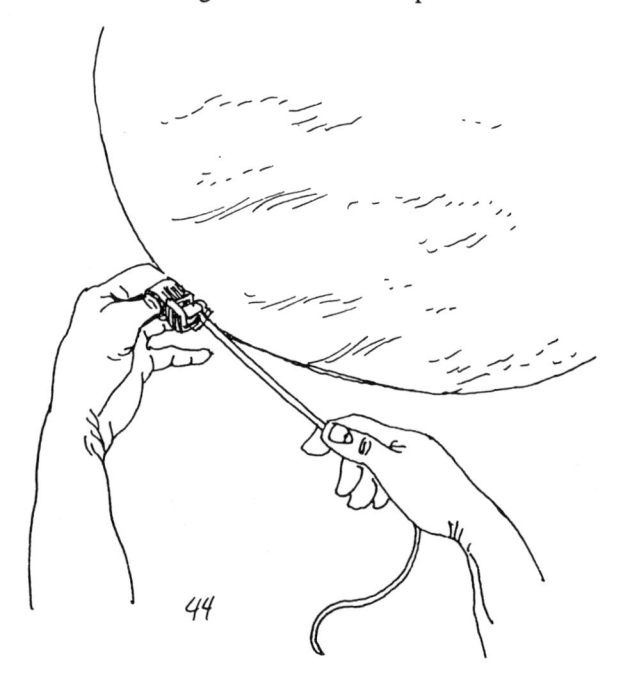

Homemade Strand Cutter

Fig. 45. A homemade strand cutter does not take long to make. The one in the sketches was put together in less than ten minutes. It is not as easy to use as the one from R.M. Williams, but it will do the job. Three scraps of timber are put together as shown; dimensions do not matter. The smallest scrap is nailed to the largest to stop the razor blade from moving backwards.

Fig. 46. The blade is put between the two pieces of timber and they are tied together. A small nail acts as a distance guide.

Fig. 47. The cutter is used as shown. The first finger of the right hand prevents the leather from rising. If you have any problem using this, put the nail on the other side of the blade and hold the cutter in your left hand.

Cutting Out Tight Corners

Even if you start with a nicely rounded skin you will find that after a certain amount of cutting has been done, tight corners will begin to develop.

Figs. 48–49. To avoid these problems you should continually trim tight corners back to smooth curves as you are cutting. Although this does waste some leather, it makes for a better-finished job.

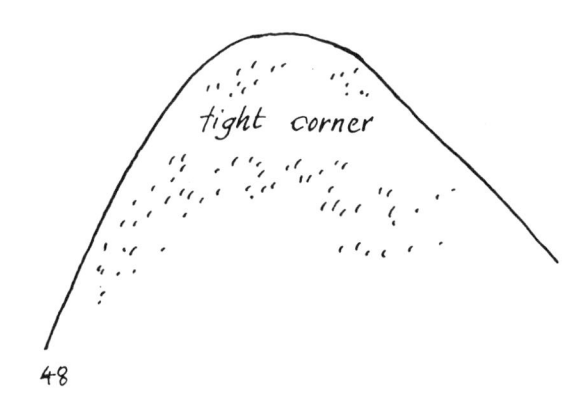

Fig. 50. If you cut around too tight a corner you will find that the strand will buckle up on one side when you try to straighten it out, because one edge is longer than the other.

It is almost impossible to run a strand like this through the leather splitter without chopping a piece out of the strand on the high side. Experiment with a scrap of leather to find out when the corner is too sharp.

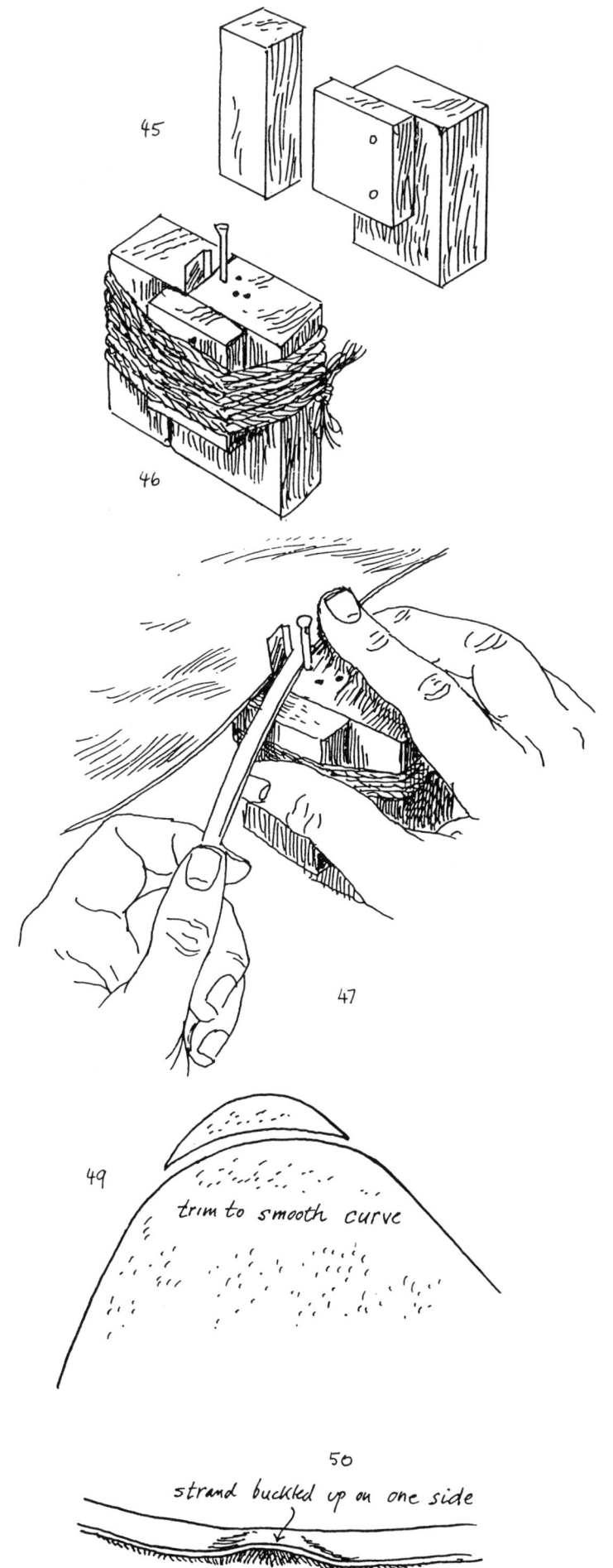

Blunt knives. One of the biggest problems in cutting out whips is a knife that is not sharp enough for the job. If you cannot shave with the knife then it is not sharp enough. If you can shave with it then it is getting close to sharp. Have a strop handy and continually touch up the blade.

A strop can be quickly made by gluing a piece of leather about 300 × 100 mm onto a board the same size. Rub jeweler's rouge into it, or valve grinding paste, or any fine grinding powder. Autosol, a chrome polish for cars, is also popular at present.

Some people glue down the leather with the smooth side up, some with the rough side up. The rough side brings the knife up sharper faster, but the smooth side gives a finer edge.

Splitting the Strands

There are two schools of thought about the need to split the leather in order to get a thin uniform thickness. One of our professional whipmakers writing in *The Australian Whipmaker's Journal* said that he never used a splitter but always made sure that he bought skins of the thickness that he wanted and checked that they were even all over. On the other hand there are other professional whipmakers who always split the strands before beginning to plait.

The beginner will usually have the decision made for them according to whether they already have a splitter or not. Buying a splitter is not worthwhile unless you plan to do a great deal of leatherwork. In our saddlery we seldom have to use the splitter because we have access to a good variety of leather in various thicknesses.

Skiving

Skiving (rhymes with diving) is the technique of cutting a bevel on the edges of the leather. By thinning down the edges the strands sit flatter and the finished job looks better. There is another advantage to skiving if you have been a little uneven in cutting the width of the strands, for while skiving the strands tend to get evened up.

Skiving kangaroo leather requires a delicate touch with the knife. The professional starts at one end of a 3-meter-long strand and pares off an unbroken strip the full length of the strand and not much thicker than a needle. Yet this strip is still so strong and even that I have seen people work a 4-plait string with these offcuts in order to make a necklace!

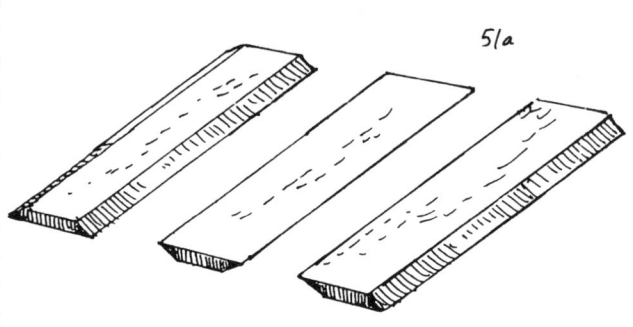

Fig. 51a. Some professionals skive the top edge of the strand on one side, and then skive the opposite edge underneath, while others skive both sides on the top (the beginner may find this the easiest way).

Harry, a leather worker who used to make whips for our saddlery business, skived his strands on the underside, but this is difficult for the beginner as it is harder to take a thin strip from the rough side of the leather.

Leather Chattering While Skiving

If the leather is at all dry it may chatter while you are skiving the edges. That is, instead of the strand running smoothly through your fingers it will keep gripping and releasing, and this can cause uneven work and may lead to accidentally cutting strands.

To avoid this, give the strands some sort of dressing. A rub with a bar of ordinary soap will do if you want to keep the leather pale; otherwise, any sort of leather dressing is fine.

Cheap hand lotion from the supermarket is quite good for this job: it is not too greasy and it smoothes the leather and acts as a dressing. Another advantage is that you will not have to wipe your hands clean constantly, as is the case when using fat.

A number of skin-care products can be used in this way; after all, it stands to reason that anything intended to take care of human skin will do a good job on leather of any sort. Whenever my wife tired of a skin-care product it went into our workshop to be used as a dressing, and I never found one that did not work well.

Skiving needs a very sharp knife. Since the edge of the knife is almost in contact with your first finger when doing this job, it is a good idea to wrap a scrap of leather around it, or make a small tube of leather to slip on the finger whenever doing this work. The finger out of an old leather glove is ideal, or a piece of rubber tubing.

Holes in Leather

Fig. 51b. Kangaroo skins will often have holes in them, and rather than waste a lot of leather when cutting out it is a good idea to learn how to cut around them. Here, for instance, is a sketch I did of an actual skin with a hole 12 mm long. By marking the strands out as shown it was possible to cut around it and lose only a small strip of leather.

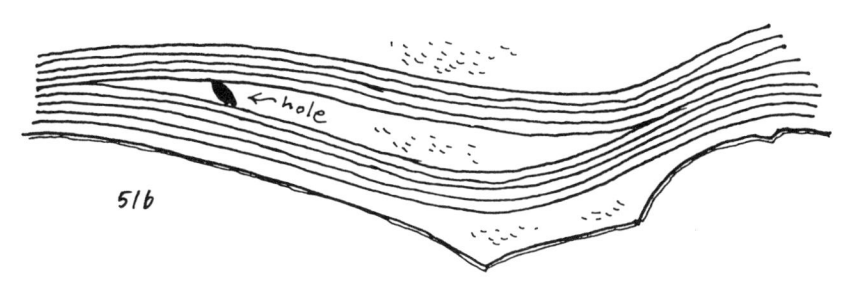

With careful planning there need not be any great amount of waste even when doing this, for the piece that is left can often be used to make a keeper for a whip handle.

Professional leatherworkers get very canny about using up scraps. Short lengths of lace can often be cut from the outside trimmings of a skin, and even scraps of lace as short as 300 mm can be used to form a Spanish ring knot on the narrow end of a whip handle.

Leather Dressing and Greasing the Strands

A tighter whip can be made if the strands are given some form of dressing. In the bush fat is the usual standby, and we always put a little kero or eucalyptus oil with it to stop vermin from chewing the surface of the finished whip. Mutton fat from around the kidneys is said to be the best, but in practice any good clean fat will do. For people who do a lot of plaiting, large quantities can be bought clean and clarified from hotel suppliers.

Ready-made leather dressings are also good, and there are a number of brands such as Coacholine, Jay-el, Gee-wy or Dubbin (Dubbin is good for whips and for all sorts of other jobs). As I wrote on the previous page, some whipmakers also use unusual things such as hand and body lotion, on the theory that anything that is good for the skin will be good for leather.

I also make up my own dressings using a variety of mixtures. For instance, one can be made by melting together some beeswax, neatsfoot oil, and fat. Use enough of each to make a firm, workable paste when it cools. Grated soap that has been dissolved into a thick jelly in a little water will make a good plaiting soap when mixed with some fat, and this is a good mixture in cool weather.

Temperature does play a part in it, and the overseer of a large tannery told me that they had one soft leather dressing for winter and another harder one for summer. While revising this book I have been making whips, and as the temperature has been rising each day I have noted that my normal home-made leather dressing has been getting softer and softer.

Not only that, but it has been soaking into the leather much faster. As a result, the leather is darker and stretches a little more during plaiting, so that on the last two kangaroo full-plait handles that I made I ended up with 50 mm more waste on the end than normal.

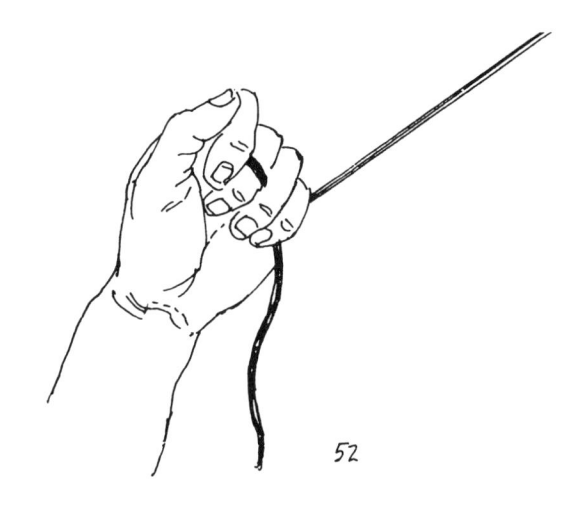

Fig. 52. Whatever is used the strands will be slippery, and it may be necessary to wrap them around the fingers in order to get a good purchase when plaiting.

Pull Tight, Plait Loose

This is an old plaiter's saying, and it means that you should take the strand you are going to work with and pull it firmly into place *before* you work it through the other strands into its next position. Many beginners have trouble understanding this and will work the strand into position and then pull it tight before picking up the next strand. This does not give as tight a finished job as will be the case if you pull each strand firm first before you do anything else with it.

STEP 5: PLAITING THE OVERLAY

The top plait (or overlay) is the slowest and most complex part of the job. Here whipmakers show their skill and knowledge, and the expert whipmaker may sometimes introduce a few fancy plaiting patterns. However, the thong is most often worked in a plain pattern as this is the working part of the whip.

Although it is tempting to try fancy patterns, the beginner is advised to stick to the method shown here, as it is both neat and fast.

Most of the fancy work found on good whips is done on the handle. I have written a small book about the various patterns called *Whip Handle Designs* and this also forms a chapter in this book.

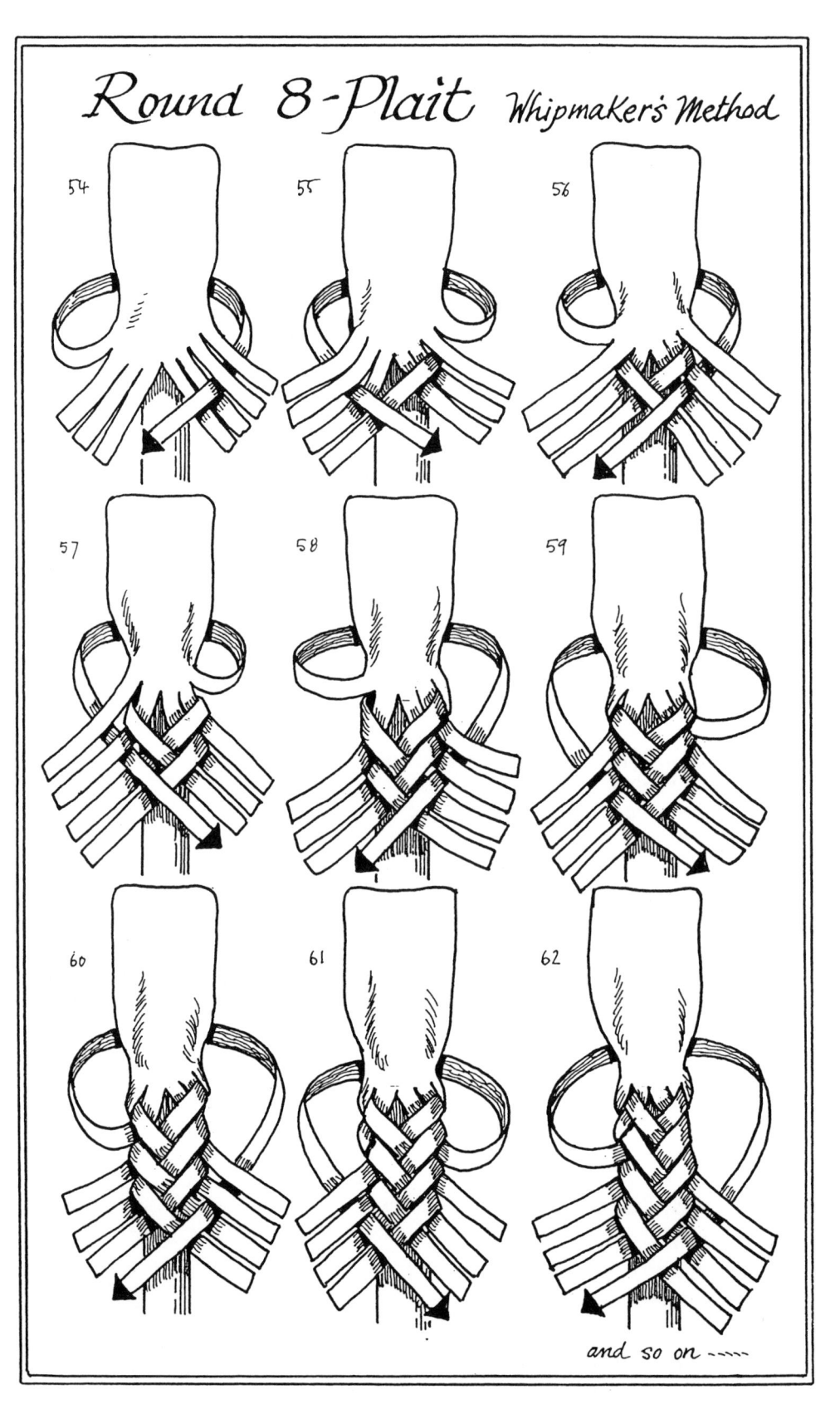

Round 8-Plait — Whipmaker's Method

54 55 56
57 58 59
60 61 62

and so on -----

62

Fig. 53. Place the belly on the end of the overlay set, leaving about 100 mm of plain leather for the keeper. Put plenty of dressing around the keeper, as this will be hard to grease once it is attached to the handle. Note that the keeper will now have two layers of leather (the loop on the belly is the other), and this will add life to the whip.

Using fine thread tie the long strip of leather (which will form the other part of the bolster) onto the belly, forming it around so that, if possible, it touches but does not overlap the bolster piece that has already been tied to the belly. This may mean trimming this strip of leather and some messing around, but the extra work will be worth doing when you get a nice round finished whip.

It may even help the finished job if you give the belly and bolster another good rolling at this stage, though this may not have to be done. Many professionals do not bother tying on the bolster but just work everything in as they go; but then again, they have been doing this for many years and the beginner cannot expect to be able to easily gain these skills that take a long time to develop.

Round 8-Plait

Figs. 54–62 (previous page). This is the basic 8-plait, which will be used on both the thong and the handle. It is easy to do and easy to remember.

Round 8-Plait

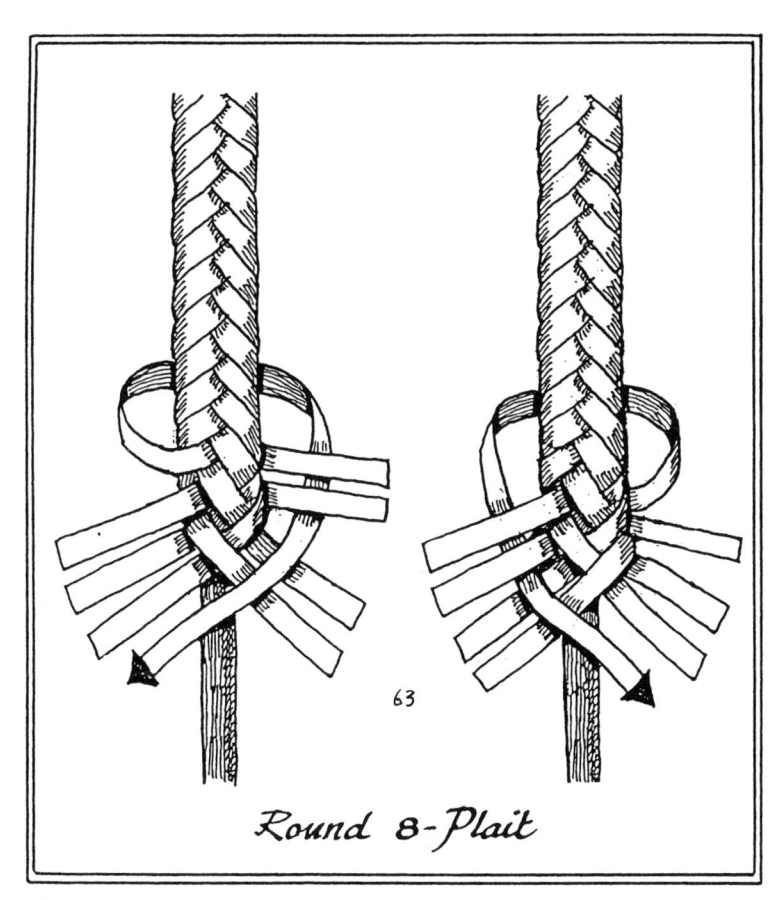

Fig. 63. Once you have got the plaiting started it continues in the same sequence all the way as shown, with only these two moves to remember.

(If you have begun with only 4 strands at the top, as illustrated in figure 39, then you will begin with the 4-strand plait as illustrated in the section on beginning the belly. When you come to the 8 strands you will find it easy to change to this 8-plait sequence)

Bundles

When plaiting begins you will soon be confronted with a tangle of strands below the work and around your feet. The secret to avoiding them is not to try to untangle all the strands, but to simply pull free of the bundle the strand you are about to use. This alone is enough to stop a tangle developing.

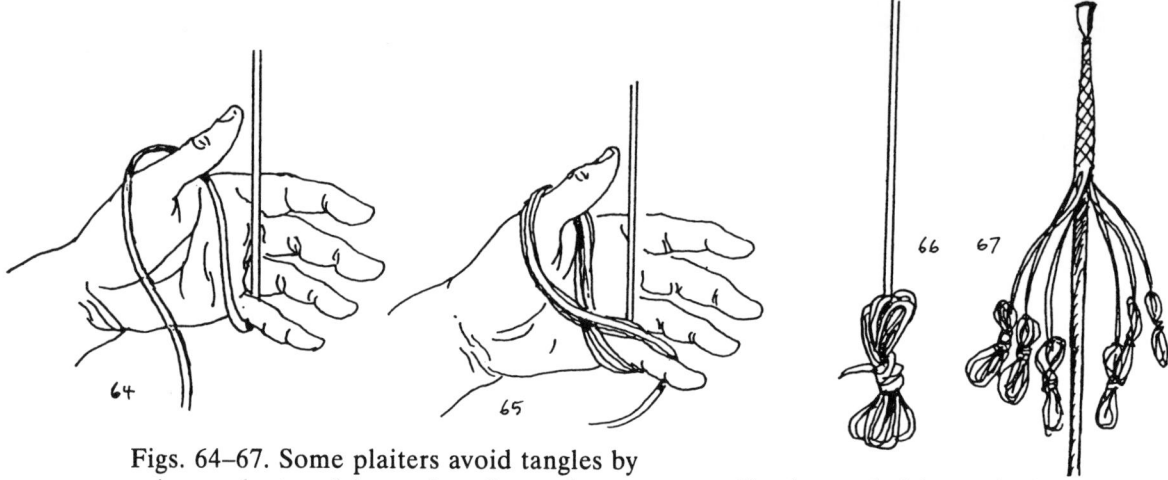

Figs. 64–67. Some plaiters avoid tangles by wrapping each strand into a bundle as shown. By pulling downward on the bundles more lace is freed as required. The bundles can be tied up as shown, but it is even easier to slip a couple of rubber bands around each one.

However, I find the bundles (called *tamales* in South America) a mixed blessing unless making very long whips and usually work without them, but some plaiters find them useful—it is a matter of personal choice.

Self-Greasing Lace Holder

Jim McDowell, a member of the Whipmakers Association who liked to work with many strands of fine lace, used this idea not only to manage strands but also to grease his lace as he was working. The greaser was made from a plastic thimble glued to a short length of plastic tube. A hole was made in the top of the thimble just large enough for the lace to pass through.

The lace was bundled up into a hank, and this was held with a couple of rubber bands and the end of the lace was pushed up through the hole in the thimble. The tube and thimble were then filled with leather dressing. This meant that as the lace was pulled through the hole it was greased at the same time.

Because the materials were cheap, Jim made one lace holder for each of the strands that he was working with. This is the same as tying all the strands up in the *tamale* style as illustrated above, but with the added advantage of the grease.

Jim learned this method from his father, James H. McDowell, on Lakefield station, north Queensland, in the 1930s. His father used the tips of wallaby tails for the same purpose, and would tan them himself, then pierce a hole through the end.

Looseness in Plaiting the Overlay

When I was learning to plait thongs I had a lot of trouble with getting a tight finished job. It seemed that no matter how hard I pulled the strands the finished job never had a good firm feel about it. It took some time before I realized that pulling hard is only part of the answer.

A round plait is by its very nature a hollow construction. The nature of any plait from 4 strands to 24 strands is such that the strands cannot be pulled into a solid unit. There will always be a hole down the center, and it is this hole that creates the loose effect later.

The belly and the core inside the whip are needed to create a solid leather foundation. If the belly is too small, the final overlay cannot properly lock together around it. There will be an air space, and this will create a loose effect.

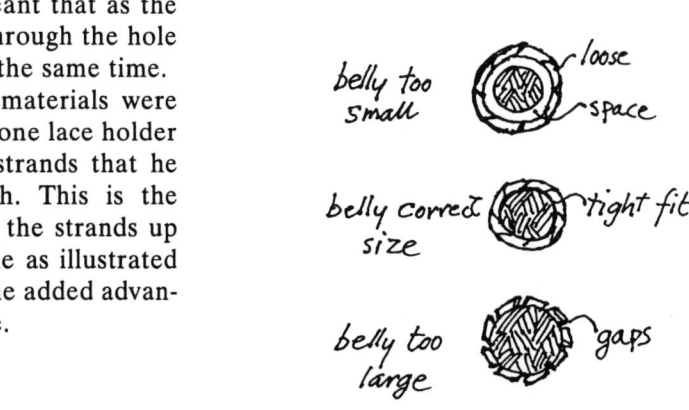

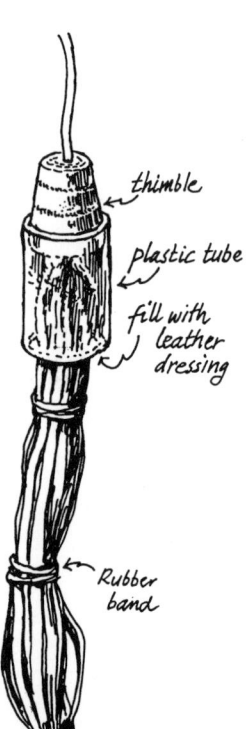

The drawings on the previous page show three cross-sections of a whip. Note that when the belly is too small for the size of the strands, the whip is loose, but when the belly is too large there will be gaps in the plaiting.

For example, you complete a thong and notice that while the top and bottom ends are firm, part of the middle section is loose, and when you twist the thong you can see individual strands standing loose. You wonder why this has happened because you were pulling the strands at the same pressure all the way down the job. The problem here will probably be found to be that the belly narrowed down too quickly, or that the outer strands of the overlay did not narrow down quickly enough at that point.

Whichever it was, the result will be the same—a section where the strands of the overlay cannot be pulled down tightly around the belly. When the strands lock together there is still air between them and the belly. Here are three useful rules:

1. Use plenty of plaiting soap, leather dressing, or just plain fat so that the strands will slide together better.

2. Make sure that you have stretched the strands in your hands before you begin; using strands that still have a lot of stretch in them will result in a loose job.

3. Pull each strand in firmly before working it into the next sequence. Remember the old saying "Pull firm and plait loose." In other words, pull the strand firm before you begin each sequence rather than after.

4. Make sure at all times that the strands are fitting firmly around whatever is underneath them, whether it is the belly, bolster, or filler.

Gaps in the Plaiting

If gaps develop between the strands as you are plaiting it could mean one of two things:

1. You are not pulling at the correct angle. Try adjusting the position of your hands and see if this helps.

2. Your strands are too narrow for the size of the belly. Quite often beginners make the belly much fatter than it needs to be. In this case you could remove part of the bolster or belly and see if this helps. It is possible to add in extra overlay strands, but this makes the job more complicated for the beginner. Getting the belly the right size in the first place is a better idea.

Plaiter's Knot

Figs. 68-71. Interruptions can be a problem when plaiting, as the strands from one side can get confused with the other. If the sides are tied up as shown, this problem can be avoided. With a little practice this simple knot can be tied with one hand.

A simple pull on the end of the strands will release the knot ready to continue work. As you may have forgotten which side you finished on, you should have a look at the job. One strand will be nearer the top than the others, and this is the next one to use.

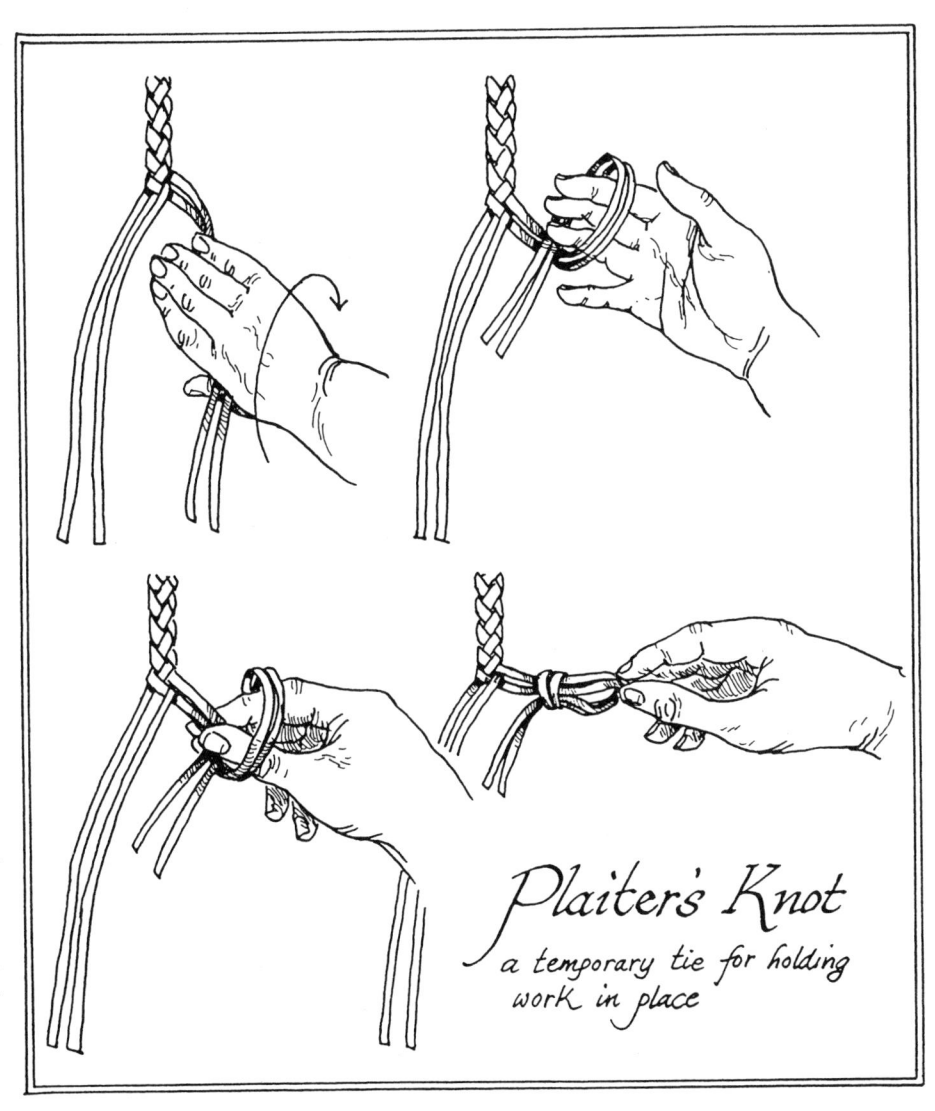

Plaiter's Knot — a temporary tie for holding work in place

Broken Strands

Sooner or later a strand will break, or you may find that you are running short on a number of strands. There are various ways to add on extra strands, and these are discussed later (see figures 171–79).

Dropping Strands

It is quite possible to begin plaiting with 8 strands and continue right down to the end of the thong with the same number of strands. However, to do this you have to taper the ends of the strands down very fine, and while professional whipmakers do taper their strands, they usually find it more convenient to taper down to a certain extent and also drop strands as they go. (There are exceptions to this rule. A whip that came into my hands for repairs while I was writing this had 12 strands right down to the very end, but this had been made by an expert and the strands were so fine as to be beyond the skill of a beginner.)

There is no fixed point at which to begin dropping strands, so I am not giving any measurements for this step. You must just watch how the strands are fitting as you plait. There is no need to drop any strands if everything is sitting down nice and flat.

Changing from 8-Plait to 7-Plait

Figs. 72–74. When you see the strands beginning to ride up onto the ones next to them, you know that you have too many and this is the time to begin dropping them. At this point a lot of whipmakers prefer to drop two strands at once, and jump from 8-plait to 6-plait in one operation. However, a neater transition will be achieved if you go from 8 strands to 7 as illustrated.

The strand to be dropped is shortened (but not too much for a start) and tapered down and then covered by the plaiting. After a few more passes pull the end carefully to make sure it is lying properly at the point where it was dropped. If you pull it too hard it will create a small gap where it is dropped, so take some care.

After you have plaited another 25 mm or so, stop and have a look at how the strands are lying. If there are any small gaps, you have dropped the strand too early and the only thing to do is to undo that bit and carry on with the 8-plait for a little longer. This is why it is a good idea not to trim off the dropped strand too early.

The dropped strand can be trimmed short if the plaiting begins to bunch up; otherwise it can just be left on the belly if it is not forming a lump.

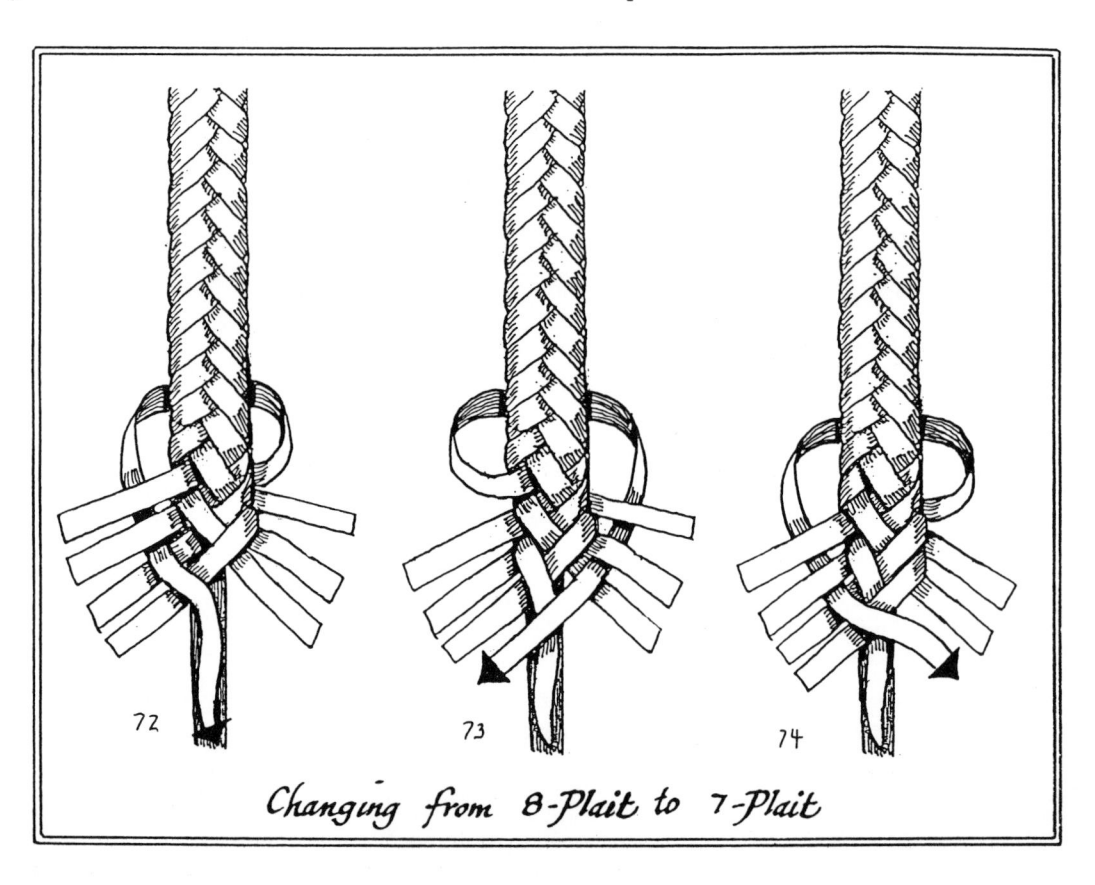

Changing from 8-Plait to 7-Plait

(Method 1) Changing from 7-Plait to 6-Plait

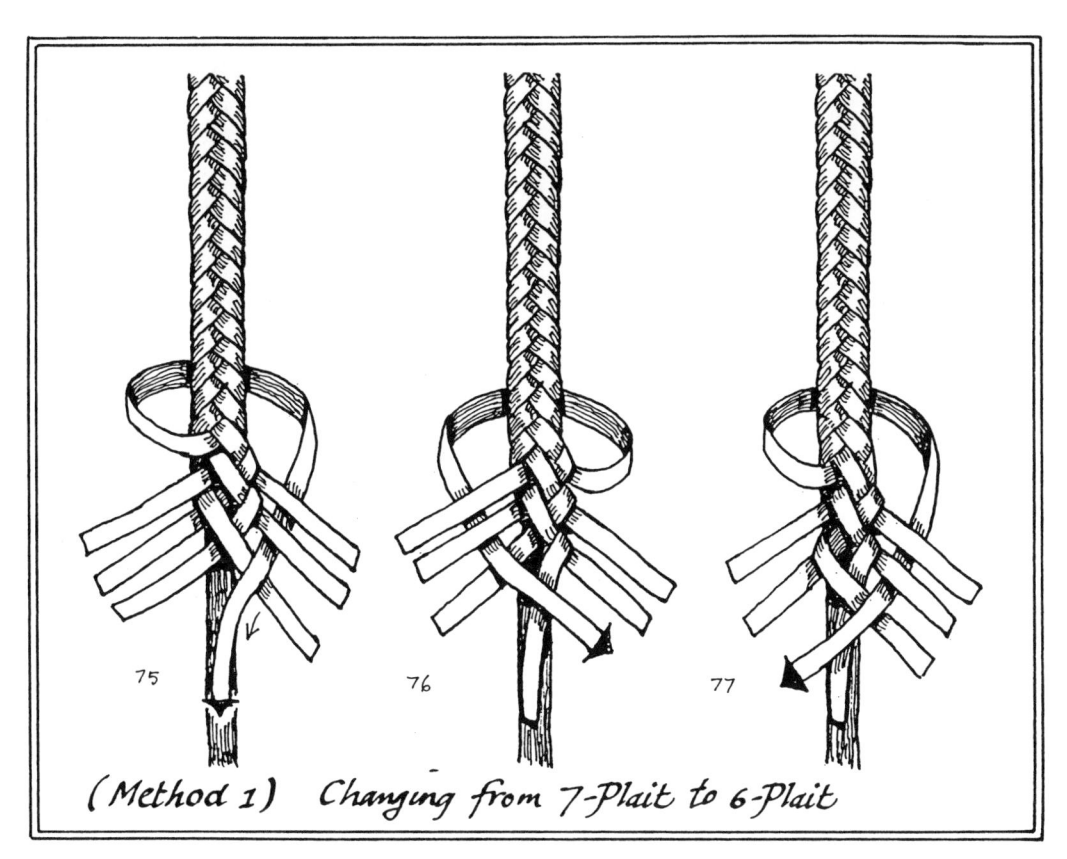

Changing from 7-Plait to 6-Plait

Figs. 75–77 (Method 1). Continue now with a 7-plait until the strands start bunching up once again (if they do not start bunching up then you can continue with the 7-plait for the rest of the whip). When you are ready you can change from 7 strands to 6 as shown. This is the easiest method and the one that most whipmakers use.

Figs. 78–80 (Method 2). This will give a somewhat neater result but is much slower to do.

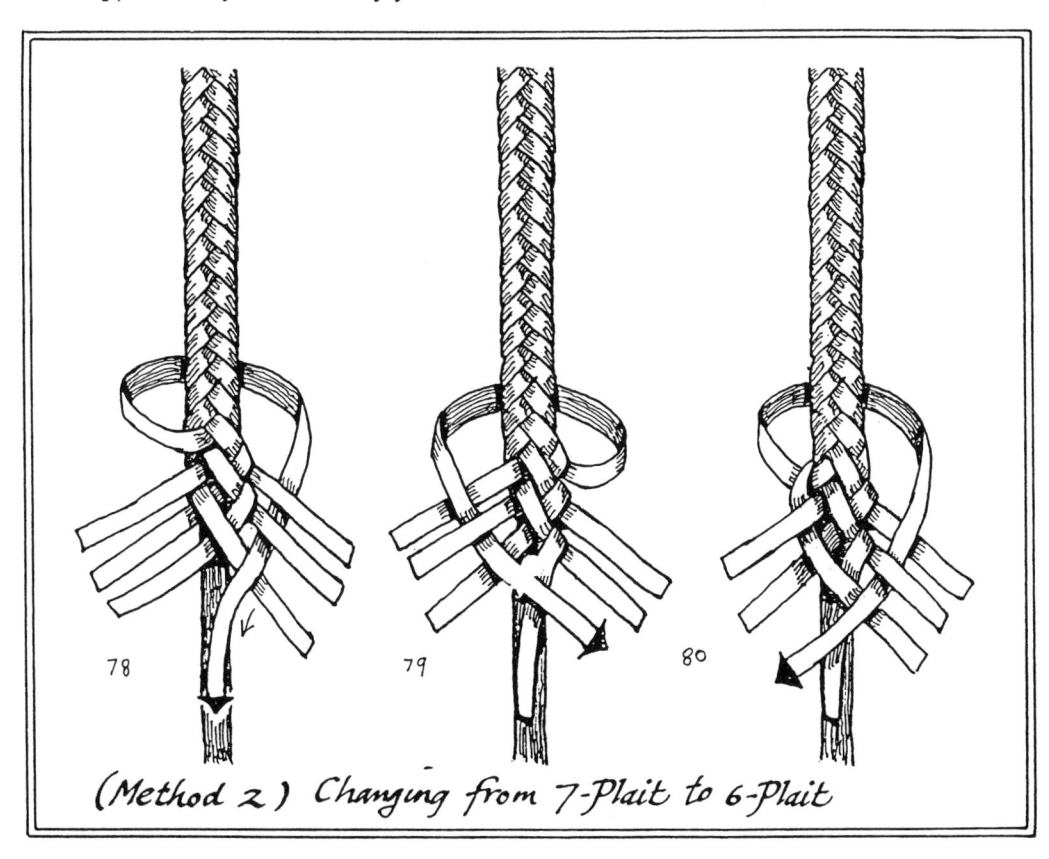

(Method 2) Changing from 7-Plait to 6-Plait

Uneven Taper

It is very annoying to spend a lot of time making a whip and then when it is all finished discover that there are ugly lumps on it or, even worse, one section that is narrower than the rest.

The answer to this is to constantly take a rest and have a hard critical look at how the job is going. You also have to be tough enough to see when it has gone wrong and be prepared to undo it back to that point.

Lumps

A badly shaped belly may cause lumps. If that is so, undo the plaiting back beyond the bad patch, unwrap the belly, and repair the trouble. This can usually be done by a bit of fine skiving with a very sharp knife and then firm rolling.

If the lump has been caused by a dropped strand sitting against the belly you must decide whether to taper it, thin it down, or trim it right off.

Narrow Sections

It takes some care to repair narrow sections. Undo the plaiting well back from the trouble spot and then build up the thickness of the belly at that point with fine thin leather tapered to a featheredge. Make sure that the work is solid and that there are no air pockets.

Round 6-Plait

Fig. 81. This is a simple way to do the 6-plait. There is another sequence illustrated in figures 79–80 in which instead of just going over the lower strand as shown here you take the working strand over the top one, under the middle, and over the bottom one. This makes for a more even-looking job, but as it takes longer most whipmakers do not bother.

Continue the 6-plait until you have almost run out of strands. Usually one strand will end up a little shorter than the rest, so when this is about 75–100 mm long you can stop.

At this point you should still be plaiting over the belly but it should be very fine.

Finishing Off the Thong

If this is your first whip then you will probably find it convenient to tie the end of the plaiting up tight with a couple of turns of fine black thread. Professionals do not do this, but it is helpful for the beginner. Otherwise, when tying on the fall the plaiting near the end can often work loose and spoil the whole job. Tying the finished work tightly will prevent this and also give you time for a breather and a chance to see whether the job has gone well.

Check that the loose ends of lace are as thin as you can conveniently trim them. The width of the lace is not so important at this point, but its thickness is. Thick lace will create a large and ugly knot when you come to attach the fall, and this will spoil the look of the finished job.

When you have checked that the plaiting is firm right down to the end, then you can put on the fall.

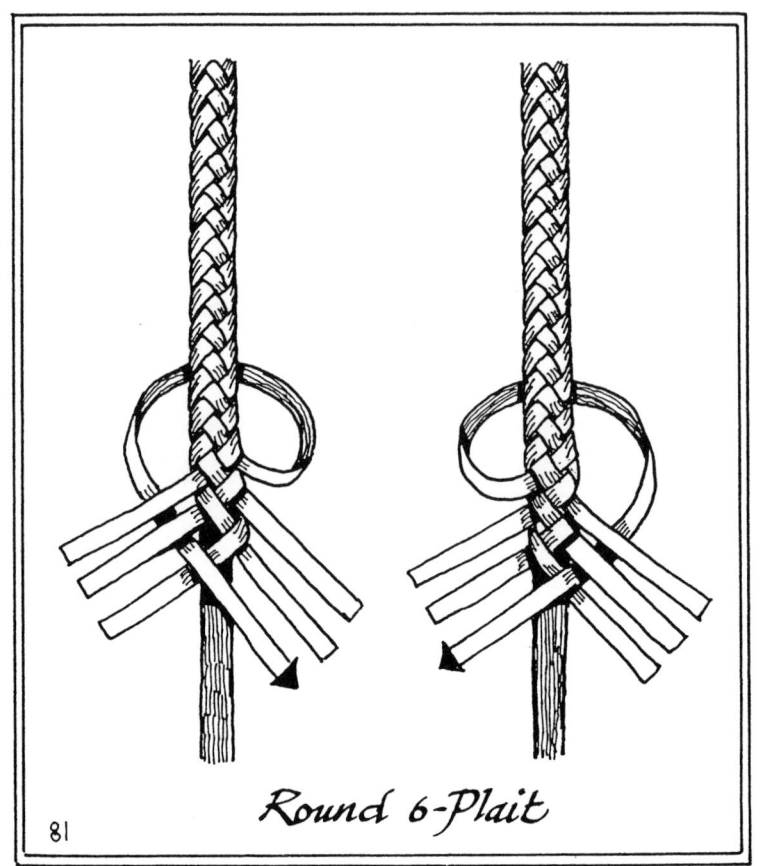

Round 6-Plait

STEP 6: THE FALL

The fall of the whip serves a useful purpose, but it is not meant to last the lifetime of the whip. Many people when cracking a whip will let it hit the ground, sometimes with considerable force. If there was no fall, then a plaited section of the whip would be taking this punishment and in time would get worn down and finally break.

Once the strands of a whip start to break it is difficult to repair them and, as a result, the whip will tend to get shorter and become useless. The fall is there to prevent this. It fits on the end of the whip where the damage usually takes place and is replaced whenever it has been worn out or broken. The fall can generally be replaced without losing any of the length of the whip.

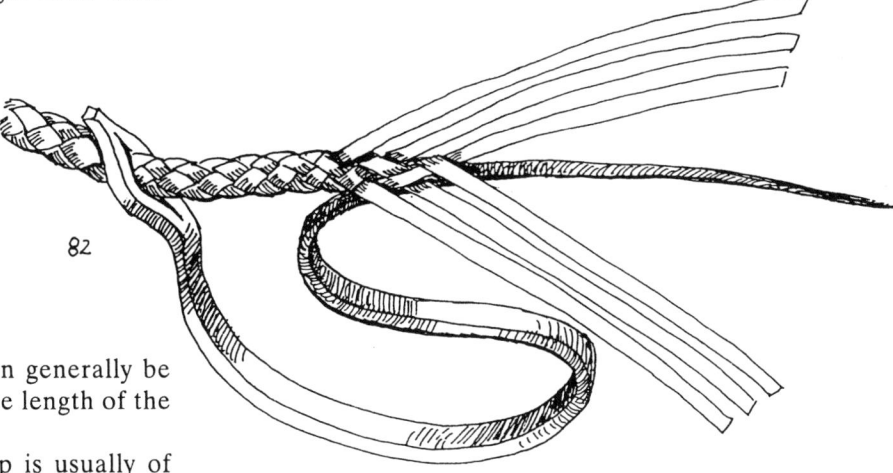

Fig. 82. The fall of the whip is usually of redhide or greenhide. If you have neither, then a heavily oiled strip of any good strong leather can be used. It can be cut to whatever length you like, but 500–600 mm is the most common. However, some people who follow the sport of whip cracking prefer short falls of around 300 mm.

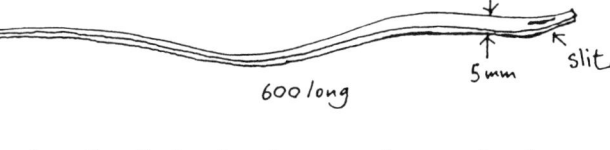

Some professional whipmakers prefer flat falls of the type illustrated here, and these can be 5–6 mm wide at the thickest and cut from 3–4-mm-thick leather.

Other whipmakers prefer to use the thickest leather that they can find, cut a strand that has an almost square section, and then round it so that the final job is as round as possible. Because this takes a little longer than the first method, it is not used as much.

Fig. 83. Wrap a scrap of leather around the fall two or three times and have the top of the fall attached to a hook. Pull the scrap backwards and forwards fast and firmly and it will not only round the leather but give it a good finish. Use plenty of leather dressing or fat.

A flat fall should also have its edges skived and be partly rounded by applying fat or leather dressing and rubbing the fall firmly with a scrap of waste leather.

The falls on kangaroo whips are usually better finished and narrower than the robust falls found on heavier redhide whips, though made from the same materials.

Fig. 84. One of the secrets to getting a neat, tight joint between the plaited section and the fall is to bind the strands around the narrowest part of the fall as shown. Grease the fall very well before beginning the binding and it will pull through easier.

Attaching the Fall

Figs. 85–90. (See next page.) This is a common method used to fix on the fall. It is easy to remember and works well. It can be used for any number of strands. A similar method, but with slight variations and using only 4 strands, is shown on page 22.

There are other methods of attaching the fall (see pages 149–53), but this is the most popular, partly because it does not have to be undone when it comes time to replace the fall.

Replacing the Fall

To replace the fall: cut the remains of the old fall off close to either the top or bottom of the knot (depending on what is most convenient), apply a good layer of fat or leather dressing, and then use pliers to pull out the remains of the old fall.

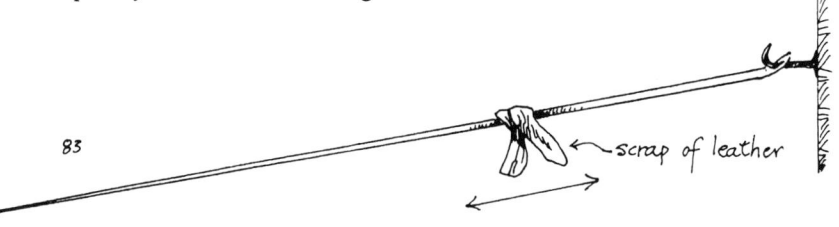

Attaching the Fall

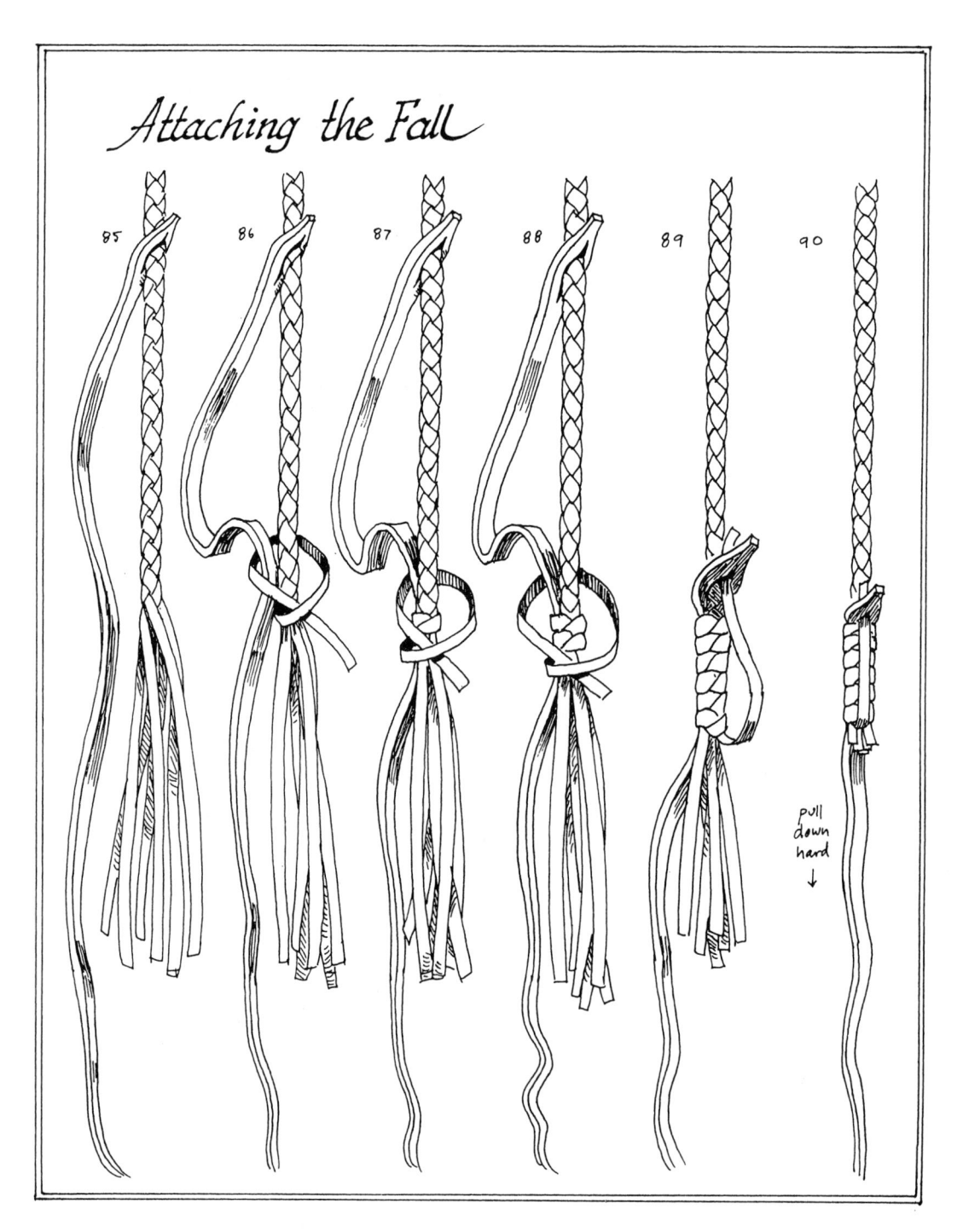

If this can be done without interfering with the knot, then the new, greased, fall can be slipped up the thong, the point of it fed through the hole where the old fall had been, and pulled down tightly into place.

Fig. 91. Professional whipmakers who have to cut a lot of falls often cut a number of them in gangs, hang them up on a hook, and cut one off whenever it is needed.

This sketch is of a gang cut by Peter Clarke, a maker of fine kangaroo whips.

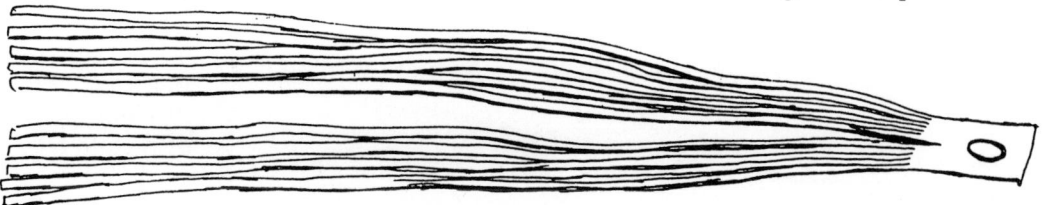

STEP 7: MAKING THE CRACKER

The traditional way of making a cracker is to pull a few hairs from the mane or tail of your horse and twist them as shown in the sketches of a stockman friend.

We find that nylon twine, classed as 210/18 ply makes excellent crackers, but any fine hard cord can be used. One whipmaker uses dental floss and says that it makes good crackers. A lot of professionals use the synthetic twine that comes around hay bales. Silk was used in the old days.

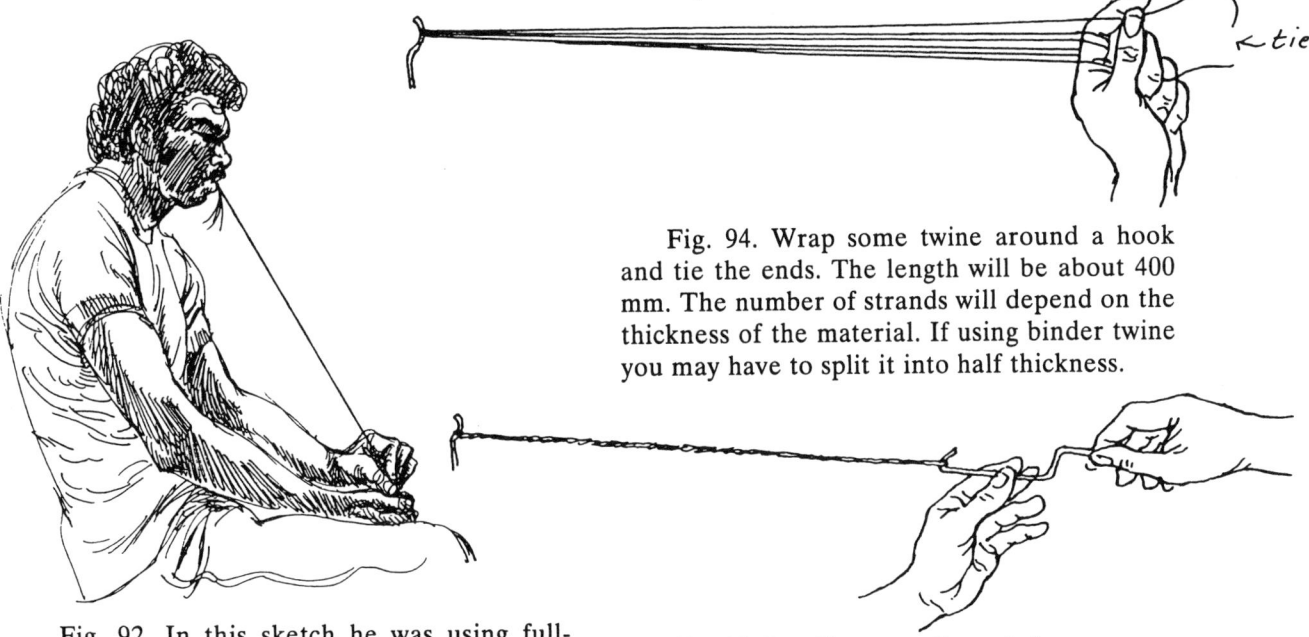

Fig. 94. Wrap some twine around a hook and tie the ends. The length will be about 400 mm. The number of strands will depend on the thickness of the material. If using binder twine you may have to split it into half thickness.

Fig. 92. In this sketch he was using full-length tail hairs. A more usual length would be around 450 mm. The hairs are twisted until they begin to kink.

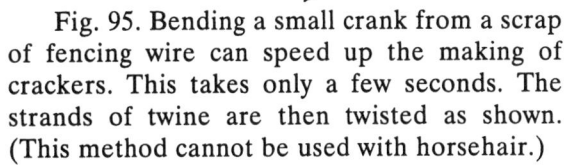

Fig. 95. Bending a small crank from a scrap of fencing wire can speed up the making of crackers. This takes only a few seconds. The strands of twine are then twisted as shown. (This method cannot be used with horsehair.)

Fig. 93. The middle is grasped and gently pulled. As this is done it will form into a twisted cord. A knot is tied in it to stop it from coming unwound.

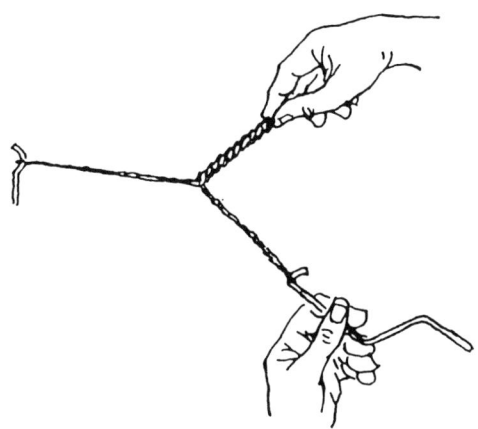

Fig. 96. When the strands have been twisted enough they will start to kink. When this happens, grasp the middle firmly and twist it with the fingers while still retaining a little tension on the thread with the other hand.

You will find that it will only twist in one way, and once twisted will stay twisted even when you remove your fingers.

Finishing the Cracker

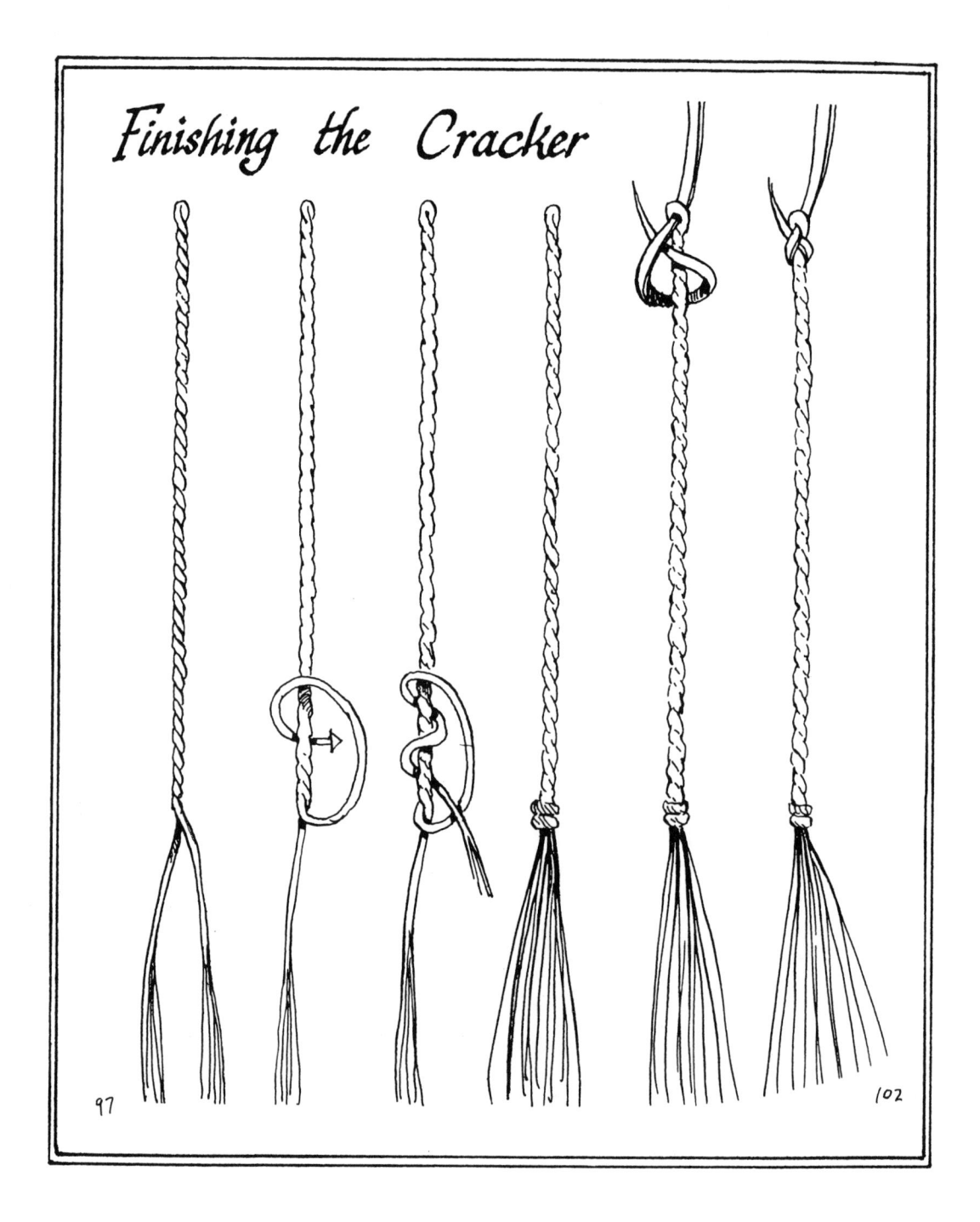

Figs. 97–102. This shows a neat way to finish off the cracker. This is a variation of the blood knot and is popular with a lot of stockmen. Other knots can also be used to finish it off, and a selection of them may be found later in the book (see pages 146–47).

The last two drawings show how to attach the cracker to the fall. Although this is a very simple hitch, it is also a very strong one.

It is at this point that the fall is at its weakest, so try to ensure that you have good quality leather at this end. When the whip has been completed, give it a few good cracks just to make sure that everything is holding properly. It is very annoying for a customer to buy a new whip and have the cracker fly off at the first crack.

There is something to be said for using colored material for the cracker rather than black, for it is a little easier to find if it does come off.

On the subject of material for crackers, while nylon does make a good cracker it also wears down to very fine filaments at the end, and this fine stuff is the very devil to pick up burrs and bits of rubbish. Synthetic binder twine is nowhere near as bad in this respect.

Fig. 103. For the final roll, use a solid board and roll it firmly until the whip comes up smooth and round. For a beginner's whip, this may take some time and effort, but attention to this part of the job will prove to be well worthwhile in the appearance of the finished whip.

Fig. 104. Some whipmakers roll the whip on the floor; some roll them on the bench. A number of them use a pair of boards—a wide one below and a narrow but heavy one on top. The sketch shows the two rolling boards used by Maurice Doohan and their dimensions. He picked up the top one from a heap of firewood and it is very heavy.

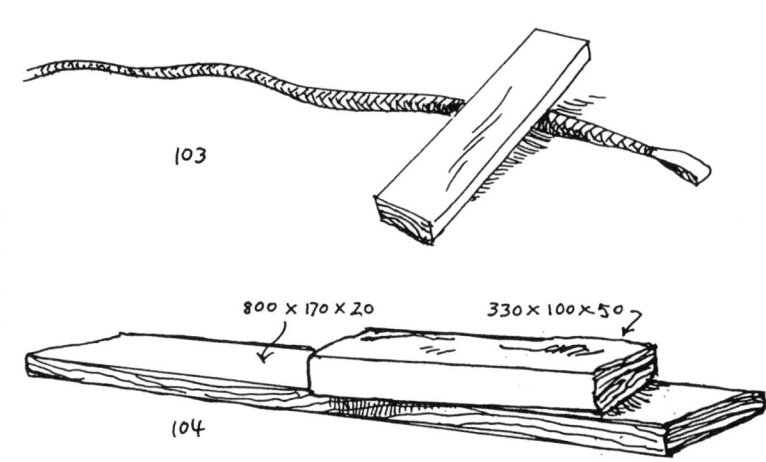

Fig. 105. The late Tom Cluff used to roll his whips with a leaf from a set of truck springs. He said it was a good length, and the curve made the work easier.

The sketch shows Tom rolling a whip. The curve in the spring helped keep his fingers clear of the table.

Fig. 106. If a lot of fat has been used on the whip, the board may start to slip and will not roll it properly. The cure for this is a light dusting of powdered resin (used by roughriders, golfers, etc., to keep their hands from slipping).

The sketch is of an old sock in which Maurice Doohan keeps his resin. The weave of the wool allows a light dusting of resin to come through so the sock does not have to be undone to get the resin. I use a square of cheesecloth with some resin tied up inside it, and a good shaking will release enough dust through the weave of the material.

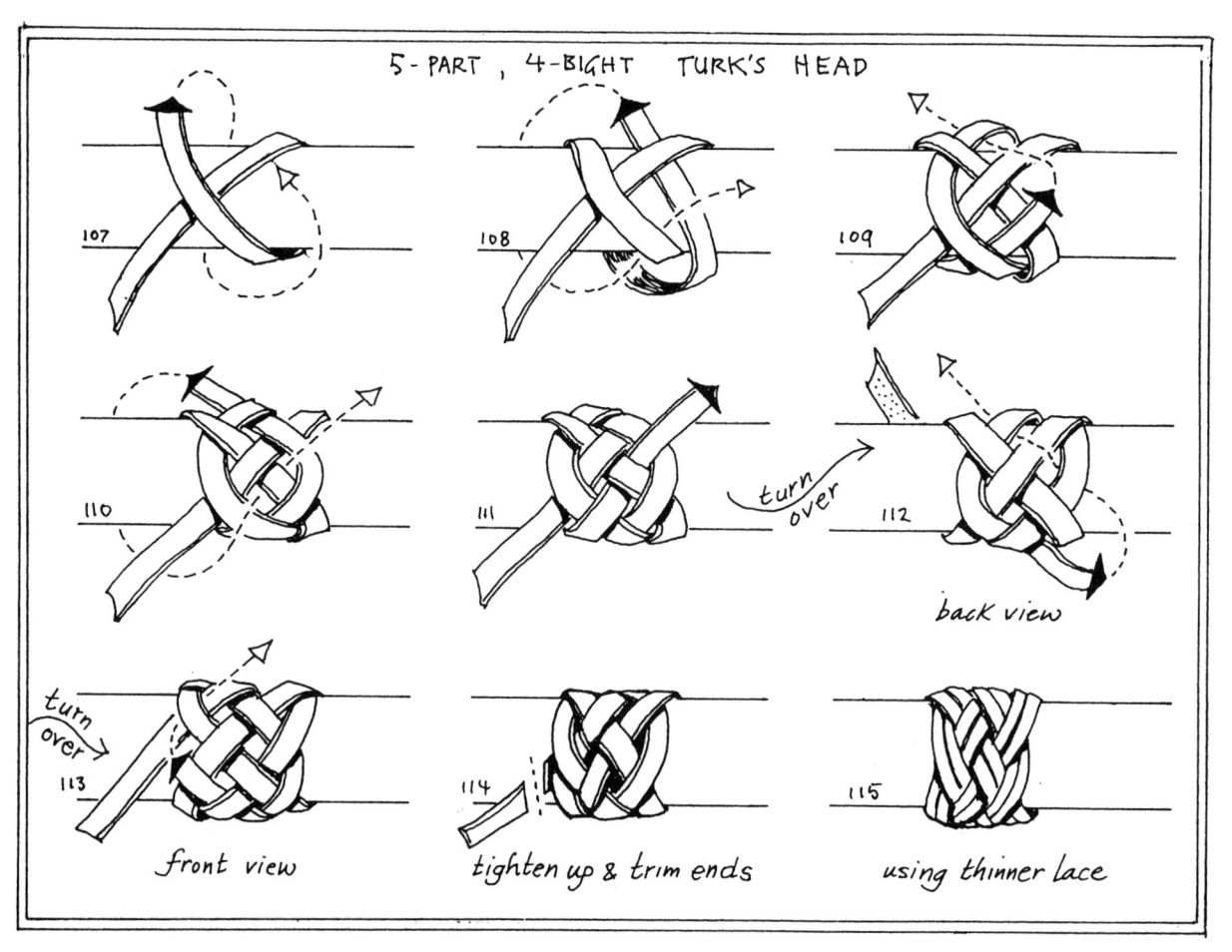

5-Part, 4-Bight Turk's Head on the Thong

Figs. 107-114. The final touch is a small Turk's head at the beginning of the plaiting. There are a great number of Turk's heads, and this one is known as a 5-part, 4-bight. It is a favorite with whipmakers and is often used to cover the knob on the end of the handle. (A few pages on, this knot is shown being tied on the handle knob, together with an explanation of the way it is formed.)

About 300 mm of 4.5-mm-wide lace will do the job, but cut 500 mm to be on the safe side. This knot is only added for decoration and is a matter of choice.

Fig. 115. It is also possible to use thinner lace, say 3 mm wide, and go around twice (or even three times) following the same path, once the basic knot has been completed.

You can even make the first knot with one color of thin lace, then go around the second time with a length of lace of a different color and so create quite a decorative effect.

Fig. 116. This is how the finished knot should look on the end of the thong. A similar knot can also be put on the handle at the keeper end.

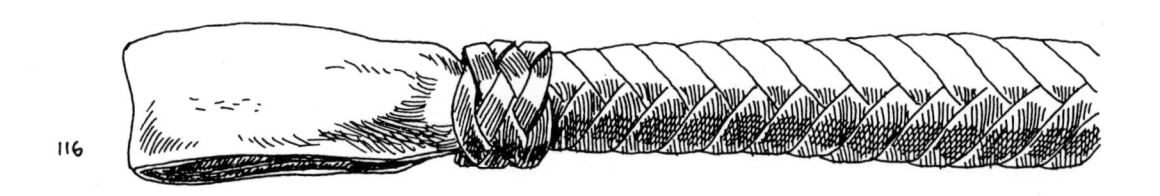

STEP 8: THE HANDLE (OR STOCK) FOUNDATION

Stock is the old term for the handle, but as handle is more readily understood I will use that term for this book.

There are two main types of handle, and the first is the solid handle that tapers a little towards the keeper, but often only as much as the natural material has tapered while growing. The strength of this handle is in the material itself, and it may be made from native timber or from cane.

Handles of solid timber (without any steel reinforcing) are usually only plaited over just far enough to give a good grip for the hands, and the rest of the timber or cane is left exposed. This type of handle can be used on the kangaroo thong but is commonly found on the redhide whip, and the making of it is explained on page 29.

Fig. 117. The handle we are going to describe here is the second type, which is a finely tapered cane handle, lined with a spring steel core. The use of the steel allows the cane to be tapered down far more than would be possible with an ordinary piece of timber, no matter how strong it was. A steel-lined handle will usually be tapered down to 5 mm in diameter at the narrow end. (Cane can be obtained from the makers of cane furniture.)

To make this type of handle, the cane is split down the center and a groove cut into it. A piece of spring steel 400 mm long and of around 5 mm in diameter is put in place and then the two halves are glued together again.

Once the glue has dried the handle is shaped as shown. In old saddlers' catalogs this was called the foundation. Today you can no longer buy shaped handles so you will have to make your own unless you have a whipmaker friend.

Fig. 118. The end of the steel is grooved as shown in the sketch so as to give a good grip to the leather overlay when it is tied on.

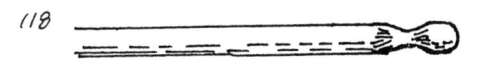

Using Bush Timber

Fig. 119. If you cannot make a good tapered foundation as described above then you may have to use bush timber. Try to select timber known for its strength and one that will not split readily. Stockmen have been badly injured by whip handles that have split and pierced them when they fell from their horses. Try to find something of around the dimensions given here.

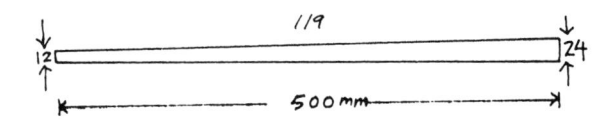

Note. If using bush timber remember that all the following leather dimensions are for the narrow steel-lined foundation, and you will have to allow more according to the thickness of the timber that you are using.

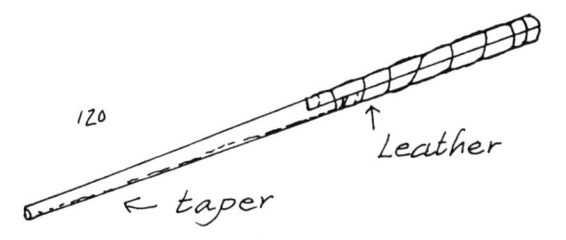

Fig. 120. If your bush timber is not wide enough at the end, it is quite possible to build up the shape with pieces of leather. Bend and twist the timber at this point to test its strength. It is better if it breaks now than when you have put a lot of work into it.

STEP 9: THE OVERLAY FOR THE HANDLE

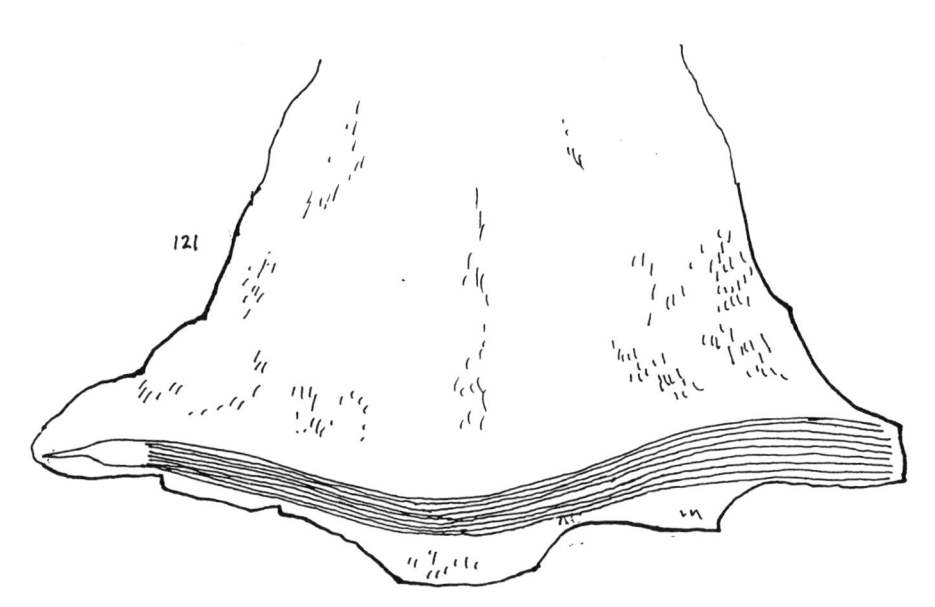

Fig. 121. The overlay is the leather plaiting that goes over the handle. For convenience the overlay set for the handle may be cut from the lower part of a kangaroo skin, for this leather, while good enough to cover the handle, might not be the best for use in the thong of the whip. Also, the leather here may be just the right length for the job, and this helps even up the skin.

The strands are cut from one back leg to the other, dipping down where the tail has been so as not to waste any leather. Before cutting just check that there are no very thin or stretchy patches in the skin. A certain amount of stretch can be tolerated, and in that case the strand is cut a little wider at the stretchy part, and when the strand is later pulled it will come down to the correct width.

Fig. 122. An overlay like this is intended for the tapered and lined foundation illustrated on the previous page.

When the strands have been cut out it is a good idea to put them through a splitter to get them all to an even thickness. However, a person who is only going to make one or two whips will probably not have a splitter, and so the best that can be done is to select a skin which has the best available finish underneath and an even thickness.

Do not worry about this, because there are some professionals who do not use a splitter for this part of the job but rely on selecting leather of even thickness.

Skiving the strands. The strands should be skived on either side in order to make them lie well when they are plaited into position. A smooth final job is difficult unless this is done. However, like splitting the leather, it can be a traumatic sort of job, and it is very annoying to slit through a strand by accident just when the job is nearly completed.

If this does happen, do not despair, for the loose strand can be worked into the job later. A good woodworking glue like Aquadhere, or a leather glue such as Leather Weld, can also be used to glue the broken strand back, taking care to scrape or taper a good surface on both strands for the glue to grip on. See figures 171–86 for more on this.

Tying the Set to the Stock

Fig. 123. Notice in the sketch where the keeper tapers off to a point. The exact shape of this bit will depend on the size of your handle foundation. Wrap it around the handle and make sure that it is not too bulky. If it is, then trim it a bit more. The aim is to have strength in the leather at this point but not bulk, so it is a fine balancing act.

Skive this pointed end of the set down as fine as possible with a sharp knife to a featheredge, as it has to sit flat and smoothly on the end of the foundation. If you do not do this properly the narrow end of the handle will have lumps in it when it is tied on and plaited over.

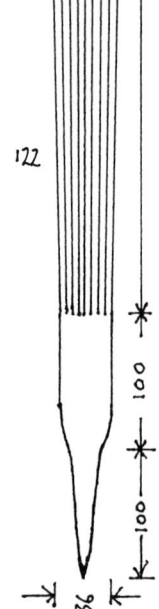

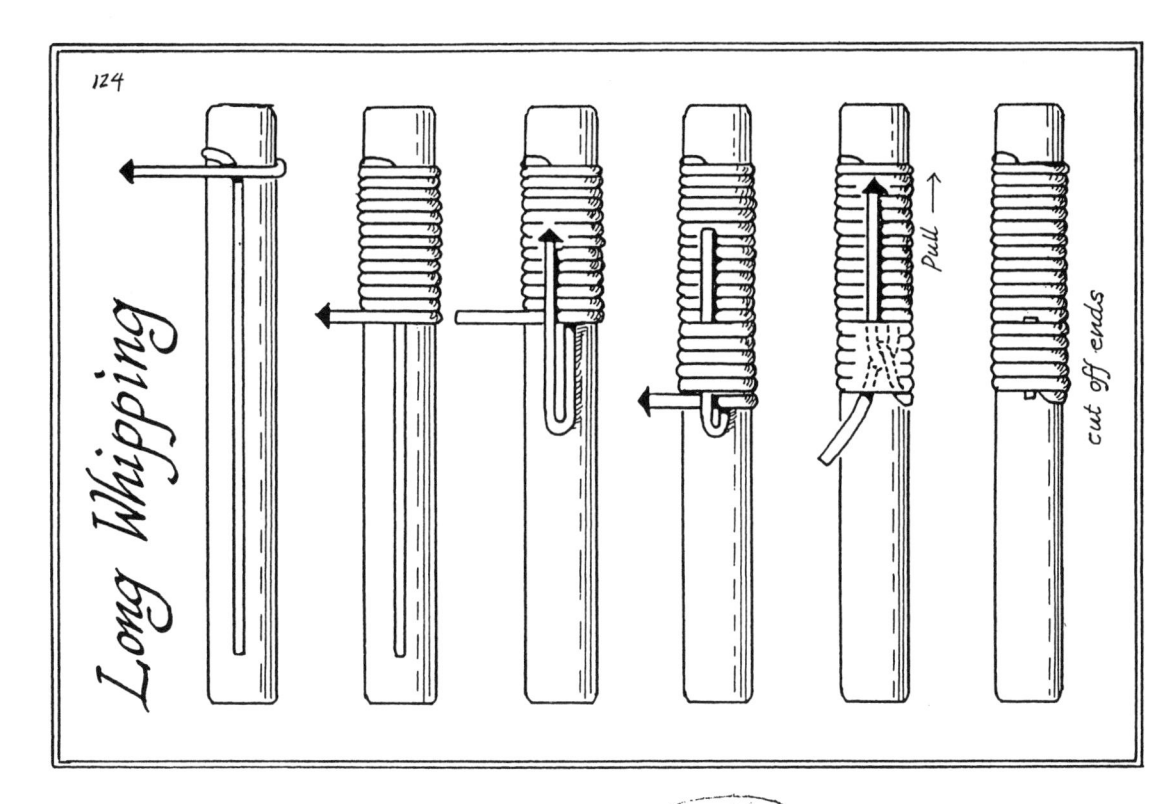

Long Whipping

Fig. 124. Bind the point on with fine strong twine. It needs to be fine so that it will not add too much bulk and it needs to be strong so that it can never come loose. A long whipping can be used for this job.

Fig. 125. This shows the set bound to the handle foundation. The leather will be folded over to form the keeper.

Fig. 126. This is a sketch of north Queenslander Lindsay Whiteman beginning to cut out a set, with the kangaroo skin on his knee. He is holding a strand in one hand and using his thumbnail as a gauge for his knife.

Lindsay Whiteman   Jan 25 1993

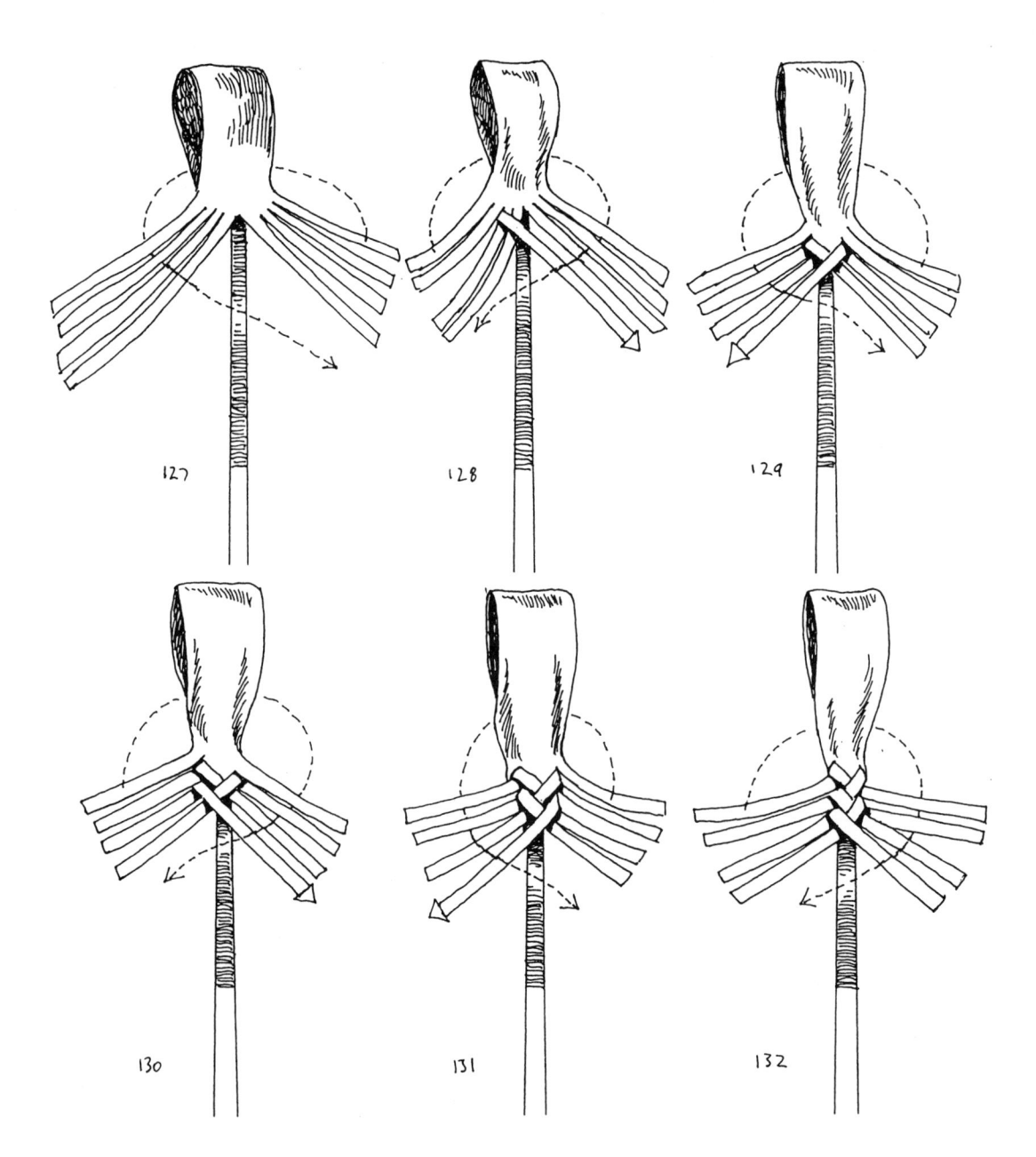

Figs. 127–32. Once the end has been tied on, fold the leather down so that the strands are against the top of the handle; then plaiting can commence as shown. This sequence continues for the full length of the handle.

Should you wish to try other patterns a number of them are illustrated in chapter 5, but for a first whip the plain plait will be the best.

Fig. 132. When the handle has been plaited over, tie the end very firmly and then trim off the surplus. Try to do this neatly so that there are no gaps or bumps.

Fig. 133. Both edges of the keeper can be folded in after being given a good coating of leather dressing. This looks better than leaving the keeper as a single flat piece of leather, and it will also last longer as the leather is now doubled.

Fig. 134. Holding the handle while plaiting can be a bit of a problem. Pages 140–42 show the plans for a large clamp to do this job, but this is far too elaborate for the beginner who just wants to make a couple of whips.

Here is an idea for a simple clamp that will do the job and which can be made quickly. First take two scraps of timber and cut a groove in each as shown. This can be quite rough.

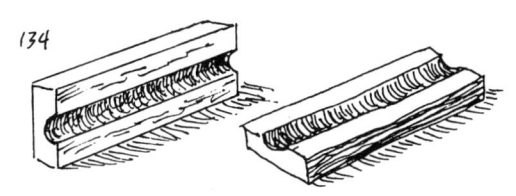

Fig. 135. Put a grooved piece on each side of the handle, place this on a wedge-shaped piece of timber, clamp the whole lot to the corner of a table, and you have a quick solution that will allow you both hands free to do the plaiting.

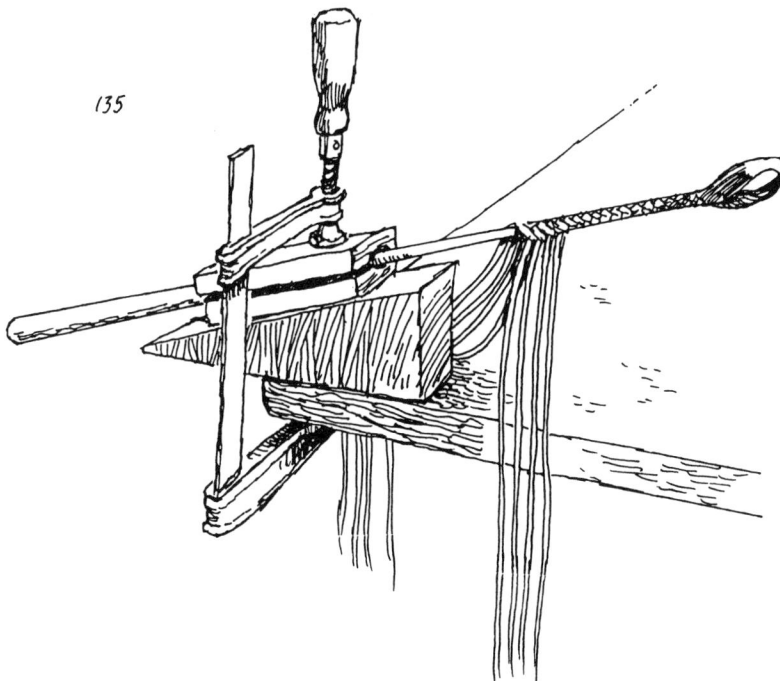

STEP 10: THE KNOB ON THE HANDLE

The Turk's head that goes on the knob on the handle is a great mystery and source of worry to many beginners. However, if you take it quietly and learn just one step at a time you should be able to complete this part of the job without trouble.

Professional whipmakers today approach this job in two different ways. Some of them close the Turk's head up completely over the end of the knob, while others leave a gap so that the top of the knob is showing.

It is easier if the knot is formed with an opening at the top, for the knot can then usually be worked neatly and without any gaps. If the knot is to be closed at the top, there is less room for error, for it has to cover the knob without any gaps, but also without bunching up too much. This can be a problem for a beginner.

If you are going to leave an opening, you will need to follow this next step, but even if you are not going to leave one it is not a bad idea to do this, because it does make a nice smooth surface on which to build the knot.

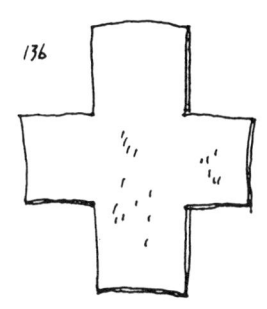

Fig. 136. Take a scrap of kangaroo and cut it into a cross; you will soon work out the size.

Fig. 137. Smooth and round off the end of the handle so that there are no bumps on it. This is an important step no matter what sort of a handle knob you are making. Wrap the leather cross over the end of the handle and tie it firmly in place. Rub it on a smooth tabletop, or with a smooth piece of bone, so that the shape is as good as it can be made.

Fig. 138. Place the knob over the edge of the table, or your lower rolling board, and give all the plaited surfaces a good firm roll. Also roll the knob section, but with some care so as not to loosen the new cover.

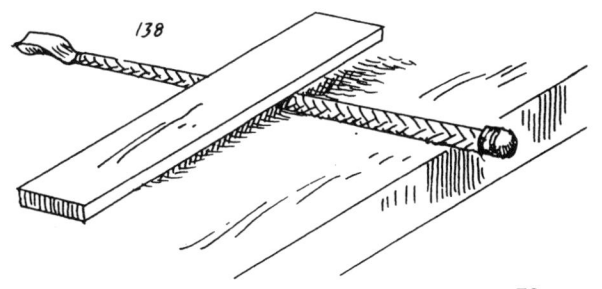

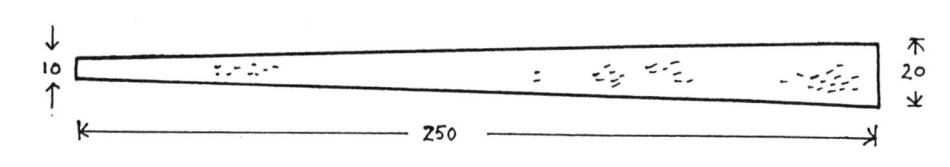

Shaping the Knob

Fig. 139. Here is a chance to use up some scrap of soft, flexible leather. Cut a strip as shown; the measurements are only a rough guide, for it will depend upon the thickness and the stretch in the leather, as well as the size and shape of the knob that you are aiming for.

Fig. 140. Skive both ends of this strip so that it will lie down without forming a bump. Tack one end and then pull it around the knob tight and tack it in two or three places. Do not put tacks where you are later going to trim the leather—it is hard enough to keep knives sharp without having to cut tacks.

Because every job is different, you must not go by my measurements but instead watch the job and make sure that the leather builds up to a knob of the diameter that you want, and one that is of even thickness all the way round.

If the leather scrap has any thickness about it you must take care where you finish it up so that the layer will not be thicker at this point.

Fig. 141. Now take a sharp knife and carefully trim the edges of the leather to make a smooth knob. You must get this part nice and even; otherwise the Turk's head will not be a good shape.

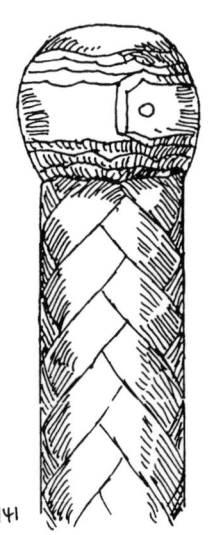

The Shape of the Knob

Three basic shapes are found in knobs. The upper one in the sketch is a flattened knob, and this is often found on whips that use the faster 3-part, 4-bight Turk's head. On this shape of knob the knot is always closed over at the top.

The second shape is a ball, quite a common shape.

The lower one is an oval, and this is the shape most often seen when the knot has been formed so as not to close at the top.

5-Part, 4-Bight Turk's Head

(See next page.) There are dozens of Turk's heads and they are all described by parts and bights. Bights are the loops that you can count around the top of the knot, and parts are the number of strands if you were to cut across the knot with a knife and then count the ends. So this knot has 5 strands across and 4 loops or bends around the top (and bottom).

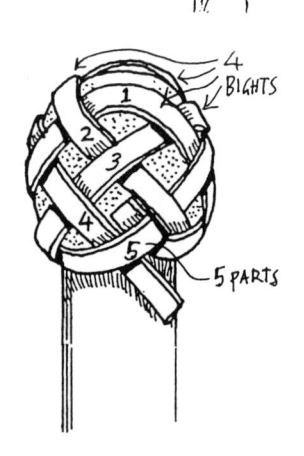

It is a good knot for this type of whip—a little more elaborate than what would be found on a cheap whip but not too difficult for the beginner. Cheap whips commonly have a 3-part, 4-bight Turk's head—the same number of bights as this one but with less parts. As a result it is faster to do, but does not cover as much area. The 3-part, 4-bight knot will be found on page 36.

For the knot we are using here you will usually need a little over a meter of 4.5-mm-wide lace, but the amount will vary from knob to knob. To avoid waste I do not cut the lace off the roll until after the knot has been tied. When the knot is complete I tighten it and then trim it off. When firmly tightened the ends will never come loose.

When you do the Turk's head it is a good idea to try to break it down into three steps, because it is easier to remember it in this way rather than trying to learn the whole sequence by rote.

The steps consist of first forming a very simple Turk's head, making tracks, and finally splitting the tracks, creating a larger and more complex knot than the first one. This process can be repeated again to create an even larger and more complex Turk's head, but this will not be necessary for this knob.

Figs. 142–44, Forming the first Turk's head. This is a complete knot in itself, but too simple to use for a knob. When you have done it, you can let go of the lace and have a good look at it.

5-Part, 4-Bight Turk's Head

142 — over 1

143 — over 1 under 1

144 — O1 U1
This is a 3 part 2-bight Turk's head

145 — making tracks O2

146 — making tracks U1 O1

147 — splitting tracks O1 U1 O1 U1

148 — splitting tracks O1 U1 O1 U1

149 — spread out the strands evenly & follow round 2 or 3 times

150

You will notice that all the lace follows an under-over sequence.

Figs. 145–46, Making tracks (also called making pairs). This means that you are following the path that the lace took at the start of the job, going up alongside it on the right side and then crossing over and coming down on the other side.

Figs. 147-148, Splitting the tracks. The lace now goes between the tracks that have just been made and pushes them apart to create an under-over sequence all over the knot. Take care at the top of the knot to follow the sequence.

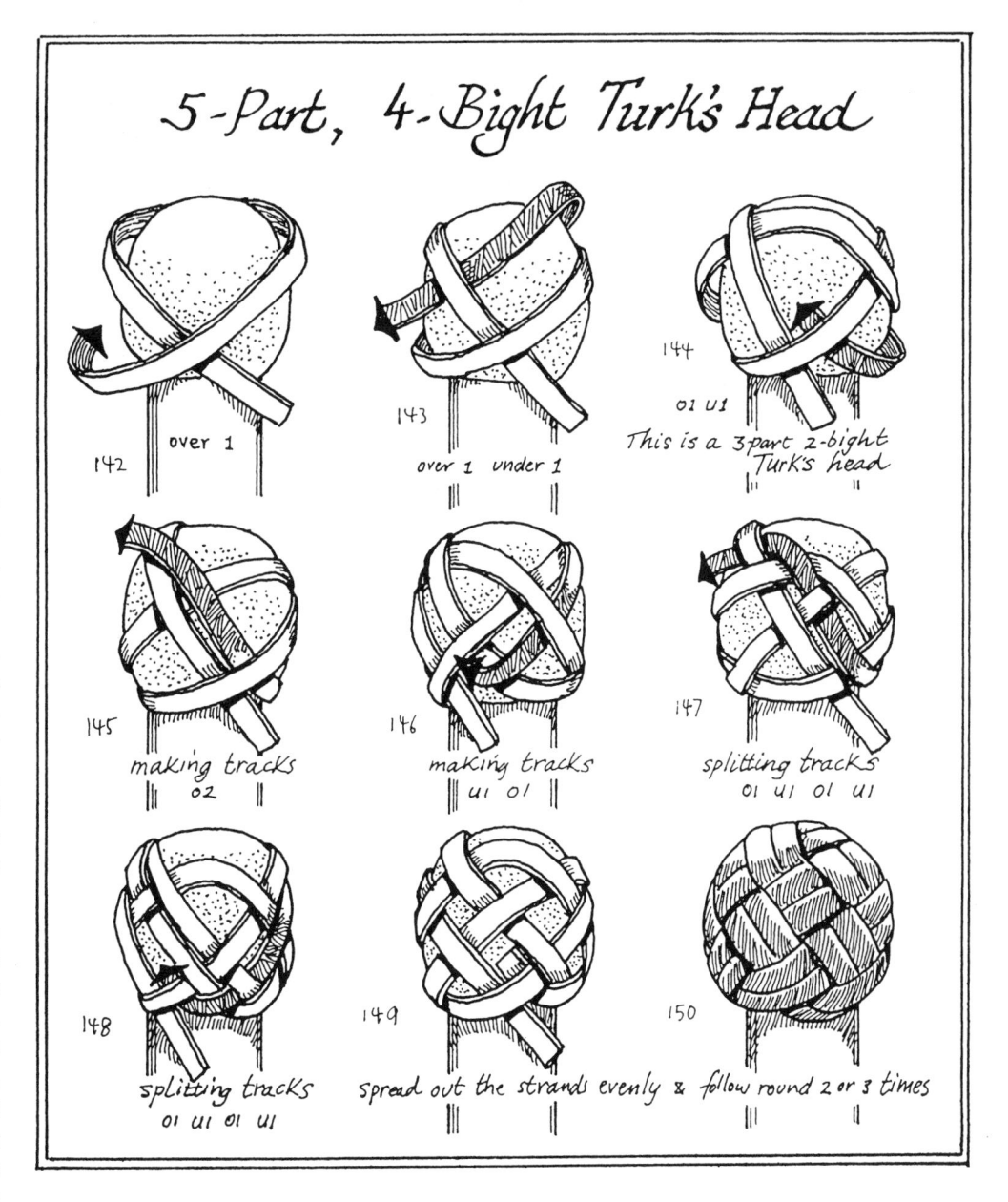

Fig. 149. When the knot is completed you should carefully arrange it so that all the strands are evenly placed around the knob, and also have the knot firm enough so that it is sitting properly and will not slip off.

Fig. 150. Now you can decide whether you want to go around the second time on the left or the right of the original strand. There is no fixed rule about this despite what some whipmakers say; you can make up your own mind. Go around on the right if you want to close the hole in the middle, on the left if you want to leave it open.

Gaps in the Turk's Head

Fig. 151. It may be when you have gone around the Turk's head twice there is not enough room to go around for a third time but there are still narrow gaps. The way to get around this problem is to cut a narrow strand and work this around as the third one. If you choose a contrasting color of leather, it will look very fine and appear as if that is what you had intended to do all the time.

(In this example the smooth leather put over the knob before the Turk's head is showing at the top of the knob, while in the next one the knot has been closed at the top.)

Fig. 152. Going around three times. If there is enough space you can go around the Turk's head three times, and this looks good. However, it is best to limit it to three. If there are still gaps then it means that you have made the knob too large, or are using lace that is too narrow. My book *Turk's-heads* will give you some knots that will cover a larger area, but for the beginner it will probably be easier to reduce the size of the knob or get wider lace.

Finishing the Knob

When the covering of the knob has been completed it should be rolled to make it smooth. Some of this can be done in the same way that the handle was rolled, but a piece of bone or the back of a large spoon will help rub down smooth those parts that cannot be rolled on the board.

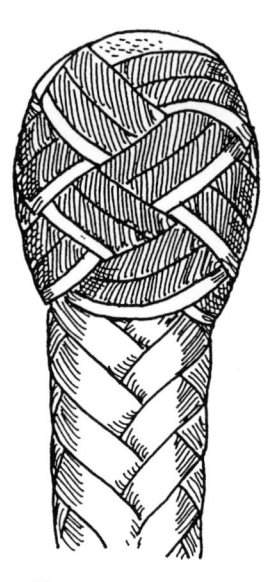

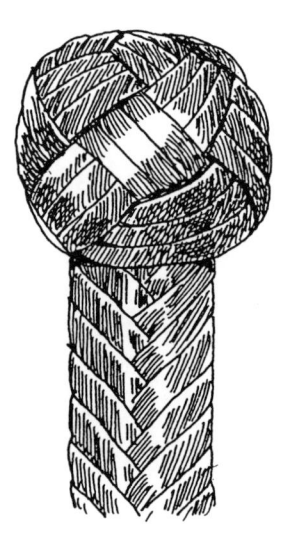

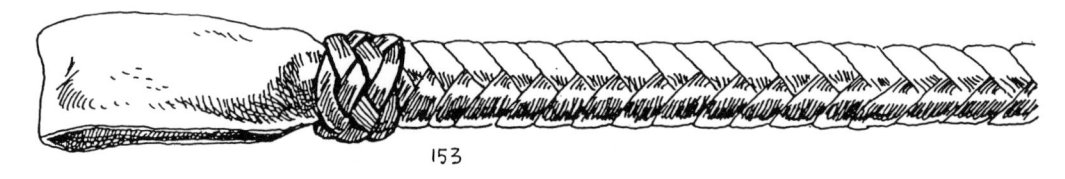

Turk's Head on Keeper End

Fig. 153. The same Turk's head used on the end of the thong (p. 74) can now be put on the end of the handle near the keeper. This is not essential but it makes for a neat finish.

Once this has been done the handle should be given a good coating of shellac or a clear leather finish. Not only does this give a good-looking surface, but more importantly it acts to bind the whole thing together under a protective skin.

Shellac is the traditional coating for a whip. It not only protects the surface but also acts to lock all the strands together and thus prevent any of the ends of the knots working loose.

It is bought in flake form and soaked in methylated spirits, where in time it will dissolve into a useable liquid. It can be put on with cotton wool. Several coats may be needed.

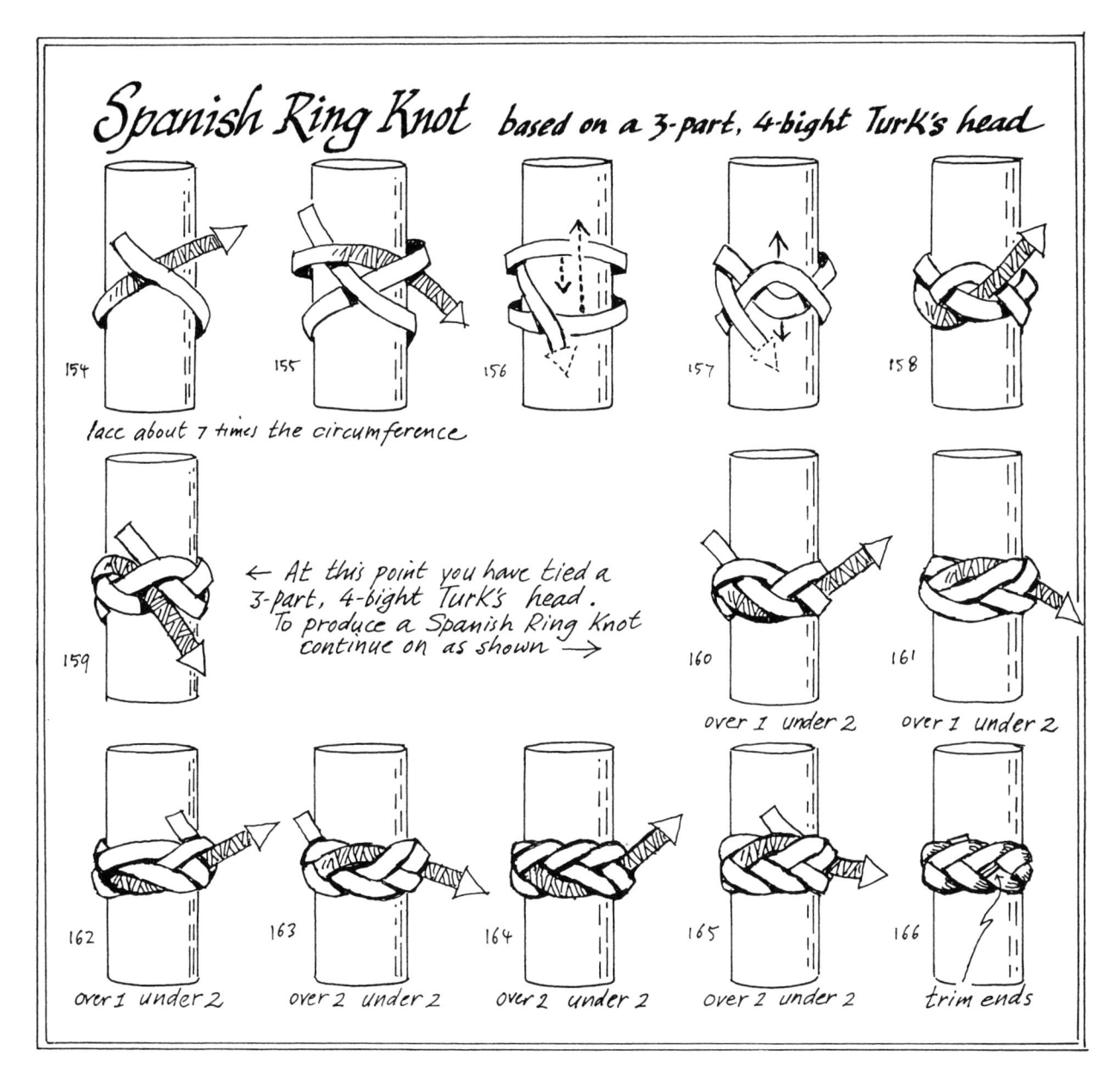

Spanish Ring Knot based on a 3-part, 4-bight Turk's head

154 155 156 157 158

lace about 7 times the circumference

159 ← At this point you have tied a 3-part, 4-bight Turk's head. To produce a Spanish Ring Knot continue on as shown →

160 over 1 under 2   161 over 1 under 2

162 over 1 under 2   163 over 2 under 2   164 over 2 under 2   165 over 2 under 2   166 trim ends

Spanish Ring Knot

If you would like to try something different you could put a Spanish ring knot on the narrow end of the handle instead of the Turk's head. It may take a little longer to get it right the first time, but once you understand how it is done it becomes simple.

Figs. 154–59. The Spanish ring knot can be built up from a number of Turk's heads. It can easily be built on a 3-part, 5-bight Turk's head (as shown on page 10), while in these drawings it is built on a 3-part, 4-bight Turk's head.

It is the same 3-part, 4-bight Turk's head that is popular for basic whips because it is quick and easy to tie (though the beginner may think otherwise).

Figs. 160–66. Once the Turk's head is tied the next step is the interweave, and this is where you must take care because if the strands are taken under in the wrong place just once then the even pattern will not work out. If you do have any problems be prepared to undo it as far back as figure 159 and have another try.

Fig. 167. By now the handle should look like the sketch on the left. The Spanish ring knot can be seen at the narrow end, just below the keeper.

A More Elaborate Handle

Fig. 168. Once you have made a couple of whips with a plain handle you can begin experimenting with some patterns. For instance, the handle can be commenced with the 6-plait shown in figure 81, page 68. Then, after a third has been done it is changed to the 6-plait shown in figures 79–80, page 67.

After a section of this has been completed the strands (which have been previously split into two up to this point) change to a 12-plait (p. 31). This follows the same system as the 8-plait previously described, each strand going around the back and coming out halfway between the strands on the other side.

Two-Tone Work

Interesting effects can also be obtained by using leather stain to change the color of some of the strands. Traditionally only two colors are ever found in a whip—one dark and one light.

The problem with leather stains is that many of them fade, especially with use, and sometimes the kangaroo leather will have been given a finish in the tannery that is hard to stain.

Two-tone work needs several coats of shellac to seal it in.

Fitting the Handle and Thong Together

Fig. 169. The final step is to fit the handle and thong together by this simple action. Work them together until they are tightly locked.

Care of the Whip

Even as I write this the bugs have been chewing the corners of the half dozen whips that I had to make while preparing the sketches for this book. They had all been given a good coating of leather dressing, as mentioned earlier, but it seems I did not put enough kero in the mixture, so I have had to add more.

I cannot give any proportions, as I tend to make the dressing up by eye and it differs each time, but perhaps two teaspoons of kero to a liter of the mixture would be better than the one teaspoon that I probably put in. Or perhaps a bit more eucalyptus or teatree oil would help.

So make sure that your leather dressing has something in it that will deter vermin (most of the leather dressings that you buy are all right in this respect).

After the dressing has been allowed to soak in, or has been rubbed in, leave the whip for a day or two to make sure that the surface is no longer greasy. Then give the whole whip a number of coats of shellac, or use one of the clear leather finishes which can be bought at a saddler's or leather shop.

According to the amount of use the whip has it should be given a good rub with leather dressing every few months. If this is done it will last fifty years without any trouble.

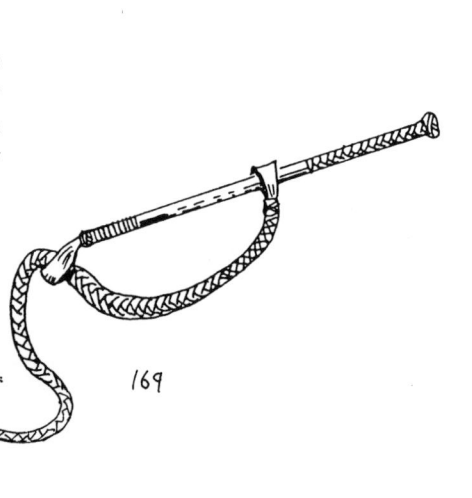

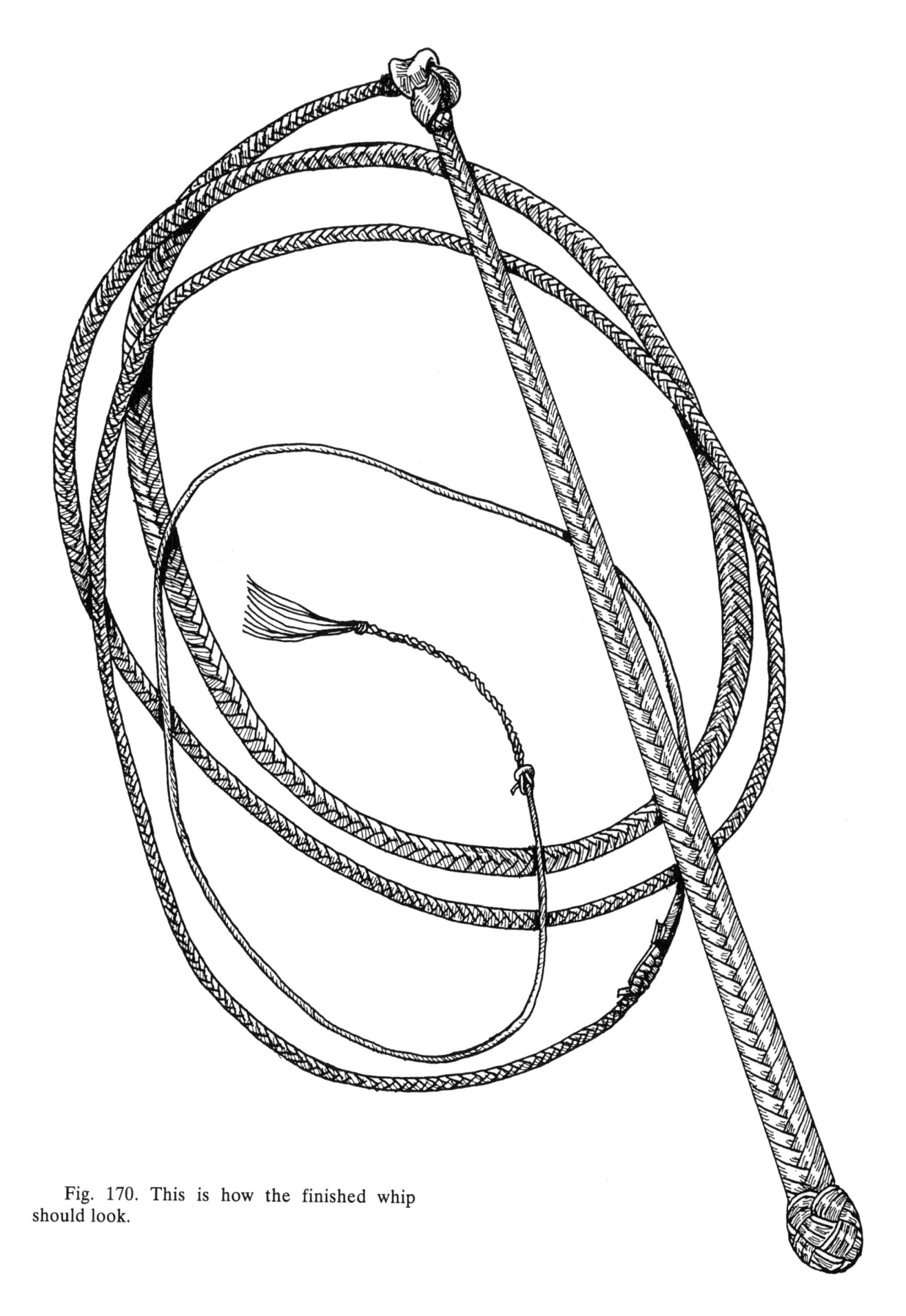

Fig. 170. This is how the finished whip should look.

A FEW TIPS

Broken Strands

Sooner or later a strand will break, and although this is very annoying it is usually possible to repair it without weakening the job. Whenever using a repaired strand try to position it so that the joint is covered by other strands in the plaiting.

Fig. 171. This is the neatest way, but it has to be done properly. Wipe all the grease off the strand before skiving in order to get a clean surface for the glue. Both ends of the lace are skived back for as long as possible—25 mm is good. The ends are then glued together with Kwik Grip, Leather Weld, Aquadhere, Contact Cement, or some other similar glue. When done properly the joint will be almost undetectable.

Bought lace will often have strands joined like this, and quite often they are not noticed unless you are trying to get the lace through small holes where the extra bulk will make itself felt.

Joining without Glue

Fig. 172. It is possible to join the strands without gluing them if you can ensure that an overlapping strand in the plait will hide the joint. This first method is the neatest. Cut a small slit in the short end of the lace and two angled cuts in the new piece.

Fig. 173. Push the new piece through the old one and then pull them together.

Fig. 174. This shows the back view. The angled cuts will act like arrows and hold the pieces together. The idea of having a 20-mm overlap on the pieces is so that when the lace is plaited in, the weakness of the lace at this point will be minimized.

Fig. 175. This is what the completed joint will look like from the front.

Another Method

Figs 176-178. This is an easier method of making a joint without glue by simply putting a slit in each end and joining them as shown.

Fig. 179. This is how the finished joint looks. This type of joint is easy to remember, and is stronger than the previous one, but does not look as neat.

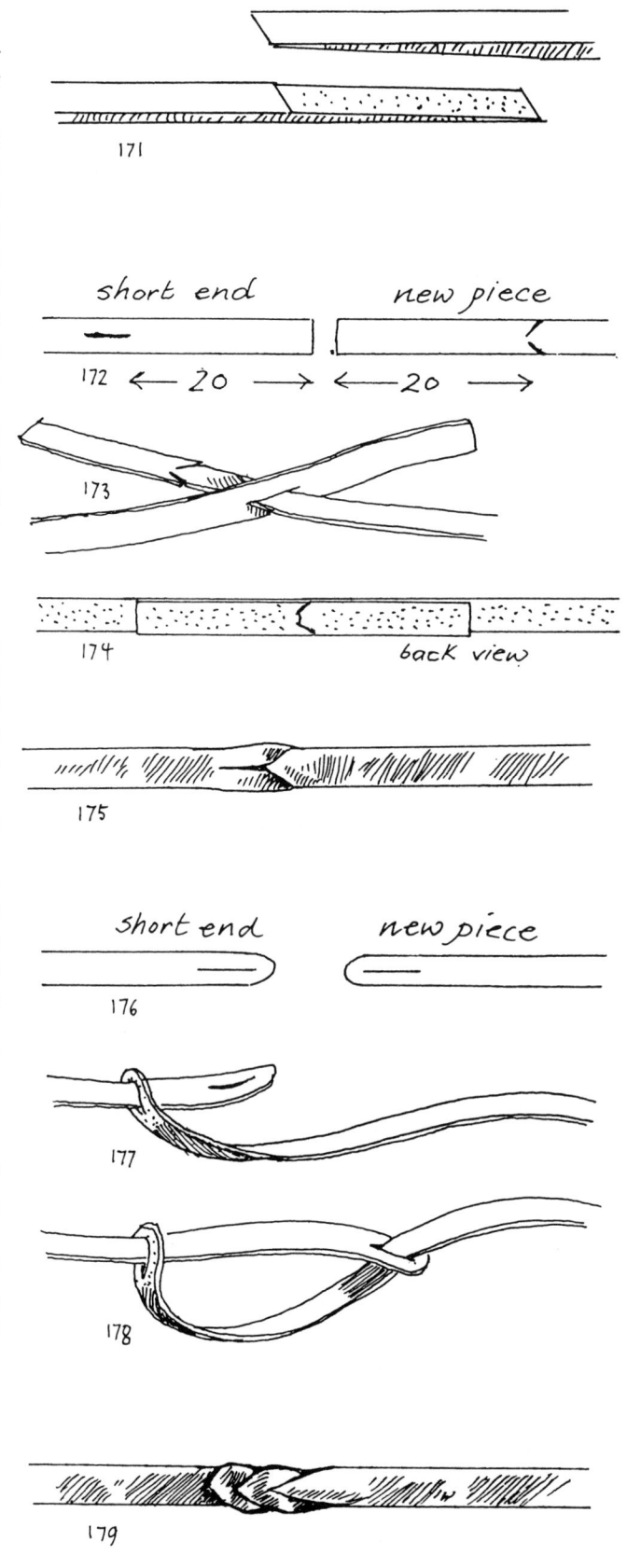

Adding in a Strand

It sometimes happens that a strand will break and you do not wish to join it again because it will make it too short. Or it may be that you wish to add one or more extra strands because you are developing gaps in your plaiting. Even the professionals break strands from time to time, but they always make sure that the new strand cannot be detected and that the job is not weakened in any way.

Fig. 180. There are various ways to add on extra strands and this first method is the fastest. The new strand is simply laid over the broken end and plaiting continues. Because the new strand is only held in place by the pressure of the other strands, this method will only work if you can plait tight and firm.

Fig. 181. After a few strands have been worked into place, the new strand should be quite firm and the end can be trimmed off.

Fig. 182. This is probably a better method of adding in a new strand, for I have seen more than one professional use it. The new strand is simply laid on the job and plaited over. Continue plaiting until you are sure that it is firmly in position.

Fig. 183. Pull down carefully until the end just goes out of sight. Drop the short end, pick up the new strand, and continue plaiting.

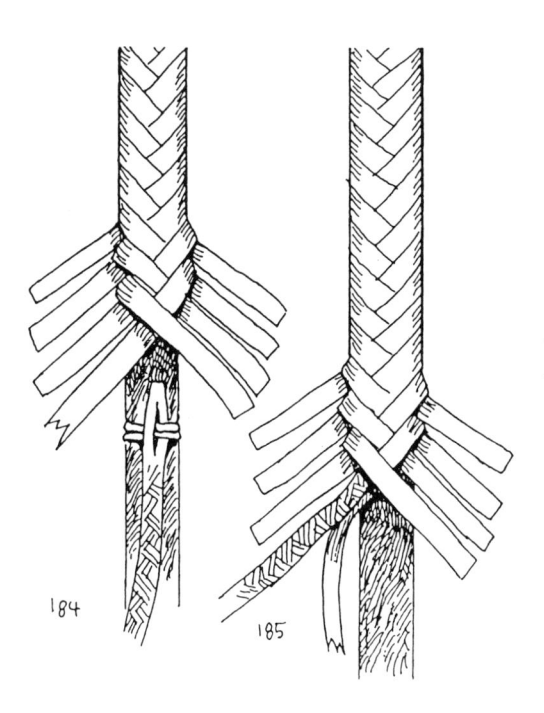

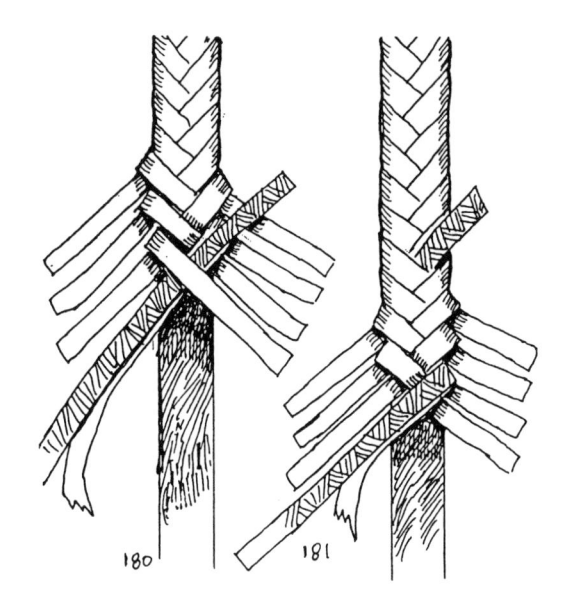

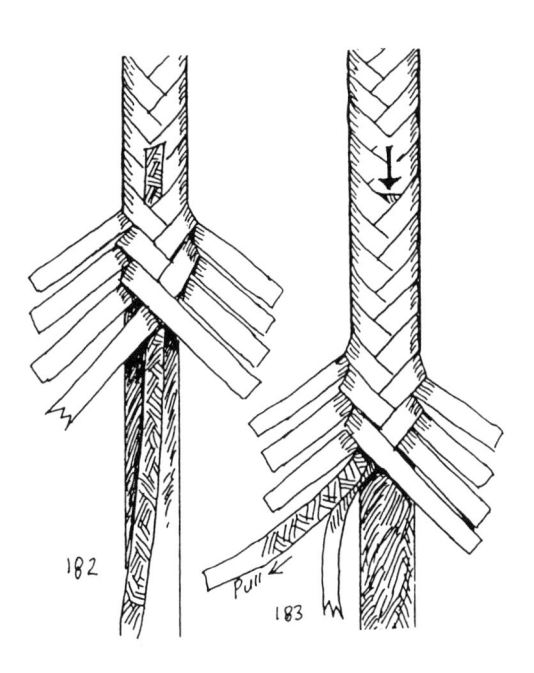

Fig. 184. It is also possible to tie new strands to the belly. Although this is the strongest method (because the strand cannot come loose), it is not used much because it takes longer than the previous methods, and also because the twine can cause a lump in the finished whip unless care is taken.

Fig. 185. Continue plaiting until the new strand feels quite firmly in place. Then drop the short end and pick up the new strand.

Adding in Two Strands

Fig. 186. It is simple to add pairs of strands by doubling a long strand over and tying it on to the belly. Then plait a little more so that the tie will not show.

Portable Plaiting Rack

Fig. 189. A portable rack allows you to work wherever you want, and the sketch shows Peter Clarke at one of the Whipmakers Association gatherings at Jondaryan Woolshed on the Darling Downs of Queensland. The rack can be clamped to anything that will hold it and has a stout hook to hold work and a clamp to hold anything that needs to be gripped, as well as a shelf for tools. The height of the hook can also be adjusted.

Only a few whipmakers bother to make anything as elaborate as this, but most of them will have a few ideas to help make the work easier.

I have only been able to describe the bare bones of making a whip in this book, and there are many more tricks and techniques to help with every aspect of the craft. Whenever you have the chance, try to watch an expert at work and you will find your own work will improve as a result.

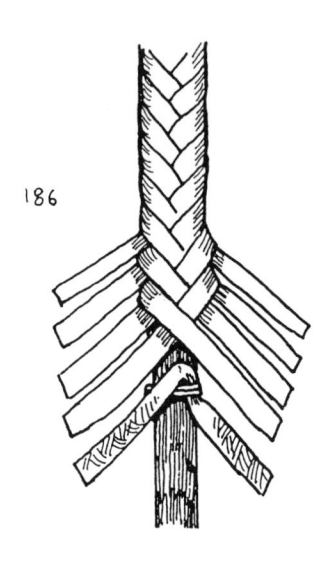

The best place to learn is at a get-together of the Australian Plaiters and Whipmakers Association, but other organizations put on classes from time to time, often with good instructors, and although books are good to learn from, there is nothing like watching a skilled pair of hands.

Chapter 3
How to Make a Bullwhip

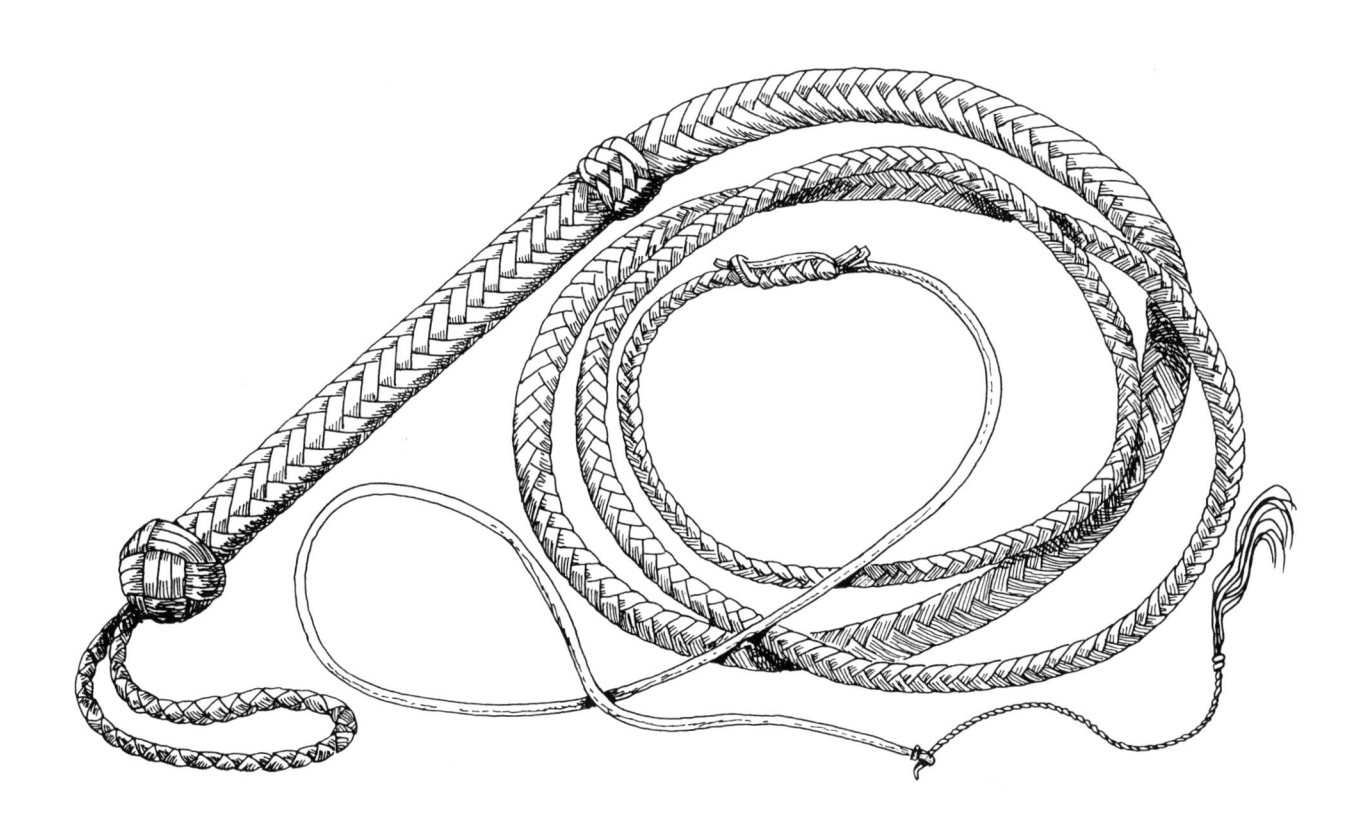

MAKING A BULLWHIP

The bullwhip is common in America but not popular in Australia for a number of reasons, one being that it does not crack as easily as an Australian stockwhip. Also, it has no history in our cattle industry. However, some people do want to make them, and so here are instructions for a basic one.

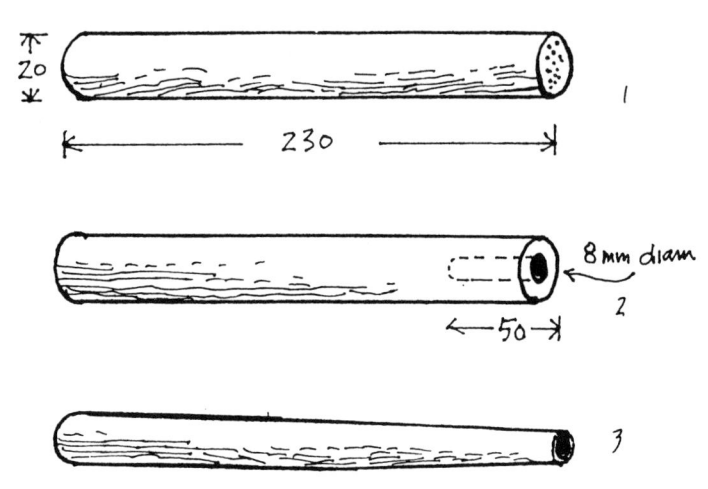

The Handle

There are many ways of making the handle, but this one is simple and strong. This is a fixed handle but some bullwhips have swivel handles, allowing the thong to rotate in the handle. Sometimes the handle is left as bare timber, but in this example the handle is covered.

Because the handle does not come under any stress, due to its short length, almost any timber can be used for the job.

Fig. 1. Select a piece about 230 mm long and 20–23 mm in diameter. The actual diameter will depend on the thickness of the leather that you use to plait the overlay over the handle. If you had leather 3 mm thick and no way to split it any thinner, then the handle timber would only need to be about 15 mm in diameter, while a whip covered in kangaroo leather might have a handle 23 mm in diameter.

Fig. 2. Drill a hole into the end around 8 mm in diameter and 50 mm deep.

Fig. 3. Starting halfway along the handle, taper it down to as thin as possible around the hole.

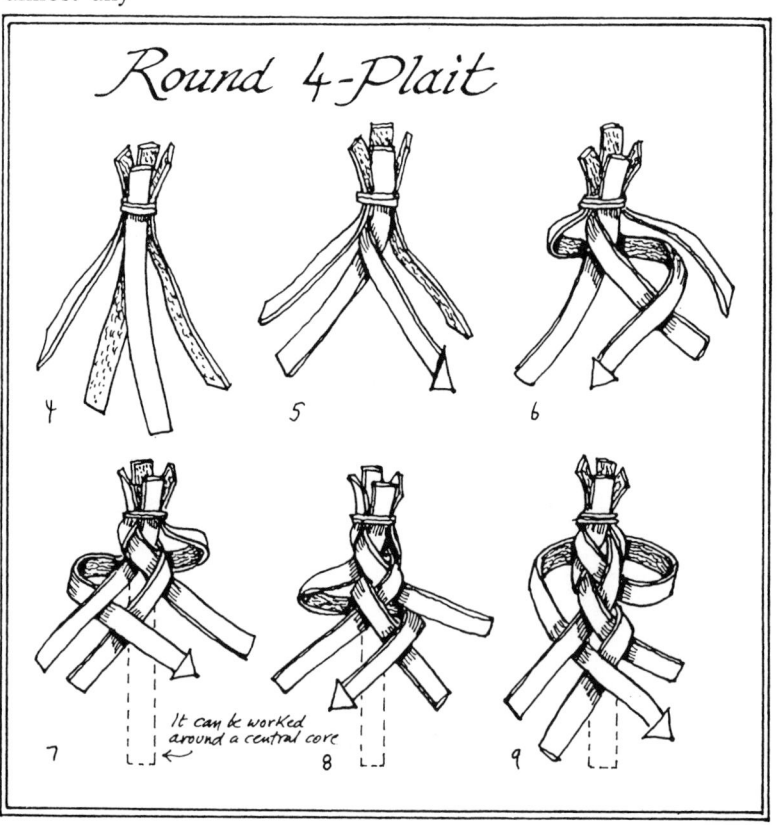

The Belly

The belly can be made from greenhide, kangaroo, or any suitable leather, but for the one described here redhide was used, so the measurements are those that would suit this type of leather.

Cut 4 strands 7 mm wide and 1,250 mm long. Taper and thin them down as much as possible towards the end.

Round 4-Plait

Figs. 4-9. Tie the four strands together, all facing inwards, and then begin the plaiting as shown.

Use plenty of leather dressing on the strands. This will not only allow you to plait a tighter job but the finished whip will last longer if the inside has plenty of dressing on it.

You can buy many brands of leather dressing from leather shops, or make your own. The most simple is just clean fat with a little kero in it. (The kero is to make it unattractive to vermin—all sorts of things will chew a whip that has been dressed with only fat.)

When you have plaited about 75 mm, roll the plaited section as smooth as possible and see whether it will fit into the hole. If it does not, you may have to undo your work and thin down the leather a little.

If it is not large enough then you may have to plait the belly around a single strand of leather (known as a core) in order to get the right diameter.

Fig. 10. When the strands have almost been used up, put some fine thread around the end to stop it from coming undone.

Get two boards and roll the belly between them. If you are going to learn to make whips of any sort, you will have to get used to rolling the whip whenever it has been plaited.

The boards can be of any size. A scrap 500 × 200 × 20 mm or larger will do for the bottom board while the top one can be 600 × 100 × 75 mm or larger. Use plenty of pressure and you will be surprised at how it improves the look of the job.

If the plaited work does not want to roll, and this will happen sometimes if you have been using a lot of leather dressing, then shake some powdered resin on it.

Fig. 11. Put some glue into the hole in the handle and push in the belly. If there are any gaps put in some slivers of wood, such as matchsticks, to make it all firm.

It is important that the belly is well fixed into the hole, because this is the spot that takes a lot of strain when the whip is cracked. Also, you will probably find some idiot who has been watching too many films and thinks that he can wrap the whip around something and swing from it. No whip, unless it has been specially built for this sort of stunt work, can take that sort of treatment.

If you think the whip is going to be pulled around, put a few screws through the handle and the leather belly and file off the points when they come through the handle on the other side. These combined with the glue should make a handle that will not come loose from the belly.

Fig. 12. The taper must now be made as smooth as possible and this may take a little time. If this is not done properly the finished whip will look uneven and very poor, so it is worth doing this job well.

Wrap a small piece of thin leather around the joint and bind it on tightly with thin strong twine.

Next bind on a slightly larger piece, and then another. Depending on the thickness of the leather you may need only two pieces, or you may need four; you will have to be the judge of what is needed for each whip.

Taper the edges of the leather so that there is no step where it lies on the job.

Fig. 13. The final piece of leather can go down as far as 700 mm. Bind it on tightly, as this all helps keep the belly in place.

Give the job a good rolling and then have a long look at it and also feel it. If there are any hollows or soft spots you will have to build them up with scraps of leather and twine.

Keep doing this and rolling the job until the taper is as smooth as it can be.

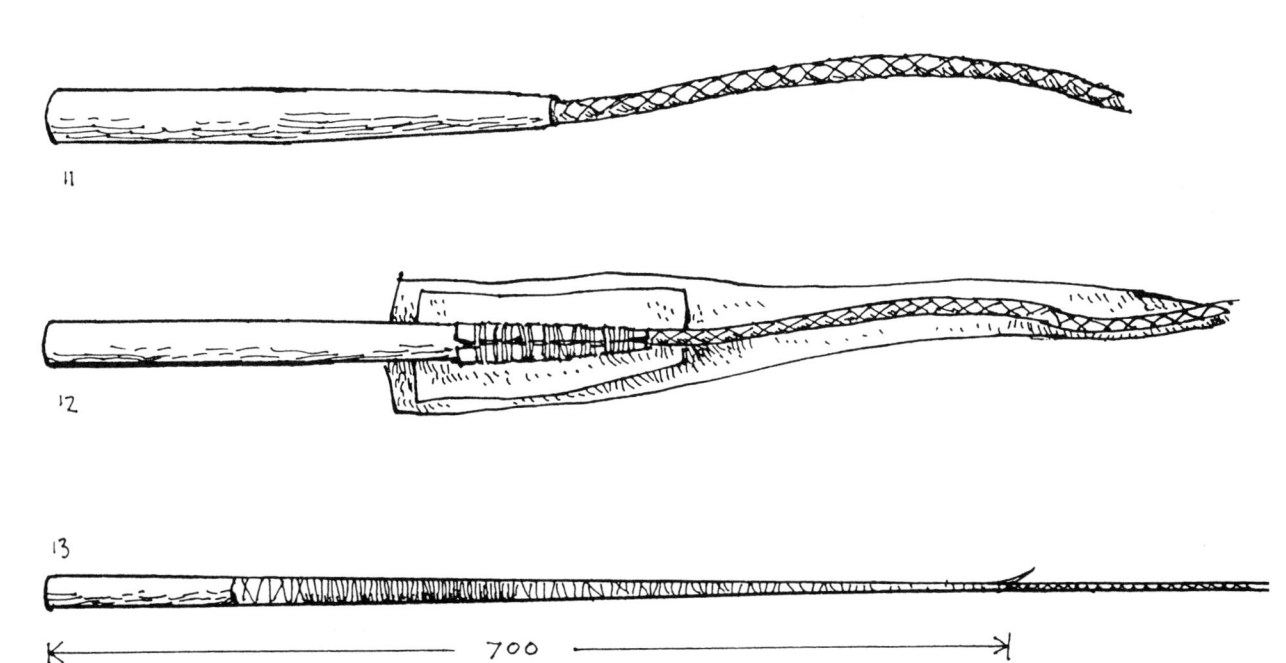

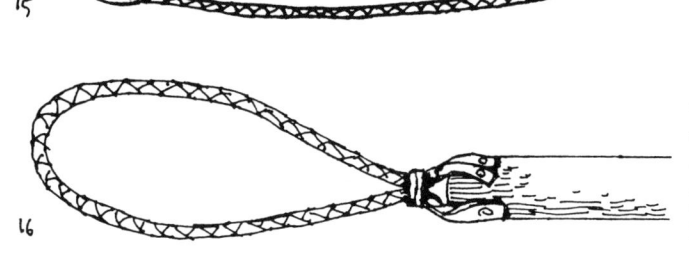

Handle Loop

Fig. 14. Take 4 strands of leather about 500 mm long and 5 mm wide, or cut 4 strands from one piece leaving the end joined as shown.

This can be the same redhide as the rest of the job, but thinned down, or it can be of kangaroo.

Fig. 15. Using the same 4-plait as shown earlier, plait the strands and bind up the end.

Fig. 16. Tack the loop onto the end of the handle and also bind it together with strong twine as shown. Do this well, as the loop will take a lot of knocking about.

Plaiting the Overlay

The overlay can be of any length that you like. Stockwhips are measured only along the thong and the length of the handle is not taken into account. Bullwhips are measured by their overall length because handle and thong are in one piece.

Fig. 17. Note that the strands taper from 7 mm wide to 5 mm. If you have a problem with freehand cutting you could use one of the strand cutters available, adjusting it as you cut from 5 mm to 6 mm and then 7 mm.

As mentioned earlier, kangaroo can be used for the overlay, but for the whip described here redhide was used. Having decided on the length, mark it off as shown and cut it out.

A problem arises here if the redhide is too thick. This may be all right at the thick end of the whip, but it can produce a lumpy effect when you get to the thin end.

The leatherworker who does a lot of this sort of work has a leather splitter, and this is used for thinning down the strands towards the narrow end. The beginner will not have this sort of tool and will have to improvise.

Some people have even used wood planes, pulling each strand through them by hand in order to shave off some of the leather.

Or you will just have to use a lot of patience and a very sharp knife. Thin the leather down only on the rough side. If you slit a strand right through, it is possible to glue it together again, but of course this will weaken the job, so it is better to take care.

Precut Lace

With this sort of whip it is possible to use precut lace sold in leather shops. This will not taper from 7 mm to 5mm, but with care and some thought it is possible to work around this problem.

Bind or tack the 12 strands on very tightly. This is easier if you have cut all the strands from one piece of leather and they are still joined at the top. Otherwise, tack the strands around the handle one at a time.

Fig. 18. In order to keep the top of the handle nice and round you may need to cut some pieces out of the overlay to fit around where the loop is tacked on.

Or you may prefer to thin down the wood where the handle loop is fitted and keep the top of the overlay straight. This allows you to put tacks through both the overlay and the handle ends, making a stronger job.

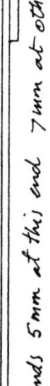

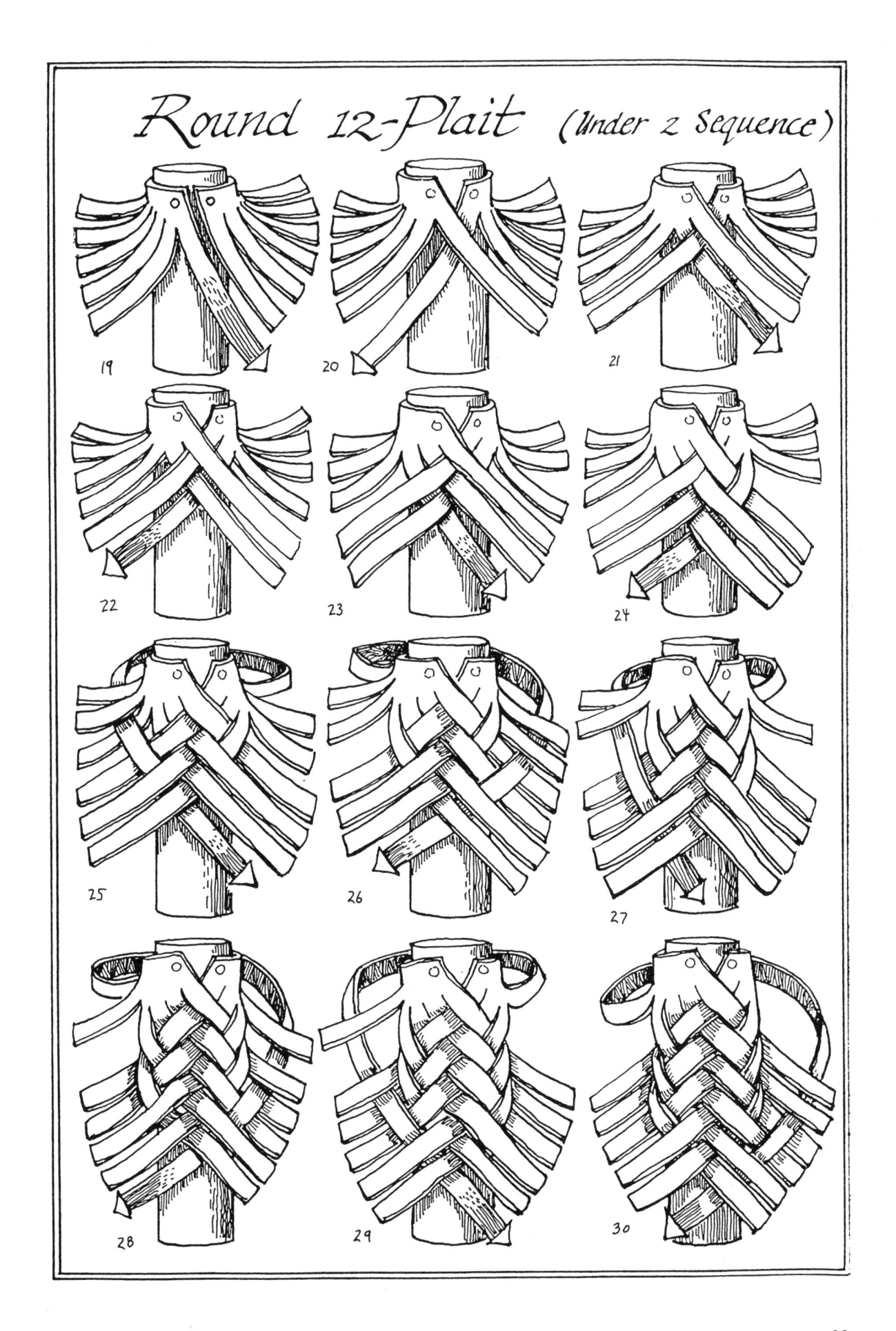

Round 12-Plait (Under 2 Sequence)

19 20 21
22 23 24
25 26 27
28 29 30

93

12-Plait, Under 2 Sequence

Figs. 19–30 (previous page). Starting at the joint, pick up 6 strands in each hand and begin plaiting as shown. If you are working with loose strands of lace, place them so that the shortest 2 are together in the center, then the next longest, and so on.

It is important that you have the short strands equally divided into each side.

This under 2, over 2, under 2 sequence is slower to do than the next one, but it looks good for the handle section.

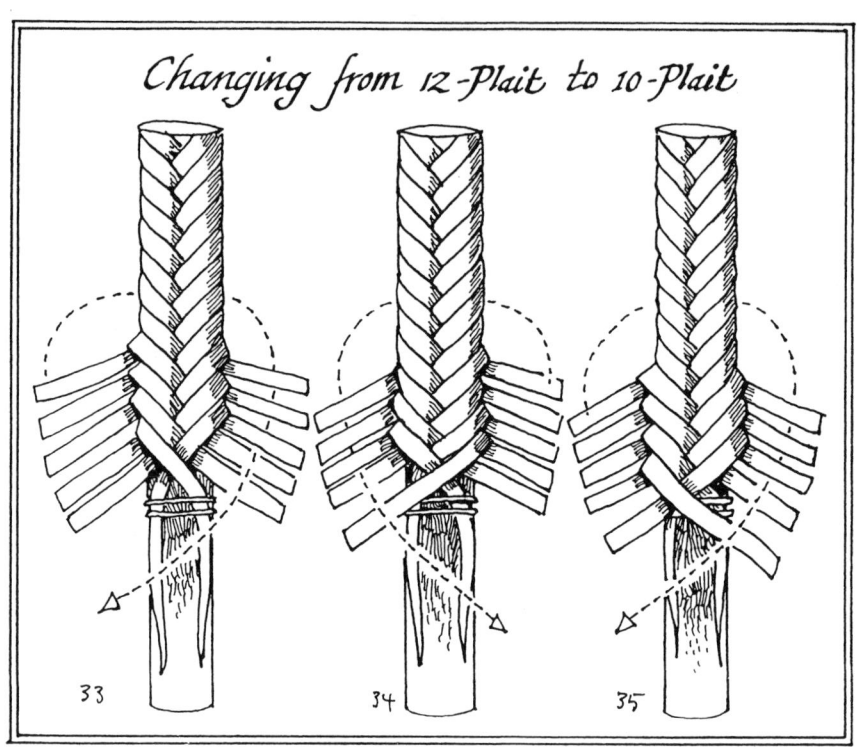

12-Plait, Under 3 Sequence

Figs. 31–32. 220 mm from the start of the handle you can switch to this faster version of 12-plait. The spot where this change takes place will later be covered with a Turk's head.

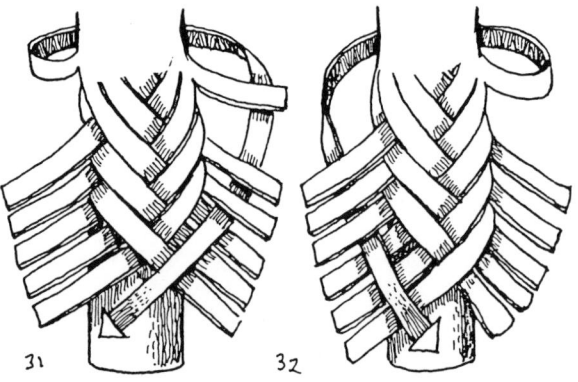

The change is simple: instead of going under 2, over 2, under 2, you change to under 3, over 3. This method of bringing the working strand halfway between the strands on the opposite side is known as a cowtail or whipmaker's plait, and the same method is used for 8-plait whips.

Continue plaiting until the strands start to bunch up. This will be about 800 mm from the end of the handle and means that you now have to drop the two shortest strands.

The exact distance at which this happens will vary from whip to whip. Remember that gaps in the work usually mean that the strands are too narrow or the belly is too thick. Strands overlapping and bunching up mean the opposite.

Changing from 12-Plait to 10-Plait

Figs. 33–35. Drop the shortest strands when they get to the lowest position. For a first whip it is a good idea to use some thread to tie them in place around the belly so that they will be out of the way.

Caution. If the strands that you drop are bulky, the whip will change from being round to being oval, and this is not a good thing.

In order to avoid this, thin the strands down as much as possible, and if they are also wide, slit them into two as well.

As you become more experienced you will find that you get a better taper by first dropping one strand only, then dropping the second one after a few more passes.

Round 10-Plait

Figs. 36–38. There are three common ways to do a 10-plait; the one shown here goes under 3, over 2, on either side.

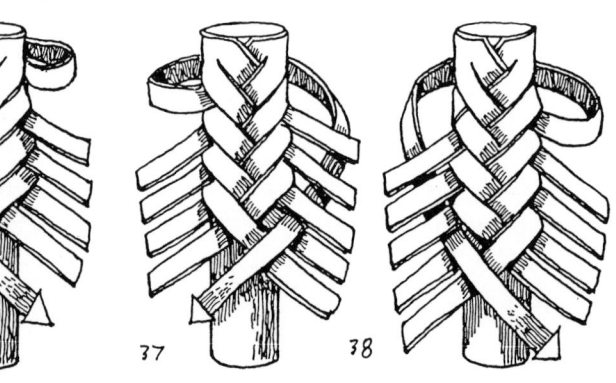

The second version ends up looking the same as the first, and goes under 2, over 3, on either side. In either version when you turn the whip around, the strands are long, long, short, short.

The third method goes under 2 on the left but under 3 on the right. The finished job shows a long, short, long, short, sequence as you turn the whip around.

Any of the three methods will do the job, but the first is easier to remember and looks just as good, although it could be argued that the third gives a more symmetrical result.

After you have done a short amount, check that there are no gaps or lumps at the point where you dropped the strands. If there are any, just undo that section and have another go.

Changing from 10-Plait to 8-Plait

Figs. 39–41. When the work begins to bunch up, drop two strands and change to 8-plait. As you gain in experience you will find you get a better taper by dropping one strand only. Then, after a few more passes, drop the second one.

Changing from 8-Plait to 6-Plait

Figs. 42–44. When the work begins to bunch up, drop two strands and change to 6-plait. Again, as you gain in experience you will find you get a better taper by dropping one strand only. Then, after a few more passes, drop the second one.

Continue with the 6-plait until there is only 80–100 mm of lace left.

Attaching the Fall

The fall is attached as has been explained for a stockwhip.

Making and Attaching the Cracker

This has already been explained in the section on making a stockwhip.

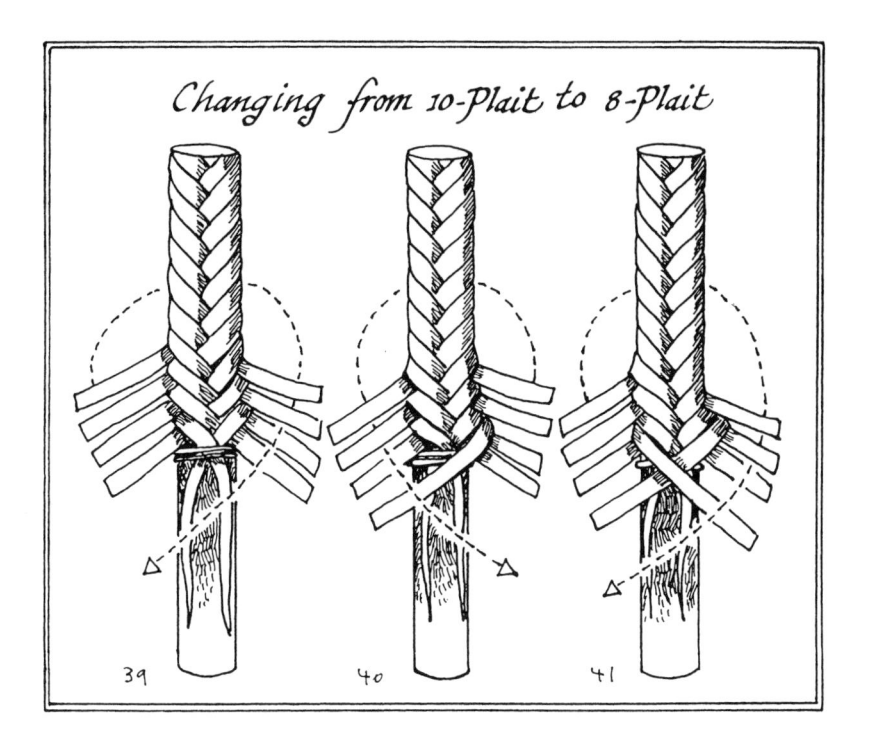

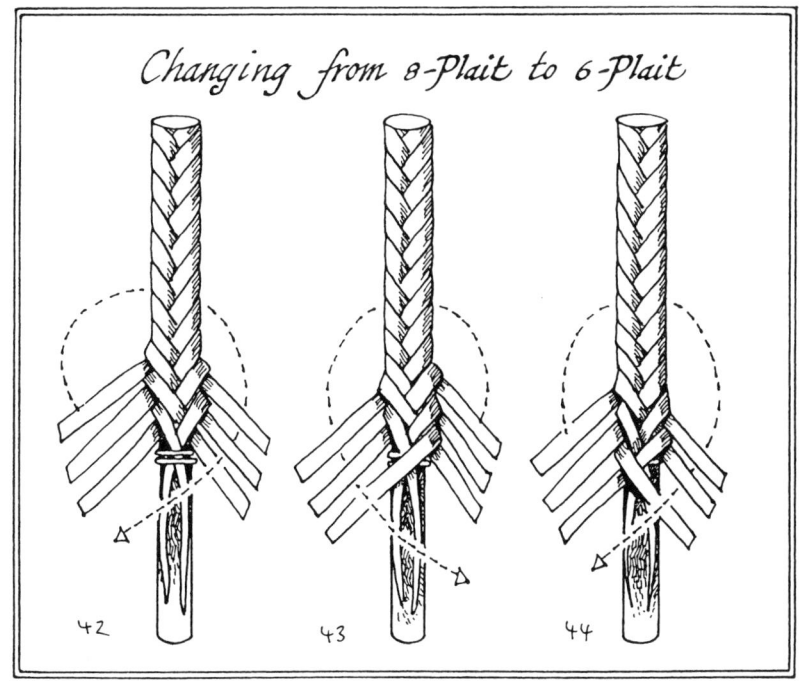

Changing from 10-Plait to 8-Plait

39   40   41

Changing from 8-Plait to 6-Plait

42   43   44

Rolling the Whip

Give the whip a good hard rolling between two boards to get it smooth and round.

The Knob

Form a knob on the whip as explained in the section on making a stockwhip and cover this with a Turk's head. A 5-part, 4-bight Turk's head looks good and is illustrated on page 81.

Turk's Head on the Handle

To finish off the job, put a Turk's head on the handle at the point where the solid section of the handle ends and the flexible section begins. This helps strengthen this section, covers the place where the plaiting pattern changed and, most importantly, gives a finished look to the whip.

5-Part, 4-Bight Turk's Head

Figs. 45–53. This is a good knot to use for the above job. When you get to figure 52 the knot is complete, and from then on you "follow the leader" two or three times as desired.

Pineapple Knot

Figs. 54–62. Instead of doubling up the Turk's head just described, you might like to do a decorative Pineapple interweave. In that case you take the previous knot only as far as figure 52 and then begin the interweave.

This can be done with one single length of lace for the whole knot, or you can tie the Turk's head with a strand of one color and then do the interweave with another strand of a different color. This can look very striking.

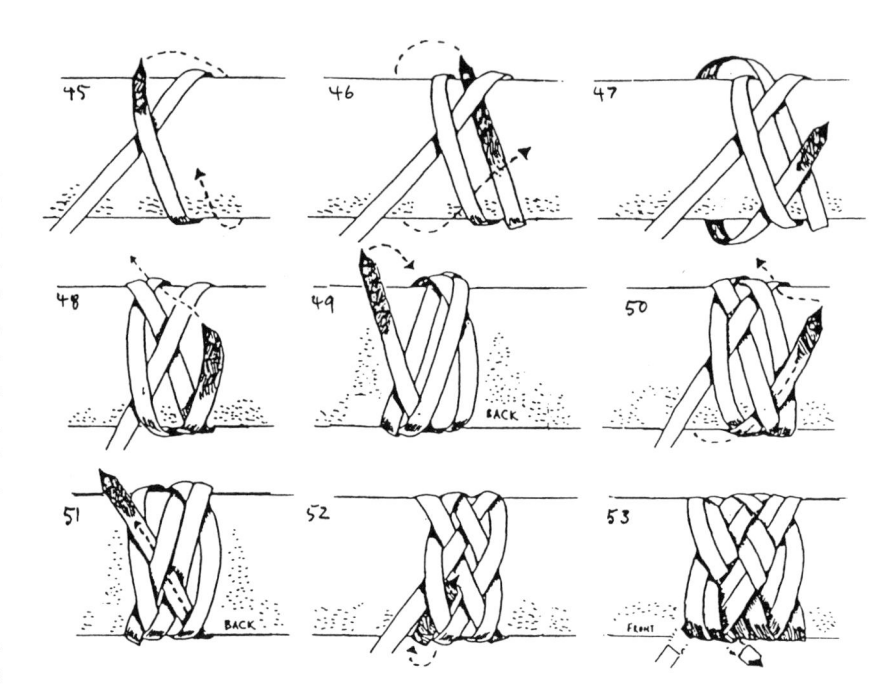

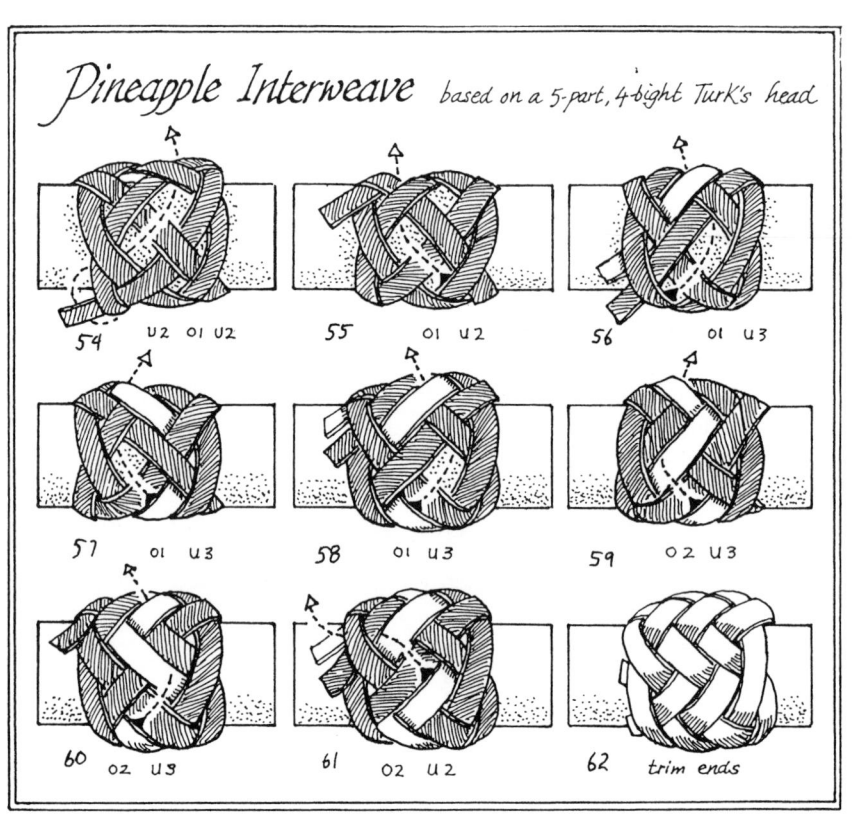

Fig. 63. The completed pineapple knot on the handle.

When the whip is completed, give it a coat of shellac, or clear leather finish, or even just a good coating of leather dressing.

Chapter 4
How to Make a Snake Whip

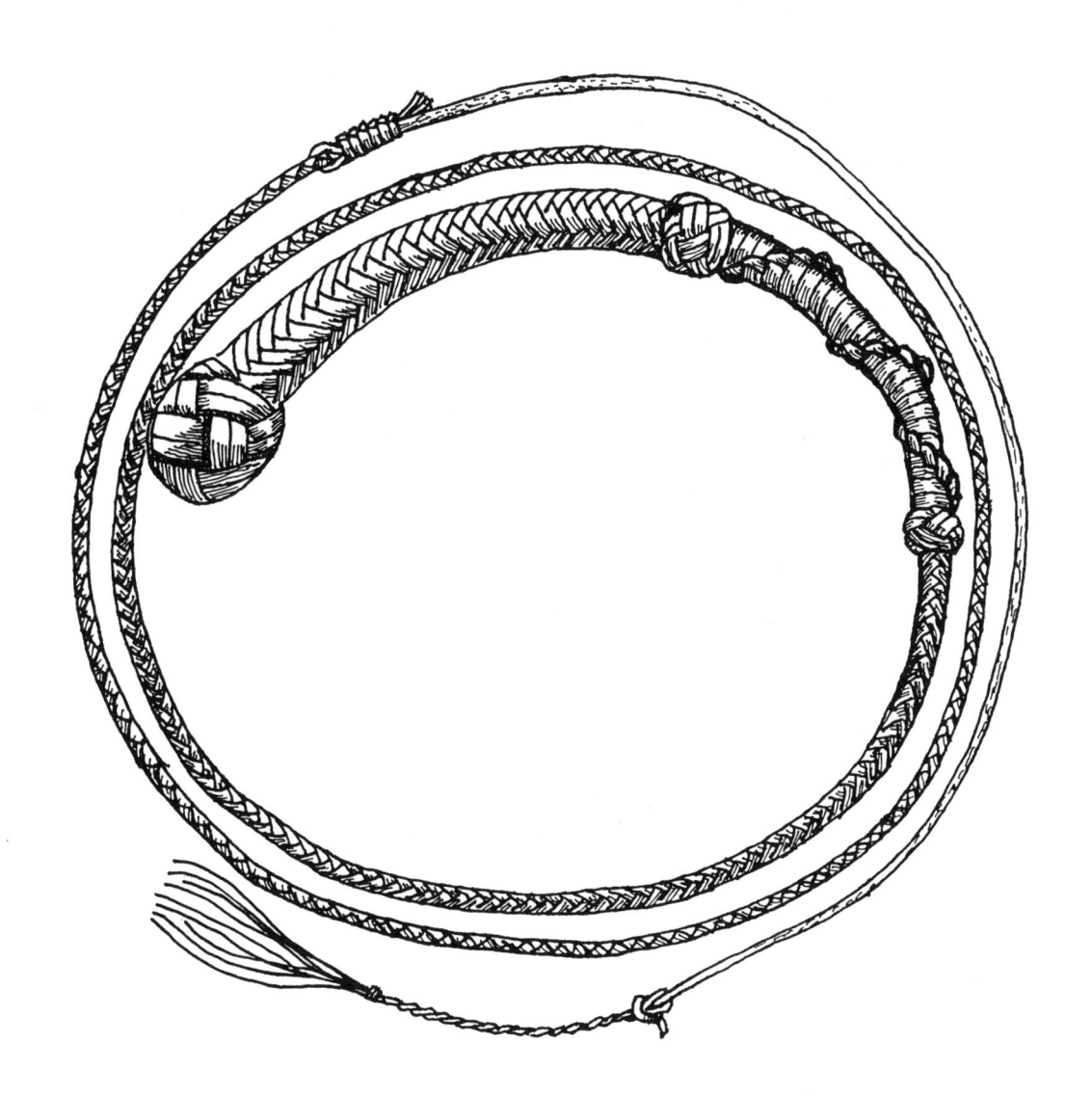

A snake whip is rather like a bullwhip, except that the handle is also flexible. It is usually also a lighter whip (though there have been some quite long and heavy ones). Its main advantage is that it can be rolled up and slipped into a large pocket out of the way when not needed. Because of its shape, it is also a favorite for playing tricks on new chums of nervous disposition, who are forever being scared out of their wits by someone throwing a snake whip beside them and shouting, "Snake!"

David Morgan, in his book *Whips and Whipmaking,* describes long snake whips heavily loaded with lead at the handle end, which were carried hung around the neck and used by farmers driving teams of horses in the wheat fields.

METHOD 1: LEAD-LOADED

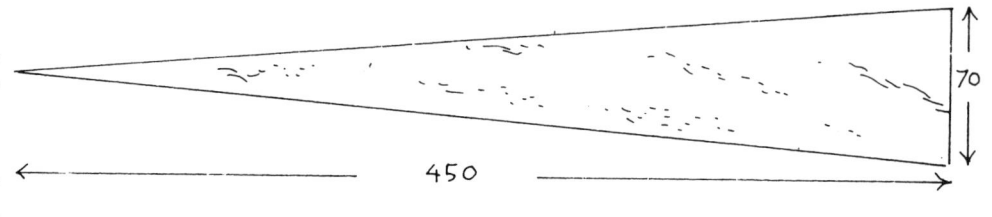

Lead-loading can also be used for stockwhips. David Morgan, in *Whips and Whipmaking*, page 3, describes large snake whips loaded with lead for "three to four feet at the butt end." However, the whip described here is only a small one and is loaded for only a little more than a foot.

Fig. 1. The foundation of the handle can be of kangaroo skin or heavy canvas. It can be 60 mm wide at the end or 70 mm as shown here. The length can also be increased to 600 mm (in fact all the measurements can be changed as desired).

Fig. 2. The core of the whip is of good-quality leather, 1,500 × 4 × 4 mm, or it can be made as long as desired.

Fig. 3. Use a sharp knife to round off the edges of the leather. It should be made as round as possible.

Fig. 4. If you do not have any 4-mm leather, thinner leather will have to be used. Soak it in water and then twist it like this.

Fig. 5. Give it a firm rolling under a board until you have a uniformly round length of leather. If it shows no signs of unwinding, you can go on with the whipmaking. Otherwise, it must be tied down and left until it has dried.

Fig. 6. The triangular piece of canvas or hide is now sewn into a tube.

Fig. 7. The core is placed into the small end of the tube and held firm with at least one stitch.

Fig. 8. The job should now look like this.

Fig. 9. The handle is filled with lead shot. Some gun shops stock this.

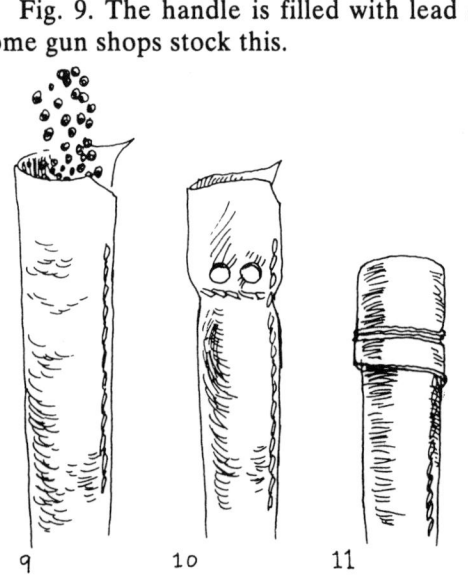

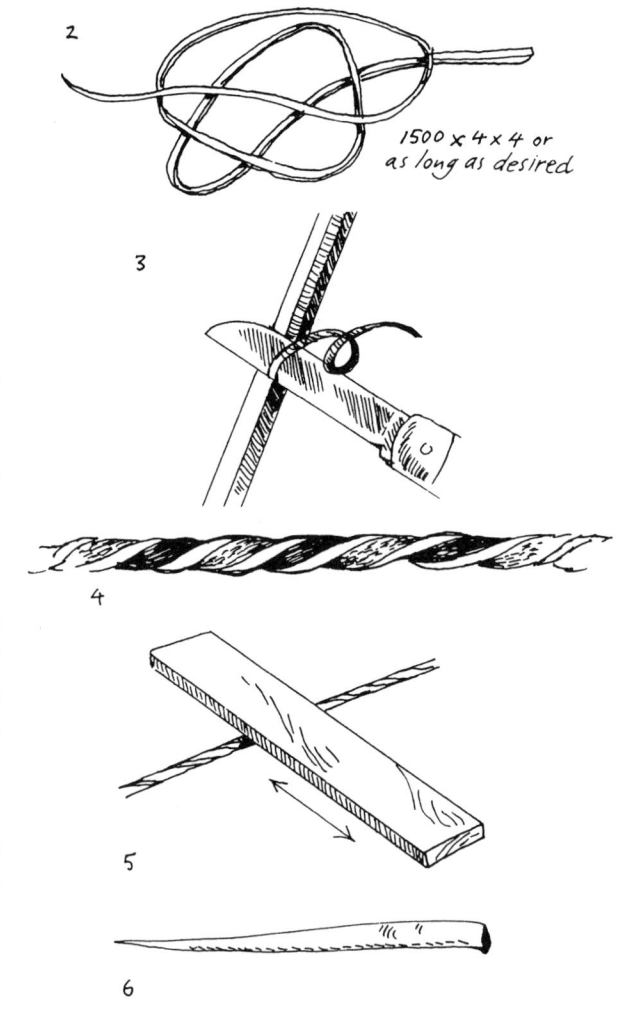

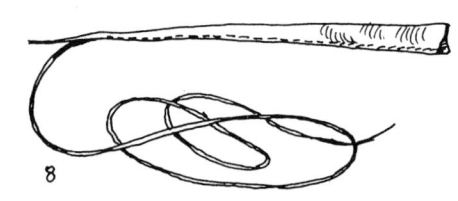

Fig. 10. Sew the end closed, leaving about 25 mm to spare. Punch two holes above the sewing if you are going to put a loop on the handle.

Fig. 11. If you do not wish to put a loop on the handle, simply fold over the extra material and tie it.

Fig. 12. If the tube is of canvas, it is turned inside out as soon as it is made to hide the seam. If it is of leather, this may be too difficult, so the seam should now be spread out and smoothed flat.

Handle Loop

Fig. 13. A loop allows the whip to be hung from the wrist and is also handy for hanging up the whip when doing the plaiting.

Take a strip of leather 60 × 3 × 3mm and roll it under a board to make it round. Tie 4 strands of 4.5-mm lace to it and begin a 4-plait. This is described elsewhere in this book.

Put the ends of the plaited loop through the holes in the handle and tie them together very firmly.

Fig. 14. Fold over the end and also tie this down firmly. The loop gets quite a lot of pulling, so it must be made quite secure.

Fig. 15. Now comes the belly of the whip. This is an extra plaited section that gives the whip its shape. This can be cut from 2- or 3-mm cowhide, or whatever leather is available. One end of the leather is cut so that it just fits neatly around the lead-filled handle. The remaining meter is cut into 4 strands, each 4-mm wide.

Fig. 16. Use fine thread to tie the belly to the handle. It should completely cover it with no overlap.

Fig. 17. The belly is plaited around the core. This is the same 4-plait that was used on the loop.

Fig. 18. Plaiting continues in this way. When completed, the ends can be tied down with thread.

Fig. 19. Use a board and give the belly a good hard rolling to get it as smooth as possible. It may be necessary to wet the leather in order to get a good finish. If this is done, also give it a good oiling before going any further.

Fig. 20. The handle and the belly are now covered with a final layer of plaiting. This is cut from a kangaroo hide.

(It is also possible to do this using ready-cut lace if a skin is not available, but the problem then is that you may have to start with as much as a 16-plait in order to cover the handle properly. By hand cutting the lace you can taper it so as to only have to begin with an 8-plait.)

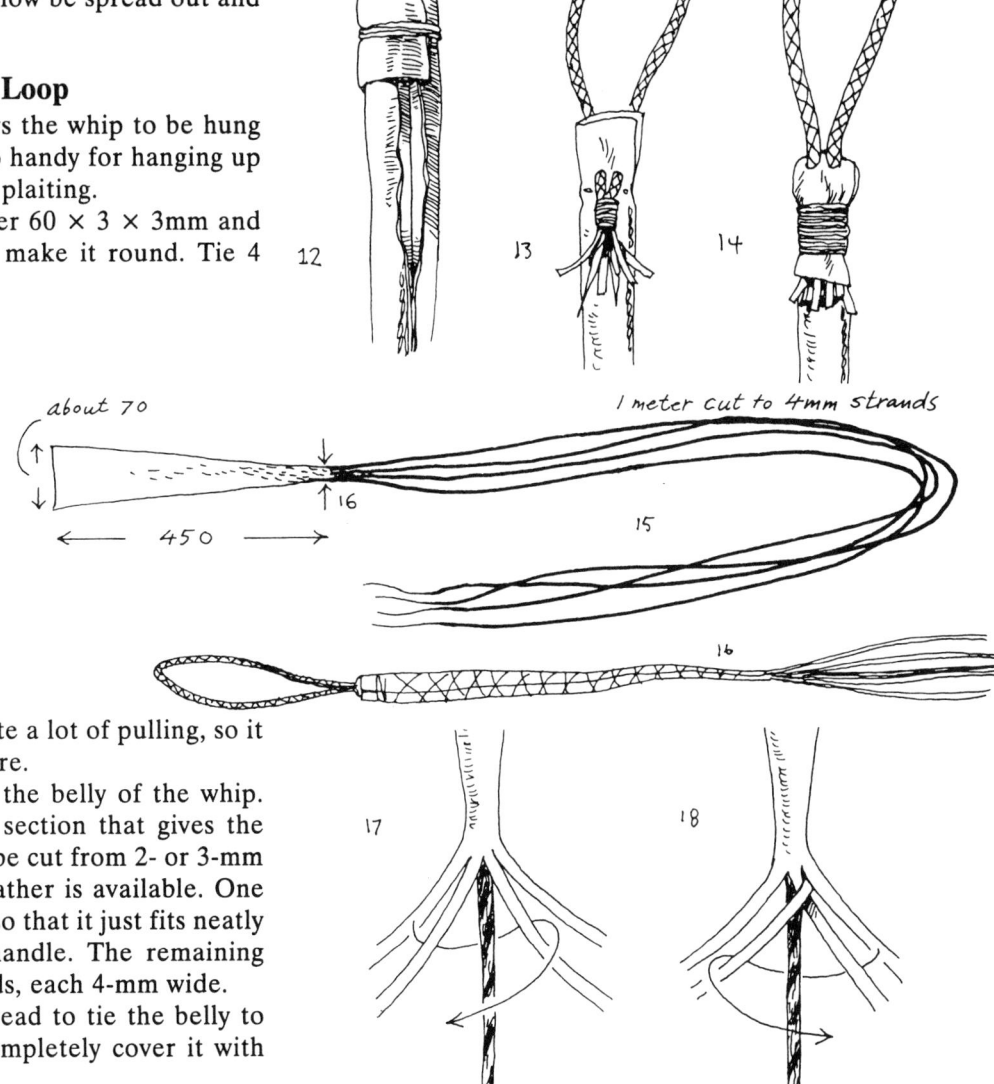

Begin by cutting 4 narrow strips, then increase it to 6 and finally 8, widening the strands as cutting continues. A very sharp knife and a steady hand are needed.

99

Fig. 21. This is how the strands should look when straightened out. The measurements are only a guide, but you will lose roughly a third in the plaiting.

The strands are tied onto the handle and plaiting begins. For the 8-plait the top strand is brought around the back, in between the opposite 4, and back to its own side. The upper strand on the opposite side is then brought around in the same way, and so on. (The 8-plait is illustrated on page 62).

The 8-plait continues until the shorter lengths of lace are nearly used up, or until the plaiting becomes too bunched up.

When this happens, you change to a 6-plait, illustrated earlier in the book (p. 68). The 6-plait continues until you again come to two short ends. Now the plaiting changes to a 4-plait (p. 19).

Plaiting continues in this way, and the 4-strand plaiting goes to the end of the whip. The fall and cracker are then fitted to the whip (these have been illustrated earlier).

The whip is now complete, except for the knob on the handle. First the foundation of the knob is built up. The making of the knob is described in chapters 1 and 2 of this book.

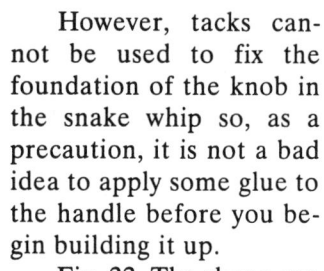

However, tacks cannot be used to fix the foundation of the knob in the snake whip so, as a precaution, it is not a bad idea to apply some glue to the handle before you begin building it up.

Fig. 22. The shape can be formed with a strip of leather as described earlier, or you can wind on string or thread to make the shape.

A couple of stitches right through the whole top of the whip will help keep the knob in place if you do not wish to use glue.

Fig. 23. A Turk's head is worked over the foundation. Either knot described in the first two chapters can be used.

Fig. 24. This is how the finished job should look.

Snake whip

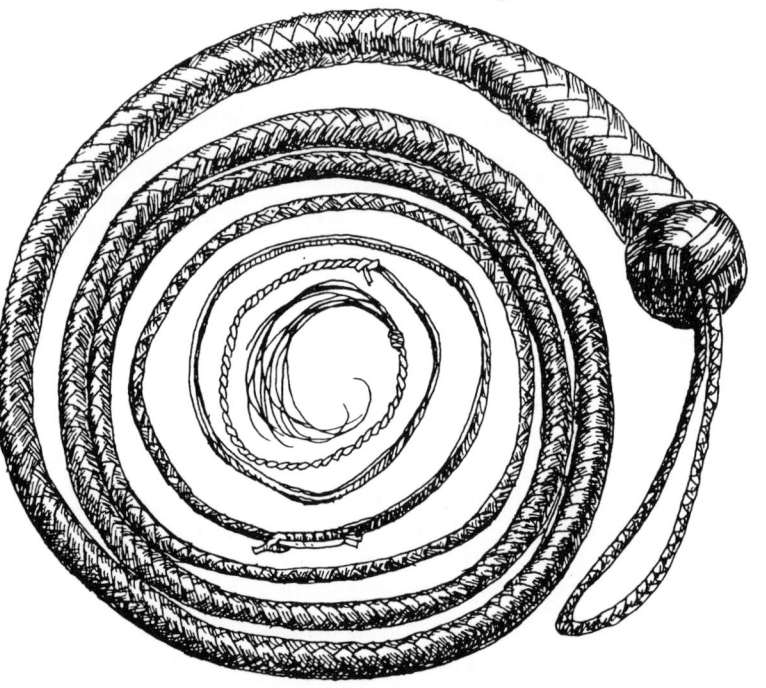

METHOD 2

Whip as a Weapon

When I first described the snake whip in one of my small leather books, I knew it only as a light and fairly useless item, good enough for encouraging an old cow through a gate but little more. But since then I have learned that the snake whip once had a darker side to it.

When I was a kid many older men, such as our neighbor George Allan, had about the house an item known as a "life preserver," which they would slip into their pocket when going into strange territory, such as a trip to the big city.

The life preserver, known in criminal circles as a cosh (or blackjack in America), was a leather instrument 200–300 mm long and consisted of a flexible handle with a ball-shaped end that would be filled with lead or sand.

A friend of my father also carried one whenever he went out alone at night, and I was told that they were illegal.

In view of this, some whipmaker with time on his hands must have worked out that a snake whip could also double as a life preserver if the knob on the end was weighted. Not only did this give the whip another use, but it was not against the law to carry a whip rolled up in the pocket.

In some ways the snake whip with a weighted end could be more dangerous than a short-handled life preserver, for it could be held farther down the thong and swung around in a circle to increase the velocity of the blow.

I have written elsewhere about Tibetan whips that I noted on visits to that country. These whips have very short iron handles that are reversed and used in the same way to fend off dog attacks.

Length. Whips of this kind are always made to order and so can vary a lot in dimensions. Those meant to fit easily into a coat pocket are not very long. It is usual to begin with strands around 2 meters long. This will make a finished whip over a meter long. There is not much point in making it longer, because this is a difficult whip to crack and is really only used for striking (with either end).

Handle

There are various ways to form the handle. Here is one of them.

Fig. 1. The first thing to find is a lump of metal that will form the core of the knob. A large nut has been used in this case, but anything can be used, even a round stone.

It is important that the handle is flexible and yet as springy and dense as possible. In this case a 400-mm-long piece of rawhide (just untanned cowhide) was soaked overnight to get it back to a flexible state, then trimmed into a long taper. It was then twisted and rolled to make it as solid as possible.

A knot was tied in the thick end and then it was tied firmly at each end, stretched out, and left to dry.

When dry it was just like a springy piece of wood. Heavy tanned leather can be treated in the same way.

Fig. 2. When dry, the leather is slipped through the hole in the nut and the knot keeps it from flying off later.

Fig. 3. Kangaroo skin or some other thin leather is then bound around the upper part of the handle to get it nearly to the right shape.

Next, cord or thread is wrapped around the nut until it forms a smooth ball.

If this part of the job has been done very well it is possible to begin the final outer layer of plaiting at this point, but it is more usual to cover this with a simple 4-plait first to provide a smoother surface for the final plaiting.

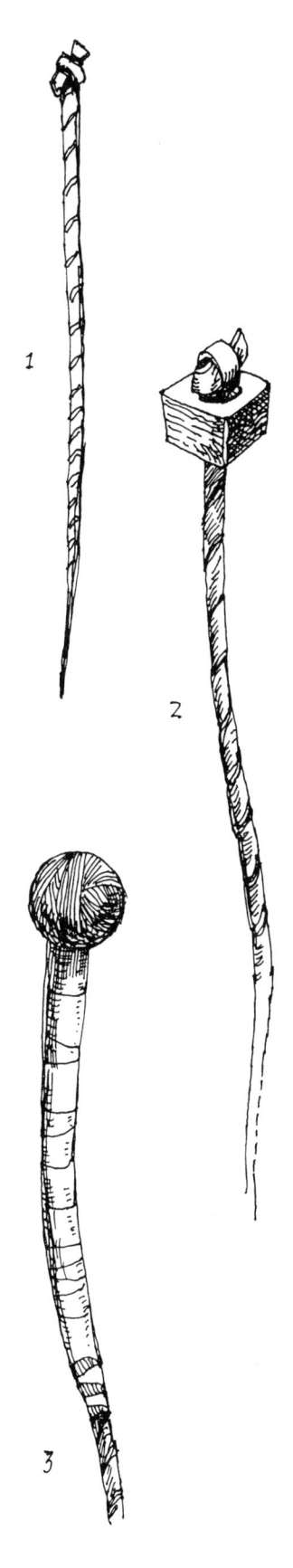

Fig. 4. A strip of kangaroo leather is pulled over the top of the knob and split into two strands on either side. This action also helps anchor the knob firmly.

Fig. 5. It is then plaited with a simple 4-plait (p. 90), which is tapered down, as is the case with normal kangaroo stockwhips, to form a tapered belly.

The next step is to plait over the whip in the same way as is done when making a stockwhip thong. The number of strands used will depend on the diameter of the whip handle and the width of strands used, but commonly it would begin as a 12-plait, then go to 10, 8, and so on to end up as a 6 or 4.

The fall need not be long; in fact, it is not really necessary, and the cracker is attached in the usual way.

A Turk's head is worked over the knob, and a 5-part, 4-bight is a good one for this job.

When the snake whip is also to be used as a life preserver, it is common to work something around the handle to act as a handgrip. This begins about 150 mm from the base of the knob, or wherever the balance is found to be best.

Fig. 6. In the example illustrated above, the grip has been covered with French whipping. This is simple to do and looks good, as the slightly raised ridge spirals around the handle. It will take about 3 meters of lace to do this. Either end of the French whipping is then covered with a Turk's head or some other decorative wrapping, such as a Spanish ring knot (p. 83).

In this case the same 5-part, 4-bight Turk's head used around the knob (p. 81) was put on the larger end and a 3-part, 4-bight Turk's head (p. 36) on the narrower end.

Fig. 7. The finished whip.

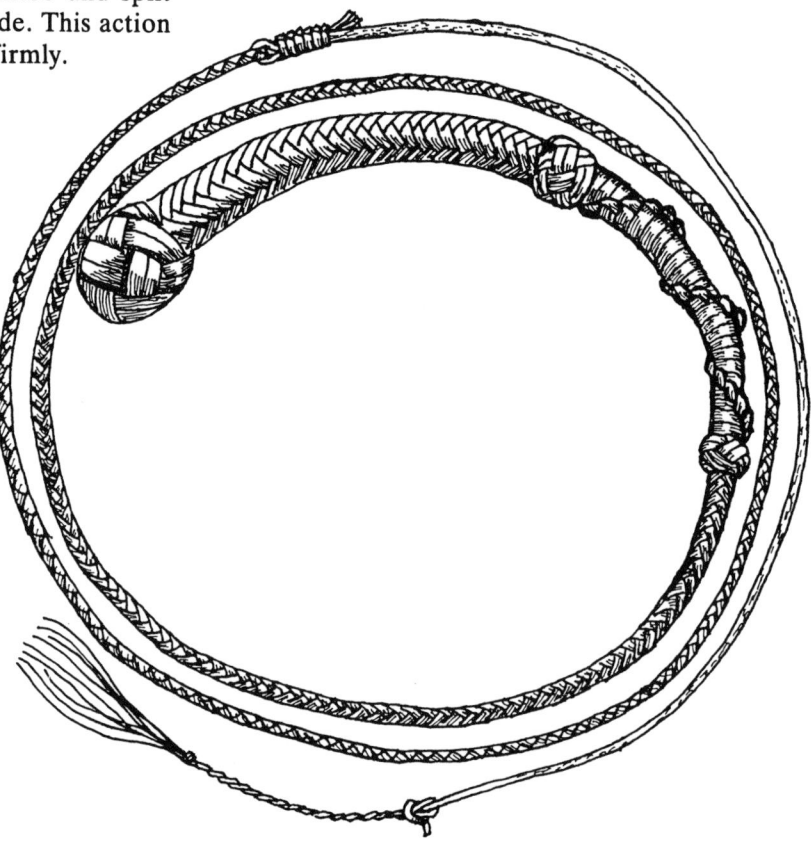

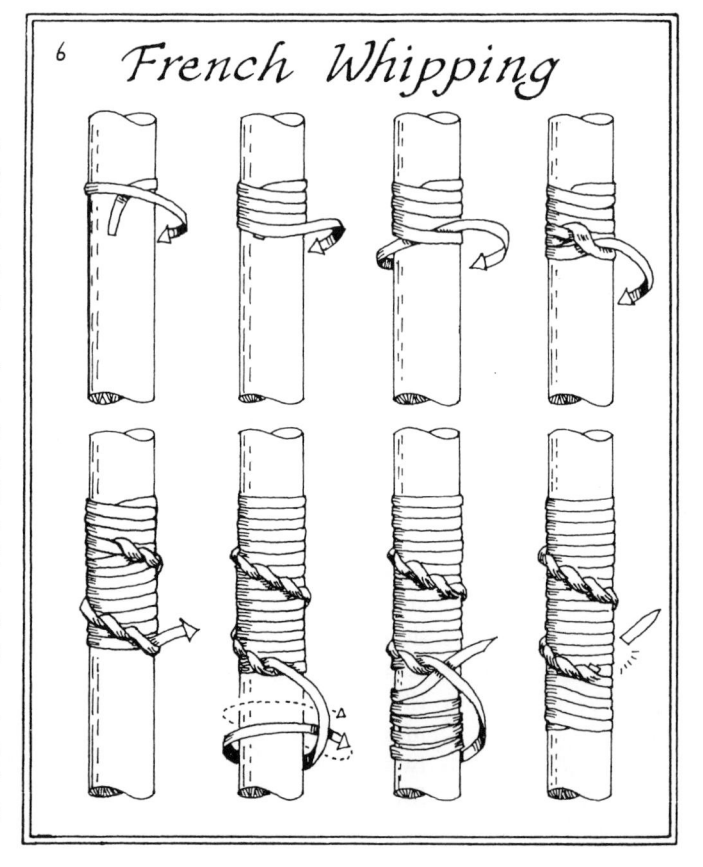

A QUICK SNAKE WHIP

This whip is much coarser in appearance than the other two but has the advantage that it takes only about a third of the time to do because of the wide strands used.

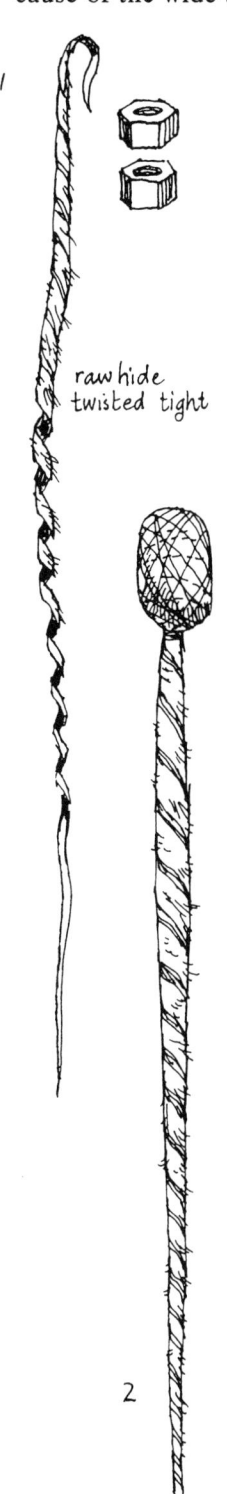

The Belly

Fig. 1. The belly can be made from twisted rawhide. In this case it was in the form of a scrap of old dried-out cowhide with some of the hair left on—not tanned or treated in any way.

As it is like a board in this condition it must first be soaked in water until it becomes pliable. It is then twisted tight; the lower part of the drawing shows how it looks when half twisted and the upper part fully twisted, so that no gaps show.

If you do not want to have the belly hollow, put a narrow strip of rawhide inside as you twist it up.

When twisted up, tack it down at each end firmly and leave it to dry.

The knob end will be loaded, either with one heavy bolt or in this case two smaller ones, or with anything that you may find suitable. The end of the rawhide was bent over and pushed down into the bolts so that they could not work loose later. They can also be tied or wired in place.

Building Up the Knob

Fig. 2. The bolts must now be built up to a smooth shape. This can be done with scraps of leather lace or string. In this case leather trimmings were used and then twine was tied over to form a smooth surface.

Fig. 3. A scrap of thin leather (or canvas) is then tied over the knob to make the surface even smoother.

Fig. 4. Four strands of tapered redhide are next bound very firmly over this. It is important to get this binding as tight as possible, or even sew right through the whole job, so that the strands cannot loosen later. The length and width of the strands will be as desired, but each strand must be a little more than a quarter of the circumference of the belly in order to get a good covering with no gaps.

An even better idea is to use one single length of leather instead of 4 strands, pulling it over the knob as shown on the previous page (fig. 4) and then plaiting it.

Plait a normal 4-plait and finish off the whip in the usual way.

Turk's Head

Fig. 5. A Turk's head will cover the knob, and a 5-part, 4-bight is suitable (see page 81).

When this has been done, a smaller version of the same Turk's head should be tightly worked over the whip just below the knob, and another one about 200 mm below this (see page 74).

The lower knot is put there to act as a handgrip in the event of the whip being used as a life preserver and is not otherwise necessary.

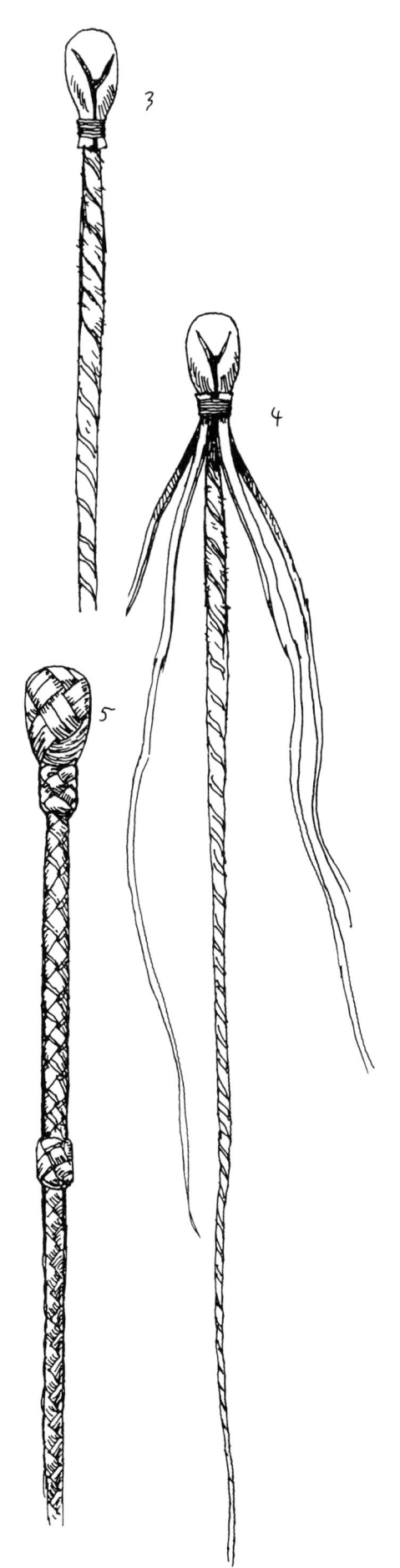

103

MINIATURE WHIP HATBAND

This miniature whip makes a most unusual and attractive hatband. A number of our good whipmakers plait them up, and this one was made by John Jellicoe of Kurmond, New South Wales. Another old friend of mine, Doug Kite of Ringwood, Victoria, also built up quite a reputation for his small whip hatbands.

There is little to say about making these miniatures because they are made in the same way as a full-size whip, except that every part is proportionately smaller. In this case the total length of the whip, including the handle and cracker, was 1,250 mm. The handle itself was 135 mm long. The strands of the whip were tapered in the same way as on a full-size whip, so it required some skill to cut them out.

There are different ways to fix this whip to the hat. It can be simply tightened up around itself or fastened with another small Turk's head to keep it all together, or sewn to the hat with a few stitches of fine thread. The latter is probably the best as it stops it from falling off, and in view of the work involved in making one of these, you don't want to lose it.

RIDING CROP

This sketch shows an attractive riding crop made by Don Russell of Buderim, Queensland. I think that Don used a fiberglass fishing-rod blank for the handle. This material is stronger and more flexible than a cane handle, as well as being of a smaller diameter. One of my students found that he could pick up broken rods very cheaply from fishing tackle shops, and these were ideal for this work.

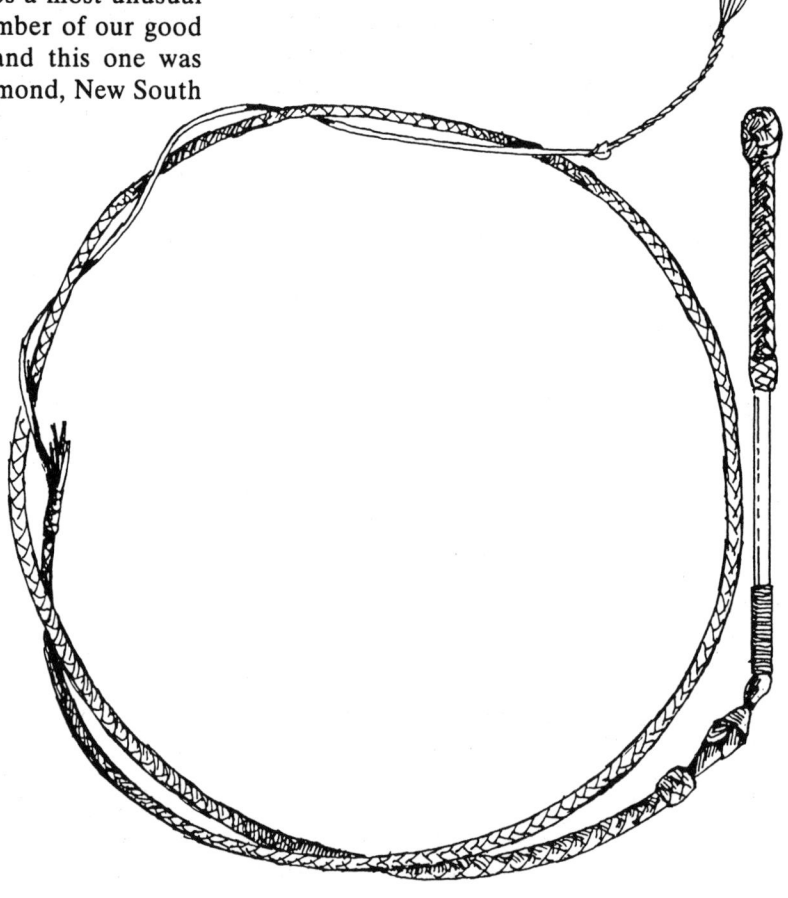

The shaft was covered at the thick end with a diamond pattern and the rest with a cowtail pattern—the ordinary whipmaker's plait.

Many beginners do not realize that a Turk's head can be used to go around a knob as well as around a cylinder, and here we have an example of each.

The flapper was made from two strips of kangaroo hide bound on tightly with black twine.

Items such as these need to be well rubbed to get them smooth and then given a high polish.

If you wish to learn how to plait kangaroo-hide whips it would be a good idea to start by making a crop like this before you tackle a full-size whip.

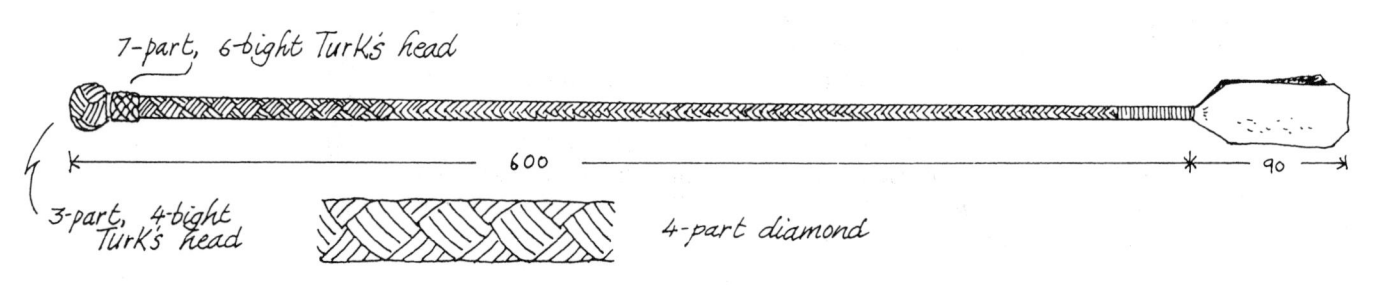

Chapter 5

Whip Handle Designs

This chapter does not tell you how to make a whip handle; you will find that information in chapter 1, and some very useful information can also be found in the pages of the journal *The Australian Whipmaker's Journal* (we publish this for the Australian Plaiters and Whipmakers Association). Nor is this chapter intended for the beginner, but rather for the person who already can make a good plain whip and who now wants to advance to the stage of working some patterns into the handle.

A very fine whip may have a handle of anything up to 32 strands or even more, but I have restricted most of the designs here to 12 or 16 strands in order to help the learner. The number of strands can easily be increased after some skill has been gained, and you will soon find that most of the designs readily adapt to being worked with a greater number of strands.

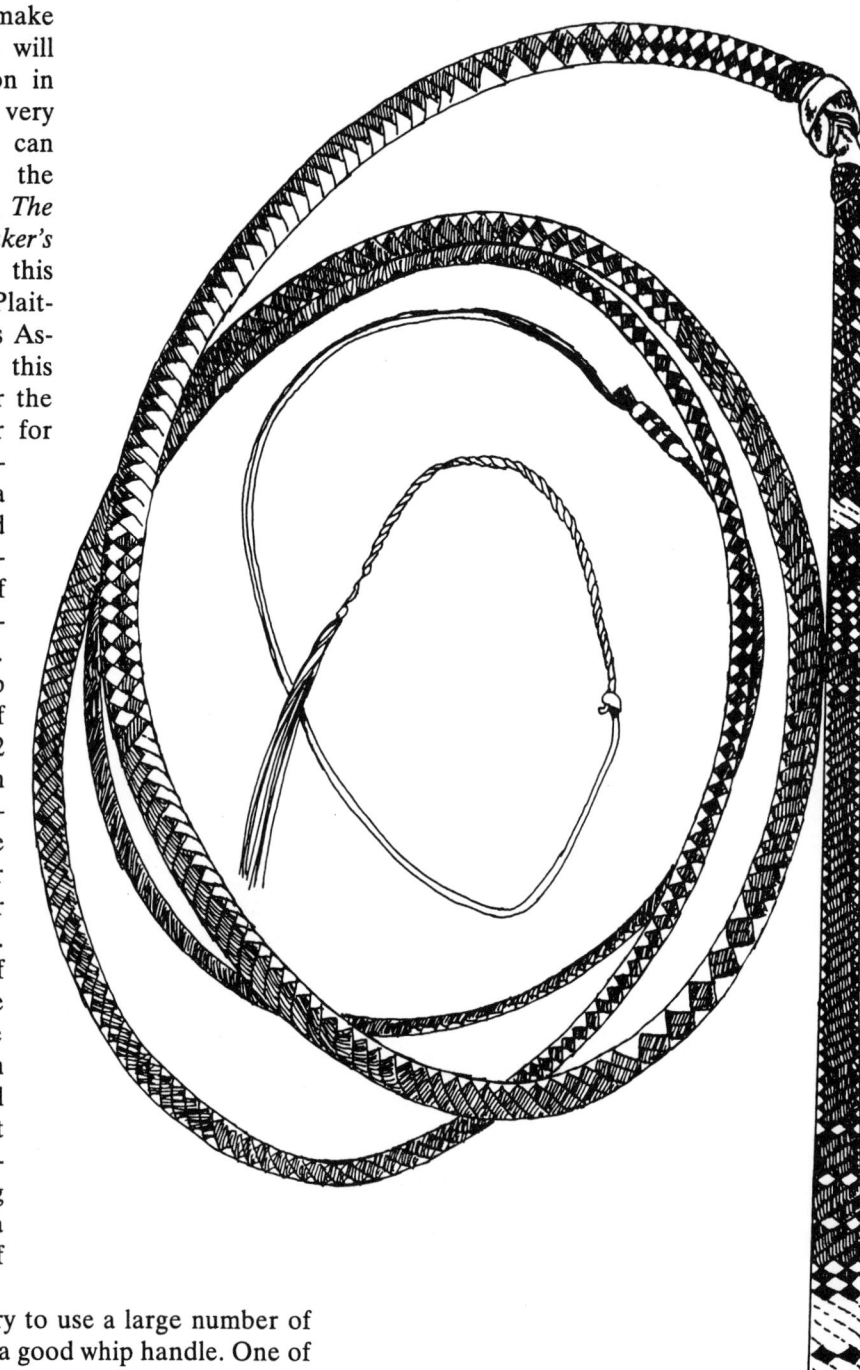

It is not necessary to use a large number of fine strands to make a good whip handle. One of the nicest two-tone whips that I have handled was made by Tony Nugent and used only 12 strands for the handle.

It is shown here in my drawing. Note how the thong also features a variety of patterns. The various patterns shown here are described in more detail later in this chapter.

Being somewhat of a slow learner, I have always assumed that a stockwhip was given that name because it was used to move stock. But one day when browsing through Hasluck's *Saddlery and Harness Making* first published in 1904, I realized that a stockwhip was so called because it was a whip with a stock, stock being another name for the handle. Of course, any good whipmaker could have told me that, and some probably have, but it did come as a surprise.

Then I had a look in the J.J. Weekes Sydney catalog of 1916 and found that the handles for stockwhips were listed as stock crops, while the longer handles for cart whips were listed as cart crops.

The problem with using the term crop today is that it is easy to confuse it with riding crops, which of course are not whips as such but consist only of a handle with a pair of short flaps attached.

From here I went to W. G. Ashford's *Whips and Whip-Making*, originally published in 1893 and to be found in the back section of Morgan's book of the same name. Ashford called the handle the stock, and referred to the men who made them as stockers. Whipmaker Maurice Doohan recently told me that the stock is really the foundation of the handle before it is covered.

Old saddlers' catalogs are very hard to get, but I do have a Walther & Stevenson catalog printed in Sydney in 1933. Both the terms crop and stock have been dropped in this and the handle is referred to as just that, a handle. You could have a 16-plait kangaroo handle for ten shillings ($1) or a cheap turned-wood handle for two shillings (20 cents). The illustration above comes from that catalog and shows the style of decoration popular in the 1930s for expensive whips up to 73/6 ($7.35).

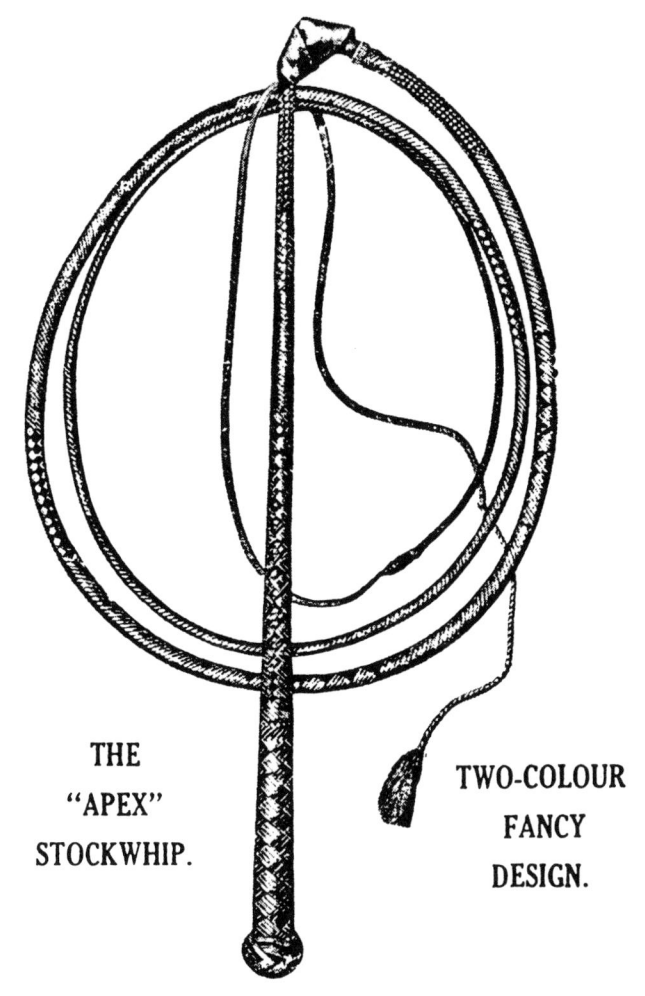

107

(Note in the illustration on the previous page the reference to the whip plaiter's art, not whip braider, which is an American term.)

So it would seem that around the turn of the century whip handles were called crops or stocks, but by the 1930s at least some saddlers were simply calling them handles.

Very few bush people know that the term stock was used in the whipmaking trade for the handle, and many will still insist that stockwhip means a whip to move stock, as in animals.

As for the other half of the whip, the end that does the work, all the catalogs agreed in calling them thongs, and this term is still the common one today.

Weekes's catalog listed hunting thongs, stock thongs, cart thongs, team thongs, buggy thongs and bullock thongs.

On the end of the thong is the fall and, though a few people today call this a lash, fall is by far the most common term. Last of all is the cracker, though many Americans call it a popper.

TWISTED HANDLES

I obtained the whip in the sketch some time ago from Tony Nugent. It was made around the 1940s or earlier by a well-respected whipmaker of northern New South Wales whose name I have unfortunately mislaid.

The handle was 530 mm long and was made of a light-colored timber (probably willow), which had been split into four and then twisted into a spiral.

Weekes's catalog of 1916 showed a similar handle and it was described as a "Twisted steel lined stock crop." I imagine that the timber was steamed and twisted, but do not really know the details and have never met anyone who has made this type of handle.

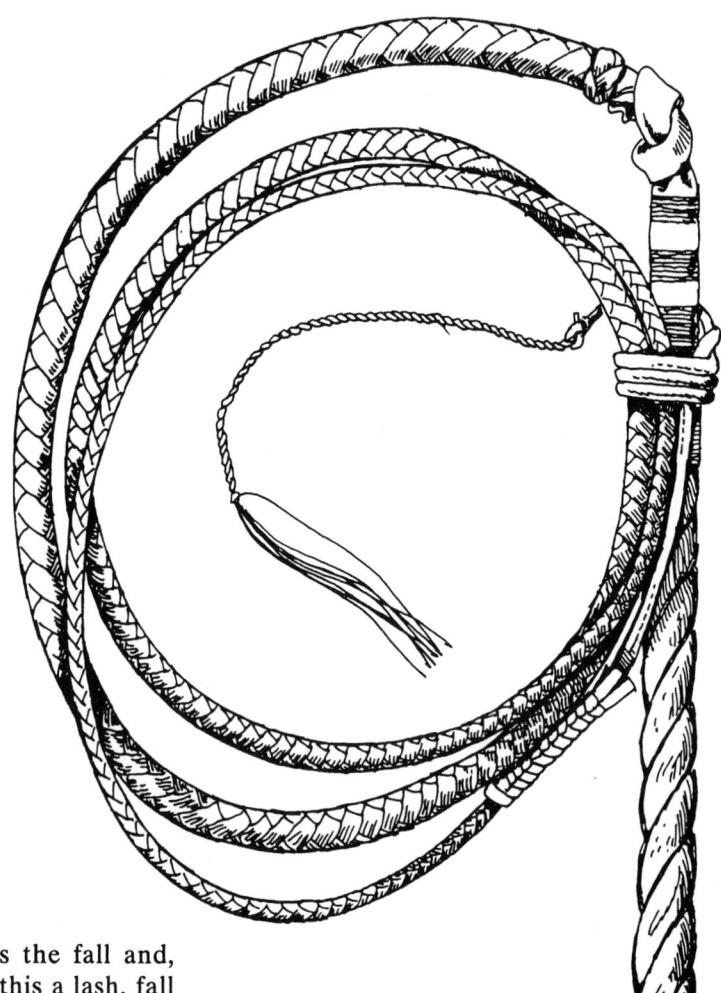

About twenty years ago we used to stock them in our saddlery, and they were sold to us as twisted-willow handles and were made in Italy. Since then they seem to have vanished from the scene, which is a pity because this was an unusual and quite attractive handle. The splitting and twisting made them much more flexible than straight timber, as well as seeming to make them stronger—especially those with a spring-steel core.

CARVED TIMBER HANDLES

Some old bushmen made quite a name for themselves carving whip handles. One became well known for his carving of handles featuring the head of Henry Lawson on the end. A number of people have told me about these carved heads, and good well-carved ones are valuable collector's items.

The handles in the sketch are considerably older than Henry Lawson and came from the collection of Kelvin Barton of Wodonga, Victoria, who had an important collection of historic whips.

They are said to have been carved by an Aboriginal who gave them to one of the men on one of John McDouall Stuart's overland explorations between 1860 and 1862.

After seeing these I tried making one for myself and found it to be an interesting project and well within the range of anyone who has done a little wood carving, though the finished product in my case was nowhere near the quality of the original.

I used a piece of our local red mahogany—not a great carving timber but one with an attractive grain and color. Silver ash is said to be another good timber for this work, and each area of Australia seems to have its own favored timber.

Because whip handles come under a lot of stress, it is important when choosing timber for them to select one that will not break and splinter under pressure.

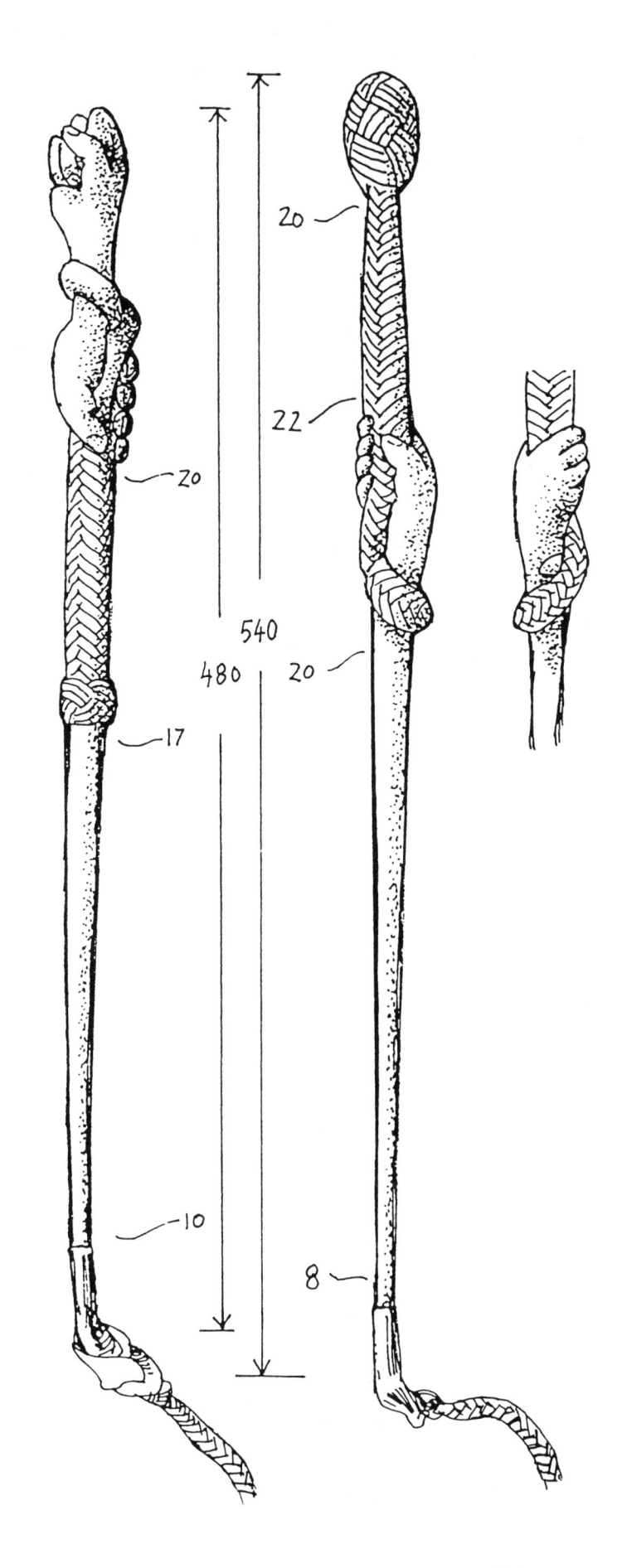

109

COWTAIL HANDLE

This whip handle, 500 mm long, was made by Maurice Doohan of Casino, New South Wales, one of Australia's best makers of redhide and whitehide stockwhips.

Cowtails (and bull pizzles) have long been traditional forms of covering whip handles, and are especially useful when the timber of the handle is of a type that might split under stress. The tail, as it dries and shrinks, puts great pressure on the timber and prevents this from happening.

For this reason tails are often used for bush repair jobs and are put over handles which have actually begun to show hairline splits, and this prevents the splits from opening up any further.

Some people put the tails on and then scrape off the hair when the tail has dried, but Maurice prefers to dehair the tail first. This is done by mixing about one part of hardwood ash by volume to four parts of water. This should be done two or three days before the mixture is wanted if it is to work at its best.

The tail (or even a whole hide) is now soaked in this mixture for three or more days, until the hair can be seen to be loosening. Maurice says it is a good idea to put the container in some place where you pass it a few times a day, and then you can give it a stir each time you pass by. When the hairs are loose they are all scraped off.

Some people also use a mixture of lime and water as a method of removing hair. Ordinary builder's lime or agricultural lime is used (around 15 parts water to one part lime). This is discussed in the section on tanning in *Bushcraft 3,* page 159.

The tail is then pulled over the whip handle and it is hung up with a weight at the lower end, about as heavy as a house brick. This pulls the whole thing tight, and as it dries it shrinks even tighter. In the handle illustrated there is a spiral pattern in the grip section. This was done very simply by fixing a cord around the handle before the tail was placed on. The leather shrinks over this and creates an attractive pattern. Both ends of the tail are cut off when it is fully dry, and a couple of Turk's heads at the thin end set it off nicely.

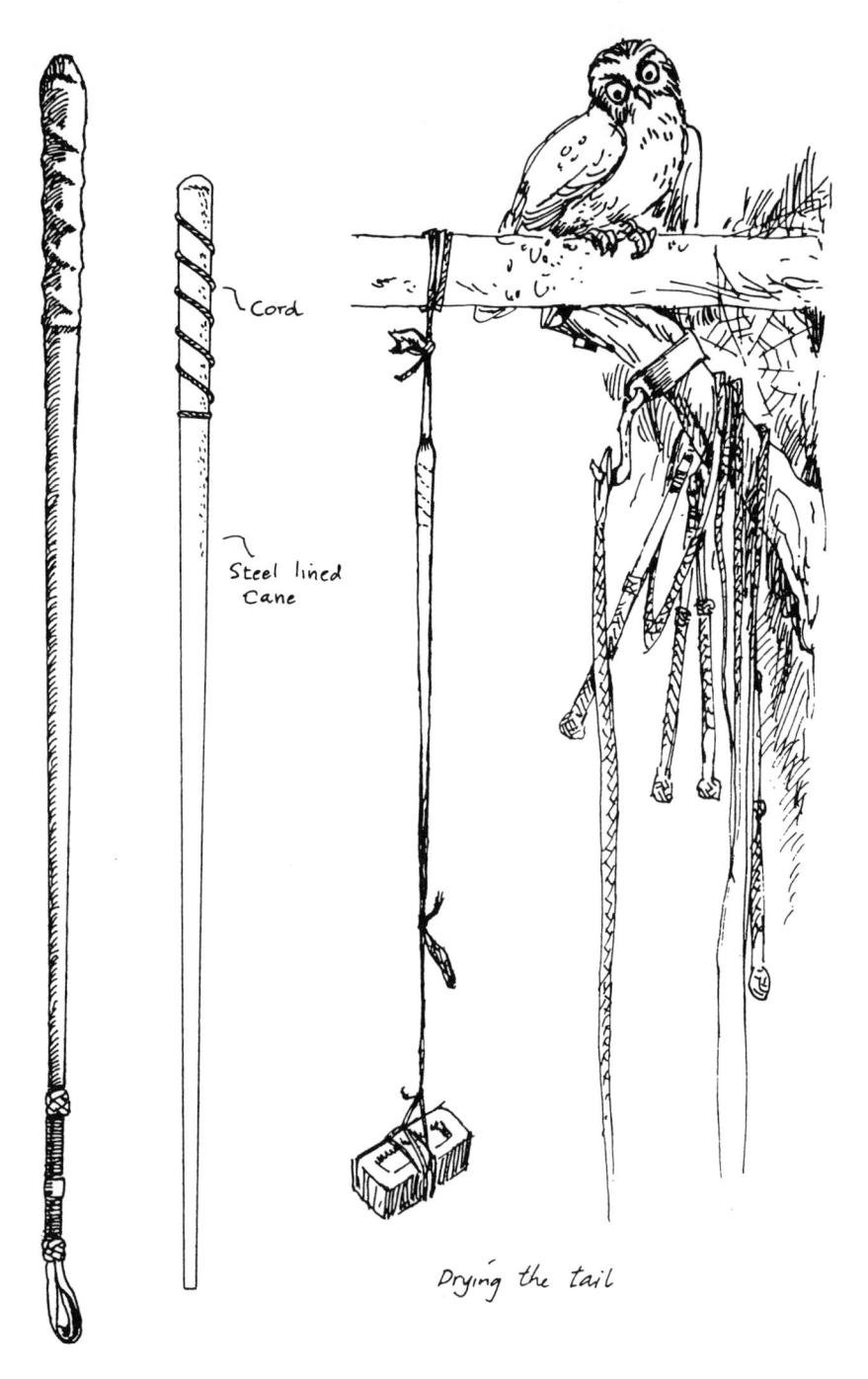

It is a good idea to give the tail a good coating of leather dressing inside and out as it is being put on, as this will help preserve the leather.

LUNGING WHIP

The handsome lunging whip in the sketch was made by professional whipmaker Bruce Cull of Cooroy, Queensland. I obtained it from him in January 1993. It was based on a fiberglass fishing-rod blank, which provided a good, strong yet flexible shaft. One end had been plaited with single-color kangaroo thonging, and a number of different styles had been used, as shown on the right of the sketch. The making of these patterns is explained in the following pages.

DESIGNS FOR WHIP HANDLES

There are dozens of designs that can be worked into a whip handle, and this section deals only with the most common ones. Handles can be worked with any number of strands, from 8 for a basic type of redhide whip to 24 and more for a fine kangaroo whip.

To make it easier for beginners I have drawn most of the following designs as either 12- or 16-plait, but nearly all the standard designs can be worked with any even number of strands. However, some will only work with strands that are in multiples of 4 or some other number. Interlocking diamonds, for instance, can be done with 16 strands but not with 14.

The names of the various designs are still a matter of argument. Whipmaker Glen Denholm contributed a list of names to our journal *(The Australian Whipmaker's Journal,* November 1991), and these have been used wherever possible here, but a number of designs have more than one name.

PLAITING SOAP

It is very hard to work handle designs in neatly if the leather is at all dry, and some sort of leather dressing is almost always necessary. For yard whips and other simple work this can be nothing more than plain fat, though this provides a feast for cockroaches, rats, and even dogs, unless a little kero is added to the mixture.

A simple plaiting soap is made from
4 parts clean fat
1 part soap
3 parts water (all by volume)

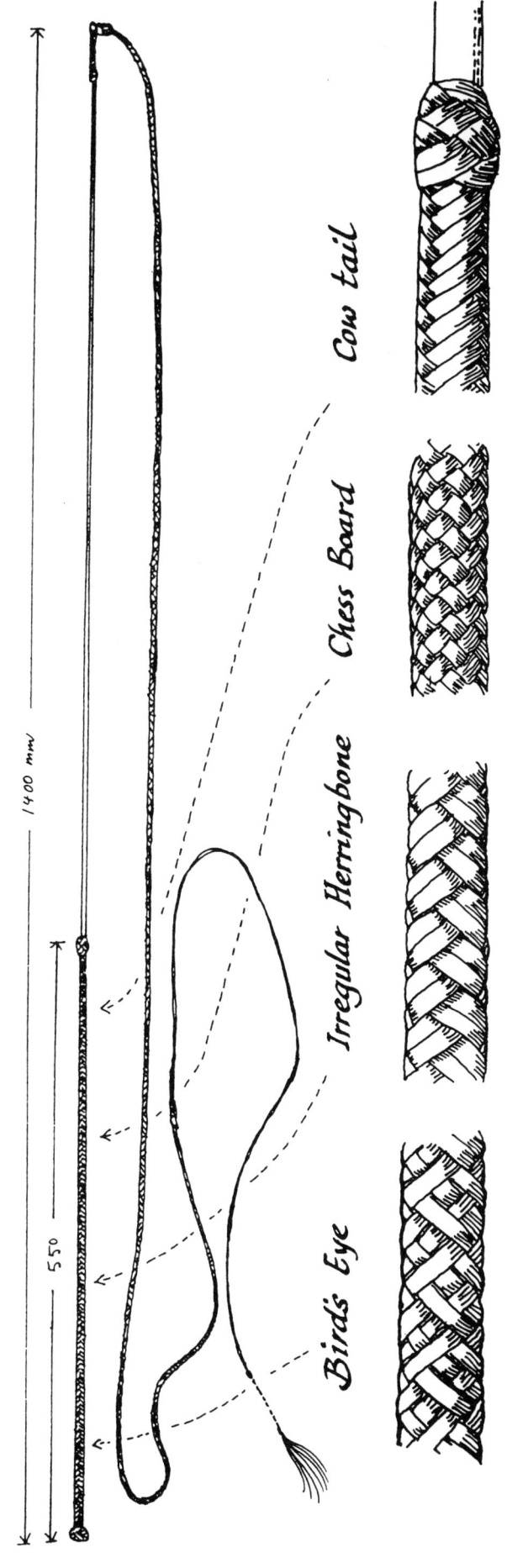

111

Heat the water and soap until the soap has dissolved. Add the fat and bring it slowly to simmer for a few minutes and let it cool. When cool it should be firm but light to the touch; if it is still watery it will need more cooking.

A different recipe used by Hugo Stephens of Mareeba consisted of
   clean fat
   emulsifying wax (from the chemist)
   ordinary soap

He heated these together until everything was melted and then beat the mixture to make it as light and full of bubbles as possible. The advantage of this mixture is that it does not make the hands greasy and yet gets the strands so that they will easily tighten up.

COWTAIL OR WHIPMAKER'S PLAIT

Let us now start with a few basic designs and then go on to some more complex ones.

This one is sometimes known as a herringbone, but this can be confusing, as there are quite a number of herringbone plaits. Some professionals just call it the whipmaker's plait, as it is the most common one used. I once heard someone call it a cowtail. I don't know how it got that name, but at least it is memorable.

I have drawn it with 12 strands and also with 16. It is also commonly used on 8-strand rawhide covered handles, and this is illustrated in chapter 1.

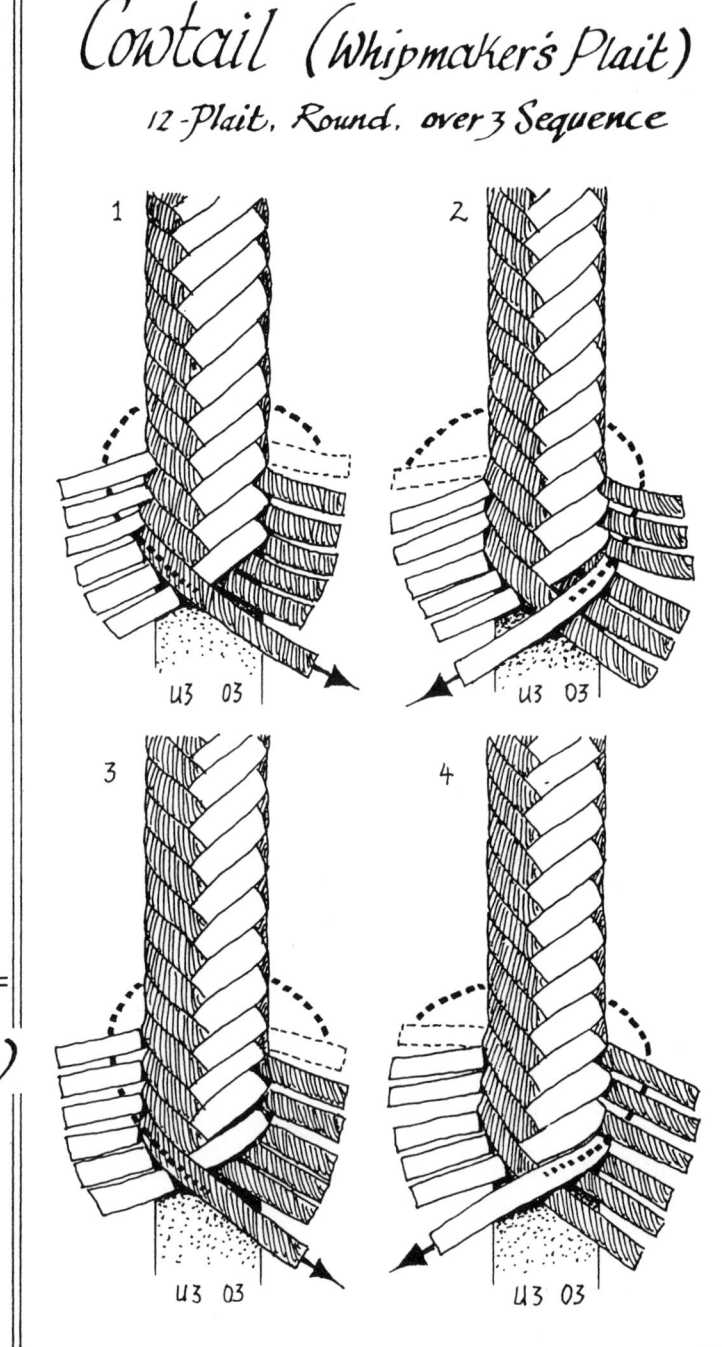

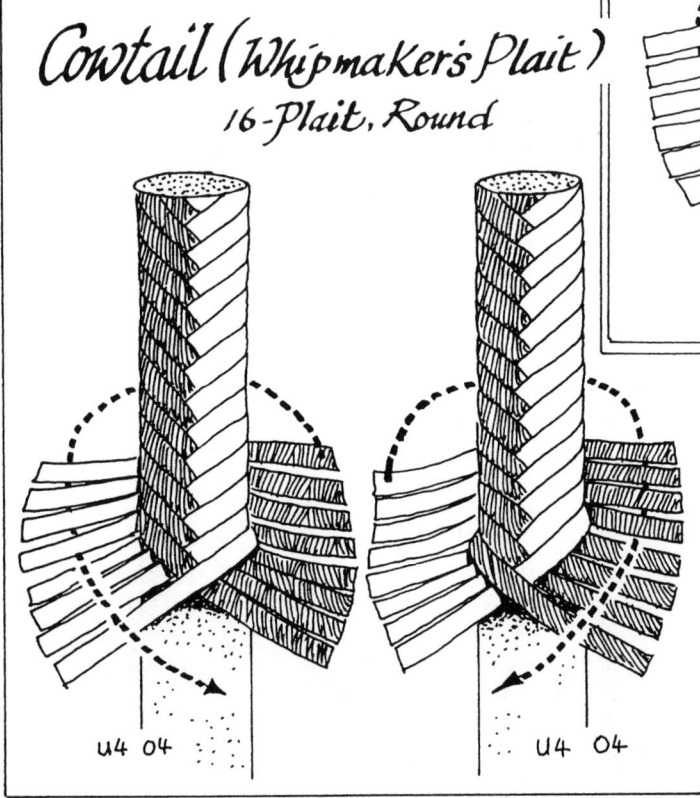

DOUBLED HERRINGBONE

If you pick up two strands at once instead of one when doing the previous plait, you will get quite a different effect and the result is shown here.

Though you may think that bringing over a number of strands at a time will be faster than one at a time, this is not always the case, and for fast work professional whipmakers work with one strand at a time.

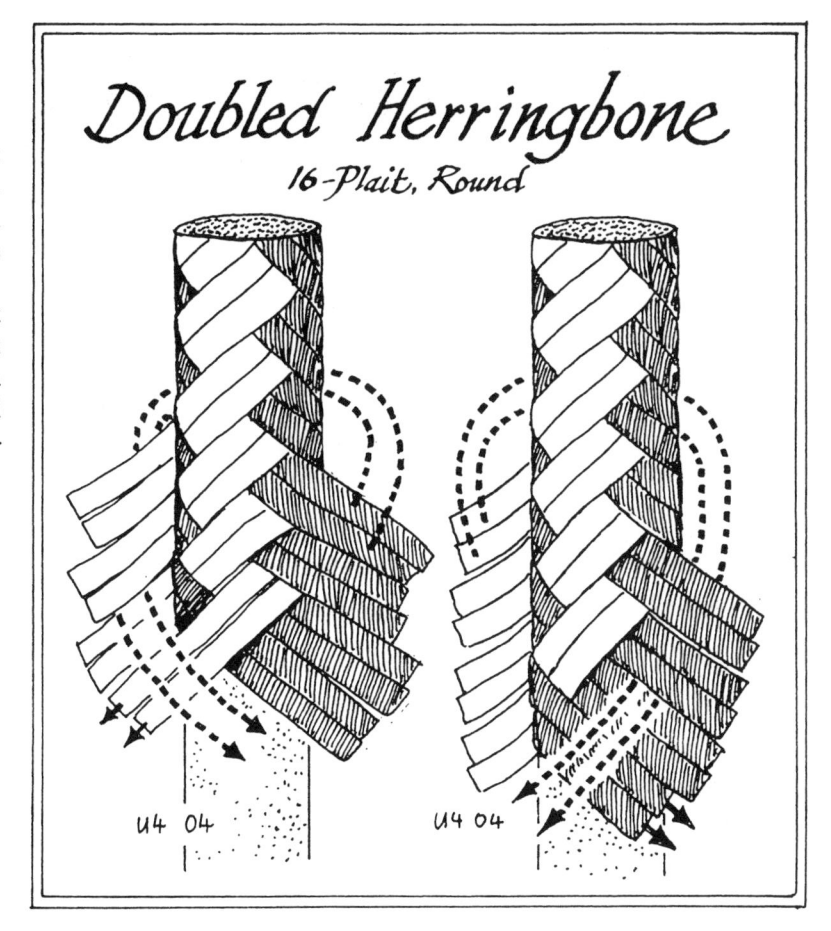

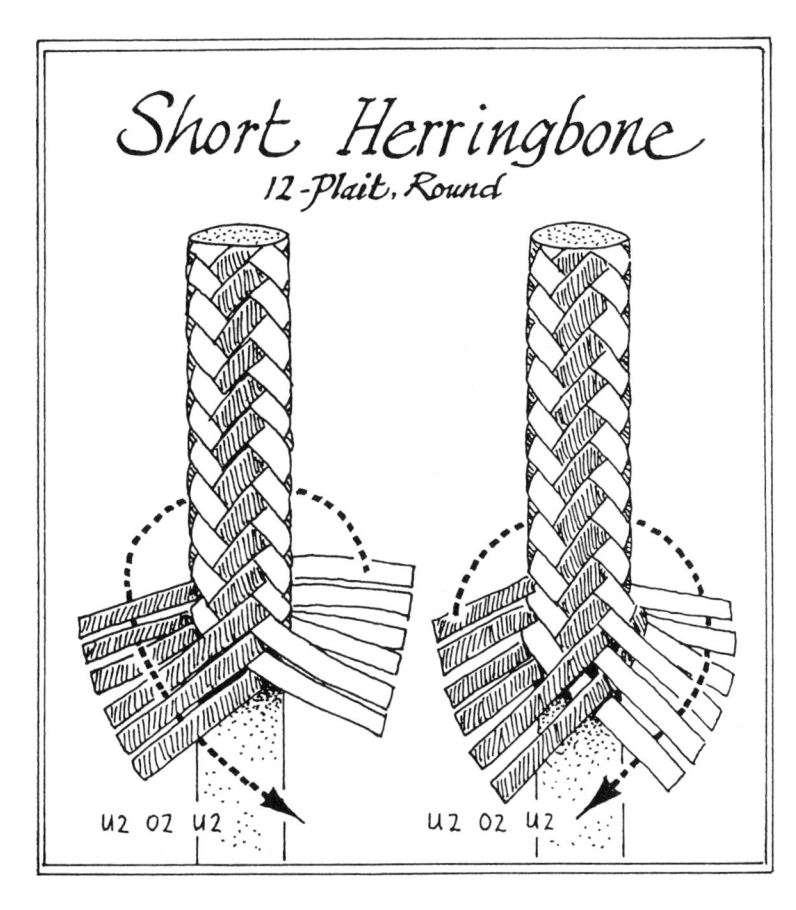

Doubled Herringbone
16-Plait, Round

Short Herringbone
12-Plait, Round

SHORT HERRINGBONE

If you compare this to the basic plait on the previous page, you will notice an important difference. The plait at the top of the previous page had the working strand passing through the center of the strands on the opposite side in an U3, O3 (under 3, over 3) sequence.

In the version on the left the working strand goes under 2, over 2, under 2, and this gives a shorter herringbone pattern.

113

Chessboard Pattern Start

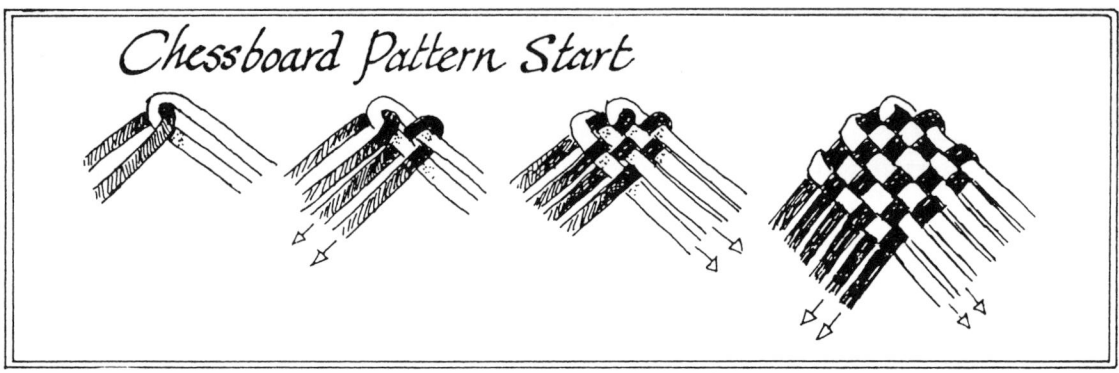

CHESSBOARD PLAIT

This is the most basic plait of all, a simple over one, under one sequence. If, however, you start it in the same way as you begin a belt, you will find that the pattern does not work out.

For that reason I have shown a different way to start that will get the colors divided into two groups, one on the left and the other on the right.

The professional does not usually begin with precut lace, but instead cuts a pair of sets out of two pieces of kangaroo hide. In this case a strip of light-colored hide would be cut out first, about 24 mm wide and a little more than one and a half times the length of the whip handle. This would then be divided into 6 strands, but a little bit at the top would be left so that they remained together at the top. The same thing would then be done with a piece of dark hide. These two pieces would then be tied to the end of the whip handle.

The beginner using precut lace finds that it is a bother trying to tie a big mob of strands to the end of the handle. One idea is to cut 6 strands twice as long as necessary and then double them over to make 12 strands—this is much easier to tie on.

Another way that I find even faster is to begin as shown here. I have shown 12 strands but you can build it up to as many as you wish. Once they are all interlocked it is much easier to wrap them around the handle and fix them as shown.

From then on you just do a normal under, over sequence as shown. This is a convenient way to start any handle when using precut lace, and then go into other patterns as you wish.

The start of this plait will be later trimmed and covered with a Turk's head.

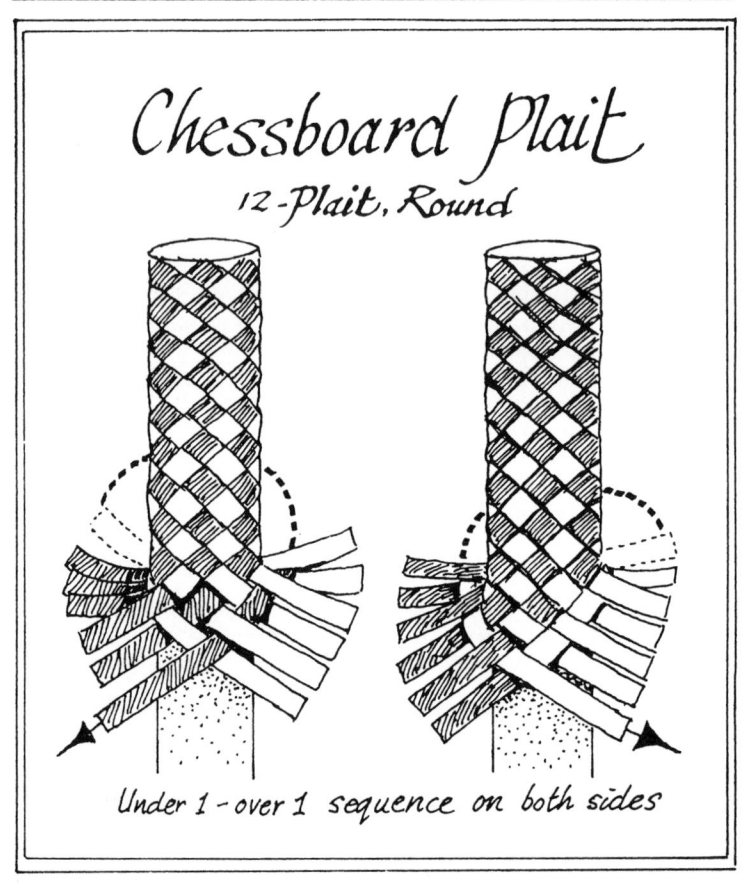

Fixing Chessboard to Handle

Chessboard Plait
12-Plait, Round

Under 1 - over 1 sequence on both sides

114

Irregular Herringbone
12-Plait, Round

IRREGULAR HERRINGBONE, 12-PLAIT, ROUND

The irregular herringbone can be done with a varying number of strands, and in each case the pattern on the reverse will be different from that on the front. In my drawings I am illustrating the 12-plait version, which consists of simply picking up two strands at a time and taking them around in an under 3, over 3 sequence. This creates a regular herringbone on the front and a slightly different pattern on the back. This is illustrated in the lower sketch of the set.

Back view

Double Diamond
12-Plait, Round

DOUBLE DIAMOND

This creates a simple but attractive pattern. Two strands are brought around each time, and they go under 2, over 2, under 2.

Strong diamond patterns like this are usually only done for a short section of the handle.

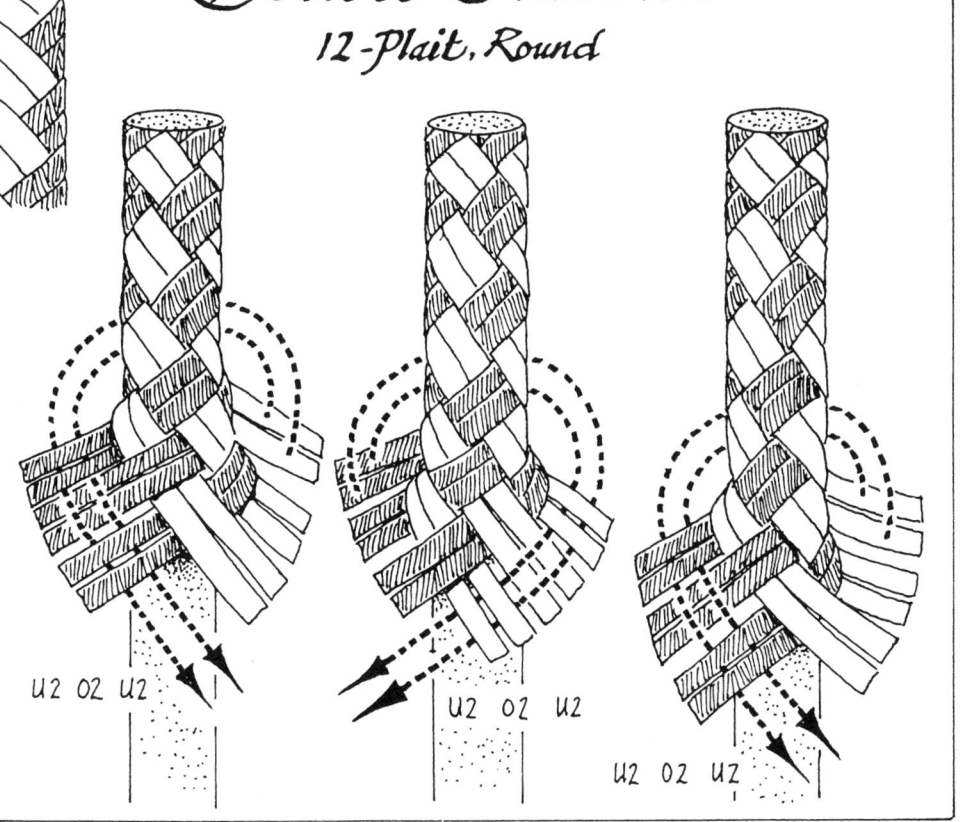

TRIPLE DIAMOND

This gives a slightly larger diamond pattern than the double diamond illustrated earlier. Three strands are picked up and brought around each time, and care must be taken to see that they all lie flat, especially around the back where they are out of sight when you are doing the work.

If this was to be done all in one color it would be called coachwhipping, as would the next pattern.

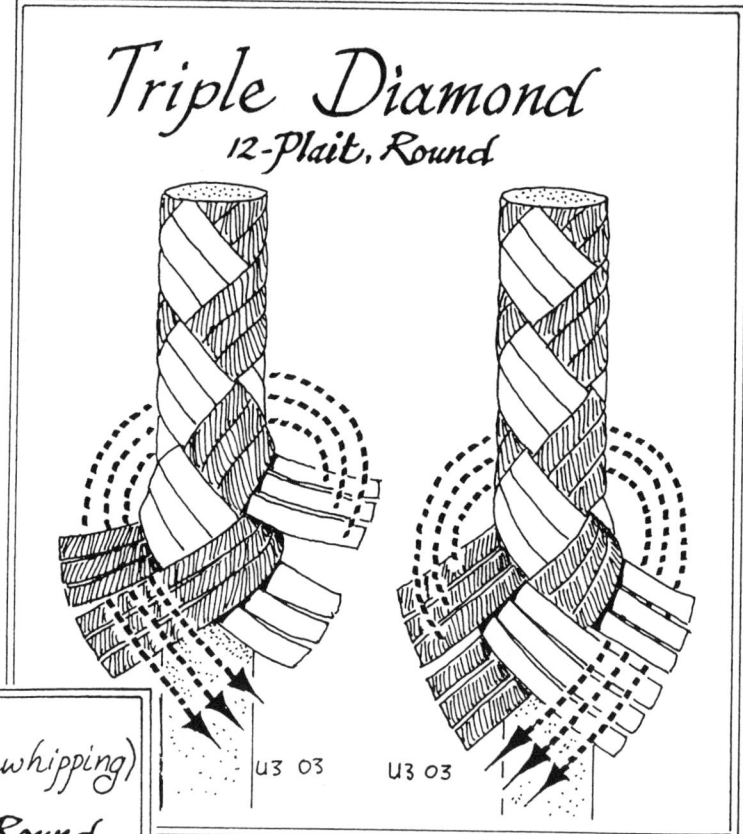

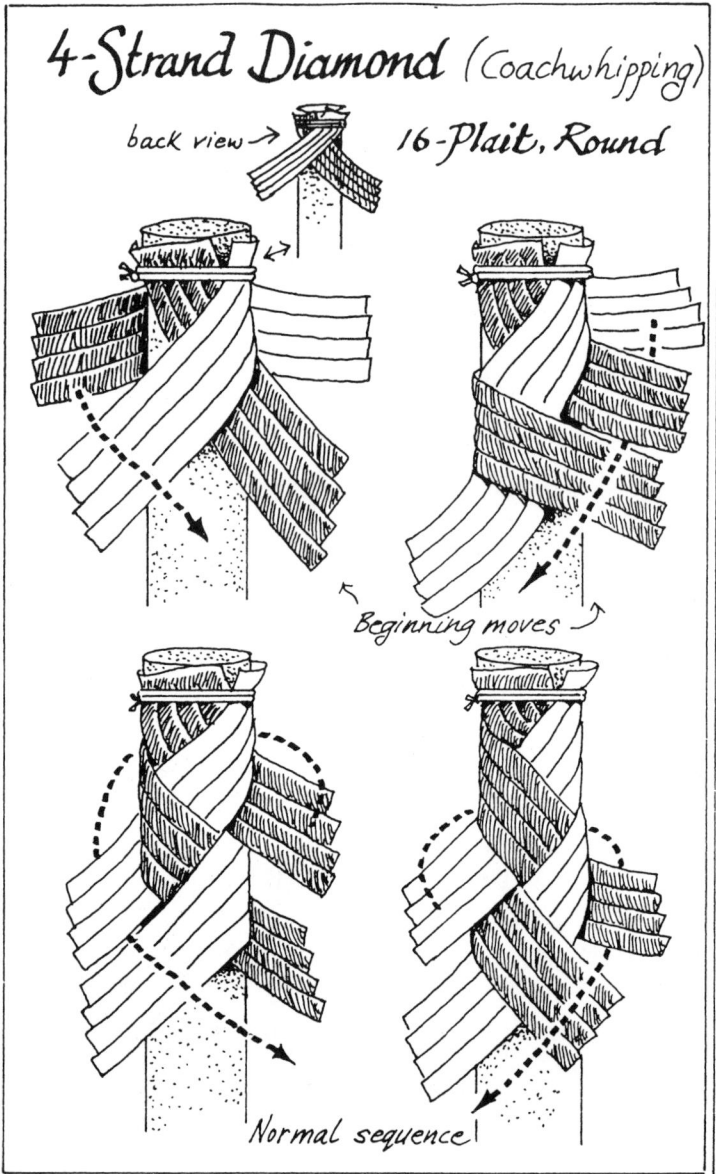

Triple Diamond
12-Plait, Round

U3 O3   U3 O3

4-Strand Diamond (Coachwhipping)
16-Plait, Round

back view →

Beginning moves

Normal sequence

4-STRAND DIAMOND, COACHWHIPPING

By the time you begin bringing 4 strands or more across at a time you are getting into the style that is called coachwhipping by sailors, who often work it in cord to cover rails. In skilled hands this can be a reasonably fast way of covering a long handle.

It used to be a favorite for covering the handles of the long whips used in coaching days, hence its name. There are quite a number of varieties of coachwhipping, and this is just one of them.

All sorts of combinations of numbers can be used, and there is a simple version using only 8 strands.

BRACELET

This is a very simple design, nothing more than a single row of diamonds around the whip handle, but even so the beginner still needs to know how to do it. As you may see from the drawings, there are two ways that this design can be done.

The first is to take a strand from one side and then a strand from the other and so on, alternating from one side to the other as is done with the previous designs.

The second method is to take all the strands from the one side until the design is formed. Both methods end up in an identical plait; it is really a question of which you find easiest.

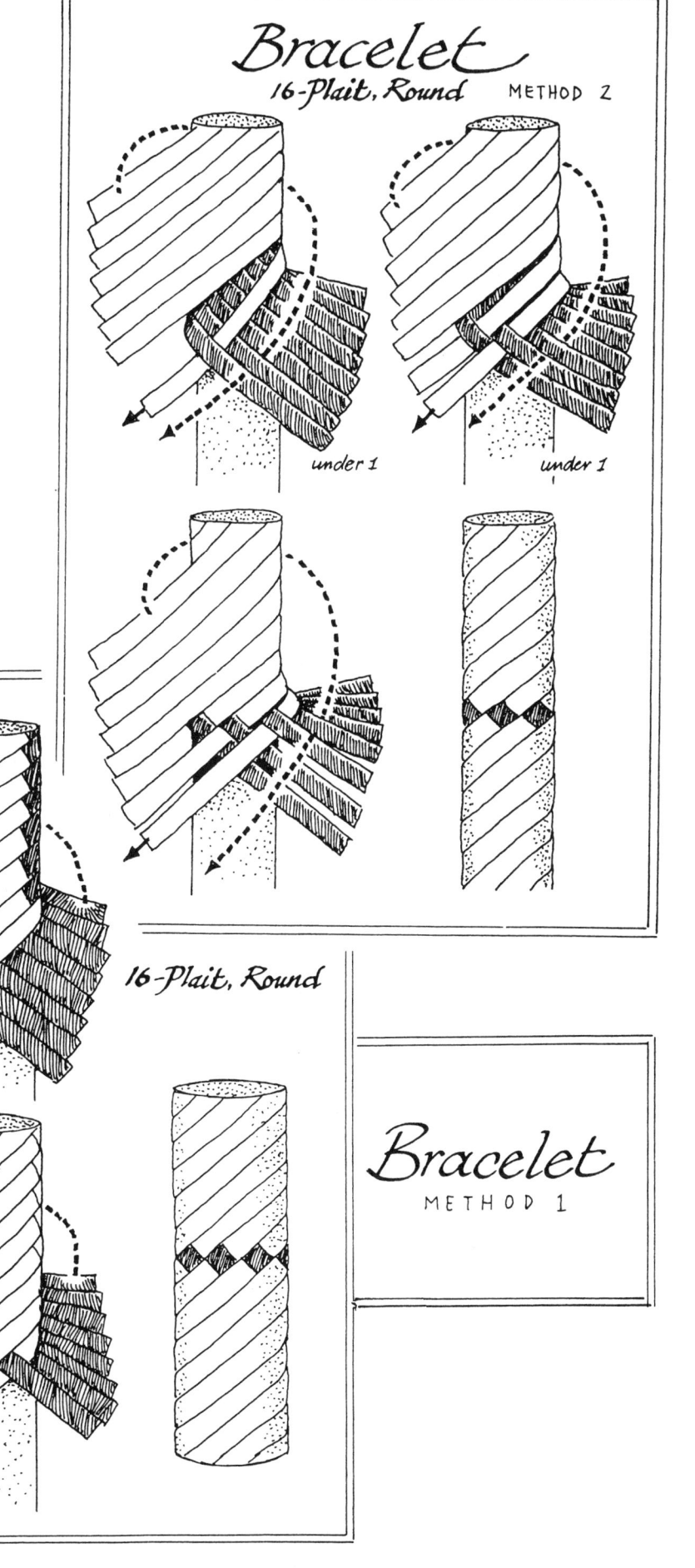

Bracelet
16-Plait, Round METHOD 2

under 1

under 1

16-Plait, Round

Bracelet
METHOD 1

117

DOUBLE BRACELET

As with the single bracelet, explained on the previous page, this one can be done in one of two ways, both of which will produce an identical result.

Once you have done this you will realize that it is also possible to do a triple bracelet in the same way.

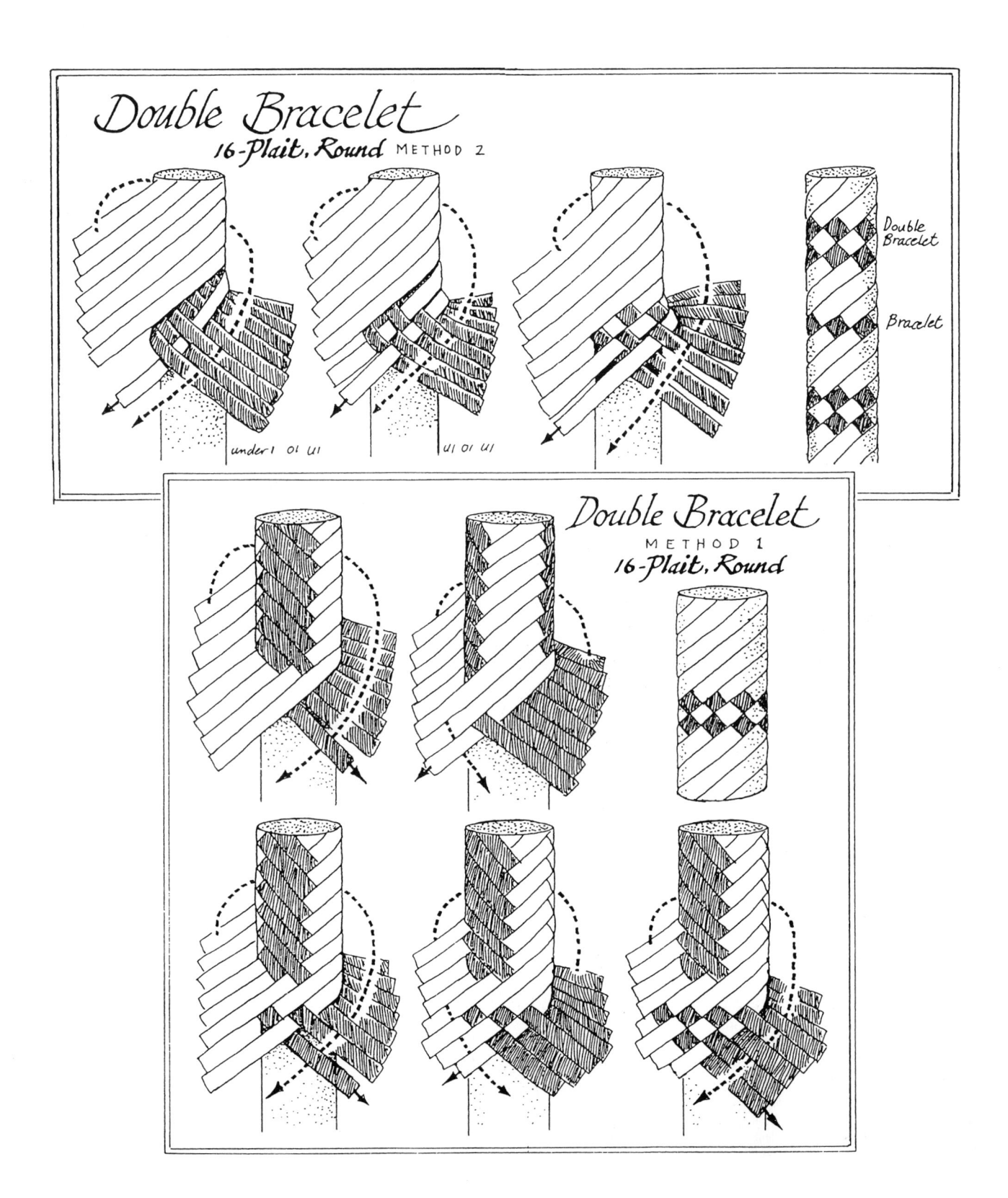

Double Bracelet
16-Plait, Round — METHOD 2

under 1 or U1

U1 or U1

Double Bracelet
METHOD 1
16-Plait, Round

118

STAIRSTEP

I got the name for this one from Glen Denholm, professional whipmaker of Cobbity, New South Wales. Like some of the previous ones it can be done in a couple of ways, according to what you find most convenient. It is like the bracelet, except that you go under 2 strands each time rather than only 1.

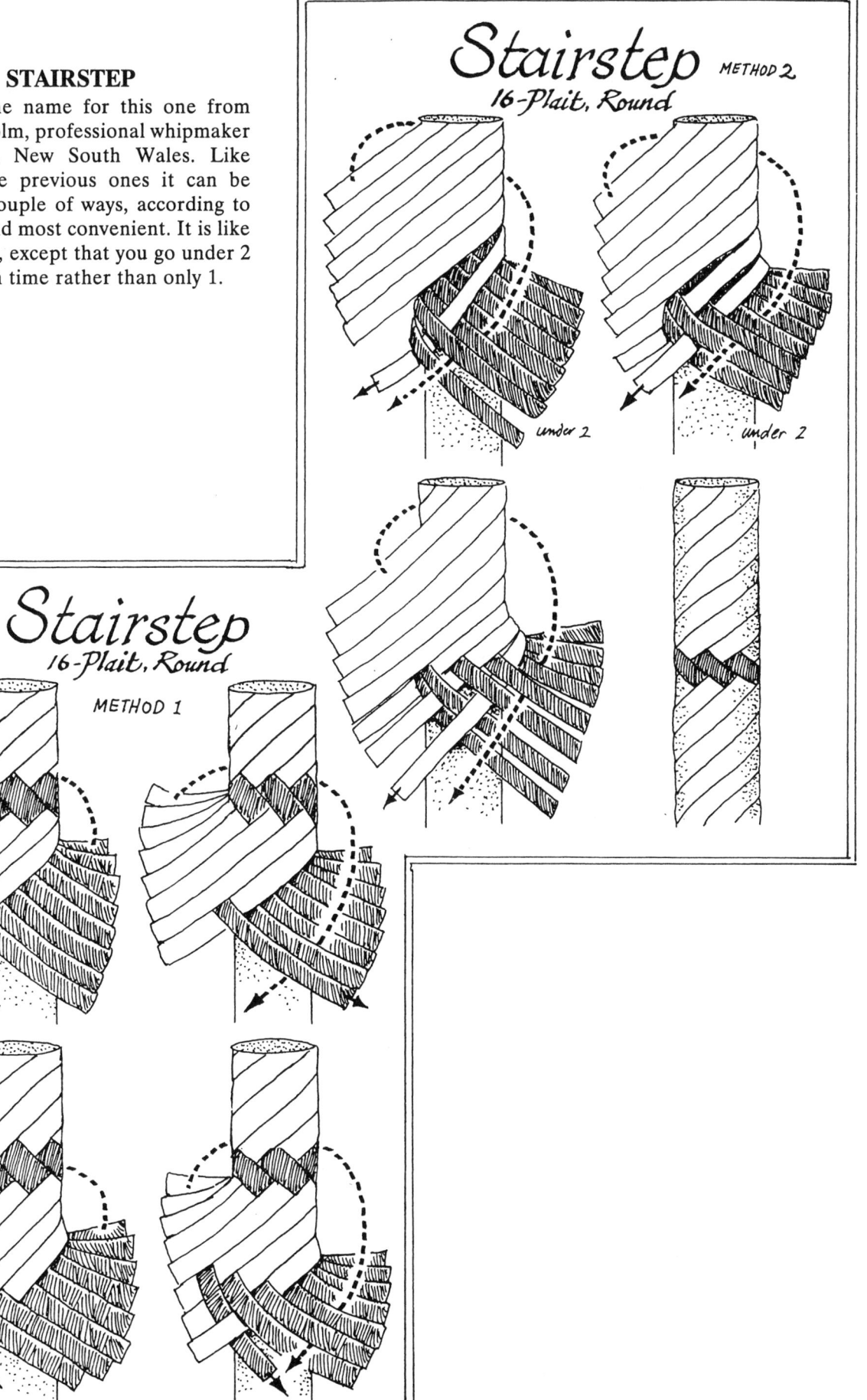

DOUBLE STAIRSTEP

The double stairstep follows a simple under 2, over 1, under 2 sequence. I have shown it here only as done by method 2, but you can easily work out how to do it by method 1 if you wish.

If you have been following the diagrams through in order you will have noticed that for the last few I have shown two methods of tying, and perhaps this is a good time to talk about the difference between them. Method 2 is often used for name plaiting and other complex work.

TWO METHODS FOR COMPLEX PLAITING

Alternate Strand Method

This is the standard method for all simple round plaiting. You simply take a strand from one side and work it down, then a strand from the other side and work that down, and so on. You really need to have your wits about you to use this method for jobs such as name plaiting. Some professionals feel happy with it; it is the same as their ordinary plaiting method and so allows them to go back into a simple pattern as soon as the name is finished.

Spiral Method

The other method is used by some whipmakers for complex designs. Despite what you may think, it uses exactly the same number of strands as the previous method. There are two ways to use the spiral method, and the first short spiral method is probably the most common. First you spiral all the dark strands down the handle once, as is shown in the drawing for the double stairstep on this page. Then you work all the light-colored strands into the dark ones as shown. Once you have formed a particular design you can easily return to the alternate strand method for the simple parts of the job.

The second way of using the spiral method is quite different. First you take all the dark strands and tightly spiral them around the handle from top to bottom so that no timber is showing.

The spiraled dark strands are tied firmly top and bottom, but the white strands are only tied at the top. You now work the white strands down one at a time, forming the design as you go. The advantage of this is that you are holding only half the number of strands in your hand and the whole lot can be released at any time while you have a rest and look at the job.

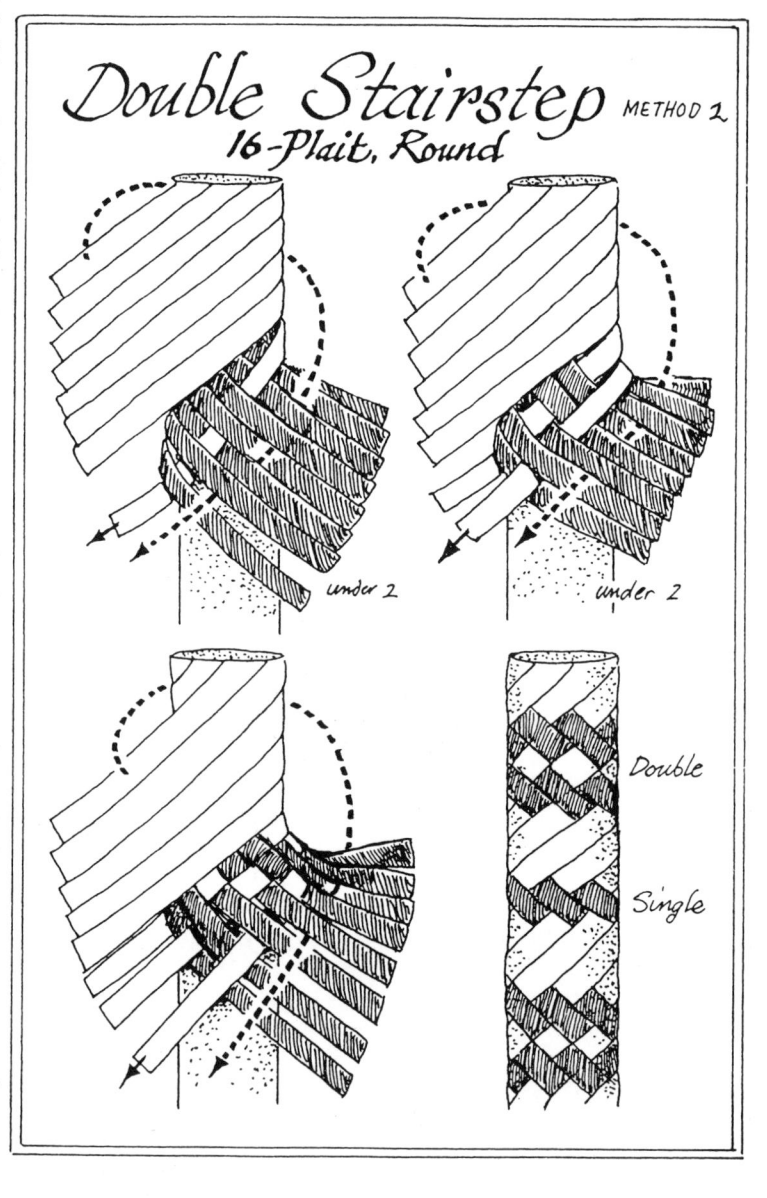

The disadvantage is that you have to lift up the black strands with a pointed tool of some sort to get the white ones under the black ones, and this can be a lengthy job. You also will probably have to go back and tighten everything up later, as it is hard to keep the work tight when you follow this method. Even so you may find it an easier method for complex designs.

Peter Clarke, a whipmaker of Bilpin, New South Wales, told me of an old-timer who worked with up to 50 very fine strands on a handle using this method.

The sketches show three ways to do spiral work. One way is to use long strands and dye one half of each strand a darker color. One half is spiraled around the handle and the other half is ready to work. Another method is to simply use two sets of lace, one dark and one light, and tie them both to the top of the job. This tying is often a fiddly job. Professionals usually cut their strands in sets with a strip of leather left at the top to hold them together, as shown in the top right-hand sketch. This makes it so much easier to attach them to the handle.

left light; dyed dark

SOLID BAND

For this solid band the white strands go under 4 of the dark strands, but it can also be done by going under 3, 5, or even more. To be effective the dark strands have to lie very neatly together so that no light strips can be seen showing through from below.

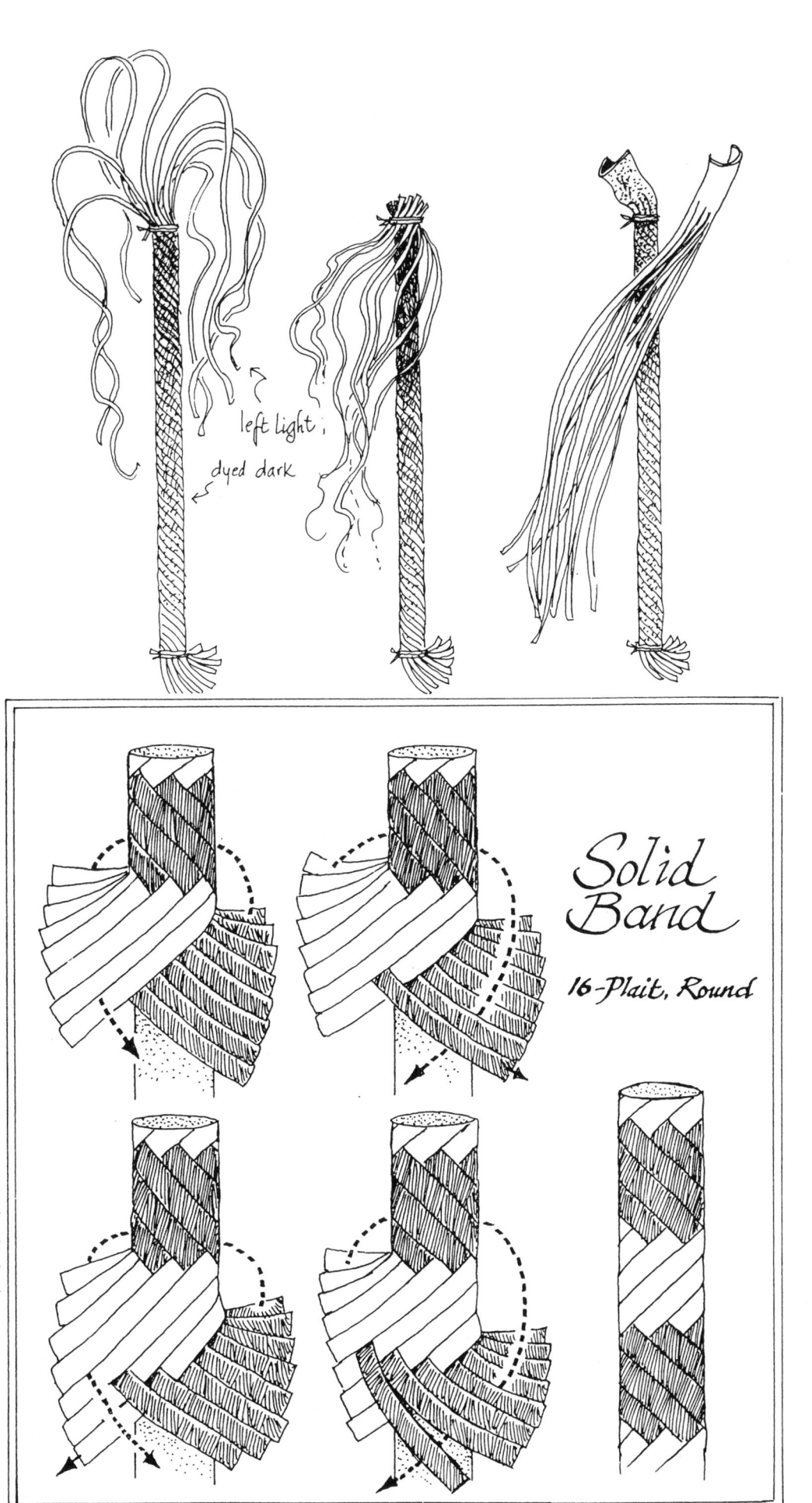

Solid Band

16-Plait, Round

121

Bird's Eye Plait — 12-Plait, Round

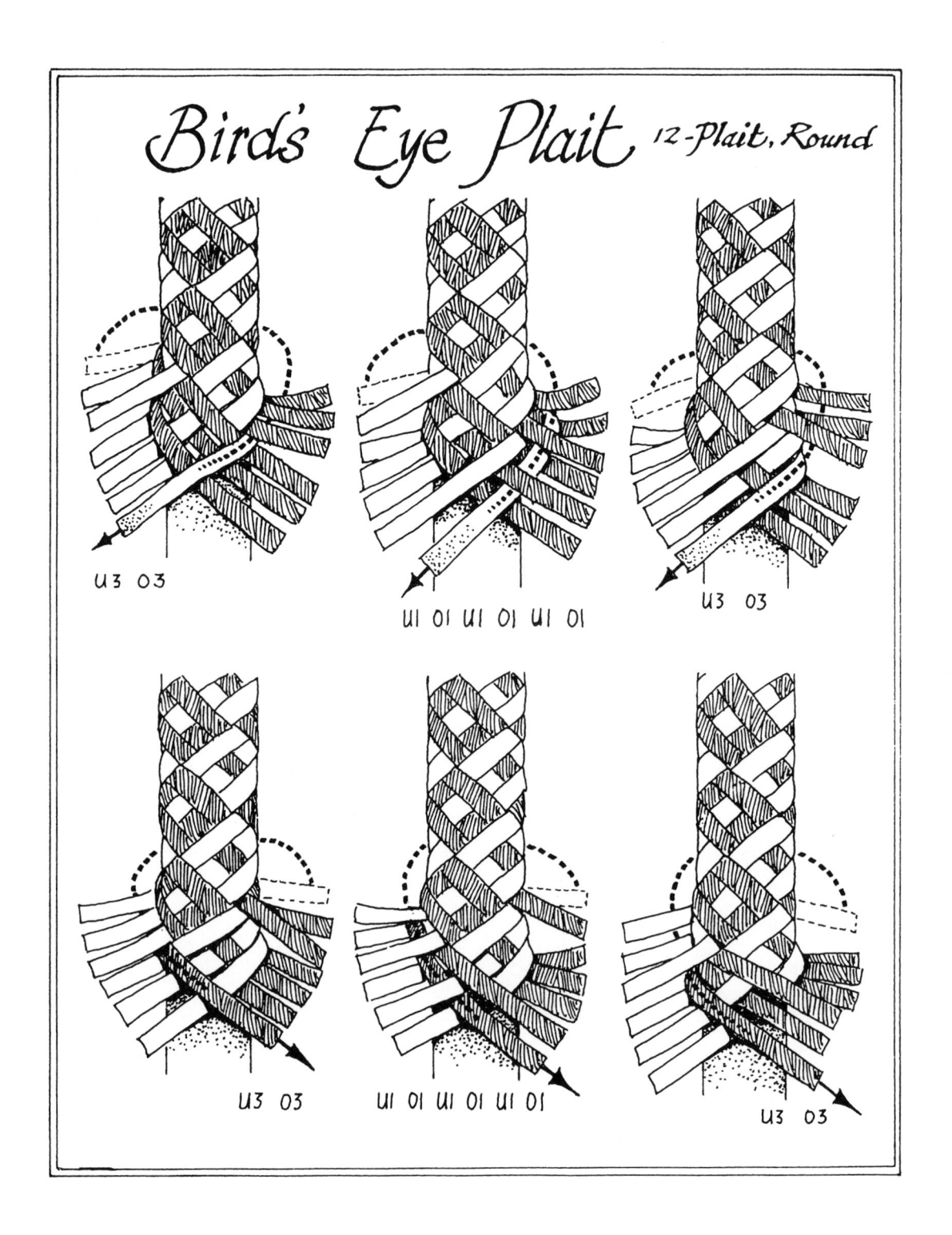

U3 O3

U1 O1 U1 O1 U1 O1

U3 O3

U3 O3

U1 O1 U1 O1 U1 O1

U3 O3

BIRD'S EYE, 12-PLAIT, ROUND

The bird's eye is an attractive plait, but one that looks best when done in moderation and balanced with longer areas of plainer patterns. This also makes sense to the whipmaker because plain designs can be done faster. Quite often one or two rings of bird's eyes are enough to nicely set off a whip handle.

Bird's eyes are nearly always done with two colors, but on the lunging whip illustrated earlier Bruce Cull used only a dark brown, fairly thick thong. As a result of the dark color the design was not obvious, but what it did do was create a good handgrip on the section of the handle that most needed it.

Egyptian Eyes

16-Plait, Round

SPIRAL METHOD

① O6 U1 O1 U1
② O6 U1 O1 U1
③ O3 U4 O1 U1
④ O4 U1 O3 U1
⑤ O5 U1 O1 U1 O1 U1
⑥ O6 U1 O3 U1
⑦ O6 U1 O1 U4
⑧ O6 U1 O1 U1

ALTERNATE STRAND METHOD

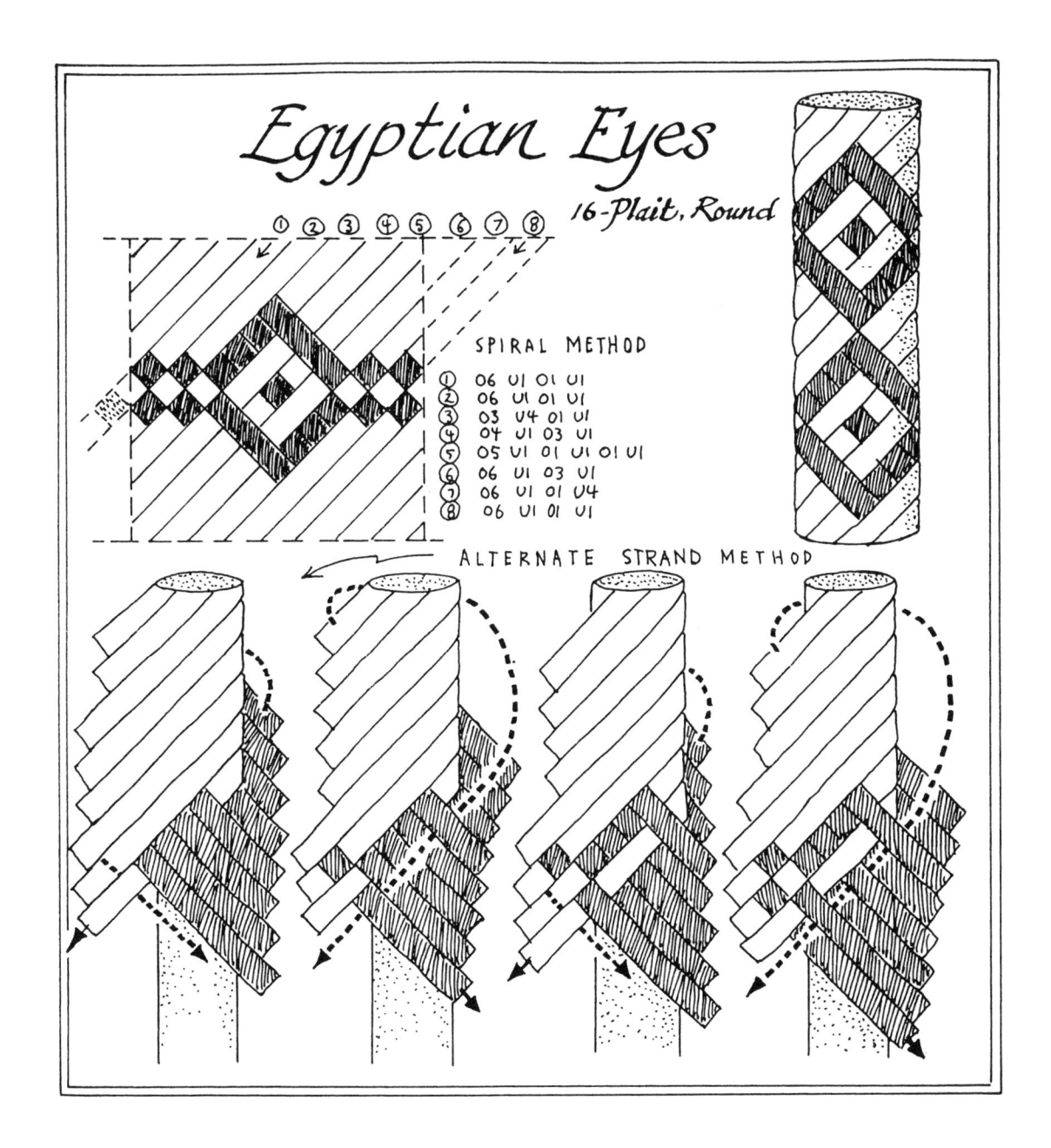

EGYPTIAN EYES

You can call this design by whatever name you choose, for the name that I use has nothing to do with either Egypt or eyes. This is an old bush term for a breakfast dish that seems to have been totally forgotten. A circle would be cut in a slice of bread and it would then be thrown into the frypan and fried on one side. When done it would be turned over and an egg broken into the hole so that the other side of the bread and the egg fried together. The results were known as Egyptian eyes.

I have shown two methods for making this design. In the spiral method you first spiral the dark strands around the handle and then follow the code given on the drawing. For the alternate strand method you simply take a strand from one side and then one from the other, working down and forming the pattern as you go.

Sun
16-Plait, Round

SPIRAL METHOD

① 02 U1 O1 U1 O1 U1
② 02 U7
③ 04 U1 O3 U1
④ 04 U2 O1 U1 O1 U2
⑤ 06 U1 O3 U1
⑥ 06 U7
⑦ 08 U1 O1 U1 O1 U1

ALTERNATE STRAND METHOD

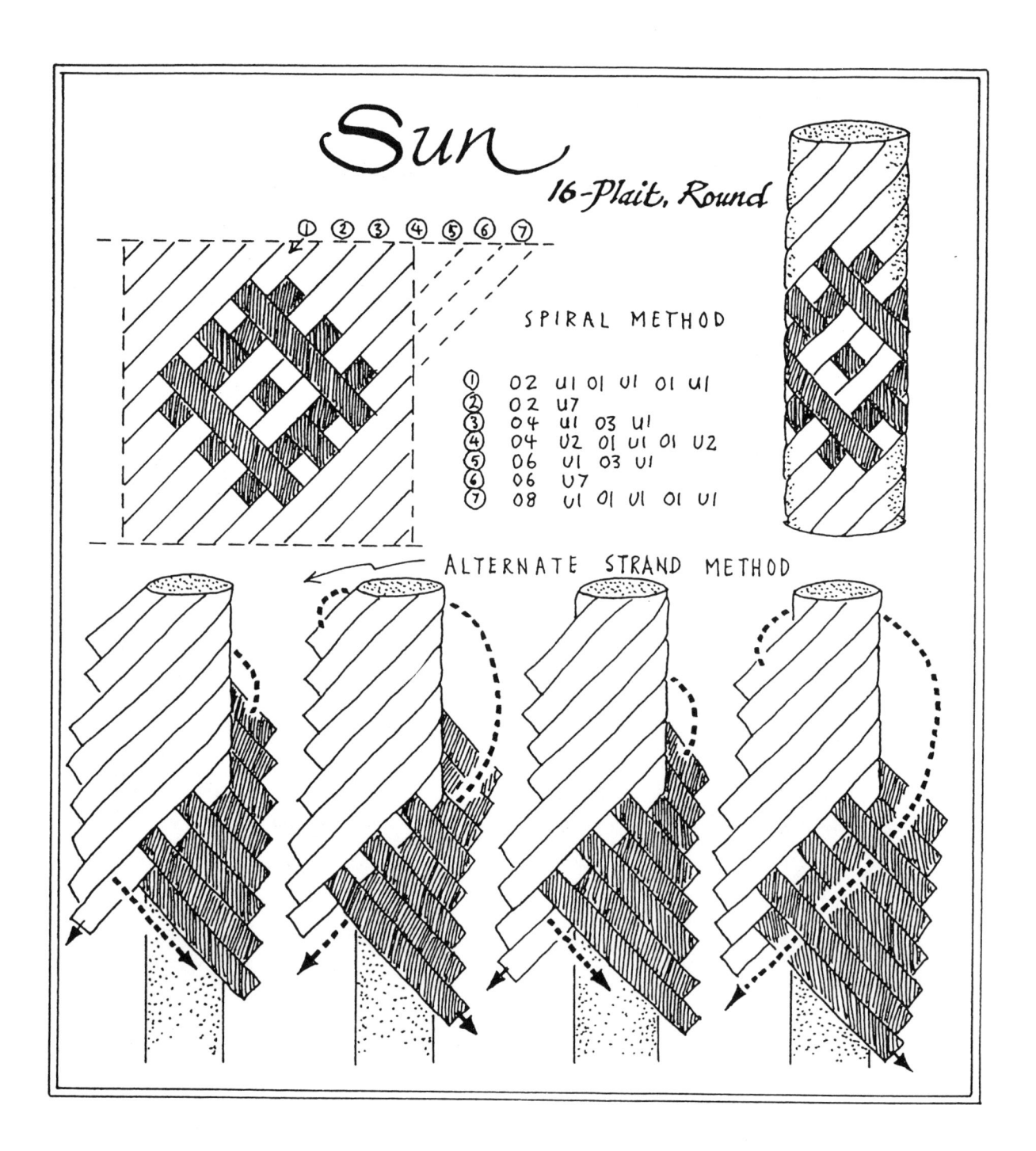

THE SUN

As you would expect, the sun design is a very old one and is to be found in woven and plaited work all over the world. For a relatively few number of strands, such as this 16-plait, the design is very simple, but with 24 or more strands it can be made much more complex.

As with the previous design two methods are illustrated, and the method that you choose will depend on whichever you find the most simple and convenient. In either case the end result is exactly the same.

Flowers & Zigzag
16-Plait, Round

① O4 U3 O1 U3 O2 U1 O1 U1 O1 U1 O1 U1 O2 U3 O1 U3 O4
② O5 U1 O3 U1 O3 U2 O1 U2 O5 U1 O3 U1 O5
③ O4 U3 O1 U3 O5 U1 O5 U3 O1 U3 O4
④ O5 U1 O3 U1 O5 U2 O1 U2 O3 U1 O3 U1 O5

Flowers

Zigzag Bracelet

FLOWERS AND ZIGZAG

This provides quite a decorative band around a whip handle, especially when contrasted with sections of fairly plain plaiting such as cowtail (or whipmaker's plait). The two parts of the design can also be done separately, and this is shown on the next page.

In this drawing the code is given for doing this design by the spiral method, but it can also be done quite easily by the alternate strand method shown in earlier drawings. In that case you just work it out as you go.

DOUBLE ZIGZAG

This and the following design are both shown on the previous page as part of a combined design. They can also be used by themselves and are quite attractive.

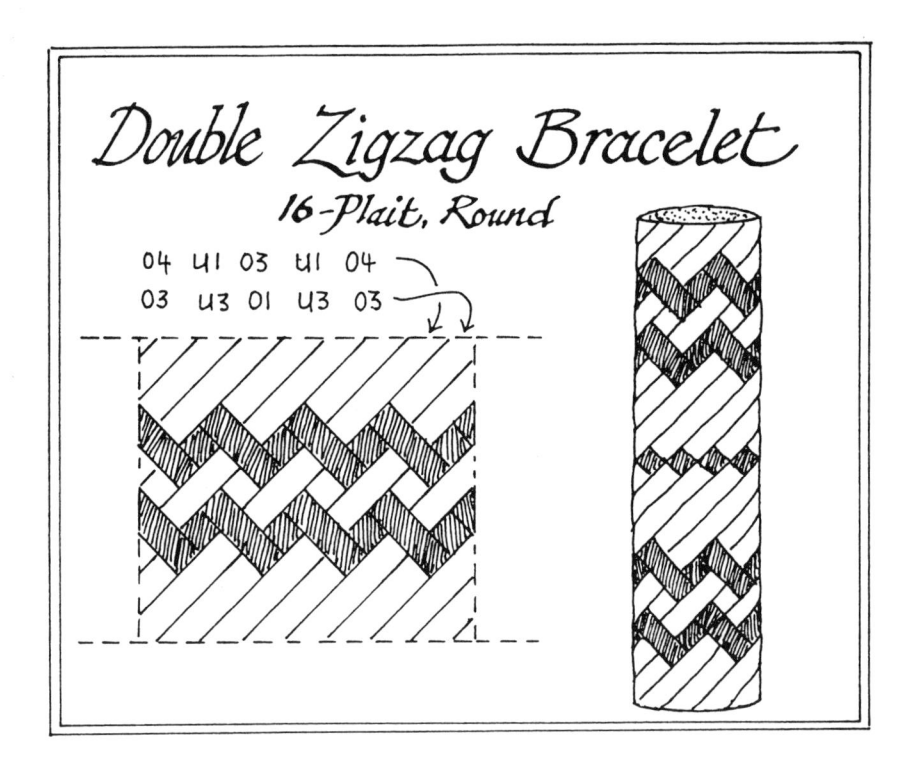

Double Zigzag Bracelet
16-Plait, Round

04 U1 03 U1 04
03 U3 01 U3 03

FLOWERS

There are two or three different designs that are called flowers, but this is one of the most attractive and is an easy one to work.

In this drawing and the one above, the code is given for doing this design by the spiral method, but it can also be quite easily done by the alternate strand method shown in earlier drawings, just working it out as you go.

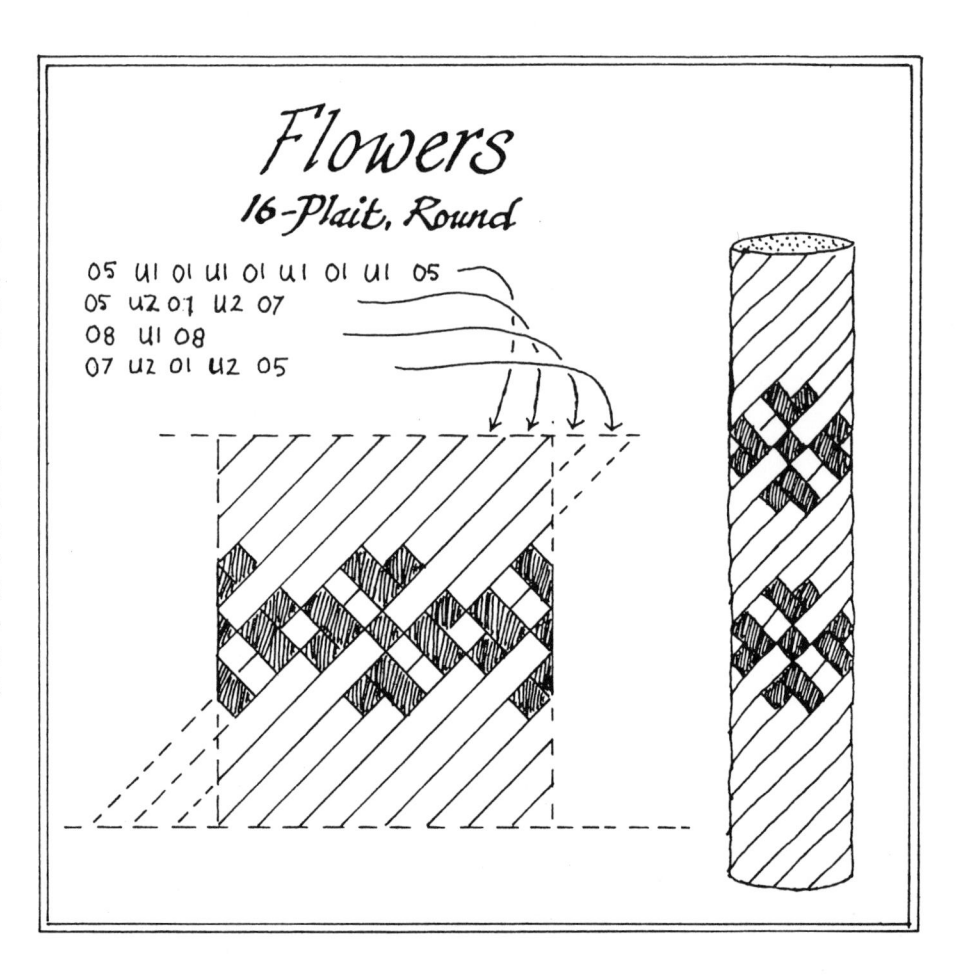

Flowers
16-Plait, Round

05 U1 01 U1 01 U1 01 U1 05
05 U2 07 U2 07
08 U1 08
07 U2 01 U2 05

Interlocking Diamonds
16-Plait, Round

O7 U1 O4 U1 O1 U4 O4 U1 O1 U1 O9
O7 U1 O3 U4 O1 U4 O5 U1 O1 U1 O9

Bracelet

Interlocking Diamonds

Double Bracelet

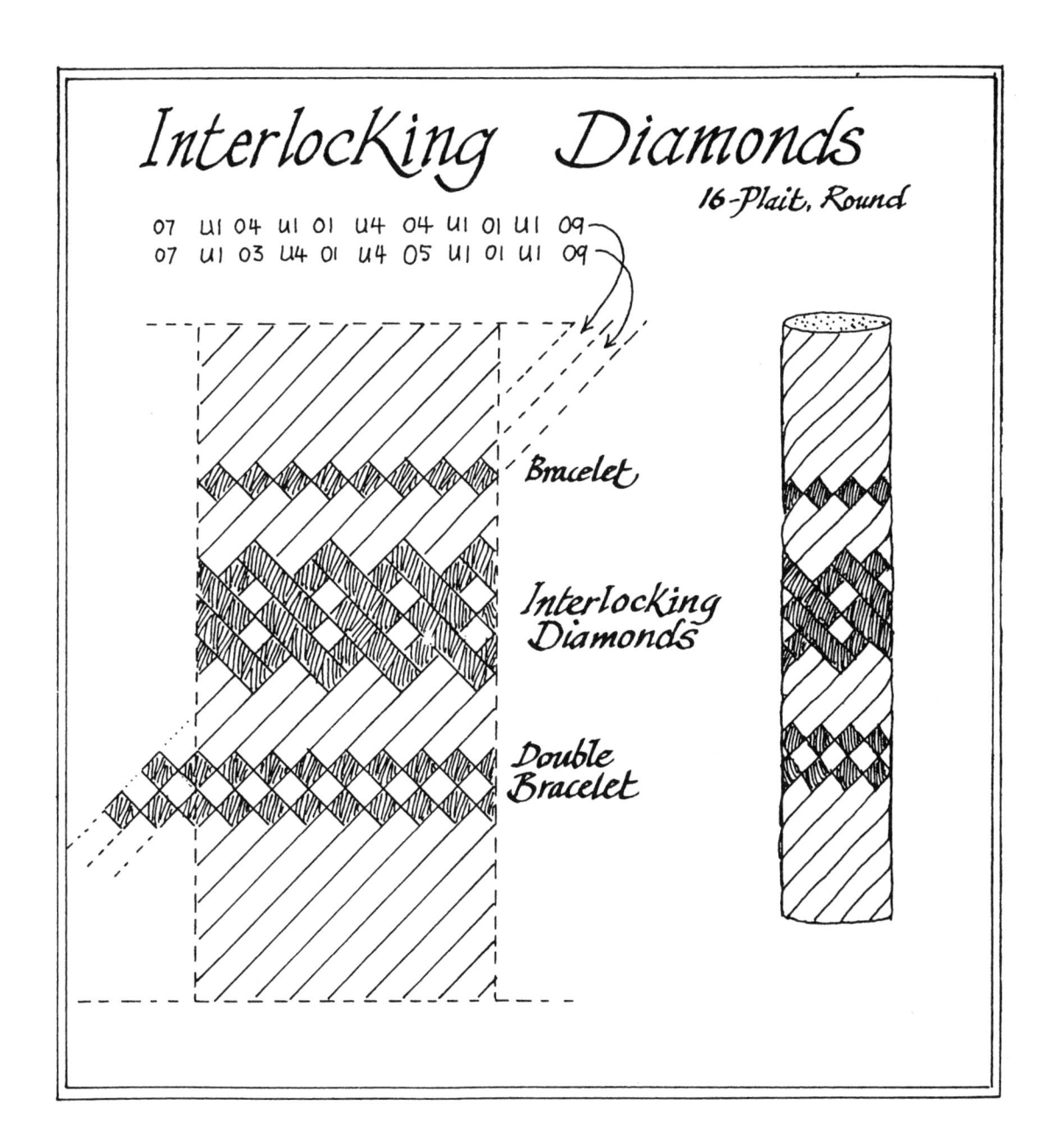

INTERLOCKING DIAMONDS, 16-PLAIT, ROUND

As I mentioned elsewhere, there are two basic methods of plaiting complex patterns on whip handles. One is to hold all the strands in the hands and work down one strand at a time. The other is to first spiral the dark lace around the handle and then work the light lace into this. Beginners will probably find the spiral method the best for designs such as this one, but it can be done quite easily with the ordinary alternate strand method.

The design begins with a bracelet, then interlocking diamonds, and then a double bracelet. You will notice that though the design looks complex, there are in fact only two runs of lace, as given at the top of the drawing that shows the design opened out.

Both runs begin with O7 (over 7) and end with O9 (over 9), but you can alter this to make whatever amount of blank space you need above and below the design.

If you are going to do the design with the alternate strands method you will not need the code given in the drawing, but will work the design out as you go along.

THE SHIP OF THE DEAD

The Ship of the Dead is a very ancient Viking design and has been found engraved on rocks in Scandinavia. To modern eyes it does not really look like anything, but to the ancients it had a lot of supernatural meaning.

There is a fir tree in the center of the boat, for it seems that in ancient ship burials a tree was cut and placed in the boat, and above it is depicted the sun, the symbol of life.

In this drawing the code is given for doing this design by the spiral method, but it can also be done by the alternate strand method as shown in earlier drawings, just working it out as you go.

The drawing at the bottom left shows how it looks when using the alternate strand method (interweaving left and right side strands one after the other), while the drawing next to it shows how it looks when you first spiral down the dark strands.

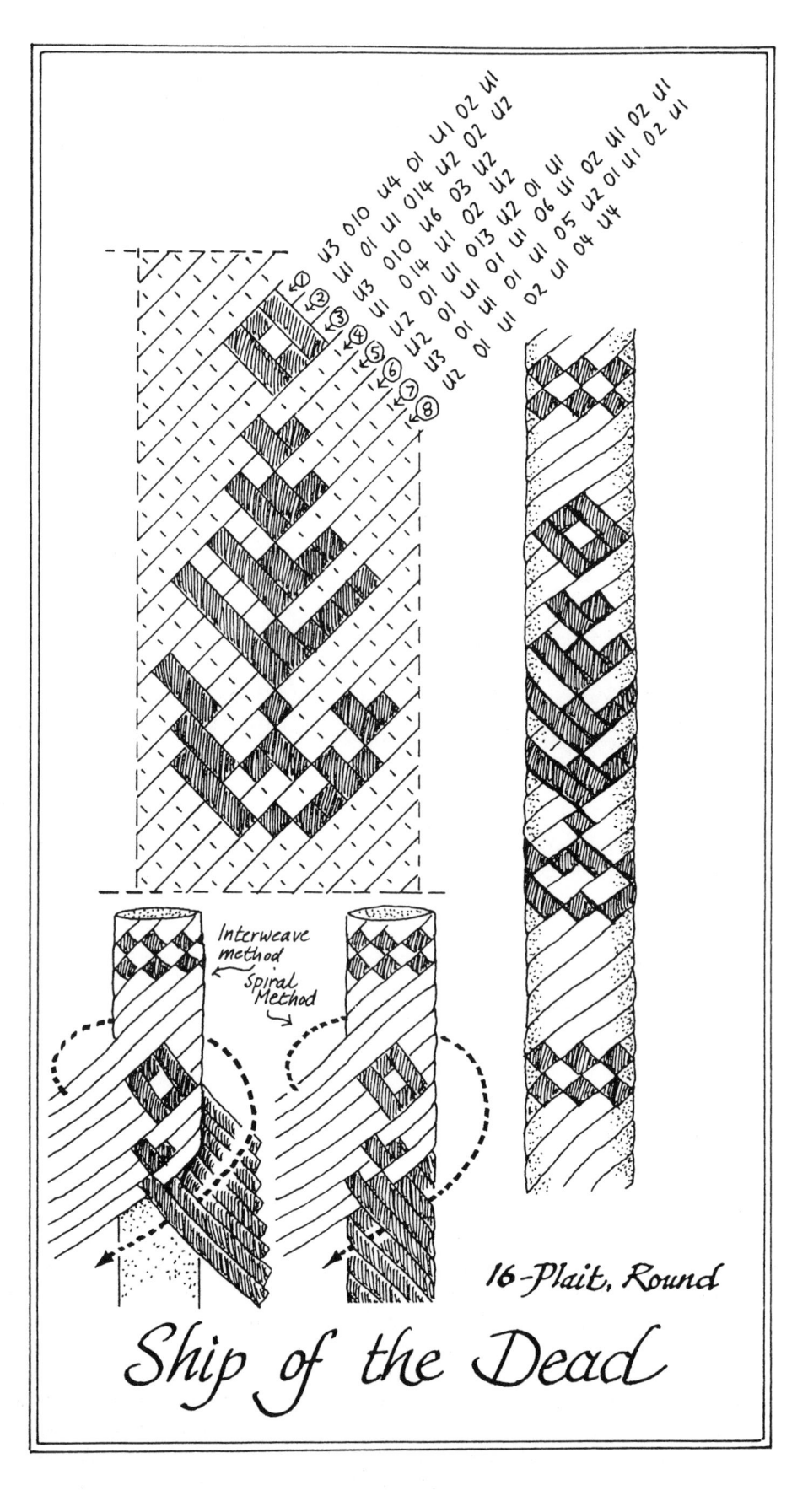

16-Plait, Round

Ship of the Dead

TWO-SEAM PLAIT

Professional whipmaker Peter Clarke used this name for this particular design and it is probably the most appropriate, as there are only two seams in the pattern. As a result, one half of the handle is dark and the other half light.

Although it might look like the cowtail (or whipmaker's plait) shown earlier, it is quite different, as the cowtail divides the handle into four bands of color while this only divides it into two.

It is very simple to do as you can see from the drawings. Each strand simply wraps around the other. However, it is not used by itself all that often, but can be used as the basis on which to plait names in whips.

For instance, I was told that whipmaker Richard Taubman often used this plait and would work dark letters on light on one side of the handle, and at the same time work in the date in light letters on dark on the other side. This requires considerable skill and patience.

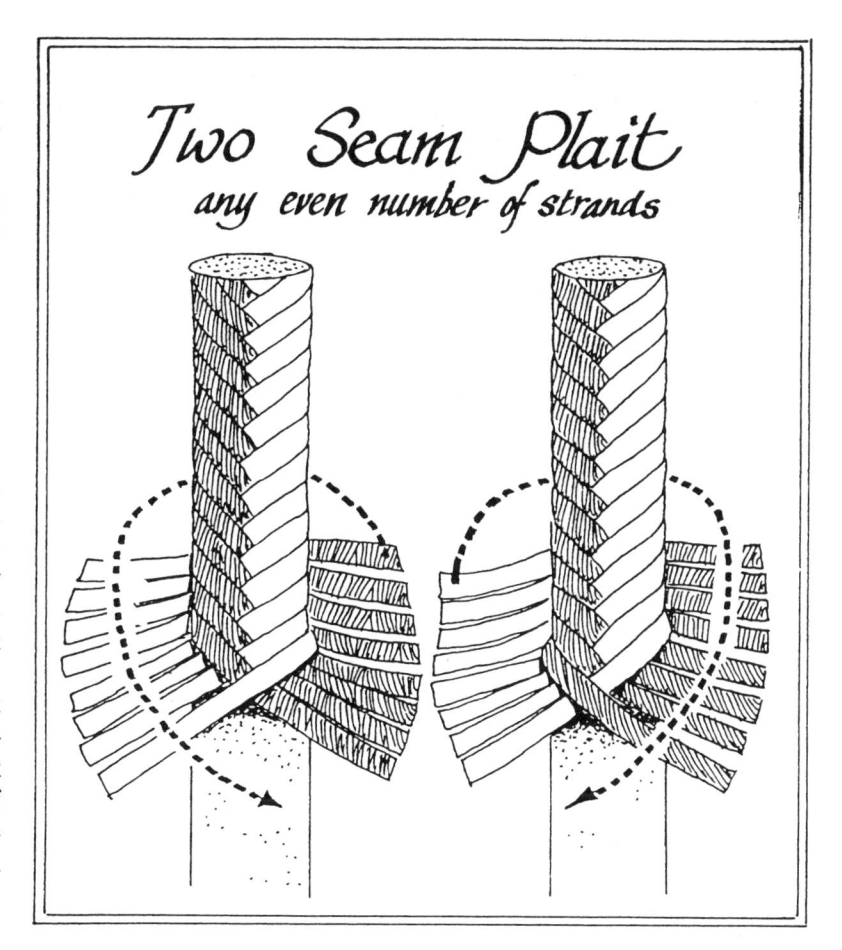

VEE PATTERN, WHIPMAKER'S PLAIT

All the designs in this section shown up to this page have been based on the rule of having all the dark strands in one hand and all the light strands in the other.

However, if you change the pattern in which the strands are laid, then a totally different set of designs can be worked out.

In this example the strands are alternated, one dark, one light, one dark, and so on. When worked in a cowtail (or whipmaker's plait), a series of vees are formed.

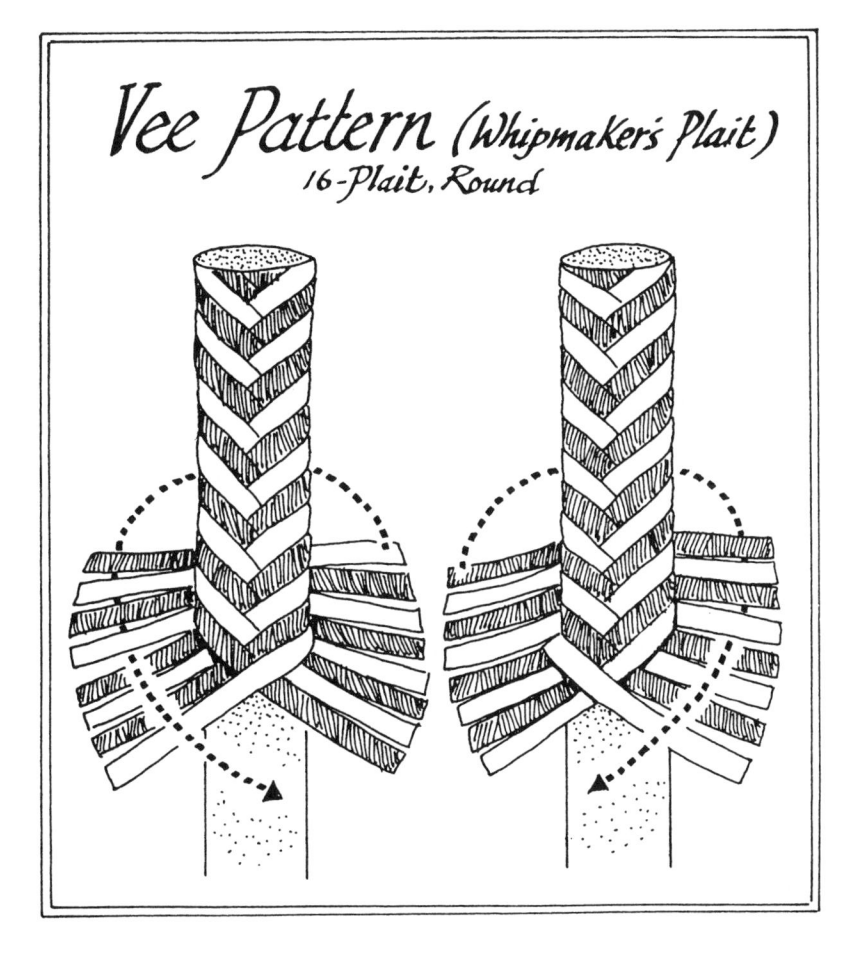

129

The effect of this is unusual, but tends to be a bit too bold, especially if done in dark and light lace. It looks better if done in two tones that are not too far apart, say a light and a middle tan.

The whip in the sketch was made by Eric Fuerst as an experiment and gives a good idea of some of the effects that can be achieved. Note that towards the knob on the handle the strands have been split so that you have a sequence of two light and two dark strands. There is also an experimental zigzag pattern at the thin end of the handle, and the striped effect has also been carried through to the Turk's heads at each end of the handle.

BARBER'S POLE PLAIT

This is the same sequence as the Chessboard Plait, a simple over one, under one sequence, but done with strands of alternating colors instead of having all the dark strands in one hand and all the light strands in the other, as is the usual case.

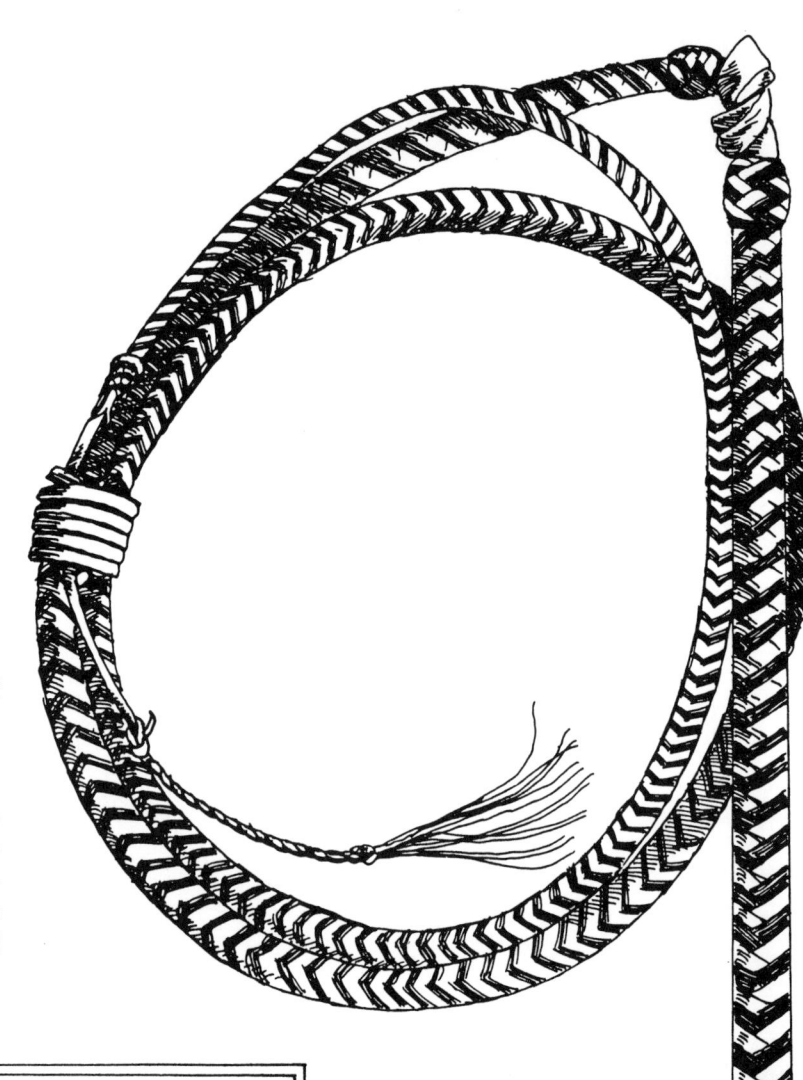

The effect is a spiral from one end of the handle to the other, like that found on a barber's pole. As in the previous design, this is best done with, say, light and dark tan rather than with black and white lace, as the effect can be far too bold if strongly contrasting colors are used.

Barber's Pole Plait
12-Plait, Round

Under 1 - over 1 sequence on both sides

130

Chapter 6
Plaiting Names in Whips

NAME PLAITING

The plaiting of names into the handles of whips represents the highest form of complex braiding, and while there are quite a number of whipmakers who can plait names, there are very few who can do it well. I am not one of these because I simply do not have the patience to do it. But I can do basic name plaiting, and in this section we will look at some of the techniques.

Joining One Pattern to the Next

Name plaiting is usually confined to the handle of the whip (though people have plaited names into thongs), and it is always combined with some of the decorative patterns shown in the previous section.

All the patterns shown in chapter 5 can be combined one with another, but because there are so many possible combinations, it would be impossible to show all the various ways of changing from one design to another. When in doubt, put in a bracelet, or do a band of double diamonds or some other simple pattern. A well-designed whip handle should be planned in advance, and you should try to avoid putting too many different designs on one handle.

It is usual to put a bracelet at either end of a name so that it stands clear of other designs.

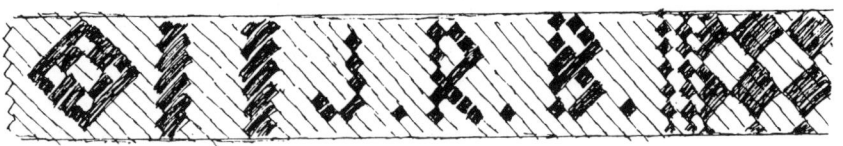

Plaiting Names with Short Pieces

In *Leather Projects 1* I described a simple method of plaiting names into a belt and explained that this method could also be used for a whip handle. The handle is first entirely plaited over with an even layer of plain light strands. Using a fid to open up gaps under the strands, dozens of short lengths of dark lace are then worked into the weave to form the letters, tiny spots of glue helping to fix them in place.

The only problem with this method is that if the article is handled roughly, or if poor glue is used, then parts of the letters can come adrift in time.

For this reason the method is not recommended for whip handles, though I must admit that I have seen quite good work done this way.

Working the Letters into the Weave

The next method is the one used by many of the old-time whipmakers. It is more difficult to do, but the result cannot come loose no matter how the whip is handled.

It can be used on any part of the whip thong or the whip handle, but is nearly always found on the thickest part of the whip handle, as this gives the best display area for the work. This method is not suitable for belts.

I must warn you that this is not for the beginner. You must first be able to plait over 20 strands onto a handle without even thinking about it before you can tackle this work, and you should also be able to handle two-tone pattern plaiting before you move onto name plaiting.

Colors to Use

The colors used are your decision. However, traditionally, jet black and snow white are considered too much of a contrast. In fact, many of the old-timers regarded black-and-white work as a bit flashy, unless it was done with black-and-white horsehair, which is another skill again.

Dark brown and light flesh color are considered to be better looking, but I have also seen beautiful work done with black and deep red.

In November 1990 I visited Burton's Saddlery in Armidale, New South Wales, and John Burton showed me a whip that he said had been made for him by John McMaster of Baringo. This had John Burton's initials worked into the handle, which was of 24 strands, so I did a sketch of it on the spot (shown here) and then later decided to use the same initials to illustrate this method of name plaiting.

First I had to plait up a handle with the same initials in order to show the step-by-step method used. However, I did not want to waste time plaiting up a whole handle and so only did a half handle, finishing it off with a pineapple knot.

I also spiraled the strands in the opposite direction and finished off with some different patterns just to show that you have a lot of variety available in this sort of work. My version is at the top of the page.

Never Believe What You Are Told

Years ago I was told by an old bushman that the method used to calculate the number of strands was to lay them as shown in the first sketch, and then count them.

I believed him, and so did a lot of other people, because I have heard this method talked about quite often. I think that I even wrote about it in one of my books and said that this is how you calculate the strands.

Nonsense! That method is quite wrong and you can easily prove it for yourself, as I should have done all those years ago.

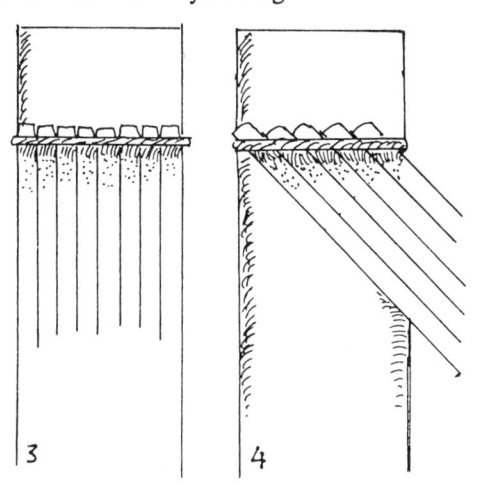

Figs. 3 & 4. Take a few strands and tie them around a handle as shown in figure 3. Go all the way around so that all the wood is covered and then count the strands. Now tie them at an angle as shown in figure 4 and again cover all the wood, and you will see that you need far less.

I tried this experiment around the timber that I was going to plait over. When I hung the strands down as in figure 3 it took 16 strands to cover the timber. When I put it on the diagonal it took only 12 to cover it.

However, this did not mean that I would be working a 12-plait. Think about it for a minute: in all plaited work you always have one strand going over the top of another. In other words, the work is always 2 strands thick. So in this case it would take not 16, not 12, but twice 12, which is 24, to do the job.

In name plaiting the rule is that the finer the lace, the better the letters will be. Twenty-plait is okay—24 is better. The most common and convenient numbers for this sort of work are the multiples of 4; that is, 20, 24, or 28. If necessary, you could use 16, and if you are very good at this sort of work you could go up to 32.

Fig. 5. To give you an idea of how fine plaiting compares with less fine, have a look at figure 5. The vertical stroke of the left-hand B is made up of 4 diamonds, one on top of the other. The next B has a vertical stroke of 5 diamonds and is a little better. The right-hand B is worked with lace twice as fine as the others and, as a result, the finished letter is very much better and is 10 diamonds high. However, for most practical whip work, the middle example is the most useful.

When making a whip handle it is customary to begin at the keeper end and do some patterns first, then the letters, and then some more patterns. Even if you are only practicing with the method, it would be best to do some ordinary chessboard-type patterns first, in order to get everything locked in place around the handle.

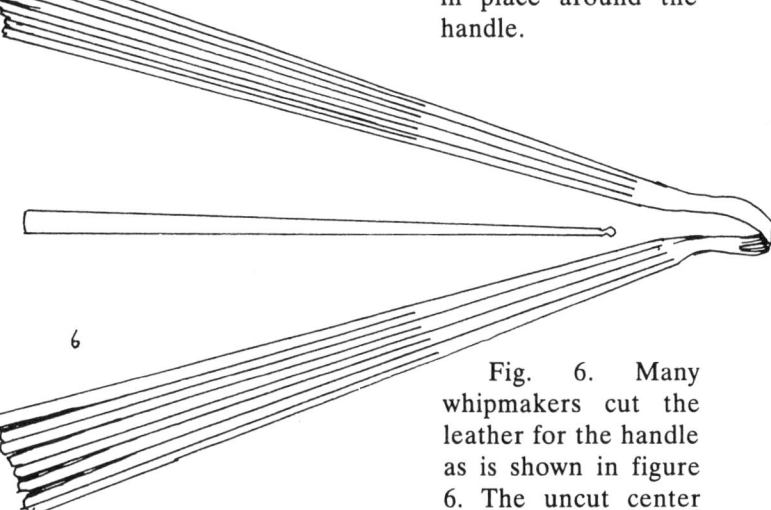

Fig. 6. Many whipmakers cut the leather for the handle as is shown in figure 6. The uncut center section forms the keeper of the whip and they then begin plaiting with an 8-plait. As the handle gets thicker, this changes to a 16-plait, and it is at this end that the name plaiting takes place.

For two-color work one end of the leather is stained a dark color before the plaiting begins, using a good, permanent leather stain.

If you are using this method, ignore the next section and go on to figure 14.

Using Precut Lace

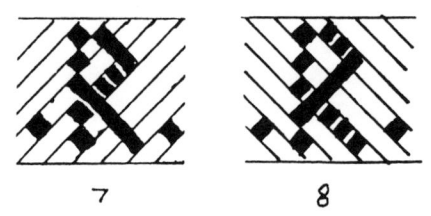

If you are using precut lace, as I have done in this example, you have two choices. The first is to tie the individual strands around the handle—a slow and often annoying job (but then name plaiting cannot really be described as laugh-a-minute work). The second choice is to use the chessboard start.

Fig. 7. If following the first choice, begin by tying the dark lace to the handle. When this is spiraled around the handle diagonally it should entirely cover the timber and at the same time not overlap itself anywhere.

The direction is which it winds does not matter—it can go to the left or right. Figures 7–8 show the same letter worked into lace, the first spiraling in the opposite direction to the second. Note that the final shape of the letters is exactly the same in both drawings, even though there are slight differences in the construction.

Having attached the dark lace, you now tie on light lace in the same way, but this time they will go in opposite directions as you form the letters.

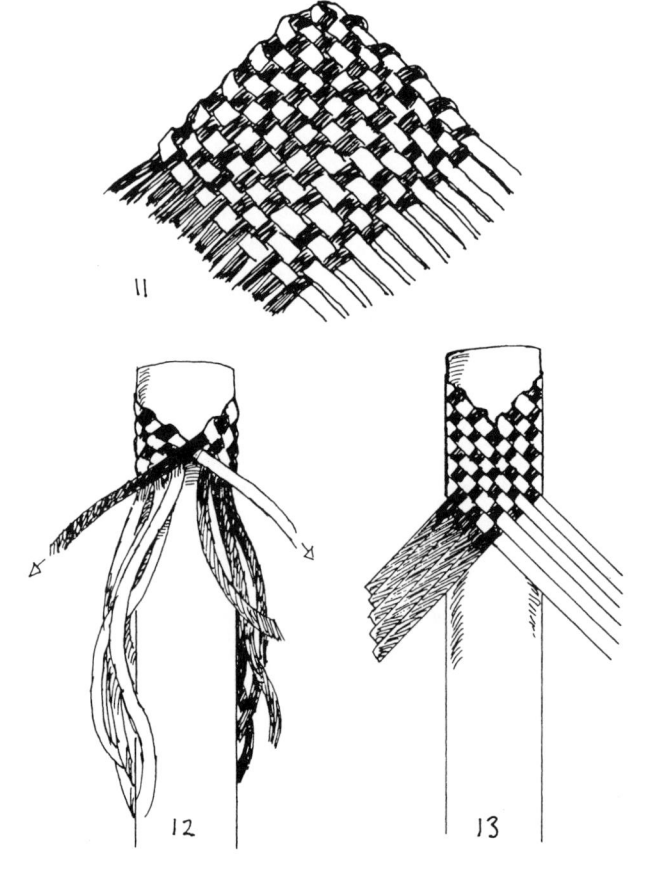

Chessboard Start: Calculating the Length of the Lace

Keeping to a 45-degree angle, spiral a length of lace all the way down the handle in order to calculate how long each lace will need to be. Add a little to be on the safe side. (But do not forget that the chessboard pattern is made up of pairs of laces, so cut accordingly).

Fig. 10. If you find that tying on the lace is a problem (and it can be), then here is a simpler method. First hold the lace in your hand and make a chessboard pattern start as shown, just as if you were beginning a belt. Keep on doing this until you have enough to wrap around the handle.

Fig. 11. For my example I used an extra-thick handle and so ended up with 24 strands as shown, but you may get by quite well with 16 strands.

Fig. 12. Just keep building up the plait until it reaches right around the handle and meets without either gap or overlap.

Fig. 13. When the plaiting meets around the back, begin to work each strand in so that the plaiting becomes a complete unit, as shown in figure 13. Before going any further take a good look at the job. If there are any gaps, you may need to undo it and add in extra lace. However, if the work begins to get too crowded, then you may have to remove some strands. It is best to do this right now rather than have problems later on.

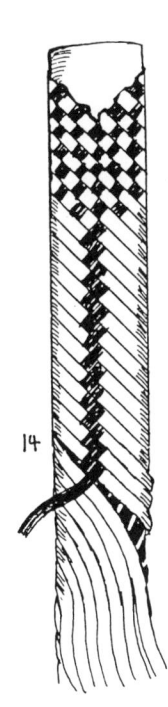

Locking the Back

Fig. 14. If you are working on a wide handle it may be that you will find it best to interlock the black and white laces on the reverse side to the name plaiting; otherwise, the white laces can ride up on each other with rough usage.

The type of interlocking pattern you use is your choice. The one I have shown here is about the most simple. This is not all done at one time but progressively, as the letters are worked into the front section.

Working in the Letters

Figs. 15–21 show how the letters are worked in. In my drawings the strands are shown all neatly sitting together in groups, but in reality it is nothing like that at all and more like a can of worms. But this is the only way to draw it so that it can be understood.

Fig. 15. The white strand goes under one black strand. This forms the top of the letter J.

Fig. 16. The white strand goes under two of the black strands, thus forming the start of the lower hook of the letter J.

You must fully understand how you are going to form the letters before you begin to do them, otherwise you will be forever picking out the work and doing it again. For instance, first have a look at the alphabet (figure 26) and you will see how the loop of the J is formed at the same time as you are working in the main down stroke.

Fig. 17. Now you can see the J beginning to be formed.

Fig. 18. The J is now formed, and at the same time as you complete it the next letter is begun.

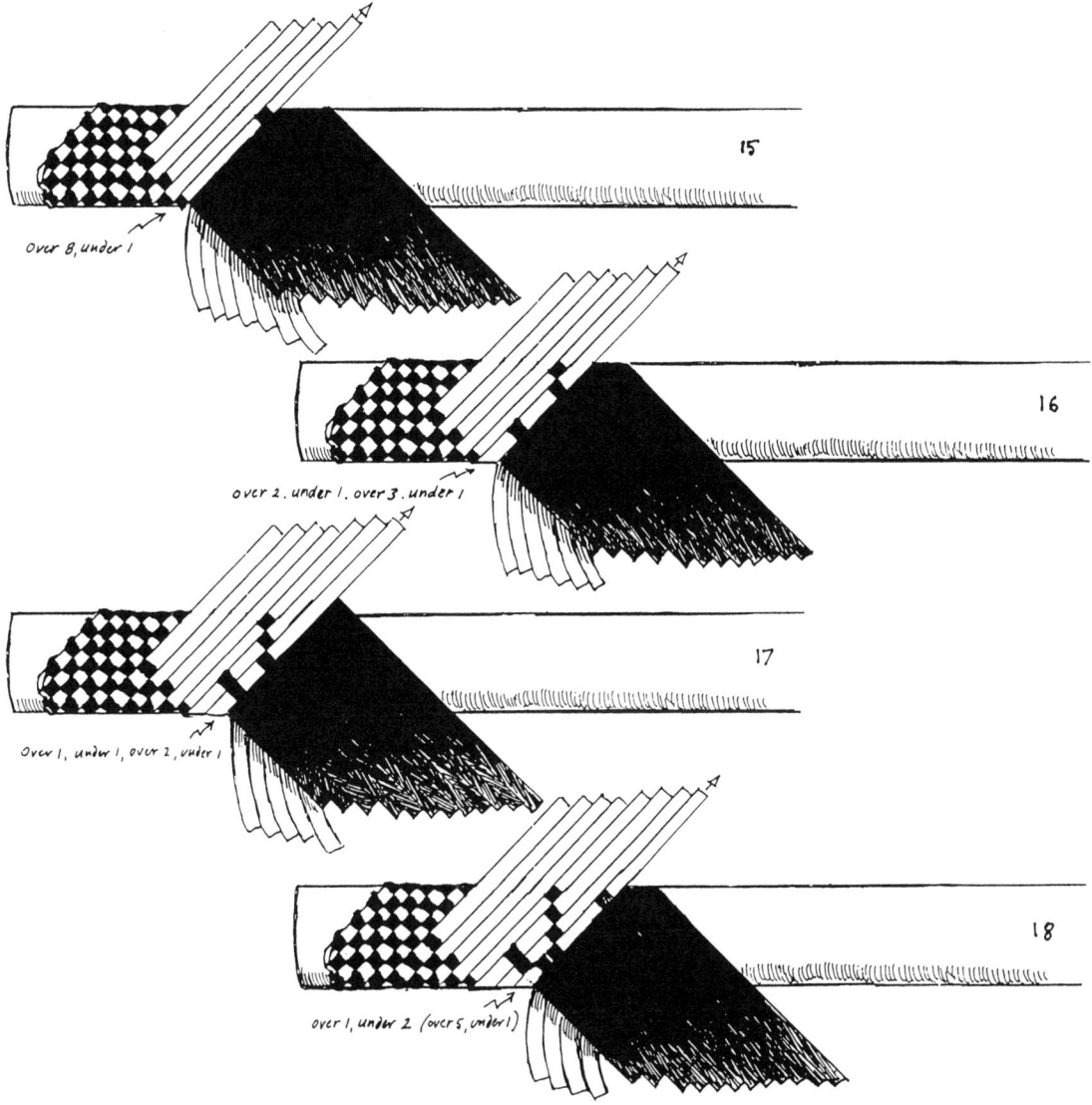

Fig. 19. This is the start of the letter R.

Fig. 20. The letter R is complete and the shaded section shows how the B is begun.

Fig. 21. B is complete and some decoration has begun. This is simple. Take the white strand under 1, over 1, under 1.

Fig. 22 shows how it looks when completed.

Fig. 23. The next band is also simple: under 1, over 1, under 1, over 1, under 1.

Fig. 24. The wider band is made by taking the white strand under 3, over 1, under 1, over 1, under 3.

Fig. 25. Once you have covered as much of the handle as you wish, tie some twine around the end of the strands and trim them off neatly. But before trimming make sure all the letters are as neat and as straight as possible. You might have to spend some time getting everything in just the right position, but this is time well spent.

Turn the whip over and look at the back; the black line that runs down it (fig. 14) should be straight. If it is not straight, then your letters cannot be straight.

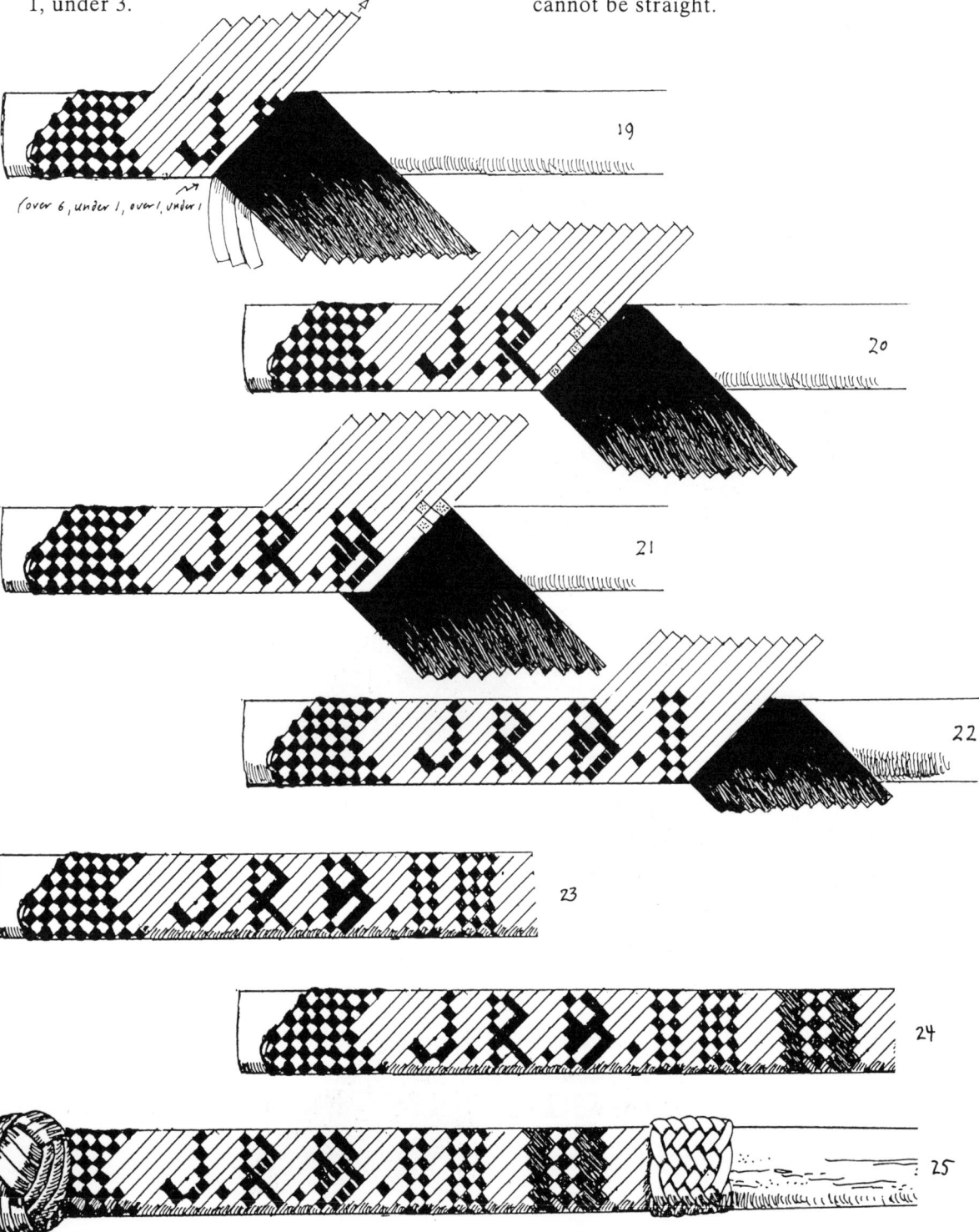

Having got everything straight and worked tight, the end of the handle can be covered with a Turk's head (page 81) and the end of the plaiting covered with a pineapple knot (page 96).

Rub the handle with something smooth, such as a piece of bone. This will push down any slight bumps and also burnish the leather. Then give it a clear leather dressing or a couple of good coats of shellac.

Fig. 26. Here is an alphabet to work from—this one is 5 diamonds high. A smaller alphabet, 4 diamonds high, may be found in *Leather Projects 2* in the section on how to plait letters using small scraps of lace.

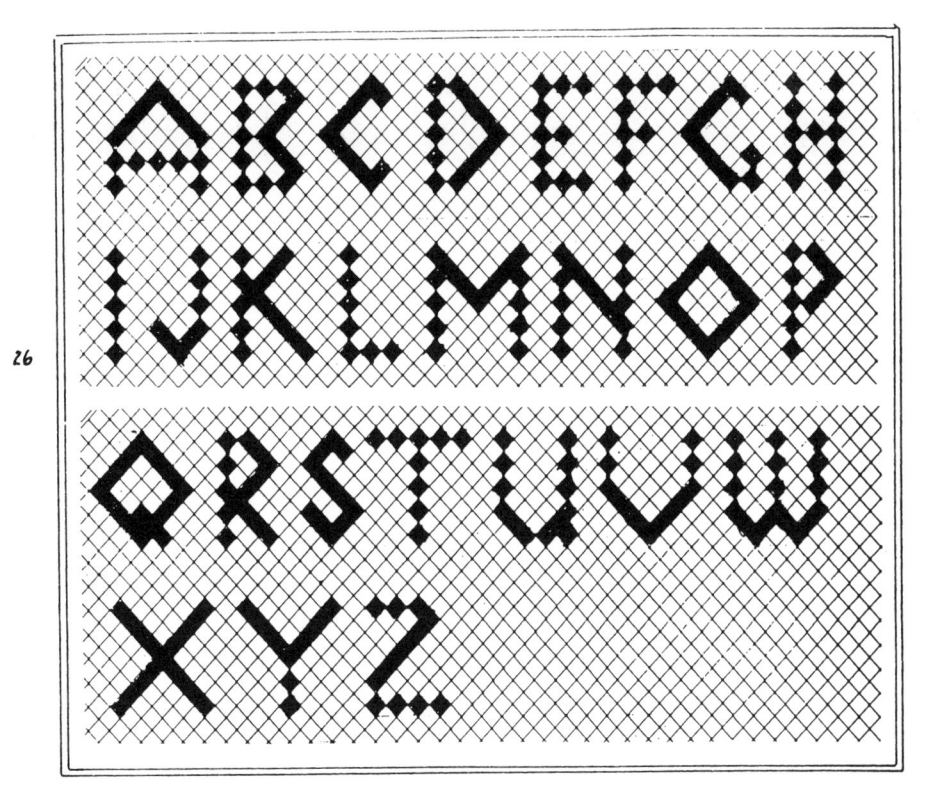

White-on-Black Letters

For the purposes of these examples I am talking about having black lettering on a white background. It is just as easy to have white lettering on a black background; you just begin by reversing the instructions given above and attach the light layer first.

Vertical and Horizontal Letters

Figs. 27–28. The same skill is required to produce letters that can be read when the handle is held upright, as in figure 27, rather than on its side, as in figure 28. It is just a question of planning.

Name plaiting is all about planning. You must think in terms of just one letter at a time. In fact, for the beginner, it is probably better to think in terms of just one stroke at a time even though this will mean a slower job.

Glen Denholm of Cobbity, New South Wales, finds it easier to work the letters so that they are read when the handle is held vertically, as in figure 27, rather than placing them so that they are read when the handle is horizontal, which is the more common practice.

Technically, there is really no difference in the way the letters are formed, but the advantage seems to be that when you are plaiting the handle it is pointing away from your body, and so the letters are easier to read while you are forming them.

Fig. 29. As an example I decided to work the word CAIRNS into a whip handle, as that is where we have our saddlery. It was not until I had plaited in CAIN that I realized something was going wrong!

I have illustrated just the beginning of plaiting to give an idea of the method (not to demonstrate my bad spelling). The white strand is the next to be brought around, and then the top black one will follow.

Letters can be plaited in by the spiral method as shown in this chapter or by the alternate strands method explained in chapter 5, whichever you feel happier with. Having tried out a variety of methods of plaiting names, I think that the best for the beginner is to spiral the dark strands around the handle first.

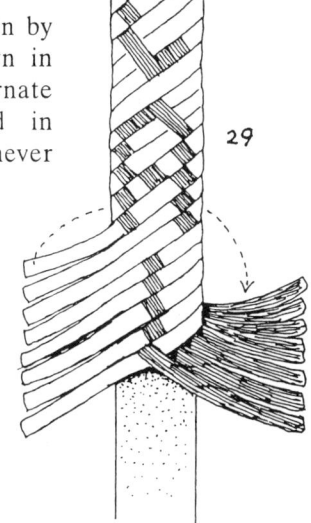

PLAITING LONG WORDS

The photograph above, not a very good one, is of a whip handle that I worked up with the word Australia on it. Because the handle is round and the photo is flat, the bottom part of the letters cannot be seen in this illustration.

Plaiting two or three letters into a whip handle can be done in the course of ordinary plaiting work, without any special preparations, but if you want to do long words it might be worthwhile making up a rack to hold the handle while you do the work.

You will discover the reason for the rack if you try and do long words without one. Maybe some experienced plaiters can work in letters without having the handle held firmly in some way, but a learner needs all the help he or she can get. The rack allows you to lay the words out carefully and lessens the chances of them slipping out of position whenever you have to stop for a minute and let the job go.

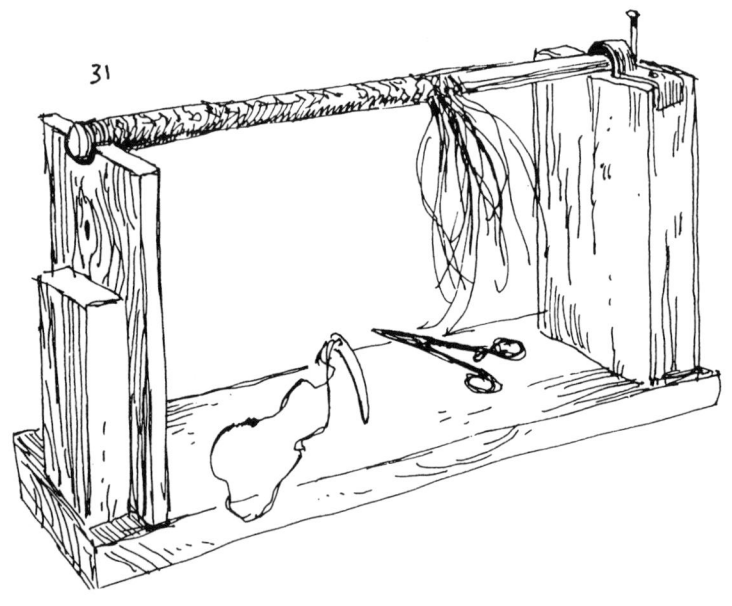

With a rack it is easier to carefully lay out the mass of strands that you will be working with, and so keep both your hands and mind much freer to sit quietly and work out the job one step at a time.

My rack is quite primitive, knocked together quickly from some scrap timber that was lying around the workshop. The dimensions do not matter; you just make it up to fit the job in hand.

I have a groove for the handle in the left-hand end, and a hoop iron loop in the right end, but you could have a groove in each end or a loop in each end—it does not matter.

Because you pull to the right end, there is a nail sticking up there so that the whip handle cannot move in that direction.

For the person who intends to do a lot of handle plaiting, it might be worthwhile building a more substantial clamp, as shown further on.

Setting Out

Planning is important in doing long words. Rather than calculating as you go along, it is a better idea to draw out the word on a piece of squared paper. Graph paper can be easily bought, but I rule up the paper myself to the right size. I do this in ink and then write in the letters in pencil; that way I can rub them out later and use the squared paper for the next job.

(Of course, experts who do a lot of this work have no need to plan it ahead like this. They can work out in their head where each strand will go. But such skill takes years to master, and the beginner is advised to make as much preparation as possible. In the long run it will be found to be quicker this way).

One advantage of having the design on graph paper will be seen when you have finished one letter and move on to the next, because it is often difficult to know exactly where the next one is to begin. By consulting the graph paper you can work it out.

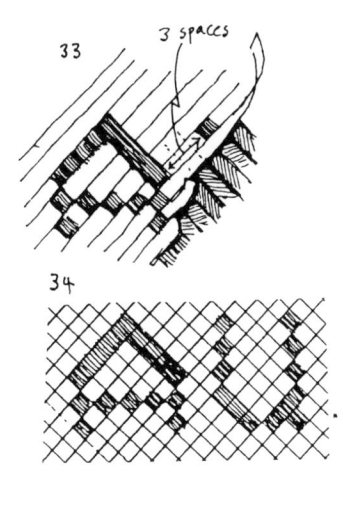

Fig. 33. For instance, say you have finished the A in my example and want to know where to begin the U.

Fig. 34. If you look along the diagonal line from the top of the U, you will see that it begins 3 strands away from the sloping stroke of the A.

Although an expert will be doing parts of the next letter as he completes the first one, the beginner is advised to do just one letter at a time; it is a little slower but easier.

Amount Needed

For the sample I chose a cane handle 18-mm in diameter. In order to cover this I needed 24 strands of 3-mm lace. The strands were each 700 mm long because I was only covering three-quarters of the handle; a full handle would need strands over a meter long. Twelve of the strands were dark tan, the other 12 natural.

Because I was using precut lace, I did not taper the handle where the word was going to go. Had the handle been tapered at this section, the lace would also have had to be tapered down.

It takes a long time to plait in a word like this. When you have the word completed, it is a good idea to tie a string around the ends of the lace to hold everything firm and then carefully work all the strands tight, at the same time making sure that the letters are in line.

When the job is finished and everything is firm, tie the ends down permanently and then cover them with a Turk's head, as shown on page 81.

Try to smooth down the surface as much as possible. One way to do this is to bone it. A beef rib makes a good bone, or you can shape one from a shoulder bone. Rubbing the leather firmly with a bone, a piece of heavy plastic, or even the back of a spoon will smooth it down as well as giving it a gloss.

After doing this give it a few coats of shellac to get a good smooth finish. Shellac can be bought in hardware shops and is mixed with methylated spirits. Apply it with a piece of cloth and give several thin coats rather than one heavy coat.

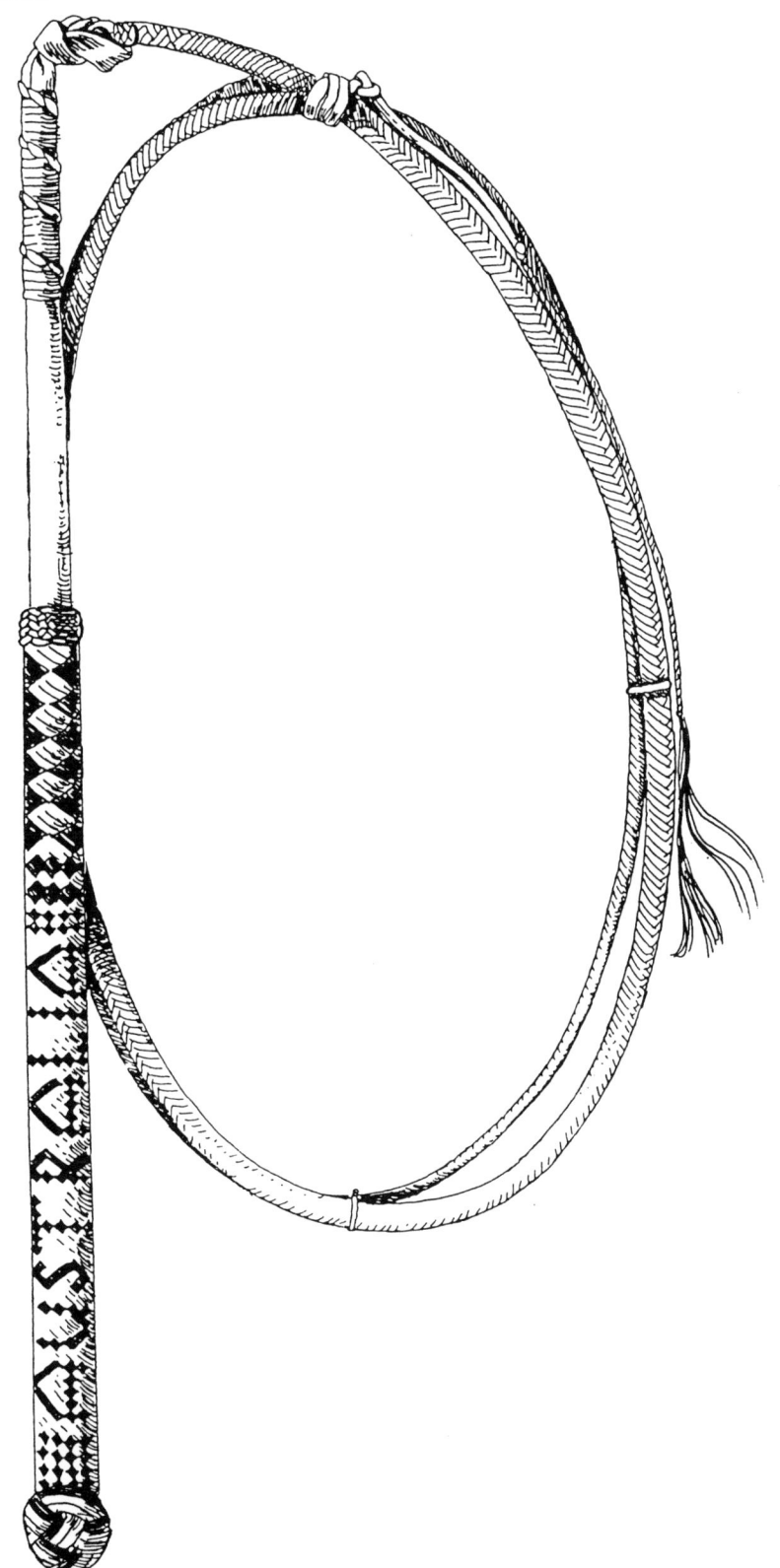

WHIP HANDLE CLAMP

I saw this clamp in an old photograph and decided to build one for myself. The principle is simple, and the same idea was used by coopers to hold barrel staves in position while they shaped them. It has a great advantage over a vice, in that the pressure can instantly be removed and applied again just as quickly, and this is a great help when working complex patterns in whip handles where it may often be necessary to turn the job around.

For the normal standard patterns found on most whips, this clamp would not justify the effort required to build it, and such clamps were probably only used by professionals in the old days when very complicated patterns were regularly worked on handles. But even a modern whipmaker would find it handy when plaiting names into whips, and I find it a help when plaiting up plain handles for whips.

You use your feet to apply pressure on the clamp, and very little pressure is needed to hold a whip handle firmly in place. By moving the feet back a little the clamp is opened and the work can be removed.

The sketch shows Susie Serletto, who was assistant editor of *The Australian Whipmaker's Journal* at the time, working on a whip handle. You will notice that the clamp also encloses a small container, which is handy for storing gear needed for the job.

I made the pivot arms by finding a curved branch of the right shape on a dead tree. This was then adzed so that it was rectangular in section, and I then sawed it from end to end so as to make two identical curved pieces.

This was a long-winded process and I would not recommend it to anyone, though I rather liked the finished effect. It would be much more convenient to construct the angled arm by using a few milled lengths of timber, or cutting it out of marine plywood.

The angled legs of the stool have to be well-braced, as they are subject to considerable pressure when you sit down and, as the clamp is a working tool, the whole construction has to be robust.

There is no need to copy this design carefully; once you understand the principle you can simply adjust and alter it to suit your own style of work.

In the sketch you will notice a bit of a jumble of stuff on the stool directly below where the whip handle is sitting. This is used to adjust the distance between the sliding and the fixed part of the clamp.

This is rather a complex answer to the problem, and you may be able to work out a more simple way of fixing the sliding piece. I designed this to make use of the two holes that were already in the seat and which otherwise take the stitching pony.

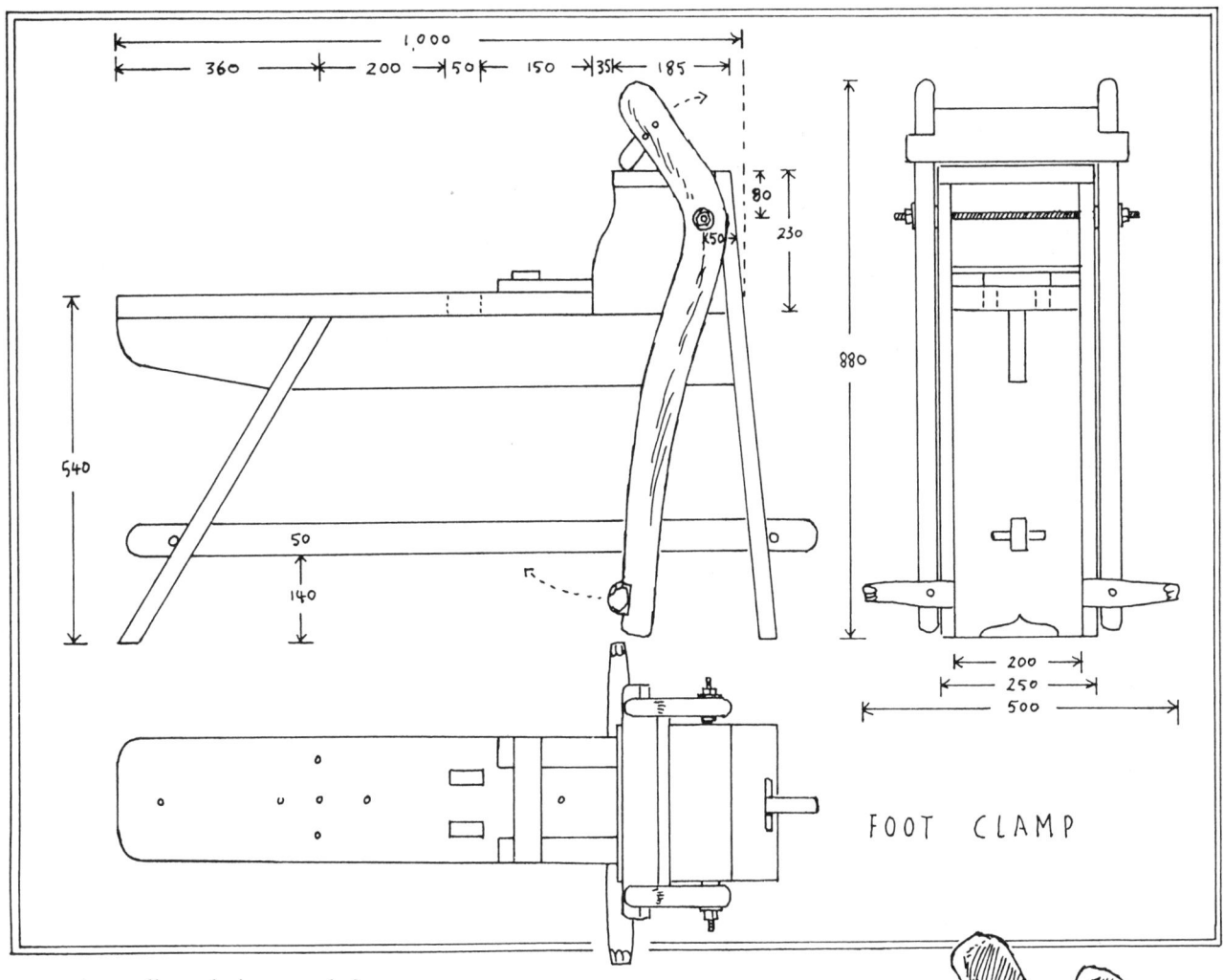

As well as being used for making whip handles, the stool can also be used as a stitching stool, as explained below. The clamp is of course not used for plaiting the thong of the whip, as it is not designed to take the considerable amount of pulling required for that part of the work.

However, by fixing a hook onto a convenient spot, it could also be used for this purpose.

STITCHING STOOL

Most old-time saddlers used a full-length saddler's clamp to hold their work while they were stitching it. This is still the best method, as it allows the work to be held at an angle that best suits the work, so that the saddler is looking down at the face side of the stitching.

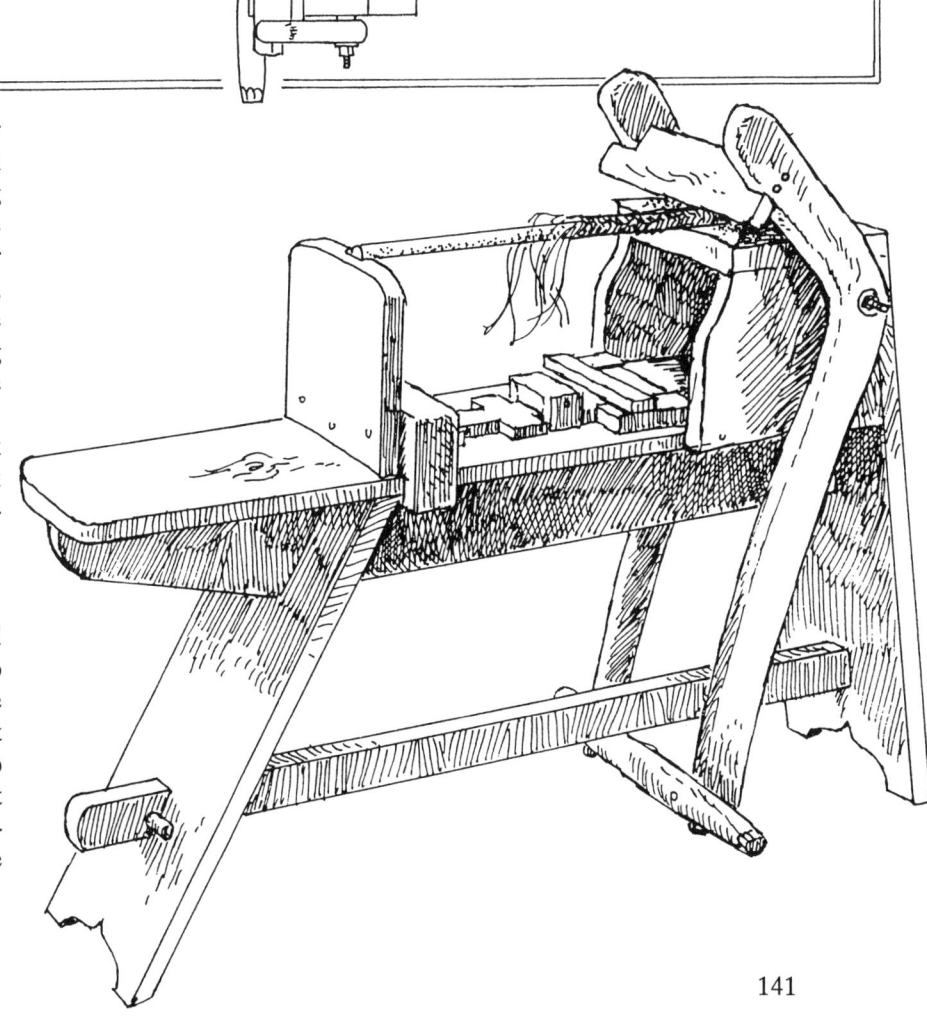

The fixed, vertical stitching pony holds the work upright and so is not so convenient; however, it is useful for certain types of work, and it is not hard to make one that will fit onto the clamp stool described here. This turns the stool into a useful all-round leather working stool.

The stitching pony is made from two lengths of timber held together by a length of threaded rod. When the pony is needed, it is dropped into two holes in the stool and is then ready for use. When you wish to use the whip handle clamp, the pony is simply lifted from its holes and put away.

For ease of use the threaded rod should be fitted with wing nuts. I did not have any of these and so brazed a couple of short lengths of rod onto ordinary nuts. This only takes a few minutes (if you have the gear) and works just as well.

It is best to make the pony out of hardwood and plane it well so that it will not mark the leather. The measurements given suit me, but you can adjust them as you wish.

On my stool I have also fitted a couple of leather loops so that the traditional saddler's clamp is close at hand and can be reached without getting up.

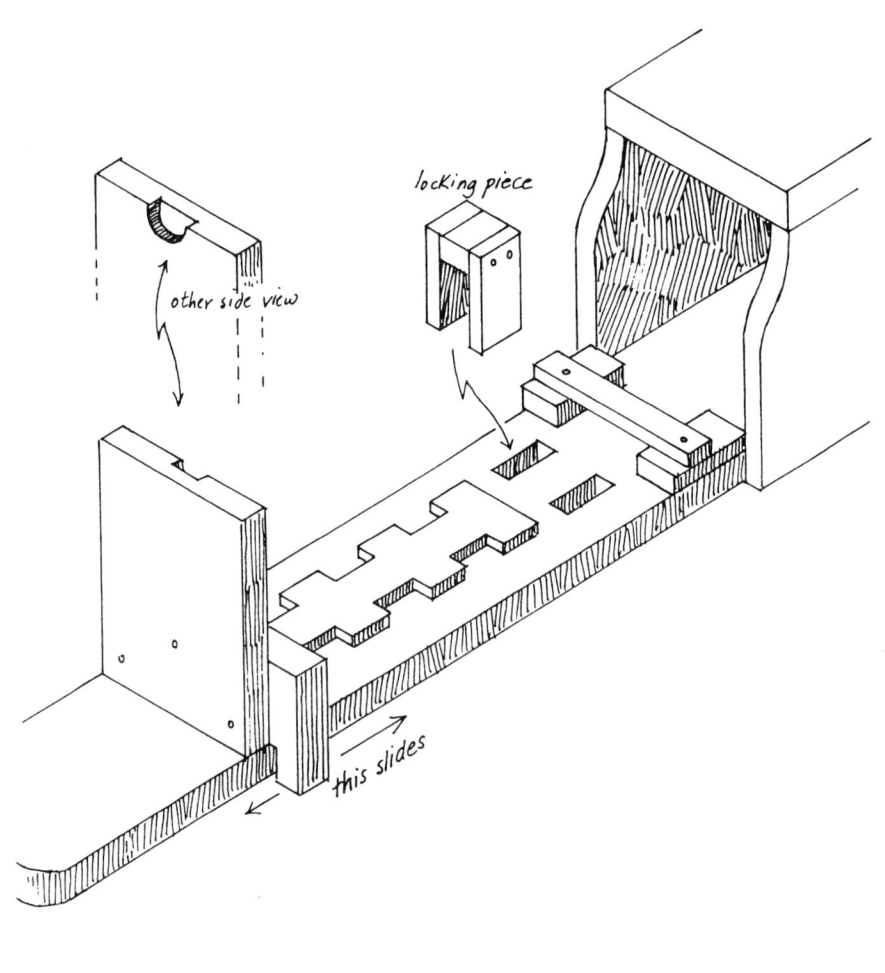

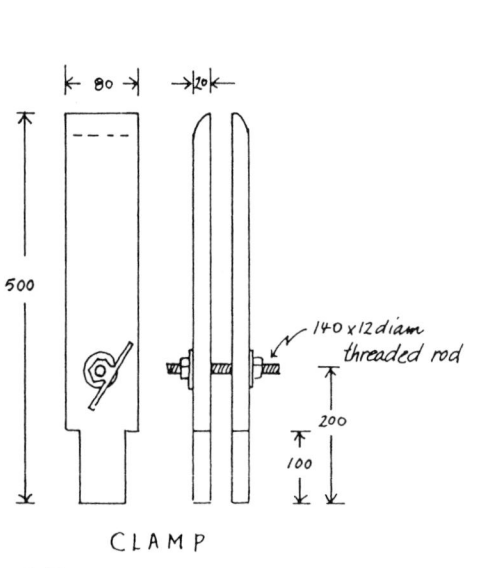

CLAMP

142

Chapter 7

Some Useful Tips

MAKING A WHIP WITH BOUGHT LACE

Because of the complexity of their shape, whips are usually cut from a kangaroo hide, with the strands being cut to a long taper. However, for a person who wishes to make a whip and cannot obtain a hide, it is possible to make one with bought precut lace, obtainable from leather-craft shops or saddlers.

This is not to be recommended for a number of reasons, not the least of which is that the plaiting is more complicated and precut lace is more expensive than cutting your own. Also, it cannot be tapered, so a different technique for making the whip must be used than that described in chapter 2.

However, I have had phone calls over the years from a number of people who have made whips from precut lace simply because that is all that was available. One caller told me that he was a chauffeur and often had long periods of waiting around. Making whips with precut lace suited him because he could carry the work around in a small bag, work on it whenever the opportunity came, and put it away quickly when a call to work came.

So, reluctantly, I will pass on some hints on making a whip this way. We will assume that you cannot obtain any leather at all apart from the precut lace.

If you are patient and willing to critically examine the work at every stage, it is possible to make quite a good looking whip with nothing but bought lace.

The Belly

The belly is made using the widest available lace. First make a core. This is the foundation around which the belly will be plaited, so it should be as firm and dense as you can make it.

The Core. Take two strands of lace. One strand should be the finished length of the whip (about 2.3 meters) and the other about 1.5 meters long. Put a short taper at the handle end, 60 mm will do, but gradually taper the other end down from about the halfway point. Do this with both strands.

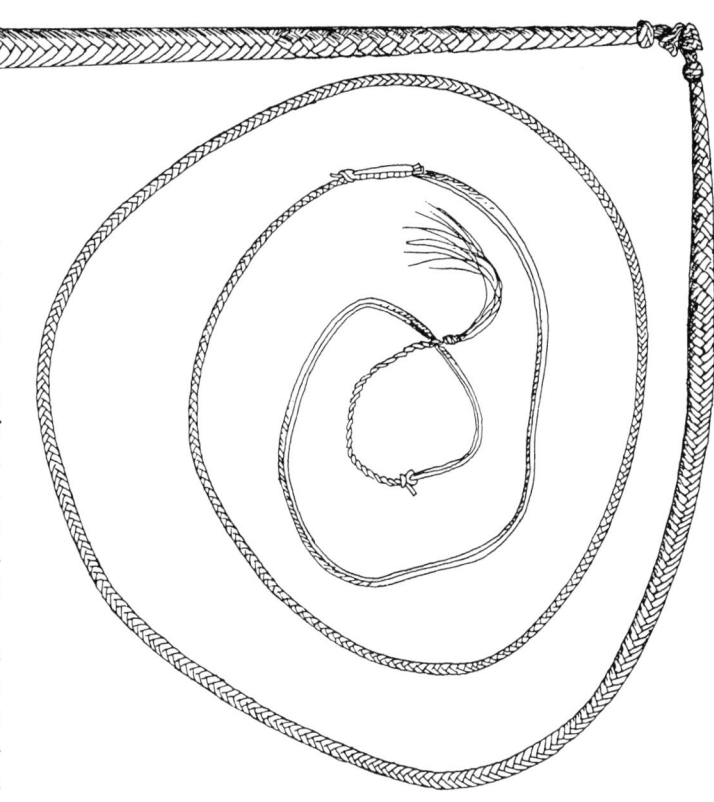

Wet both strands and then roll them under a piece of wood together until they form a single solid core. It may be necessary to tie them together with short lengths of cotton to keep them together while you plait around them, removing the ties as the plaiting covers the core.

Add another strand if the core is not wide enough for you. It is usually about 2 mm in diameter at the thickest part, but you may prefer to have it 3 mm or even more; it all depends on the amount of body in the lace that you are using for the whip.

Covering the Core

If your lace is wide enough, it should be possible now to cover this core with a 4-plait. For this you will need only 2 strands doubled over. Thin the strands in the middle so that the plaiting will be narrow at the start. Taper the ends of the strands.

143

The plaiting continues for about half the length of the whip (about 1 meter), with the core hanging out for the rest of the length. The 4 strands should have been tapered well so that there is no sudden change where the plaiting finishes; it should be one smooth taper for the whole length of the job.

Use fine thread to tie the ends of the 4 strands to the core. Take a good look at the shape of the belly, especially at the section where the plaiting finishes. It sometimes takes time to get a good tapered shape at this point, but it is important to do so, as the finished shape of the whip depends on the shape of the belly.

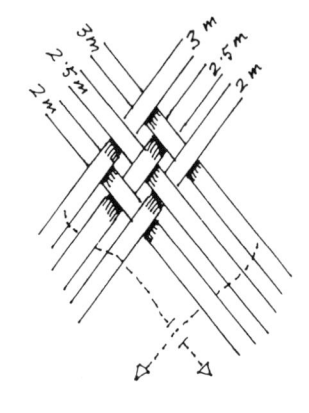

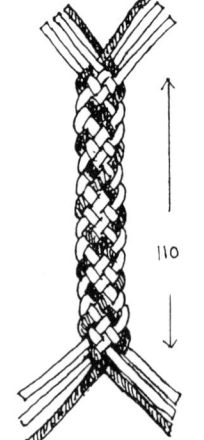

The Overlay, Quantity Needed

4.5 meter lace was used.

For the whip in the illustration I cut 2 strands each 6 meters long, 2 strands each 4 meters long, and 2 strands each 3.5 meters long.

When plaited up this made a thong 2.2 meters long.

In previous editions of *Whipmaking Book 2* I suggested using a scrap of kangaroo leather for the keeper and binding it on. However, this always creates a weak spot in the whip, and also goes against the idea of being able to make the whole thing with precut lace.

So in order to create the maximum strength at this important part of the whip, I am suggesting a rather unorthodox way to make the keeper (but this fits in with the idea of making a whip entirely from precut lace, which is unorthodox in itself).

The two 6-meter strands were folded in the middle, and the two 4-meter strands were also folded in the middle. The other two strands were then folded as shown in the illustration, at the 2.5-meter mark. This created a tapered set of strands and so saved later wastage as the whip narrowed.

Plaiting the Keeper

Plait the middle section together with an ordinary flat 6-plait. Begin by laying out the strands with the two longest ones in the center and the shortest on the outside.

Begin plaiting about 60 mm off to one side of the center point, as you want the middle of this plaiting to be the center. Plait for about 110 mm and put a temporary tie at one end until you get the next step started.

It is important to finish this bit of plaiting at the point where the 2 longest strands are again the middle. In the drawing I have shaded the 2 long strands so that you can see where they start and finish.

Because this whip is made from precut lace, there is no reason why you cannot use more than one color in the job, and a lot of interesting patterns can be created by doing this.

If you wish to experiment it is also possible to use some of the patterns shown in chapter 5, but for a first whip I would advise keeping it as plain as possible.

Round 12-Plait

(See next page for the illustrations.) Fold the plaited section over and begin a round 12-plait. This has to go around the belly, and for a start you may find it difficult to hold the belly in place until the overlay begins to cover it. Once the plaiting has begun the belly will be no problem, but getting it in place right at the start is always a trick. I would suggest that you do the first seven steps shown and then push the belly into place before tightening up all the strands.

Fig. 1. The back of the job should be laid out the same as the front, with 3 strands sticking out each way. Take the upper one on the right (as you look at the job) and bring it across as shown.

Beginning 12-Plait with Plaited Keeper

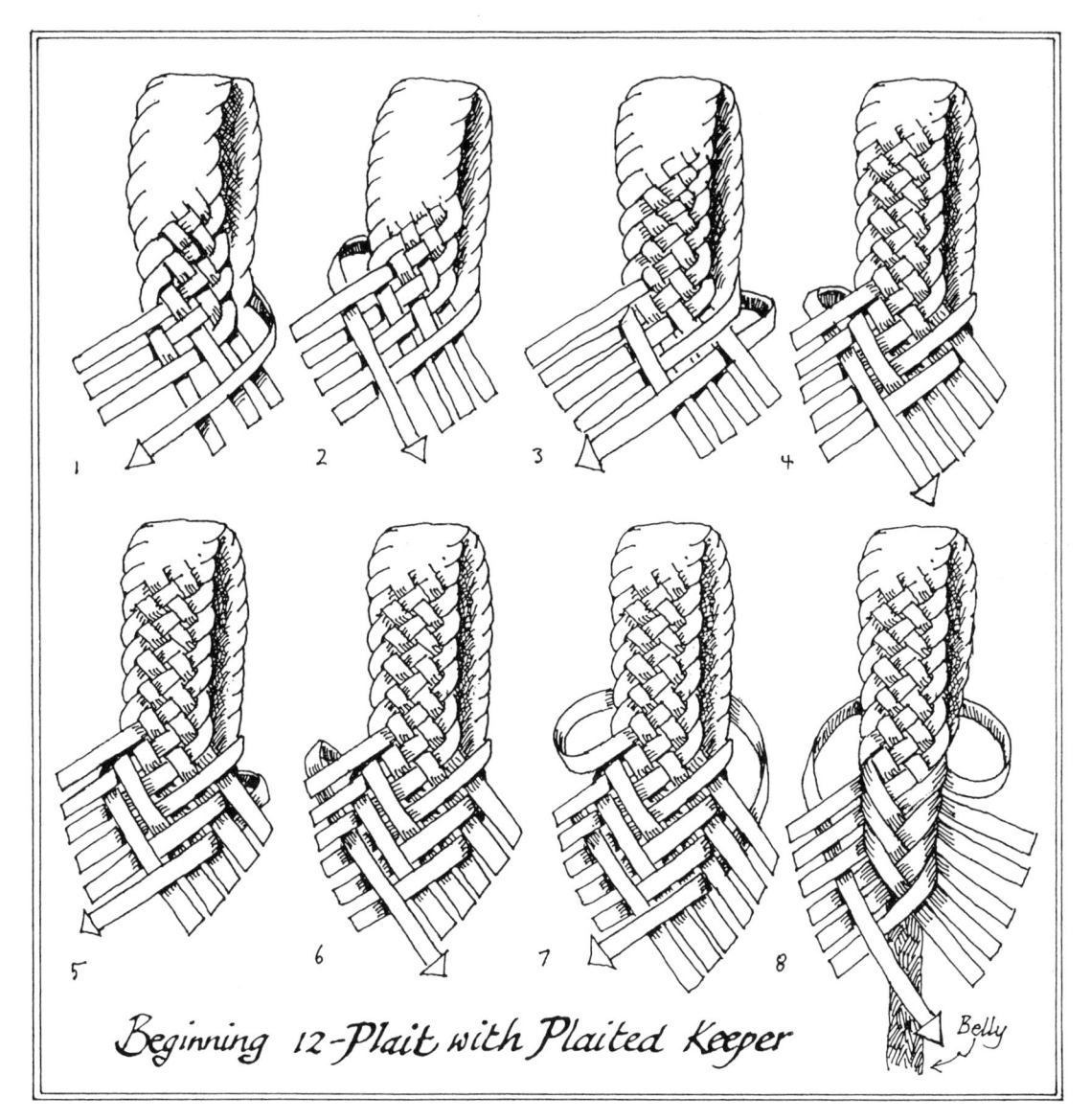

Fig. 2. Take the upper one on the left and bring it across, under one, over 3.

Fig. 3. Take the upper one on the right and bring it across under 1, over 3.

Fig. 4. Take the upper one on the left and bring it across, under 2, over 3.

Fig. 5. Take the upper one on the right and bring it across, under 2, over 3.

Fig. 6. Take the final one on the left and bring it across, under 3, over 3. All the strands have now been brought around from the back section.

Fig. 7. Take the upper left-hand strand, take it around the back and then under 3, over 3.

Fig. 8. This is a good time to fit the belly in place. Make a hole in the center and push it up and begin to tighten all the strands around it. When this has been done take the upper right strand around the back and then under 3, over 3.

Plaiting then continues in this same sequence. The taper of the whip is produced by dropping strands as the work progresses. No measurements can be given for this as it depends on a lot of factors: the stretch in your strands, the shape of the belly, and the finished shape that you are looking for.

Do not wait until each set of strands has nearly been used up before they are dropped. If the whip is looking too thick, drop them earlier and trim them off rather than let them run down beside the belly. Dropping strands is explained in chapter 2, as is making and attaching the fall and cracker and making the handle.

One last touch is to tie a Spanish ring knot below the keeper (page 83). This serves no purpose other than to cover the point at which the flat 6-plait changes to a round 12-plait.

WHIP CRACKER KNOTS

When a whip cracker has been twisted up, a knot has to be put in at the end to stop it from unraveling. There are a number of ways of doing this and I will illustrate some of them here.

Overhand Knot

Probably the most common knot seen is an ordinary overhand knot, and while this may do the job, it is not the best as it looks clumsy and part of the tip sticks out to one side as shown.

People who pride themselves on their whips do not use this knot.

Small Cracker Knot

The best advertisement that I know of for this cracker knot is that I noticed a version of it on a group of whips made by Charlie Hassett, a highly respected name in the world of whipmaking (examples of his work have been on display in the Australian Stockman's Hall of Fame).

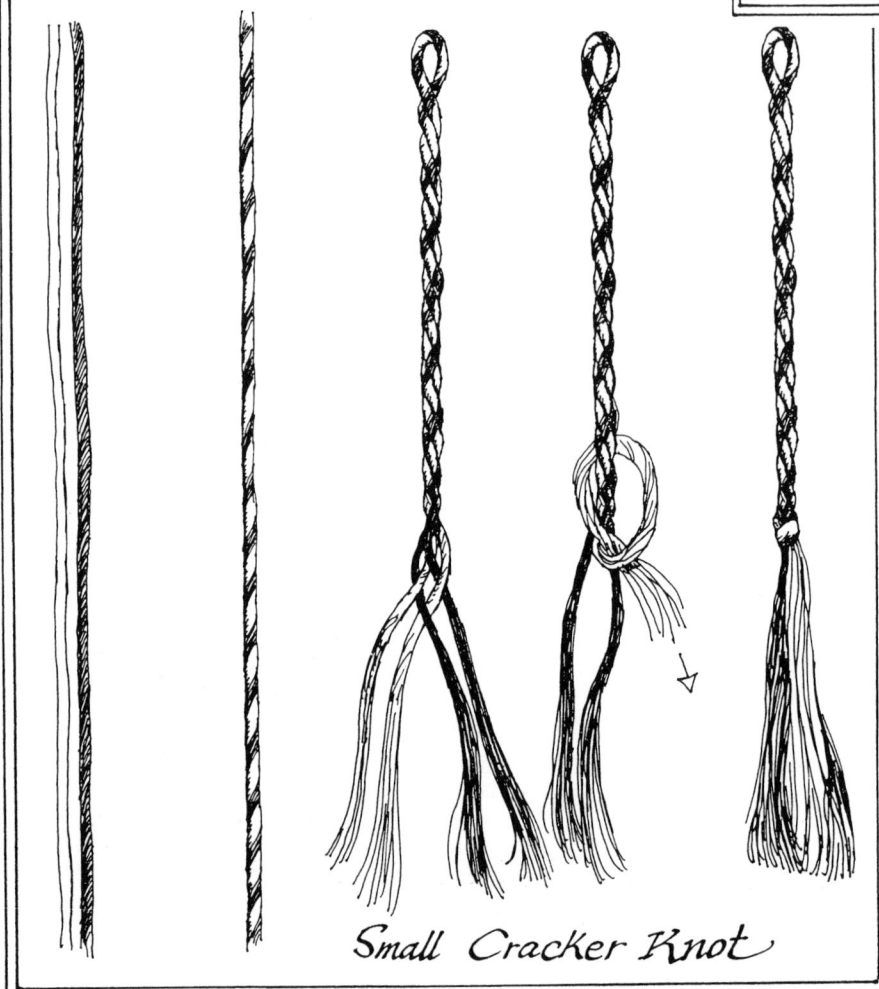

Overhand Knot

It creates the smallest knot of all those illustrated here, and so gives a clean smooth profile to the cracker.

The best way to illustrate it is by making the cracker from two different colors of material, and this also makes an attractive-looking cracker. The first drawing shows the 2 colored strands and the second what they look like when twisted together.

The strands are twisted together in the usual way as shown in the third drawing and then grasped firmly at the point where the knot is to be put. Select one group of colored strands and tie them as shown, pulling the knot down tightly.

By taking strands of all one color it means that both sides of the twisted section are tied in together.

Small Cracker Knot

Blood Knot Variation

This is one of the most popular knots for crackers, and has already been illustrated in more detail on page 24.

It is a neat and effective knot for the whip cracker, as it is a symmetrical knot and keeps the ends lying in line. I learned it from Rob Cheerio of Oak Forest many years ago. It appears to be a variation of the blood knot, but with two strands involved rather than one.

However, there is quite a knack to forming it so that it comes out neatly and so the knot does not end up below the twisted section of the cracker. This may not make sense when you read it, but if you try the knot, you will find out what I mean when you encounter the twisted section a bit loose just above the finished knot.

To avoid this a certain amount of tension has to be maintained on the ends while the knot is being formed, and the first loop is best kept as small as convenient.

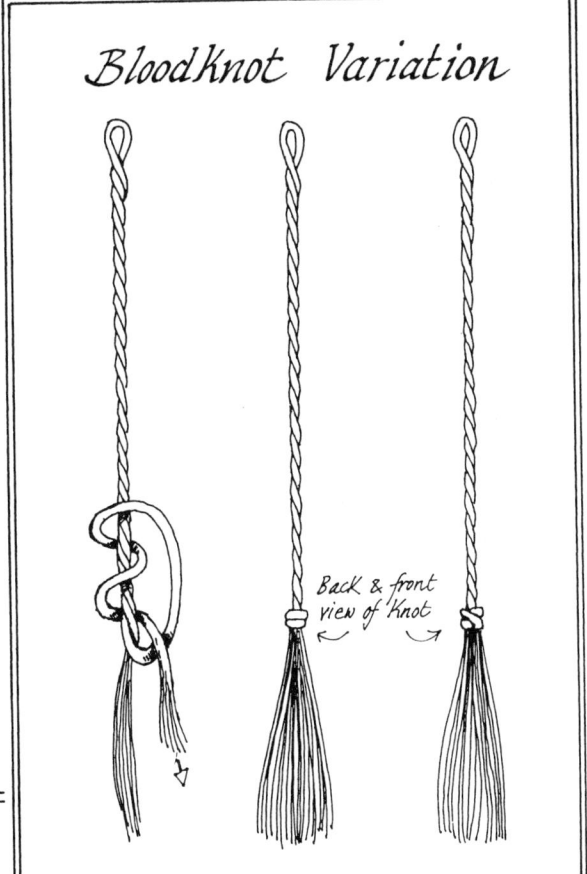

Bloodknot Variation

Back & front view of Knot

Napranum Hitch

If anyone knows the correct name for this I would be pleased to learn it. I just used this name to identify it for my own use, because I was shown it at the Aboriginal settlement of Napranum just south of Weipa.

It was here that I ran into an old friend, Les Callope, a ringer known around the Gulf country as Slippery Sam. It was Les who taught me how to make a cord girth, twist a greenhide rope, and many other bush skills which I later put into *Bushcraft 1* and *Bushcraft 2* in the 1970s.

I hadn't seen Les for some years and he looked like a battered old scrub bull. He had a long scar down one side of his chest where a knife aimed at his heart had just missed, and a pair of bullet holes, one in his stomach where it went in and one in his back where it came out. There was a recent four-inch scar down the side of his face from forehead to cheek and a whole heap of other scars that all told a story.

Napranum Hitch

Back & front view of Knot

He said that the young bucks still took turns in trying him out, but that he was still holding his own, and pointed out to me a man with a bandaged head who had required eight stitches in it after they had some disagreement two nights before.

More than twenty years earlier I had sketched Les twisting a whip cracker, and this sketch was used in a couple of my books, but I was never happy with the likeness and asked him to make one for me again.

It was while doing this that he showed me this method of putting the knot in the cracker, and he said this was commonly used by stockmen in the Gulf country. In some ways it is a little easier to form than the blood knot variation but, like that knot, care must be taken to work it down properly.

Attaching the Cracker

One rule that I have discovered in whipmaking is that no matter what you do, someone will come along and tell you that it is not the correct way. More often than not you can ignore them, but when that person is Maurice Doohan you listen.

So throughout the Gulf country ringers still twist up crackers in their teeth as I have illustrated earlier and attach them in the time-honored way as shown on the left.

However, Maurice twists his crackers around a nail or hook and attaches them with the hitch illustrated on the right. He said this is the method used by many professional whipmakers.

The theory behind the attaching knot is that the pressure of the cracker comes on the very end of the fall and not above the knot, as it does in the first mentioned method. As the fall often breaks at this pressure point, it makes sense to have it as close to the end as possible and thus not lose too much fall.

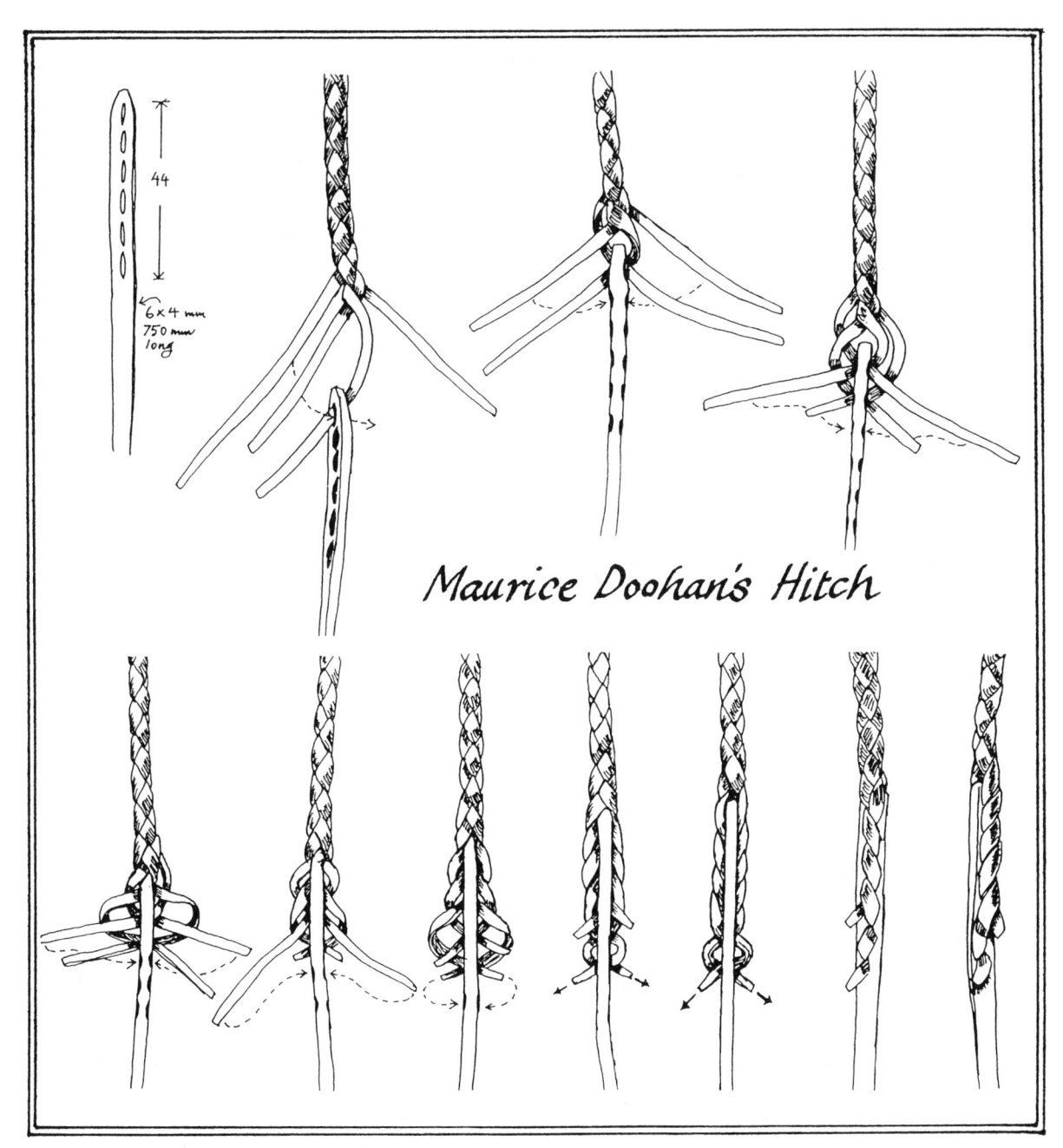

FALL HITCHES

The knot that attaches the fall to the thong must be very strong, but it should also be neat. The most common hitch is shown on pages 22 and 70, but there are other variations that are quite interesting.

Maurice Doohan's Hitch

Maurice Doohan learned this hitch from his uncle and told me that he only knew of a couple of other whipmakers who used it.

It gives a very fine taper to the end of the whip, avoiding the lump that is usually found where the fall is fixed on.

When tied and pulled up tight it is a good hitch, but it takes a little practice to learn how to do it properly. It is not a good hitch for repair work and is best used only on new whips.

Slits are cut into the fall, not holes, and the ends are then worked in as shown. The final two drawings show the finished hitch from either side.

On the next page is a sketch of the hitch on a finished whip.

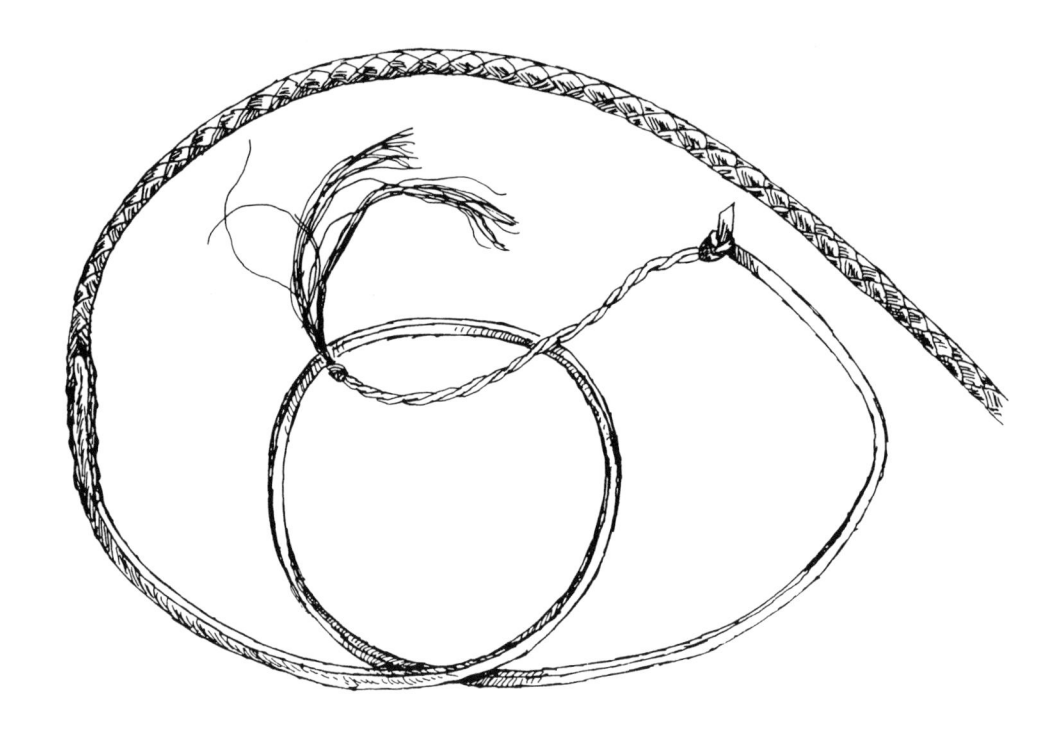

Above is Maurice Doohan's hitch, showing how it forms a low profile on the finished whip.

Snake's Head Hitch

This decorative hitch was shown to me by George Stien of Atherton, Queensland, in 1985. He had learned it from a saddler in Cloncurry, who in turn had learned it from one of the well-known whipmakers in the west.

It is usually tied in whips that end up with 6 strands and are made with kangaroo leather. The finished hitch resembles a snake's head with a forked tongue.

It shares the advantage of the common hitch in that it is possible to replace a broken fall by pulling out the old one and feeding the new one through the same hole without having to undo the hitch. This not only saves time but also makes for a stronger job, as it is hard to get old strands back again to the same degree of tightness that they had originally.

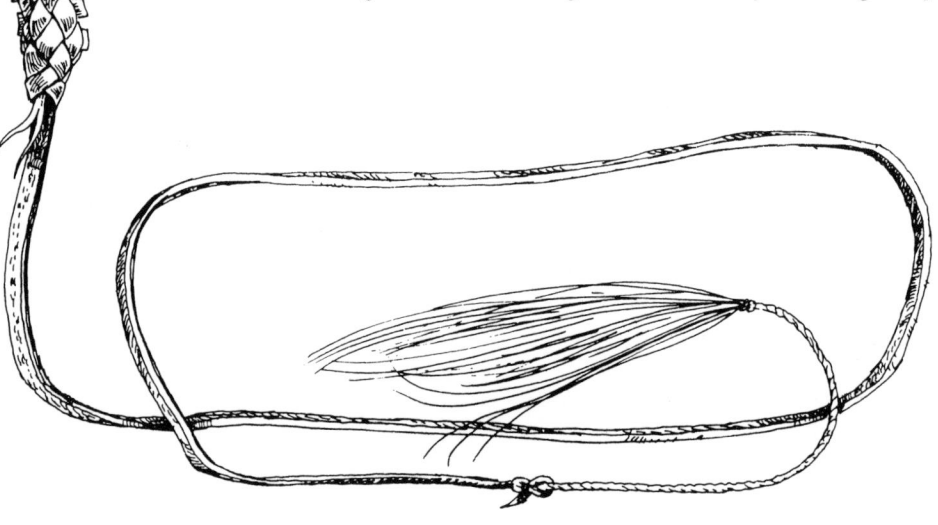

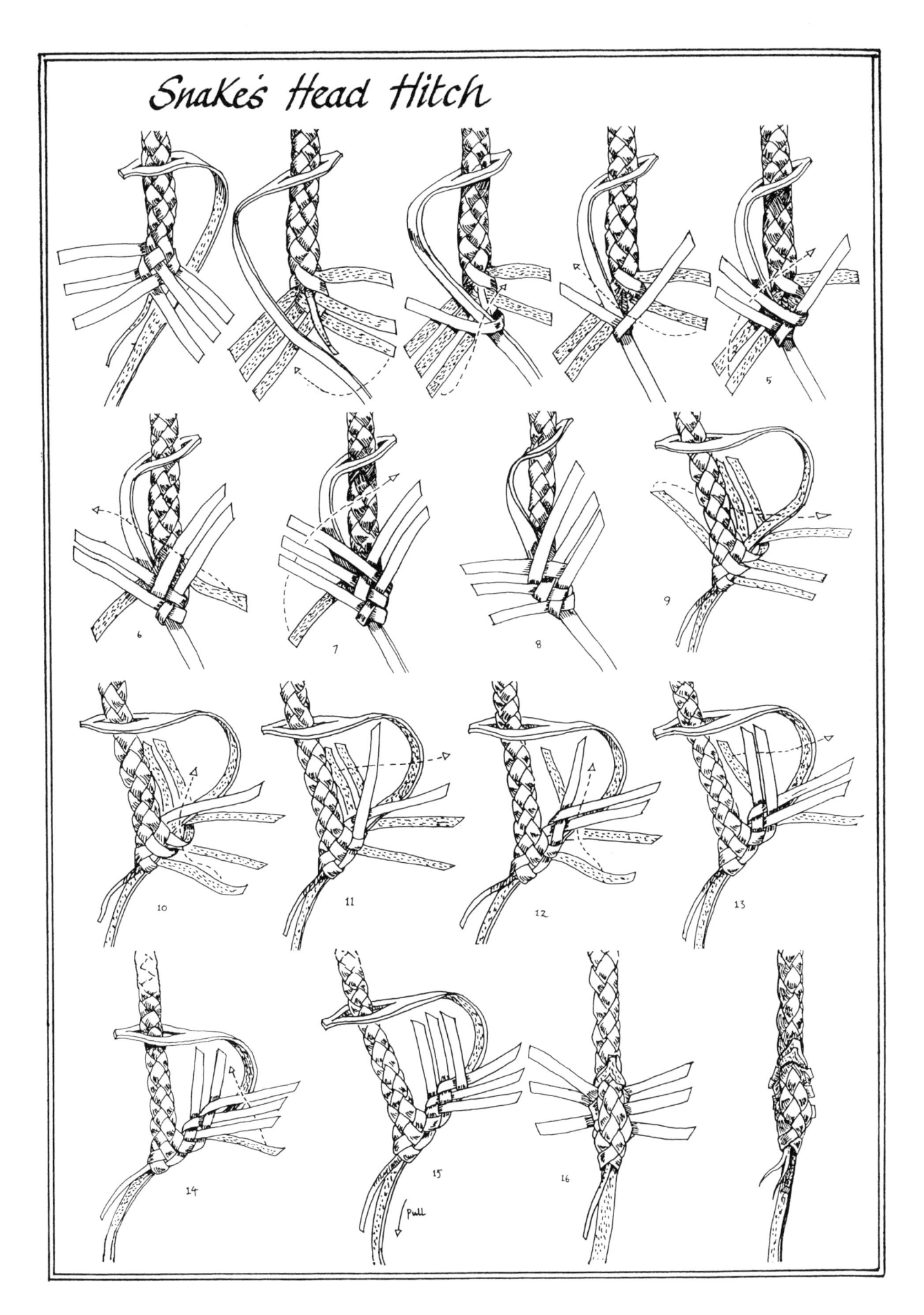

Snake's Head Hitch

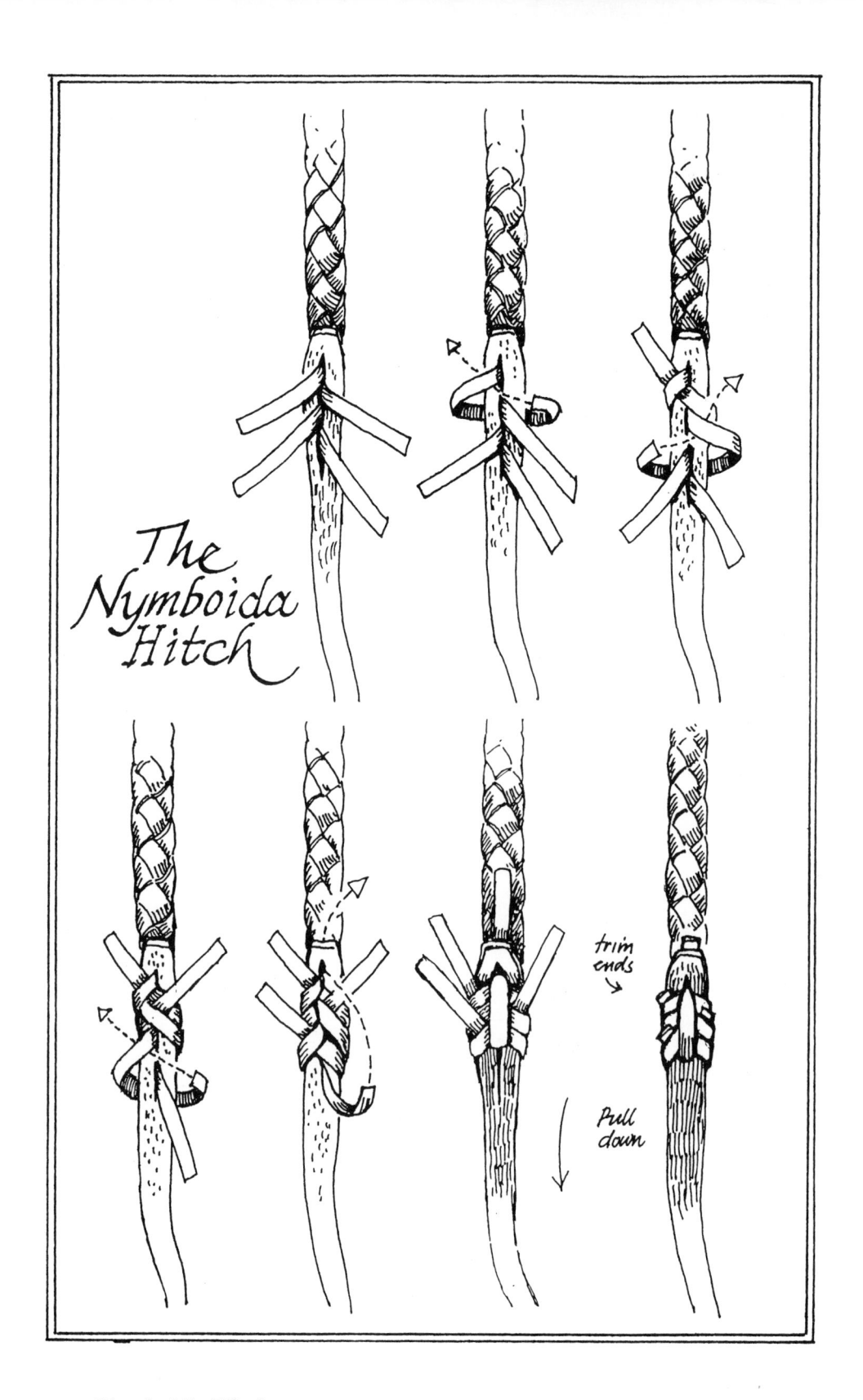

Nymboida Hitch

In May 1994 a man brought a whip into our saddlery for repairs, and I noticed the hitch that fixed on the fall. He said that it been done by an old whipmaker of Nymboida, southwest of Grafton, New South Wales, and so I gave it this name. If anyone has a different name for it I would like to hear about it.

It is much easier to do than the snake's head hitch, and faster than a normal fall hitch. When pulled tight it seems secure—in this case, the whip had worn out while the hitch was still firm.

George's Hitch

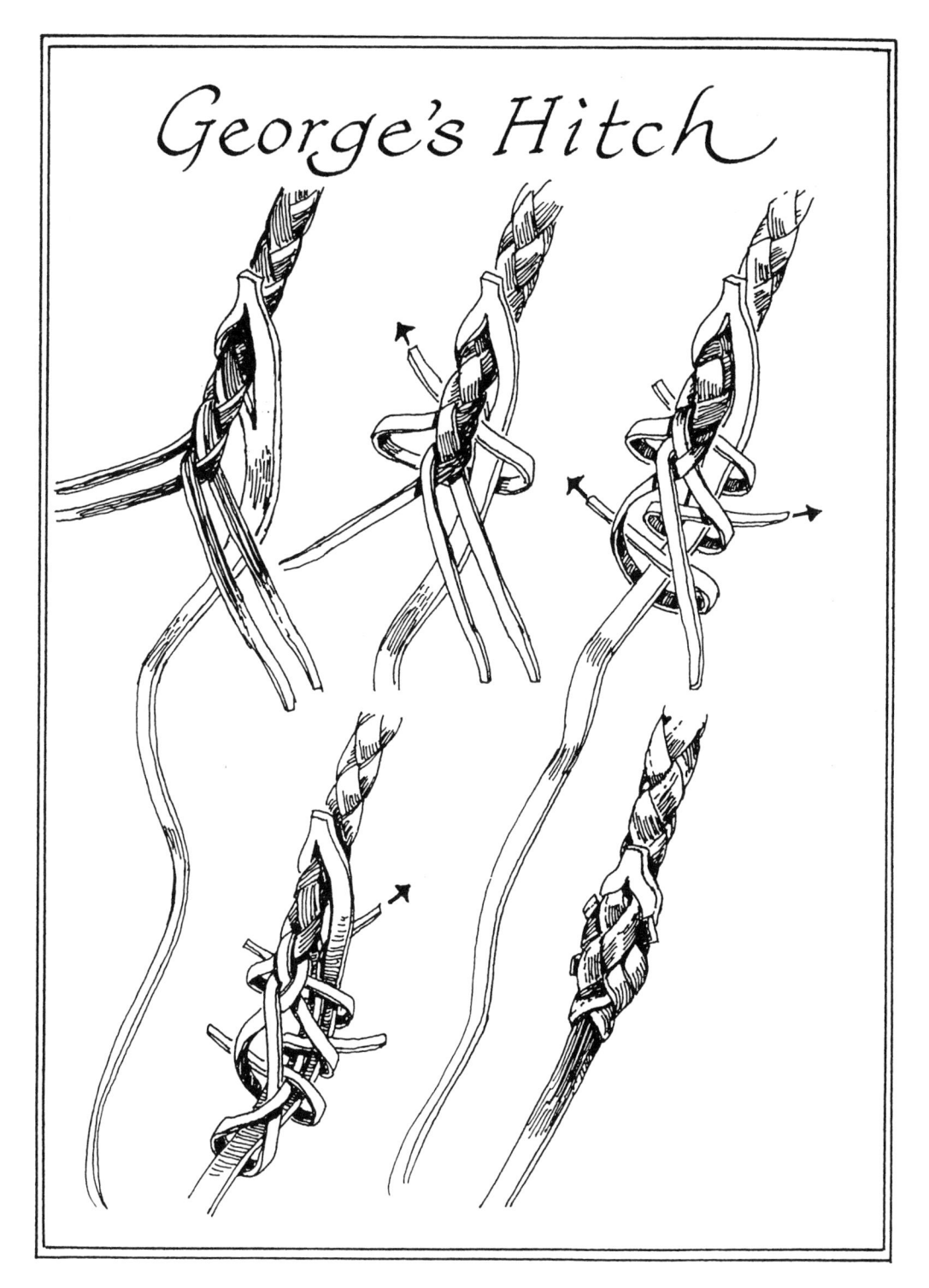

George's Hitch

After I had published the previous hitch in the pages of *The Australian Plaiters and Whipmaker's Journal* I was contacted by Lindsay Whiteman, a fine whipmaker in Townsville, who showed me another variation of the same hitch.

He had learned it from the late George Campion many years earlier and gave it this name in honor of George.

In some ways it may be even better than the previous hitch and is fairly easy to remember. But both this and the Nymboida hitch need to be put on very neatly and with well-trimmed and even strands. If not, they can end up being not only very lumpy but also very ugly.

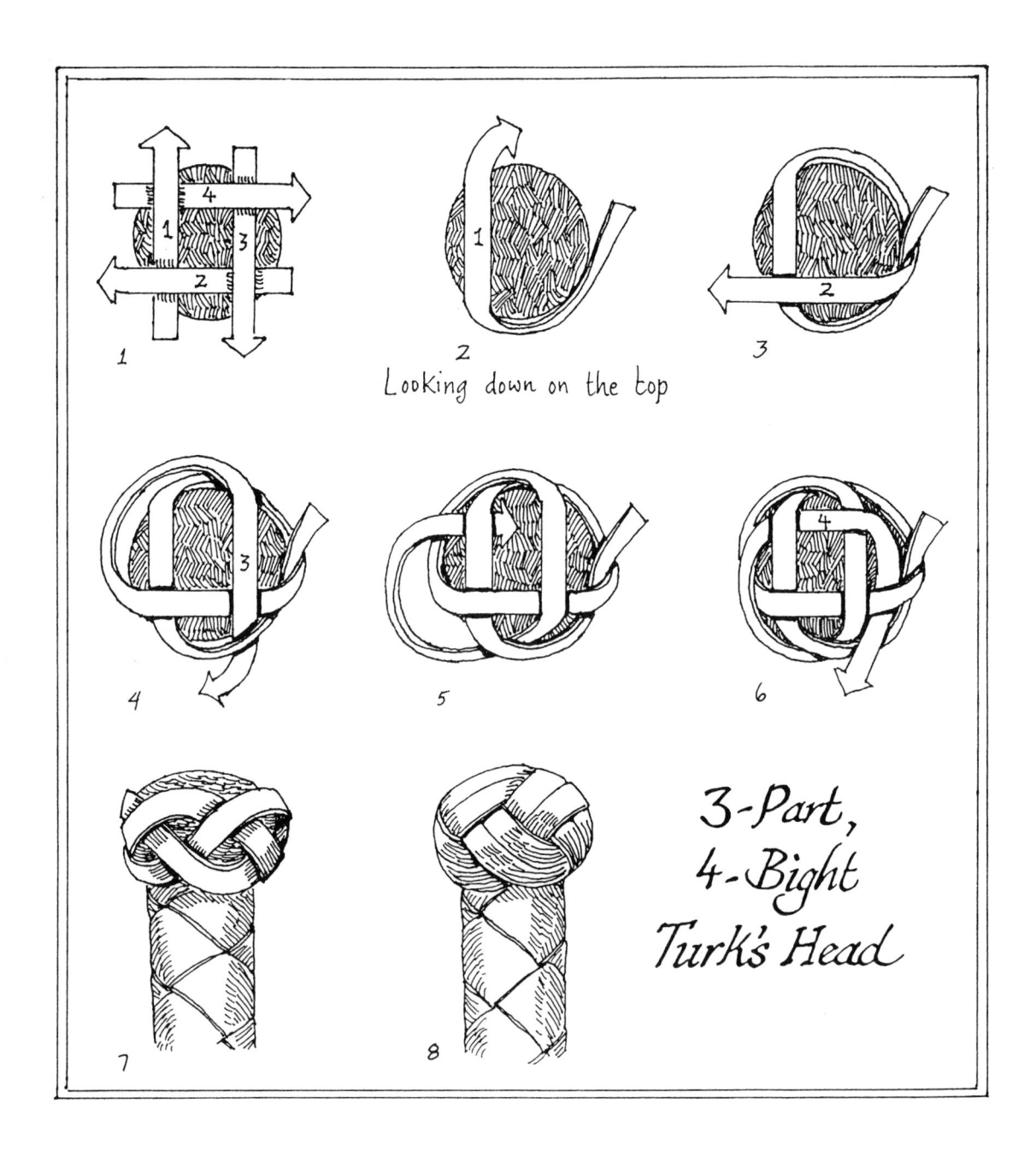

3-PART, 4-BIGHT TURK'S HEAD

This is one of the most common knots to be found on the knobs of whip handles, the reason being that it is the fastest one to form for the professional whipmaker.

I have already illustrated a method of tying it on page 36. However Turk's heads can often be a great headache for beginners, and for this reason I am including here another method of tying the same knot, which may be a little easier to understand for the novice.

In this case we are looking down on the top of the whip handle. The first drawing explains how the 4 strands will be laid down.

If you remember this order, and the way that each strand lies on top or underneath its neighbor, it will prove to be a great help in keeping the knot in your memory.

When the knot has been fully formed, as shown in figure 7, take a little time to make sure that it is spread out evenly. When this has been done do a "follow the leader" sequence, going around two or three times and following the path of the original knot.

Appendix

MAKING A SECRET 3-PLAIT

The method for making a secret 3-plait for working into a whip handle is illustrated in the figures below. In order to avoid trouble, it is important to count out each sequence as you go. The sequence for the 3-plait is one, two, three, through the top, through the bottom, four, five. The sequence is now complete.

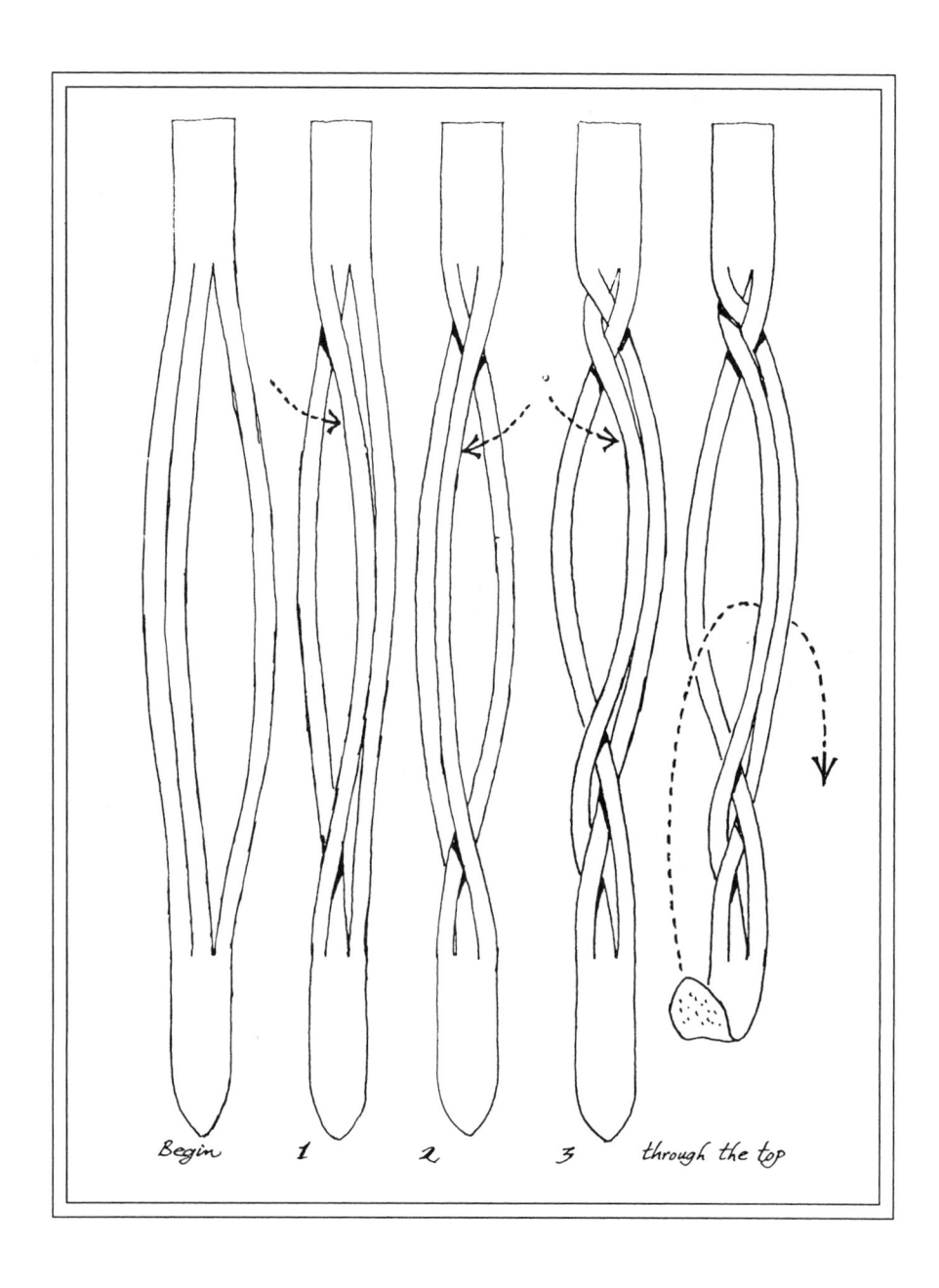

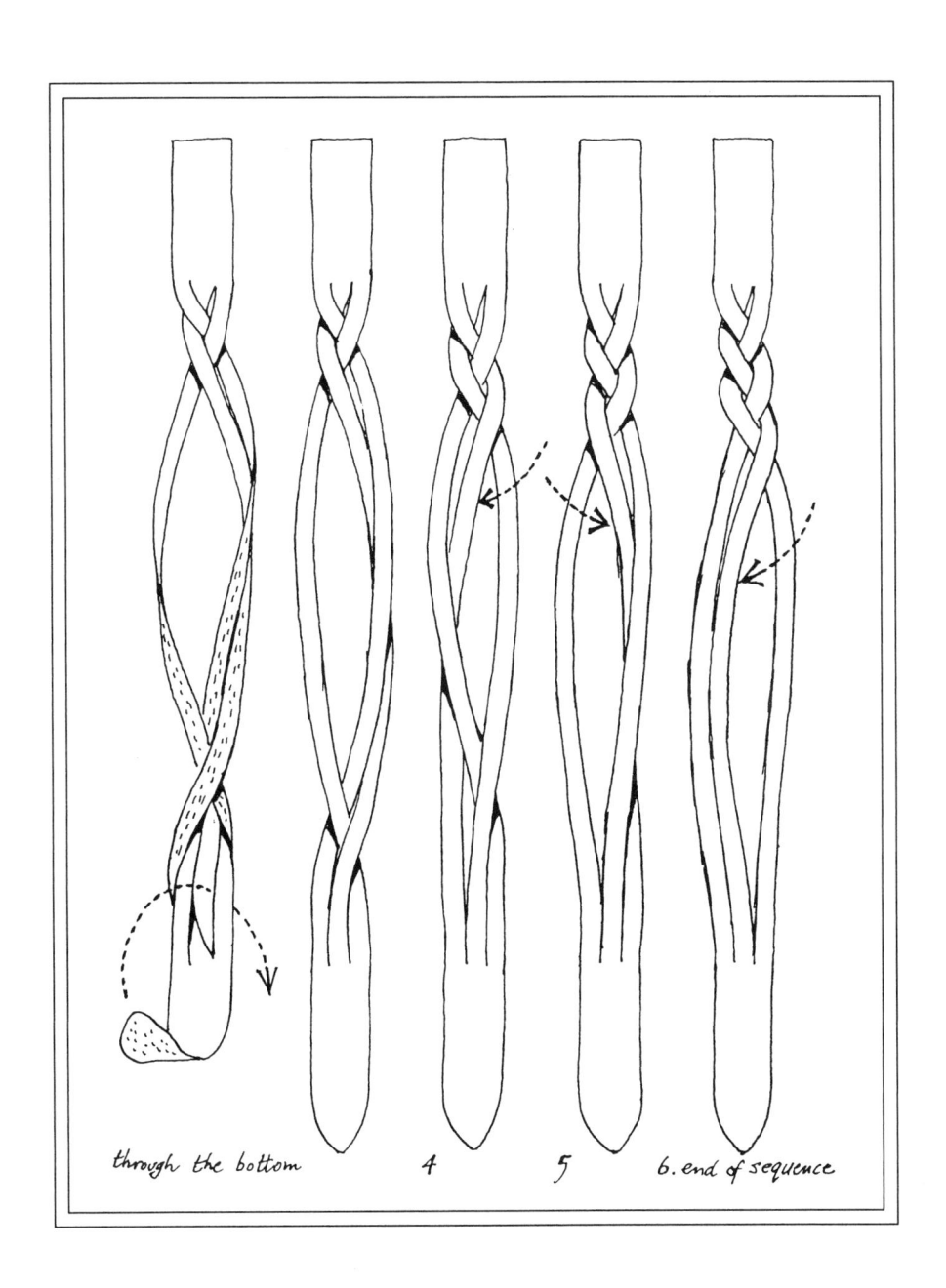

through the bottom   4   5   6. end of sequence

MAKING A BULLOCKIE'S WHIP

The bullockie's whip is quite different from the whip used by a stockman. The whip itself is often longer, and the handle is very long indeed. While stockmen usually take care of their whips this did not seem to be the case with bullock drivers. The examples I have seen are usually roughly made and have been treated even rougher.

The bullock driver did not seem to care about his whip; he would wander along dragging the end of it on the ground behind him, not worrying whether it wore out or not. When it did he would quickly put another one together as rough as the last.

The difference in attitudes was probably because the stockman not only used his whip for work but also for recreation, practicing various styles of cracking, and so his whip became a valued possession, while to the bullock driver his whip was just a tool to be used when necessary and dropped as soon as he stopped working.

The bullockie's whip was commonly made using a simple 4-strand plait (see chapter 2) with a slip keeper, but made longer than a boy's whip. It was often finished off in the same way as a stockwhip (see chapter 1) or it might be finished off with the series of locking hitches illustrated here. This same method is sometimes also used to finish off plaited reins.

The whip would usually be cut from greenhide as this was easily obtained and free. The handle was simply a strong stick, often about 300 mm taller than the bullockie, though some preferred one that only came up to their shoulder. The most common length was between 2 and 2.4 meters.

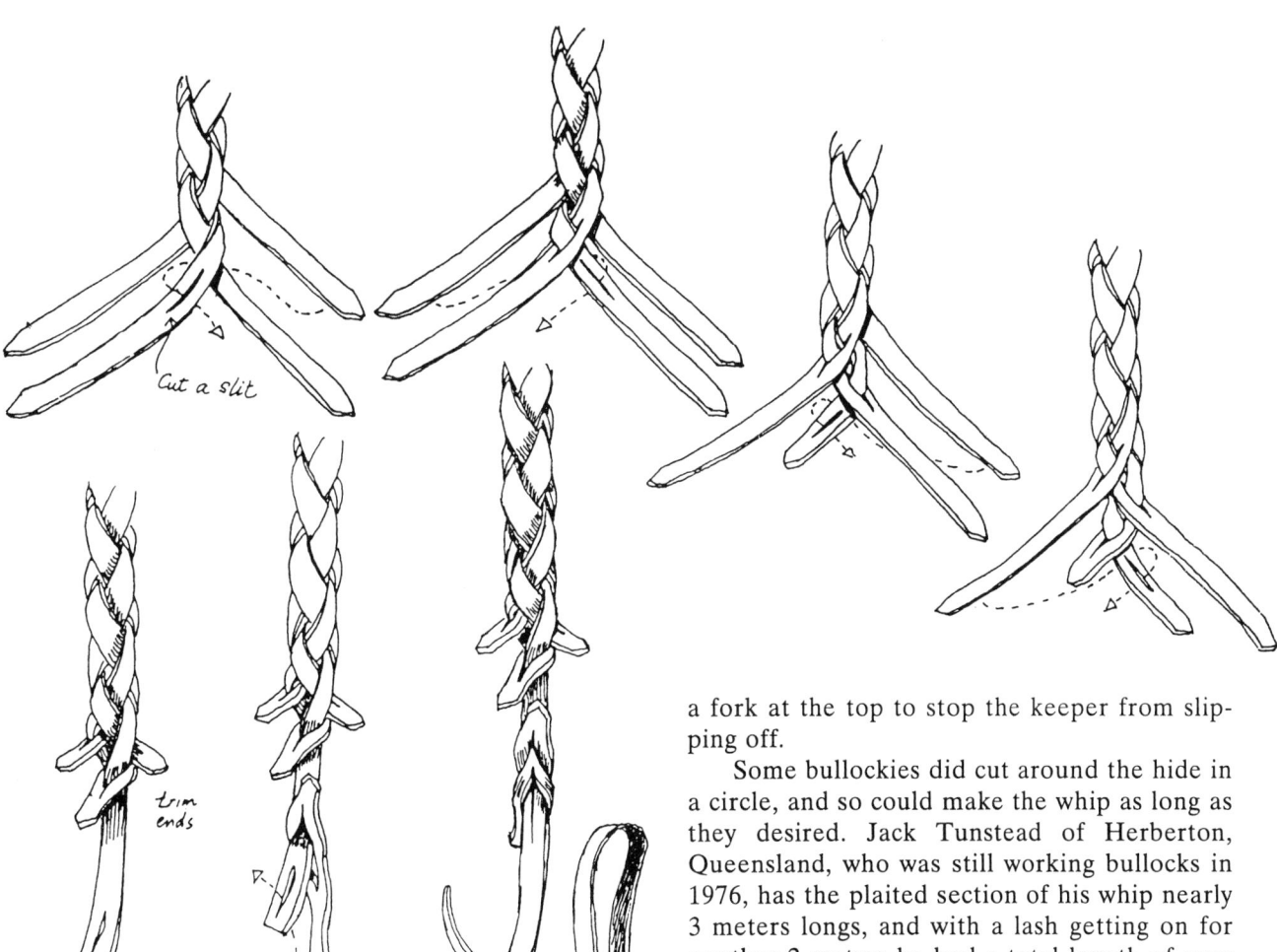

The length of the whip varied considerably. Most bullock drivers seem to have cut the whip out of the hide by taking a straight cut down the backbone, and this limited the plaited section according to the length of the hide, usually around 2 meters.

Wally Legge of Macclesfield in Victoria, who is shown on the preceding page, was an old friend of mine back in 1959. (He was the last person I saw who wore bowyangs, cords or straps tied around a workman's trousers below the knees, as a matter of course while at work.) He had a working team and used to bring in timber with it. The whip he is holding is typical, with the plaited section a little under 2 meters long and the lash about 800 mm. His handle has a fork at the top to stop the keeper from slipping off.

Some bullockies did cut around the hide in a circle, and so could make the whip as long as they desired. Jack Tunstead of Herberton, Queensland, who was still working bullocks in 1976, has the plaited section of his whip nearly 3 meters longs, and with a lash getting on for another 2 meters he had a total length of over 4-1/2 meters to drag in the dust.

Because bullock drivers were rugged individuals they attached the whip to the handle just as they pleased, but usually they used a single keeper rather than the double one that is found on a stockwhip.

The methods of attaching were pretty casual, and the illustrations show a popular style, but there were other variations. The handle was either left with a fork or natural knob at the end or one was whittled, and the keeper was looped around it. The keeper was longer than that found on a stockwhip, usually about 100 mm.

Because of the way it is made, a bullockie's whip is much harder to crack, and most bullock drivers did not bother to attempt it, claiming that the noise only startled the bullocks without achieving any purpose. For this reason the whip usually did not have a fall and cracker but only a lash on the end.

The difference is only in name, though, the lash being the same dimensions as the fall and attached in the same way, as illustrated in

159

chapter 1. Another method of attaching the lash is shown here, and this seems to have been only used for rough whips such as those used by bullock drivers.

It is not always easy to find suitable long straight sticks for whip handles, and the bullockie would keep his eyes open as he trudged along, cutting any that he found for future use. This was a necessary precaution as the long handles would often break with rough use, and it also explains why they used such a simple fastening on the handle, as it could be removed speedily when a handle broke and a new one put on.

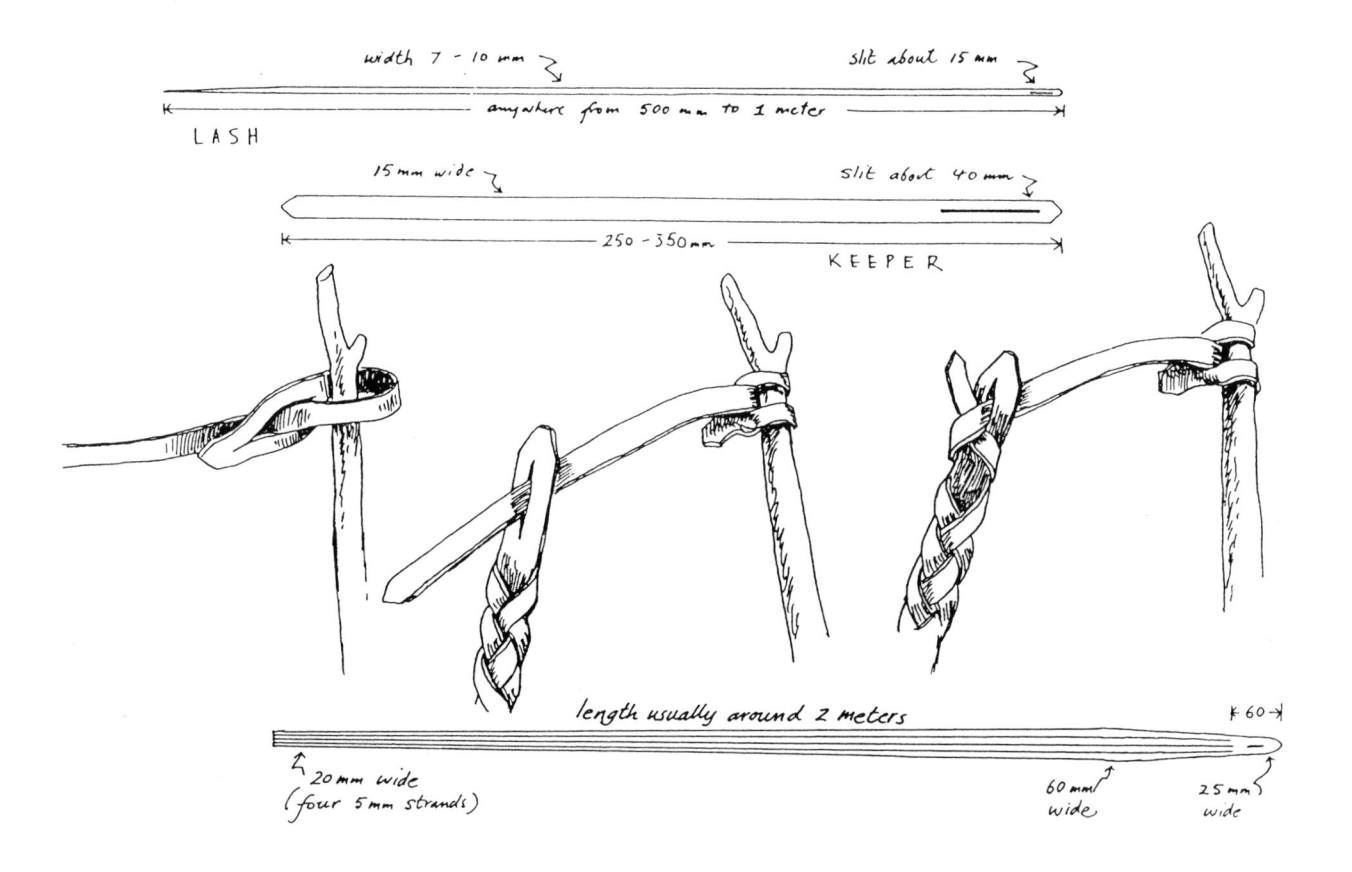

width 7 - 10 mm *slit about 15 mm*
anywhere from 500 mm to 1 meter
LASH

15 mm wide *slit about 40 mm*
250 - 350 mm
KEEPER

length usually around 2 meters *60*
20 mm wide (four 5mm strands) *60 mm wide* *25 mm wide*

Index

A
Acid used in cleaning fat 20
Angled cut to strand 17
Attaching the cracker 25, 72, 148
Attaching the fall 21, 69, 149–53
Attaching whip and handle 37, 84

B
Barber's pole plait 130
Bark-tanned leather 13
Basic whip 12
Beam, cutting on the 18
Beginning a round 6-plait 39
Belly, for bullwhip 90
Belly from redhide 53
Belly, making the basic belly 14
Belly, for snake whip 103
Belly, for stockwhip 51
Belly with bought lace 143
Binding on the keeper 33
Bird's eye, whip handle design 122
Blood knot 25
Blood knot variation 147
Bolster 54
Bracelet, whip handle design 117
Braid, definition 47
Braiding or plaiting 46
Braid, slit 42
Broken strands 86
Building up the knob 103
Bullockie's whip 45
Bullwhip, handle loop 92
Bullwhip, making a 89–96
Bullwhip, plaiting the overlay 92
Bullwhip 45
Bullwhip, the belly 90
Bullwhip, the handle 90
Bullwhip, the knob 95
Bullwhip, Turk's head on the handle 96
Bundles of lace 63
Bush timber for handles 75
Buying a strip of leather 14

C
Care of the whip 84
Carved timber handles 109
Changing from 8-plait to 7- plait 66
Changing from 7-plait to 6-plait 67
Chessboard plait, whip handle design 114
Chessboard start 134
Choosing leather 13
Chrome-tanned leather 13
Clamp for handle, simple method 79
Clamp, whip handle clamp 140
Cleaning tallow 20
Coachwhipping, whip handle design 116
Colors to use for name plaiting 132
Common fall hitch 23
Complex plaiting, two methods 120
Confined space, working in a 19
Core, kangaroo 49
Core or filler 49
Core, redhide 49
Covering the core 143
Covering the handle 26
Cowtail-covered handle 110
Cowtail or whipmaker's plait 112
Cracker, blood knot variation 147
Cracker, fastening the cracker to the fall . . 24, 25
Cracker, finishing off the cracker . . 24, 72, 146–47
Cracker, making the cracker 23, 71
Cracker, Napranum hitch 147
Cracker, overhand knot 146
Cracker, small cracker knot 146
Crackers, speeding up the job of making 24
Cracking the whip 25
Crop, riding 104
Crown knot 27, 28
Cutting and skiving 16
Cutting methods 16
Cutting on the beam 18
Cutting out a basic whip 15
Cutting out strands from kangaroo hide 55
Cutting out the strands 58
Cutting out the top plait or overlay 55
Cutting out the whip 15
Cutting out tight corners 59
Cutting out whips 16
Cutting out with thumbnail 58
Cutting the slit in a whip fall 21
Cutting with skiving cut 17

D
Designs for whip handles 105–30
Dividers, for marking leather 15
Dog's knot 26–28
Double bracelet, whip handle design 118
Doubled herringbone, whip handle design . . . 113
Double diamond, whip handle design 115
Double stairstep, whip handle design 120
Double zigzag, whip handle design 126
Dressing, leather 20
Dropping strands 66

E
Egyptian eyes, whip handle design 123
Elaborate handle 84

161

F

Fall, attaching the fall 21, 69
Fall, common fall hitch. 22, 70
Fall, cutting the slit in a whip fall 21
Fall, George's hitch. 153
Fall hitches 149–53
Fall, making the. 21, 69
Fall, Morris Doohan's hitch 149
Fall, replacing the fall 69
Falls cut in gangs. 70
Fall, snake's head hitch. 150
Fall, the Nymboida Hitch. 152
Fastening the cracker to the fall 24
Fat, cleaning 20
Filler and belly plait 51
Filler 49
Fingers as guides for marking leather 16
Finishing off the cracker 24, 72, 146–47
Finishing off the thong 68
First rule about whipmakers 45
Fitting the handle and thong together 37, 84
Five-part, 4-bight Turk's head 81
Flowers and zigzag, whip handle design 125
Flowers, whip handle design 126
Foundation for the handle (or stock) 75
Four-strand diamond, whip handle design. . . 116
French grapevine or French whipping . . . 35, 102

G

Gaps in the plaiting. 65
George's hitch 153
Grapevine, French 35, 102
Grapevine whipping 35, 102
Greasing the strands 61
Greenhide. 12

H

Half-plaited handle. 25
Handle, a more elaborate handle 84
Handle and thong, fitting together. 37, 84
Handle, binding on the keeper 33
Handle, bullwhip 90
Handle, calculating the length of the lace . . . 134
Handle, chessboard start 134
Handle clamp, simple method 79
Handle, covering the 26
Handle, crown knot. 27
Handle, finishing the knob 82
Handle, forming the knob 27, 79
Handle foundation, snake whip 101
Handle, half-plaited 25
Handle, joining one pattern to the next 132
Handle loop for snake whip 99
Handle loop for bull whip 92
Handle, making the. 25
Handle for snake whip 101–103
Handle (or stock) foundation 75

Handle, 12-plait handle. 29, 31
Handle, plaiting names in whip handles 131
Handle, plaiting names with short pieces . . . 132
Handle, 12-plait. 31
Handle, 8-plait 30
Handle, rib rattling 34
Handles, carved timber handles 109
Handles, cowtail handle 110
Handles, designs for whip handles 105–30
Handle, secret plait worked into a whip handle . 32
Handle, shaping the knob 80
Handles, lunging whip 110
Handle, straightening a whip handle. 26
Handles, twisted handles 108
Handle, the knob on the handle 79
Handle, the overlay for the handle. 76
Handle, Turk's head on keeper end 82
Handle, two-tone work 84
Handle, tying the set to the stock 76
Handle, using bush timber 75
Handle with an 8-plait and Turk's head 29
Handle with 4-plait and dog's head knot. . . . 26
Handle, wraparound handle 32
Hand part. 46
Hat band, miniature whip 104
Hitch, fall hitches 22, 70, 149–53
Holding strands. 61
Holes in leather. 61
Homemade strand cutter 59

I

Irregular herringbone, whip handle design. . . 115

J

Joining broken strands without glue 86
Joining one pattern to the next. 132
Joining whip and handle 37, 84

K

Kangaroo, best use of the leather 48
Kangaroo core 49
Kangaroo, holes in leather 61
Kangaroo leather, stockwhip of 44
Kangaroo leather, types 58
Kangaroo skin, selecting the 48
Kangaroo, testing for stretch 48
Keeper, attaching to handle 33, 34
Kid's whip. 41
Knob, forming the 27
Knob on the handle. 79
Knot, blood knot 25
Knot, blood knot variation 147
Knot, crown knot 27
Knot, dog's knot 27
Knot, 5-part, 4-bight Turk's head 80, 81, 96
Knot, overhand knot 146
Knot, plaiter's knot. 65

162

Knot, small cracker knot 146
Knot, Spanish ring knot 10, 83
Knot, 3-part, 4-bight Turk's head 36, 154
Knot, wall knot 27
Knot, whip cracker knots 146–47

L

Lace for overlay, quantity needed 144
Lace holder, self-greasing 64
Lace, making a whip with bought lace 143
Lace, precut lace for bullwhip 92
Lace, using precut lace for stockwhip . . . 143–45
Lead-loaded snake whip 98
Lead loading 51
Leather, bark-tanned leather 13
Leather, buying a strip of 14
Leather chattering while skiving 60
Leather choosing, points to watch 13
Leather, chrome-tanned leather 13
Leather dressing 20, 61
Leather, greenhide 12
Leather, rawhide 13
Leather, redhide 12
Leather splitter 60
Leather, stretch in the kangaroo leather 56
Leather, types of 12
Leather, vegetable tan 13
Leather, whitehide 13
Length of strands in overlay 56
Loading whip, lead loading 47, 51, 98
Locking the back for name plaiting 135
Long whipping 77
Looseness in plaiting the overlay 64
Lumps, when plaiting 68
Lunging whip 110

M

Making a bullwhip 89–96
Making the best use of the leather 48
Marking leather, using a template 16
Marking leather, using dividers 15
Marking leather, using fingers as guides 16
Miniature whip hatband 104
Morris Doohan's hitch 149

N

Name plaiting 131–39
Names, colors to use 132
Names, locking the back 135
Names of whips 12
Names, plaiting long words 138
Names, plaiting names with short pieces 132
Names, setting out 138
Names, using precut lace 134
Names, vertical and horizontal letters 137
Names, white on black letters 137
Names, working the letters into the weave . . . 132

Napranum hitch 147
Nymboida hitch 152

O

Overhand knot 146
Overlay, cutting out the top plait or overlay . . . 55
Overlay, length of strands in overlay 56
Overlay, looseness in plaiting the overlay 64
Overlay, plaiting the overlay 62
Overlay, quantity needed 144

P

Pineapple knot 96
Plait, barber's pole plait 130
Plait, beginning a round 6-plait 39
Plait, bird's eye 122
Plait, bracelet 117
Plait, chessboard plait 114
Plait, coachwhipping 116
Plait, cowtail or whipmaker's plait 112
Plait, definition 47
Plait, double bracelet 118
Plait, double herringbone 113
Plait, double diamond 115
Plait, double stairstep 120
Plait, double zigzag 126
Plait, Egyptian eyes 123
Plaiter's knot 65
Plait, flowers and zigzag 125
Plait, flowers 126
Plaiting, adding in a strand 87
Plaiting, adding in two strands 88
Plaiting, changing from 12-plait to 10-plait . . . 94
Plaiting, changing from 10-plait to 8-plait . . . 95
Plaiting, changing from 8-plait to 7-plait . . . 66
Plaiting, changing from 8-plait to 6-plait . . . 95
Plaiting, changing from 7-plait to 6-plait . . . 67
Plaiting, changing from 6-plait to 4-plait . . . 40
Plaiting, gaps in 65
Plaiting in a confined space 19
Plaiting long words 138
Plaiting, lumps, avoiding 68
Plaiting names in whips 131
Plaiting names with short pieces 132
Plaiting, narrow sections 68
Plaiting or braiding 46
Plaiting, 6-plait basic whip 38
Plaiting, 12-plait handle 29
Plaiting, portable plaiting rack 88
Plaiting soap 20, 111
Plaiting the basic whip 21
Plaiting the keeper 144
Plaiting the overlay, bullwhip 92
Plaiting the overlay 62
Plaiting the 4-plait whip 19
Plaiting, uneven taper 68

Plait, irregular herringbone. 115
Plait, round 4-plait 19, 27, 90
Plait, round 6-plait 39, 40, 68
Plait, round 8-plait 30, 63
Plait, round 8-plait, whipmaker's method 62
Plait, round 10-plait 94
Plait, round 12-plait . . . 31, 93, 94, 115, 122, 144
Plait, round 16-plait, vee pattern. 129
Plait, round 16-strand barber's pole plait . . . 130
Plait, short herringbone 113
Plait, solid band. 121
Plait, stairstep. 119
Plait, 4-strand diamond. 116
Plait, the ship of the dead 128
Plait, the sun 124
Plait, triple diamond 116
Plait, two methods for complex plaiting 120
Plait, two-seam plait 129
Plait, vee pattern (whipmaker's plait) 129
Plait, whip handle, 12-plait 31
Plait, whip handle, 8-plait 30
Portable plaiting rack. 88
Precut lace for whip 92
Problems in plaiting the whip 21
Pull tight, plait loose 61

Q
Quick snake whip. 103

R
Rawhide. 13
Redhide, belly from. 53
Redhide core 49
Redhide. 12
Redhide whip 45
Reducing from 12-plait to 10-plait 94
Reducing from 10-plait to 8-plait 95
Reducing from 8-Plait to 7-plait 66
Reducing from 8-plait to 6-plait 95
Reducing from 7-plait to 6-plait 67
Reducing from 6-plait to 4-plait 40
Replacing the fall. 69
Resin board for whip rolling 23, 73
Rib rattling 34
Riding crop 104
Ring knot 10, 83
Rolling the whip 23
Rolling the whip with truck spring 73
Round 4-plait. 90
Round 6-plait 40, 68
Round 8-plait. 63
Round 8-plait, whipmaker's method 62
Round 10-plait 94
Round 12-plait 122, 144
Round 16-plait 127
Round 16-plait, vee pattern 129
Round 16-strand barber's pole plait 130

S
Secret plait worked into a whip handle 32
Selecting the kangaroo skin 48
Self-greasing lace holder 64
Setting out for name plaiting. 138
Shaping the handle knob 80
Sharpening strop 16
Ship of the dead, whip handle design 128
Short herringbone, whip handle design 113
Shot-loaded stockwhip 47
16-plait, round 127
Skiving cut 17
Skiving 16, 60
Slit braid 42
Small cracker knot 146
Snake's head hitch 150
Snake whip, a quick snake whip 103
Snake whip as a weapon 101
Snake whip, building up the knob 103
Snake whip, handle foundation. 101
Snake whip, handle loop 99
Snake whip, method one 98
Snake whip, method two 101
Snake whip, the belly 103
Soap, plaiting 20, 111
Solid band, whip handle design 121
Spanish ring knot based on 3-part, 4-bight. . . . 83
Spanish ring knot based on 3-part, 5-bight. . . . 10
Splitting the strands 16, 60
Square start for handle 31
Stairstep, whip handle design. 119
Steel-lined handle. 46, 75
Stitching stool. 140
Stock crop or thong. 46
Stockwhip, definition 46
Stockwhip, how to make a 4-strand stockwhip. . 11
Stockwhip, how to make an 8-strand stockwhip . 43
Stockwhip of kangaroo leather 44
Stool, stitching 140
Straightening a whip handle 26
Strand cutter, homemade. 59
Strand cutters. 58, 59
Strands, broken strands. 86
Strands, cutting and skiving 16
Strands, cutting out the strands 55–58
Strands, dropping strands 66
Strands, greasing the strands 61
Strands, joining without glue 86
Strands, keeping in bundles 63
Strands, number of strands to cut 55
Strands, skiving. 16, 60
Strands, splitting the 16, 60
Stretch in the leather 56
Strop for sharpening 16
Styles of whips 12, 44
Sun, whip handle design 124

T

Tallow, cleaning	20
Tamales	64
Team thong	46
Template, for marking leather	16
Testing for stretch	48
Thong, team	46
Thong, Turk's head on the thong	74
3-part, 4-bight Turk's head	154
Thumbnail cutting	58
Tight corners, cutting out	59
Tony Nugent whip	106
Triple diamond, whip handle design	116
Turk's head, finishing the knob	82
Turk's head, gaps in the Turk's head	82
Turk's head on bullwhip handle	96
Turk's head on keeper end	82
Turk's head, 3-part, 4-bight	36, 83, 154
Turk's head, 5-part, 4-bight	74, 81, 96
Turk's head on the thong, 5-part, 4-bight	74
Twelve foot shot-loaded stockwhip	47
12-plait, round	93, 94, 115, 122
12-plait, under 2 sequence	93
12-plait, under 3 sequence	94
Twisted handles	108
Two-seam plait, whip handle design	129
Two-tone work	84
Tying the set to the stock	76
Types of roo leather	58

U

Uneven taper	68
Using precut lace for name plaiting	134
Using precut lace for a whip	143

V

Vee pattern, whip handle design	129
Vegetable tanned leather	13
Vertical and horizontal letters	137

W

Wall knot	28
Whip as a weapon	101
Whip belly	51
Whip bolster	54
Whip, Bullockie's whip	45
Whip, bullwhip	45
Whip by Tony Nugent	106
Whip, care of	84
Whip cracker knots	146
Whip cracker	23
Whip cracking	25
Whip handle clamp	79, 140
Whip handle designs	105
Whip handle with an 8-plait and Turk's head	29
Whip, kid's whip	41
Whip, loaded	51
Whipmaker's plait, vee pattern	129
Whipmakers, first rule about	45
Whipmaking terms	46
Whip, making the belly	14
Whip names	12
Whip of bought lace, plaiting the Keeper	144
Whipping, long	77
Whip, 4-plait basic	14
Whip, 6-plait basic	38
Whip, redhide	45
Whips and handles	107
Whips, main groups of	44
Whip, snake whip	45
Whip with bought lace	143
Whitehide	13
White on black letters	137
Working names into the weave	132
Wraparound handle	32

People Named in This Book

Allan, George	101	Jellicoe, John	104
Ashford	107	Kite, Doug	22, 104
Barton, Kelvin	109	Lawson, Henry	109
Baxter, Joe	20	Nugent, Tony	106, 108
Burton, John	132	McDowell, Jim	64
Callope, Les	147	McMaster, John	132
Campion, George	153	Morgan, David	97, 107
Cheerio, Rob	147	Russell, Don	104
Clarke, Peter	70, 88, 121	Serletto, Susie	140
Cluff, Tom	73	Stephens, Hugo	112
Cull, Bruce	47, 49, 53, 111, 122	Stien, George	150
Denholm, Glen	12, 46, 111, 119, 137, 160	Stuart, John McDouall	109
Doohan, Maurice	13, 15, 23, 36, 46, 49, 53, 58, 73, 107, 110, 148, 149, 160	Tarrant, Doug	29
Fuerst, Eric	130	Taubman, Richard	129
Grierson, Ross	11, 25	Turner, Les	8
Hasluck, Paul	107	Wade, William	4
Hassett, Charles	146	Walther & Stevenson	107
Henderson	53	Weekes, J. J.	107, 108
Hill, "Jimmy the Whip"	18, 34	Whiteman, Lindsay	77, 153
Hobson, Silas	1	Williams, R. M.	58